CW00801457

DESIGNING THE **CREATIVE** CHILD
Playthings and Places in Midcentury America

AMY F. OGATA

Architecture, Landscape, and American Culture Series

UNIVERSITY OF MINNESOTA PRESS   MINNEAPOLIS LONDON

Publication of this book has been aided by a grant from the Wyeth Foundation for American Art Publication Fund of the College Art Association.

Portions of chapter 2 were published in "Creative Playthings: Educational Toys and Postwar American Culture," *Winterthur Portfolio* 39, nos. 2–3 (2004): 129–56. Portions of chapter 3 were published in "Building Imagination in Postwar American Children's Rooms," *Studies in the Decorative Arts* 16, no. 1 (2008–9): 126–42. Portions of chapter 4 were published in "Building for Learning in Postwar American Elementary Schools," *Journal of the Society of Architectural Historians* 67, no. 4 (2008): 562–91, and as "The Heathcote School: An Object Lesson," *Senses and Society* 4, no. 3 (2009): 347–52.

Every effort was made to obtain permission to reproduce material in this book. If any proper acknowledgment has not been included here, we encourage copyright holders to notify the publisher.

Published by the University of Minnesota Press
111 Third Avenue South, Suite 290
Minneapolis, MN 55401-2520
http://www.upress.umn.edu

LIBRARY OF CONGRESS CATALOGING-IN-PUBLICATION DATA
Ogata, Amy Fumiko
Designing the creative child : playthings and places in midcentury America / Amy F. Ogata.
(Architecture, landscape, and American culture)
Includes bibliographical references and index.
ISBN 978-0-8166-7960-7 (hc)—ISBN 978-0-8166-7961-4 (pb)
1. Children—United States—Social conditions—20th century. 2. Creative ability in children—United States. 3. Play environments—United States. 4. Design—Human factors—United States. I. Title.
HQ792.U5O39o 2013
155.4'13550973—dc23   2012050732

Printed in the United States of America on acid-free paper

The University of Minnesota is an equal-opportunity educator and employer.

20 19 18 17 16 15 14 13   10 9 8 7 6 5 4 3 2 1

DESIGNING THE CREATIVE CHILD

ARCHITECTURE, LANDSCAPE, AND AMERICAN CULTURE SERIES

Katherine Solomonson and Abigail A. Van Slyck, Series Editors

Medicine by Design: The Architect and the Modern Hospital, 1893–1943
ANNMARIE ADAMS

Little White Houses: How the Postwar Home Constructed Race in America
DIANNE HARRIS

Manhood Factories: YMCA Architecture and the Making of Modern Urban Culture
PAULA LUPKIN

Fallout Shelter: Designing for Civil Defense in the Cold War
DAVID MONTEYNE

Designing the Creative Child: Playthings and Places in Midcentury America
AMY F. OGATA

Women and the Everyday City: Public Space in San Francisco, 1890–1915
JESSICA ELLEN SEWELL

194X: Architecture, Planning, and Consumer Culture on the American Home Front
ANDREW M. SHANKEN

A Manufactured Wilderness: Summer Camps and the Shaping of American Youth, 1890–1960
ABIGAIL A. VAN SLYCK

The Architecture of Madness: Insane Asylums in the United States
CARLA YANNI

CONTENTS

ARNOLD GESELL, the influential twentieth-century pediatrician and child-development psychologist, believed that "by nature" the child was "a creative artist of sorts. . . . We may well be amazed at his resourcefulness, his extraordinary capacity for original activity, inventions, and discovery."[1] Such awe at the child's apparently innate creativity has its roots in the romantic era, and has not only persisted but also expanded in our own age. Indeed, authentic creativity has become an unquestioned "truth" about children and childhood. At large retailers, as in small toy stores and online merchants, there are entire aisles or sections of "creativity toys." But why do we view children as having unusual insight or creative ability? Why do parents believe that taking classes and purchasing special toys, books, or furniture might help to stimulate this particular quality? Furthermore, why has creativity itself become so important to a sense of national pride and positive future gains? This book explores how a perception of children as imaginative and "naturally" creative was constructed, disseminated, and consumed in the United States in the years after World War II. I argue that educational toys, public amusements, and the plan and decoration of the smaller middle-class house and thousands of postwar schools, along with special museums across the country, were designed to cultivate an idealized imaginative child. These objects and spaces are at once the material embodiment of this abstract social and educational discourse and also actors whose material properties transformed popular understanding of creativity during a crucial period of educational reform, economic expansion, and Cold War anxiety.

Gesell's observation that children are naturally creative is, I contend, indebted to a modern discourse on creativity and childhood that is complex and historically specific. His comment, from a 1943 handbook on children in contemporary culture, seems aphoristic and ageless. Yet when it appeared, the belief in children's capacity for imagination and independent thinking was still a relatively new idea in the United States. I describe how this notion mushroomed from the province of elite psychologists and progressive preschools of the interwar era to become a widespread and cohesive national value by the mid-1970s. The dramatic rise in the U.S. birthrate from 1946 to 1964 thrust debates about raising and educating children into the public eye. Once specialized professional conversations on play, child psychology, school building, and teaching art and science now warranted coverage in mass-media publications, and as the concerns of middle-class parents came to dominate the popular discussion, questions about nurturing creativity acquired broad political significance. If the striking increase in numbers of American children appeared outwardly to suggest optimism after World War II, its impact affected debates on education, science, and art, revealing a deep sense of self-doubt and anxiety over the future of American culture.

The discourse on creativity is central to this historical moment and to the particular role children played in the Cold War imaginary. These years coincided with U.S. policy on containment, an anticommunist political doctrine that had wide-reaching effects on daily life. Theorized in 1946 as a key foreign policy for "containing" a Soviet threat, containment also had domestic applications that envisioned atomic technology for peacetime use. Scholars have also argued that containment acted socially to construct a vision of normative family life. As Cold War enmity and anxiety seeped into postwar narratives of domesticity, it affected the selling of both everyday goods and high culture, as well as the experiences of individuals.[2] Children in this Cold War domestic drama were both vulnerable and in need of protection yet at the same time a positive force whose promise appeared to answer the most pressing worries of the age.

The image of the authentically creative child as a homegrown weapon of the Cold War is difficult to reconcile with popularly held notions about postwar America. A landscape of suburban sameness, a return to traditional gender roles, and the expansion of political suspicion give the postwar era, especially viewed retrospectively, an ominous cast and make these years an unlikely moment for a resurgent interest in imagination and divergent thinking. Indeed, a renewed faith in the creative potential of children (and adults) appears paradoxical in an era of restrictive conformity. Even the more celebratory perception of postwar culture as bountiful and stable seems at odds with the spreading critique of American education. A similarly narrow set of tropes also defines a received understanding of postwar childhood. Media-driven images showed dutiful children who de-ferred to parental authority or, conversely, rebelled into a youth or street culture that fueled fears of an explosion of juvenile delinquency.[3] Although scholars have challenged many of these stereotypes of postwar domestic life, moving conspicuously away from monolithic characterizations of subur-bia, family life, economics, and gender, some of the more subtle discourses of the era, such as creativity, not only lack critical attention but have been flattened out to stretch further as universal "truths."[4] I argue that creativity was mythologized and commodified, and that it acquired a primary place in the discourse of postwar exceptionalism that has been sustained into the twenty-first century.

Because of its intangible qualities, creativity is difficult to define with precision. *Webster's Third New International Dictionary*, revised in 1961, gave the tautological definition of *creativity* as "the quality of being cre-ative; ability to create."[5] *Imagination* and *originality*, even *individual-ity*, however, were the synonyms most closely paired with the term. These attractive associations of unbounded possibility and ingenuity gained posi-tive meaning in an age of new concerns about national competitiveness. Although diffuse, the notion of creativity was resurgent in public aspects of postwar life, from the rise of a heroic abstract expressionism as an artistic emblem of American individualism to the corporate embrace of the "cre-ative revolution" in advertising and business.[6] The discourse of creativity was equally present in private life, where it took hold in a strenuous culture of hobbies, domestic science, and especially the education and upbringing of children. Raising creative children was, of course, the dream of adults, and the dynamic of enabling a child's creativity was closely tied to a par-ent's own creative choices. Inverting the norm of training children to as-sume the conventions of adulthood, the discourse on creativity valued the child's unique insight, which the parent labored to reveal, sustain, and then emulate. Mihaly Csikszentmihalyi distinguishes between "big-C" creativity, which he defines as the work of prominent artists, writers, and musicians, and the "small-c" creativity that the greater mass practices in unremark-able everyday situations.[7] This "small-c" creativity was the precise target of postwar advertisers and educators, and the activity of children, teachers, and parents. The kind of creativity envisioned in popular magazines and by toy sellers and school planners was far from monumental, yet in the period debate, the small scale of these actions augured a grand future of national achievement.

THE INVENTION OF THE CREATIVE CHILD

As creativity gained prominence as a national ideal, it coincided with an explosion of live births and an economy that enabled middle-class households to acquire ever more, but it also intersected with the well-established ideal that innocent children possessed special insightful qualities. The concept of the creative child is a notion entwined with the modern rise of childhood. Although there is evidence from antiquity and the Middle Ages that describes children's character, acknowledging familial attachment and the notion that play and encouragement helped children to learn, a fundamental shift in the concern for the individual occurred in the late seventeenth and eighteenth centuries, when philosophies on the education of children began to support the idea that specific training might result in a "better" adult.[8] In contrast to earlier notions that the child was a natural sinner who must be disciplined and trained quickly to inhabit adult society, modern concepts of an ideal childhood put emphasis on preserving innocence, curiosity, and playfulness in the growing child. John Locke's advice on raising a gentleman's son in *Some Thoughts concerning Education* (1693) encouraged the ways of the peasantry as a model for developing a healthy child into a sensible aristocratic adult. Plain foods, soft shoes and loose clothes, exposure to the elements, sufficient sleep, toys, and limited corporal punishment created the basis for a sound body and mind. Locke became known for his "tabula rasa" notion that children were essentially blank until educated. He sternly expected submissiveness to adults, yet he also showed sympathy for childish inquisitiveness. "*Curiosity*," he suggested, "should be as carefully *cherished* in children as other appetites suppressed."[9]

From the second half of the eighteenth century, pedagogues and elites fixed on children as a revelatory means of understanding and transforming the human condition. In *Émile; or, On Education* (1762), the philosopher Jean-Jacques Rousseau described a childhood that departed radically from earlier notions. Rousseau's fictional Émile was raised to exist in a state of harmony with the natural world and without the morals of bourgeois society imposed on his education. Rousseau admonished, "Love childhood; promote its games, its pleasures, its amiable instinct."[10] Baby Émile is not bound in swaddling clothes but allowed to move his limbs and nursed from his mother's breast. Child Émile is allowed to play outdoors, experience pain and beauty, and learn a trade. For Rousseau, impulse and sensation rule the child. It is the adult observer of Émile who is endowed with the faculty of imagination. Yet, as Jennifer Milam has suggested, the paintings of some of

Rousseau's contemporaries reveal how creativity and imagination became key themes in eighteenth-century depictions of children at play.[11] If Rousseau allowed that the child was fascinating and impulsive, his interpreters saw in those impulses a useful and admirable quality of invention.[12]

In the earliest years of the nineteenth century, the Swiss pedagogue Johann Heinrich Pestalozzi argued that the concept of *Anschauung*, the active, intuitive human mind, was the basis of all knowledge. *Anschauung* was translated in English in the late nineteenth century as "sense-impression" and also as the more long-lasting "object lesson." In perceiving objects through the senses, the child activated his or her higher powers of understanding, transforming fleeting sensory impressions into conscious thoughts. Pestalozzi favored an educational process that introduced the object before the word.[13] Following Rousseau, whom he admired to the extent that he named his son Jean-Jacques, Pestalozzi argued that the material world and our sensory perception of it were the fundamental sources of knowledge. Pestalozzi is best known for a system of teaching through drawing, which, while deriving from instinct, would instill skills of observation, accuracy, and patience.[14] The idea that sensory engagement with objects might not only release a child's understanding and encourage development but also promote a forceful creativity was a central theme for subsequent reformers.

Another romantic with much greater investment in identifying and molding the creativity of the child was the German educator Friedrich Fröbel. Fröbel's program of kindergarten gifts and occupations, developed in the 1830s and 1840s, aimed to train a child's senses and faculties to embody a spiritual harmony between mankind, nature, and God. Fröbel's kindergarten theory, moreover, aimed to foster what he called the "impulse to creative activity" to achieve a comprehensive expression of love and humanity.[15] Fröbel's concept of creativity was quite different from the connotations of free expression of the twentieth century. Rather, Fröbel's creativity was the acquisition of knowledge through busy manipulation, the result of an individual's self-discovery and self-instruction through observation and sensory engagement. For Fröbel, then, creativity was the child's intellect in action, the means by which he or she understood him- or herself in relation to the physical world and its metaphysical meaning. The aim of Fröbel's program of gifts and occupations was to use sensory information—to manipulate human-made and natural objects—to awaken the mind. In restating Pestalozzi's "object lesson," Fröbel established a solidly material basis for the education of children, and, more importantly, he implied that the private reflections of the individual were its ultimate aim. This aspect of Fröbel's theory, rather than its spiritual aspect, became firmly embedded in the ideal of "hands-on" learning through objects.

Adults consciously constructed the figure of the creative child, increasingly idealizing creativity as a dimension of childhood's "naturalness" and "innocence." Nineteenth-century images of children show how this enduring motif of children at play in natural settings reflected the growth of reformist educational ideas.[16] The German romantic artist Philipp Otto Runge's images of children from around 1800 suggest the painter's reverence for the state of childhood and for the especially insightful qualities he believed children possessed. Runge's *The Hülsenbeck Children* (1805–6), a group portrait of the children of his brother's business partner, depicts children as innocent and visionary (Plate 1). Runge shows the Hülsenbeck children alone, engaged in their own private world just beyond the family dwelling, which is at a distance from the city of Hamburg indicated in the background. The setting in nature, just beyond the fence, is the telling sign that the Hülsenbeck children's world is also removed from adults. Beyond documenting their childlike bodies and child-specific clothes, the painter stresses their staring intensity and absorption in play. As the two older children, August and Maria, pull along their younger brother, Friedrich (who grasps a large sunflower leaf), in a wooden cart, they engage in make-believe roles; Maria gestures maternally to the baby, and August raises his whip to his pretend horses. These ordinary playthings and the simple actions they prompt call our attention to the depth of the Hülsenbeck children's imaginative capacity. Runge's association of the children's state of enchanted playfulness with the plants and flowers of their surroundings is but one example of any number of depictions of "natural" and "innocent" children that persist in the modern era. The endurance of this motif suggests a perpetual yearning for what both Robert Rosenblum and Anne Higonnet have called the romantic child, a figure who represents what we most value and fear losing.[17] I argue that, equally with naturalness and innocence, creativity is a projected quality closely linked with the figure of the romantic child.

Modern artists and writers admired the innocent child and linked childhood positively and nostalgically with primitivism. Like the "primitive," whose apparently unselfconscious expression was widely admired, the child was endowed with special capabilities that had been deemed lost in the educated, socialized adult. In the visual and applied arts, the non-Western exotic and the European peasant possessed a childlike intuition configured as untutored creativity and spontaneity in opposition to an overcivilized, corrupt, and industrialized Western culture.[18] Furthermore, popular and scientific recapitulation-development theories, which G. Stanley Hall, a founder of the child study movement, espoused in the United States in the late nineteenth century, argued that the child passed through the stages of human evolution, thus becoming a modern primitive alive in the present.

Hall had no interest in "soft" individualism and believed children should be trained to obey authority, but another face of this primitivist discourse found a welcome home in the modernist idea of an authentic creativity that derived from a deep inward source rather than from artistic training. Jonathan Fineberg has documented how modern artists and critics viewed children as having unique, even visionary, artistic potential. The relationship between the insightful and inventive child and the child as a model artist is a modernist conceit. Artists such as Pablo Picasso, Gabriele Münter, Wassily Kandinsky, Paul Klee, and others admired and emulated children's art for its forceful and economical strategies of representation.[19] Pre- and interwar reformers in Europe established special schools to mold children's skills in drawing, painting, and the applied arts. Thus, when Gesell made his observation that the child might be considered a "creative artist of sorts," the creative child was already revered among the European avantgarde and had become a new ideal in elite American nursery schools in the 1920s and 1930s.

This modernist outlook frames the discourse of the creative child in the postwar period I discuss. The value of individual perception, the unquestioned belief in innovation, and the idealized future many imagined the next generation would enjoy all shaped the image of the creative child as an authentic figure of hopefulness. Likewise, in the architecture of postwar schools and houses and the design of toys and goods, modernist values of abstraction, timelessness, and technical achievement were articulated formally. It is no accident that some of the architects, designers, and institutions that most readily embraced the ideal of the creative child were avowedly modernist. Yet I hope this particular view of postwar modernism will complicate received notions of modern midcentury design. This is far less a story of heroic avant-gardism than that of the ways that modernism was refashioned for ordinary life and the marketplace.

The persistently romantic concept of childhood creativity—theorized as innate and at the same time responsive to encouragement—steadily emerged over two centuries. Similarly, the notion of the object lesson became firmly established so that by the end of the nineteenth century in the United States it was understood as a direct source of knowledge, a fundamental means of apprehending complex phenomena through the senses, and an effective method of teaching.[20] The same strain of curiosity and belief in practical aspects of learning resulted in what John H. Lienhard has called the "savage boy inventor," a figure that was born in the Progressive Era and lingered well into the midcentury. The inventiveness of the savage boy inventor, the presumed reader of handbooks and popular science manuals, derived from both manual competence and a streak of productive experimentalism.[21] At once hardy, virile, and inward, this notion of the American boy linked wildness with curiosity and authenticity. In the years of the American baby boom, the creative child materialized fully in psychological studies and educational literature, popular parenting texts, books, toys, television, homes, schools, and museums as the ideal future citizen. The dream of ambitious middle- and upper-middle-class parents, toy companies, and researchers, the creative child was a source of authentic imagination and insight and the regenerative answer to some of the many anxieties of postwar culture.

I want to be clear that although I explore the ways that the figure of the creative child was invented, I am not trying to suggest that creativity is an empty notion or that children are not particularly imaginative. Instead, I argue that this figure was constituted visually, materially, spatially, and scientifically. Following Bruno Latour and others, I aim to show how people, ideas, images, and objects (including buildings and exhibits) acted together to assemble the notion of creativity that we recognize as both a metaphor and the acts of real people.[22] This book, therefore, is not about individual children and their specific creations. Rather, I argue that "real" children are implied in the schemes that parents and other adults have created, but that they are nonetheless strongly idealized interpretations. What I think we can gain in analyzing childhood creativity as a historical development, rather than essentializing it as a "natural" fact, is a greater awareness of how and why we identify and value these qualities in "real" children, how we understand what we call postwar American childhood, and what those two questions together might reveal about the place of art, science, and education in the history of the United States since World War II. I also explore how creativity has become the default "answer" to social and economic problems, how it suits a mythologizing national narrative of individualism and discovery. By examining the mechanisms we adults have devised to cultivate, reinforce, study, and measure creativity in children, I maintain that we can learn more not only about what constitutes postwar material culture but also about the assumptions that underwrite our enduring preoccupation with creativity as an index of individualism.

In thinking about how the rhetoric of creativity affects our individual lives, I have benefited from Nikolas Rose's contributions to the theory of governmentality. As he argues, "Childhood is the most intensively governed sector of personal existence."[23] Rose traces the subtle alignment of institutional aims with individual pleasures and desire for self-fulfillment in the twentieth century. In my project, the nexus between scientific research on creativity, the consumption of toys and amusements in the name of raising "creative" children, and the official educational sphere of school building, art education, and elevation of hands-on "discovery" in museums shows that the authentically creative individual self was internalized as the desirable goal not only of postwar childhood but also of postwar adulthood. Although I suggest that political pressures encouraged creativity as a specifically American value, I echo Rose's assessment that the private self in the twentieth century was achieved not through coercive means but rather through the alluring image of personal freedom.

DESIGN AND THE MATERIAL CULTURES OF CHILDHOOD

Material culture has long provided scholars of childhood with a legible sign of contemporary values and beliefs. Indeed, those who recount the historical invention of childhood all rely to some degree on material objects as part of their evidence.[24] It is safe to say we generally accept that childhood is an idea that shifts over time and that the everyday things surrounding children are useful means of observing and analyzing those changes. Yet if material evidence has found its way into larger works on the history of children, it is only recently that scholars have devoted specific attention to the material culture of childhood itself. I want to make a distinction that is both historiographical and methodological. Although goods, toys, and other amusements are ready evidence for historians of childhood, they are rarely the focus of scholarship.[25] Rather than treat objects as incidental, passive reflections of larger ideas, I explore how things made for children's use redefined the ideas of "childhood" and "creativity" in historically specific ways. Things, especially those for children, are designed according to social scripts, and these are often the key aspects of signification. But objects, like users, do not always hew to a narrow set of prescribed activities or uses. In the postwar discourse of creativity, open-endedness was itself a desirable quality, and given that objects were deliberately invested with agency through their appeal to the senses, one must consider not only what they represented but also what they helped to create, both discursively and literally.

In each chapter of this book, I examine things that were created for children's use. Following Ben Highmore, whose notion of "design culture" especially embraces the unremarkable everyday things and the sensory experiences they engender, I emphasize a range of goods, from architect-designed spaces to relatively ordinary household amusements.[26] But because I attempt to trace the discourse of creativity through things and places, I am also eager to connect specific ideas with the individuals and groups that produced them. Indeed, the things, spaces, and programs I discuss were all consciously designed as object lessons. And because they are *designed,* I want to argue for the relevance of design and design history to material culture studies. Paraphrasing the late Judy Attfield, I stress an inclusive rather than an exceptional role for design.[27] This, then, is a story about how designers— some well known, others obscure—entered the quotidian world of postwar consumer culture and put the values of modernism to work in the service of raising and educating children. The creators of mass-produced toys, books, playrooms, playhouses, playgrounds, public schools, and museums, who I understand to include members of community organizations, corporate employees, parents, and independent professionals, are not, I should emphasize, unrecognized "pioneers" of midcentury design.

Resisting a teleology of greatness puts the emphasis on the cultural work of design. Historians of architecture and the built environment have begun to explore American playgrounds, public schools, and camps in important books and articles.[28] I am indebted to these scholars for suggesting how childhood operates spatially and as part of a cultural landscape. Like them, I examine a variety of everyday buildings that constitute the spaces of childhood and that, with the exception of suburban housing, are still largely unexplored. The same is also true of the design of other goods made for postwar children. Although I argue that goods are designed and that design is meaningful, I also contend that the ideal of creativity was its own powerful value, slogan, and agent, which animated some very ordinary things. Strings of wooden beads, mail-order science kits, finger paints, and stacking furniture are among the everyday goods that not only gathered around but also perpetuated discourses of creativity in American households and schools. Although created with an eye toward aesthetic and cognitive improvement, many of these goods were part of an everyday texture of middle-class life.

New scholarship on consumption has brought common goods and their use into the history of the material culture of childhood, showing how modern childhood in the United States was tethered to a developing and then mature consumer economy. These studies of toys, novel foods, radio clubs, movies, television shows, clothes, and books highlight the role of things and desire in relationships between children, parents, and advertisers. Tension between shifting parenting models from the early to the mid-twentieth century is mapped in children's access to spending money, in the advertising strategies and marketing promises of individual products, in the goods themselves, and in children's own opinions of them.[29] This scholarship makes it evident that consumption and childhood grew up together. Likewise, media studies and communication scholars have examined how media shaped children's goods. Unlike the historians and sociologists, they have tended to view children's consumption as either an illusion dangled by media corporations or the creative enterprise of an authentic children's culture.[30] Scholars have now come to understand the vexed relationship between children and consumption in more nuanced ways, as neither passive nor wholly liberating.[31]

My argument builds on this excellent research but takes a different position on the underlying reasons adults consumed on behalf of children. By looking at the material evidence (and to a lesser extent the media ideals), I explore how the educational rhetoric of creativity was commodified in objects and spaces at a time when consumer expectations were dramatically transformed. There is a good deal here about how parents were encouraged to consume in the name of raising better children. What I argue, moreover, is that as creativity entered a middle-class consumer culture, it did so in sync with the growth of cognitive psychology, educational reform, and Cold War social and political pressures. Because creativity was sold and experienced in many material forms—from educational toys, to special places for play, to new school plant designs, art materials and classes for children, and museums of art and science—it offered a transcendent value rather than just a singular commodity, and it affected children of varying economic circumstances. Beyond the aspirational consumption of middle-class parents who aimed to defy the conformist "organization man" caricature, the idea of creativity was naturalized in public spaces and increasingly popular discourses. The object lessons that constituted the abstract and powerful notion of the creative child therefore suggest a new dimension to the conventional critique that defines postwar childhood as a moment of "innocent" consumer culture of coonskin caps, Candy Land, and Mr. Potato Head, or as the now disquietingly gendered stereotypes of G.I. Joe, Barbie, and Easy-Bake Ovens. Rather, the rhetoric of childhood creativity has shaped our consumerist attitudes toward how we assess value in playthings and amusements, how we experience the built environment, from housing and playgrounds to schools, and furthermore, what kinds of civic and national policies we fabricate and embrace.

CREATIVITY AND POSTWAR AMERICAN CHILDHOOD

Creativity, as it was theorized, studied, and sold in postwar America, was inseparable from material objects. I explore these sites, which range from inexpensive toys and nursery furniture to large public schools and major museums, thematically in five chapters. Chapter 1 considers how the creative child emerged in the mid-twentieth century. With the end of World War II, the momentous demographic shift toward young families, the rise in wages, and the expansion of middle-class values, parental self-consciousness about raising children grew intensely. In the "consumer's republic" of the postwar era, as Lizabeth Cohen has termed it, the purchasing power of middle-class Americans and the goods to entice them were increasingly directed toward children's "needs."[32] This meant increased opportunities for play and for privacy and an unprecedented number of personal belongings such as books, toys, furniture, and clothes. Amid national debates on affluence and social conformity, psychologists devoted new energy to the study of creativity. The figure of the creative child was thus constituted scientifically, materially, and visually. The children who appeared in postwar picture books and on television embodied the ideals and longings of adults.

Chapter 2 shows how the concept of play, imagination, and the educational-toy market fortified the notion of childhood creativity. While established companies such as Playskool and Holgate expanded their selections of toys after the war, new businesses, such as Creative Playthings, emerged with sophisticated objects that promised to cultivate the seemingly innate curiosity of the child. In many ways, the utopian emphases of earlier educators such as Friedrich Fröbel and Maria Montessori were assimilated and reinterpreted in the second half of the twentieth century. Architects, sculptors, and designers embraced toy design as a means of teaching abstract skills and as a way to counter the proliferation of inexpensive toys on the market. Moreover, mass manufacturers were quick to adopt psychological and educational research on creativity to promote their products. In the late 1940s and 1950s, even art museums, such as the Museum of Modern Art in New York and the Walker Art Center in Minneapolis, worked to transform conventional designs for toys and playgrounds.

In chapter 3, I explore how the ideal of "creative living" affected all residents of the postwar house. Whereas middle-class nineteenth-century children were relegated to the attic or large upstairs bedrooms, postwar kids took their place at the center of the dwelling. In the new, increasingly informal houses promoted in popular magazines such as *Parents' Magazine* and *Ladies' Home Journal*, the playroom occupied a strategic place between individual bedrooms and the kitchen. Architects and designers developed child-sized furniture that looked at home in these spaces and yet remained toylike. Furthermore, the numerous designs for indoor and backyard playhouses, advertised in toy catalogs and popular magazines—transforming an elite amusement into a middle-class ideal—were sold with the aim of encouraging children to develop their own fantasy world while reinforcing the role of the parent as the model of creative activity in the home.

I look specifically at education and modern architectural design in chapter 4. The debates over education occupied teachers, parents, doctors, government officials, and architects. With the wartime population shifts, newly developed suburban tracts, and a swelling baby boom cohort, the need for thousands of new schools inaugurated a critical wave of school building in the United States. The entire school environment, from the structure and plan of the school plant to the lighting and color scheme of the classroom, and even to the type and arrangement of seats, was reconsidered between 1945 and 1975. Federal legislation and influential private organizations, such as the Ford Foundation's Educational Facilities Laboratories, put emphasis on developing schools that reflected newer theories of education. As activities such as memorization and dictation declined in favor of techniques such as team teaching, group activities, and the use of new media, the classroom itself changed in form and organization. Instead of featuring rectangular spaces with desks bolted to the floor in rows, the new classroom was organized with tables, in rooms with movable partitions, and finally in pods or clusters in the "open" schools of the late 1960s and early 1970s. Behind these changes lay the increasing acceptance of modern design as a means of helping children to learn in ways that might stimulate their attention and their imaginations.

In the final chapter I discuss how creativity was instilled through postwar art and science education. In the mid-twentieth century, "creative art" became the general name for all types of art education. Tracing the notion of "creative art education," I explore how school art instruction, art materials, and museums created a widely disseminated image of childhood creativity.

The émigré educator Viktor Lowenfeld, who wrote the influential book *Creative and Mental Growth* (1947), offered an instructional guide for teachers in postwar American elementary schools. Popular art-education programs sponsored by art-materials companies, such as Binney & Smith, which manufactured Crayola products, reinforced a growing perception that children should be encouraged in artistic pursuits both at school and at home. The education of creative children extended beyond the classroom. Many institutions opened new wings and redesigned galleries to meet the baby boom, and modern art museums developed ambitious children's exhibitions and a program of art education that stressed that all children could be creative if exposed to art as a freeing, rather than a rigid, experience. Furthermore, the children's museum, a new type of institution dedicated exclusively to stimulating young minds, expanded and flourished in postwar America. The growing business of creativity shows how these object lessons in thinking and making were transformed from an experimental aesthetic value and co-opted and commodified as an economic and social force.

Produced to instill specific values and to stimulate the senses, these toys, playrooms, playhouses, classrooms, and museums together demonstrate the enduring power of Pestalozzi's notion of the object lesson. They show not only that a romantic educational discourse persisted even in an era highly suspicious of originality, but also that a primal perceptual encounter with objects remains often unspoken but deeply embedded in our invention, understanding, and practice of modern American childhood.

1

CONSTRUCTING CREATIVITY IN POSTWAR AMERICA

THE NOTION OF THE CREATIVE CHILD emerged in earlier generations as an educational and artistic ideal, but it was newly constructed and commodified as an aspect of middle-class culture with the rapid population expansion of the baby boom after World War II. The years after the war have been called "child-centered" for the huge numbers of children born during the largest extended baby boom in U.S. history. In 1947, 3.8 million babies were born to American parents. This number reached 4 million every year from 1954 to 1964. These 76.4 million children born between 1946 and 1964 were significant in part because of their sheer number, but also because of the attitudes of their parents and the societal shifts they embodied.[1] Not only were American middle-class parents raising more children, but they also strived to raise better children.[2] Scientists argued that babies learned more and earlier than had been traditionally accepted, and it became a parent's job to stimulate and guide the growing child even before he or she entered school. Just as pediatricians and psychologists created norms and stages against which children were measured and charted, so too were matters of parental guidance increasingly analyzed. Raising IQ, improving school readiness, and developing social skills were the anxious refrains in mass-circulation magazines and parenting guides. And Cold War pressures stimulated unsettling questions about national renewal, future competitiveness, and material abundance. In the midst of these and other debates, creativity became an important subject of psychological and educational research and a quality that striving parents hoped to cultivate in their children.

The real value of creativity was, and still is, hard to define. Admired as inventiveness, problem solving, insightfulness, originality, and discovery of personal potential, creativity encompasses a broad variety of meanings. Although it is an abstract concept—and became and remained a colloquial buzzword—creativity was consumed in the postwar economy as a solid middle-class belief and was invoked in the national conversation on identity, cultural progress, and future material and political gains. Because children were widely perceived as possessing this apparently innate quality, nourishing and directing it was a common theme in the burgeoning advice literature on parenting. The widespread acceptance of creativity as a "natural" and instinctive attribute of children paralleled the scientific research on creativity. After psychologists began to study and measure creativity, around 1950, they argued that it was a vital and productive aspect of the human personality. Governmental authorities such as the U.S. Children's Bureau, toy manufacturers, and magazines quickly popularized this scientific literature, arguing for an overlooked but uniquely valuable creative child who might contribute to society in yet untold ways. As the child became an object of intense study and discussion, scrutiny and measurement of children's abilities also transformed the idea of the creative child, who shifted from a romantic agent of authentic insight to a quantifiable consuming citizen of the postwar era. The romantic ideal, however, persisted in new forms. The curious and imaginative protagonists who populated the growing market for children's picture books and juvenile television programs gave the constructed image of the creative child a lasting place in the middle-class household.

POSTWAR PARENTS

In a 1946 article about the importance of raising a new generation "imbued with a high resolve to work together for everlasting peace," a writer for *American Home* commented that parenthood was "not a dull, monotonous routine job, but an absorbing, creative profession."[3] The new parents of the baby boom children were younger than their own parents had been when they had children, were more affluent, and were greater consumers of everything from household appliances to advice literature about raising children. Furthermore, the role of the parent had shifted in the twentieth century away from a disinterested scientist model of the behaviorist to an observant coach who attended to the individual needs and developing personality of the growing child. As best-selling parenting books and mass-circulation magazines reached young families, they established a set of social and cultural expectations about attitudes, routines, and stages. Moreover, they constructed ideal roles for both the child and his or her parents.

The baby-advice industry was well established in the 1920s, but it was in the postwar era that authors of baby books became household names.[4] The most famous was, of course, the pediatrician Benjamin Spock, whose

Common Sense Book of Baby and Child Care, first published in 1946, sold 750,000 copies and, in a pocket edition, continued to sell nearly a million copies every year in the 1950s.[5] Spock's reassuring voice and psychoanalytic views made him more lenient about toilet training and feeding schedules, and more concerned with a child's personality, than earlier generations of parenting experts. Spock was renowned, yet he was just one of several figures who shifted the discourse of raising children away from the rigid management of the child's care that marked behaviorism. In the late 1930s and 1940s, the Yale psychologist Arnold Gesell and his collaborators Frances Ilg, Janet Learned, and Louise Bates Ames popularized the stages of child development in their many books and stressed that the child's own maturation process drove his or her behavior. Gesell redefined the parent's role in the development of the child, encouraging gentle detachment via correct amusements and isolation. Although later scholars and researchers pointed to the problematically small samples of upper-middle-class white children as indications of "normal" stages, Gesell's books and advice columns made him a prominent figure among the midcentury experts.[6] In his book *"Where Did You Go?" "Out." "What Did You Do?" "Nothing."* (1957), Robert Paul Smith snidely described the suburb where he was raising his three children and the reigning preoccupation with social adjustment and psychological advice: "Spock and Gesell and others of that Ilg are the local deities, the school teachers speak of that little stinker from Croveny Road as 'a real challenge,' there are play groups and athletic supervisors and Little Leagues and classes in advanced finger painting and family counselors and child psychologists. Ladies who don't know *a posteriori* from *tertium quid* carry the words 'sibling rivalry' in the pocketbooks of their minds as faithfully as their no-smear lipstick."[7] Spock, Gesell, and the anthropologist Margaret Mead all emphasized that the healthy personality and child's well-being required that parents, especially mothers, become attentive to child psychology, exert more of their energy providing correct stimulation through play, and exercise restraint in discipline.

PERSONALITY, CREATIVITY, AND DEMOCRACY

The creative child, as he or she emerged in the postwar advice literature, was a free-thinking and free-acting individual. Concern for the child's specific emotional and social development, rather than as a specimen managed according to a scientific process, marked the postwar parenting model. A child's freedom to explore and express him- or herself without fear of strong disciplinary action was equated with the democratic ideal that safeguarded the individual's personal thoughts and contributions. For postwar experts, a child possessed a "healthy personality" when parents allowed him or her to follow his or her own internal laws of development, which were nourished with love, encouragement, and guidance.[8] As the fact-finding report prepared by the Midcentury White House Conference on Children and Youth of 1950 noted, "For healthy personality development it is very important . . . that much leeway and encouragement be given to the child's show of enterprise and imagination and that punishment . . . be kept for things that matter."[9]

As experts debated the growth and development of children, their concerns grew not only for molding social and emotional adjustment but also for making democratic citizens. Wartime experience brought new scrutiny to how a totalitarian personality was formed and expressed.[10] In 1943, Gesell stated in the opening pages of *The Infant and Child in the Culture of Today*: "A totalitarian 'Kultur' subordinates the family completely to the state, fosters autocratic parent-child relationships, favors despotic discipline, and relaxes the tradition of monogamy. It is not concerned with the individual as a person. A democratic culture, on the contrary, affirms the dignity of the individual person. It exalts the status of the family as a social group, favors reciprocity in parent-child relationships, and encourages humane discipline of the child through guidance and understanding."[11] The family and the home were the first and most important sites of this process, and Gesell's concept of the household as a "cultural workshop" made explicit connections between practices at home, a child's future personality, and broader social values. Indeed, Gesell referred to the child's "cultural activities" as "creative activities."

The postwar discourse on child rearing was directed toward what some have called a "natural" American child in contrast to the image of a Soviet child raised according to directives from the state.[12] Discipline, for which Spock acquired the inaccurate reputation of being "permissive," not only was a touchstone for attitudes about the private family unit, it also was tinged with political implications. In a 1955 study of Soviet "child training" attitudes, Margaret Mead observed that recent changes in Soviet doctrine allowed the family more responsibility, and harsh discipline was rejected on the grounds that it was ineffective, but she concluded there was little recognition of the stages of a child's development and the need for privacy, rebellion, and experimentation. Soviet manuals also used psychological methods to "guide [children's] imagination, to develop it in the necessary direction, to utilize creative force in the interest of the communistic transformation of our motherland," yet Mead argued that in the Soviet system, "complete control must be maintained."[13] (In 1970, the psychologist Urie Bronfenbrenner, who made firsthand studies of Soviet attitudes, suggested that Soviet children identified with adults more closely, encountered fewer divergent views, and conformed to "more homogeneous" standards than American children did.)[14] Soviet perceptions of "creative imagination," Mead implied, were limited and activities such as play largely predetermined to produce narrowly acceptable results. The Soviet character structure, she concluded, was "equipped for a rigid acceptance of a doctrinaire view of the world, unreceptive to outside influences, energetic in the pursuit of Soviet national purposes."[15] For Mead, then, the American child, whose individuality was recognized and encouraged, whose parents noted developmental shifts, and whose imagination was apparently unfettered, was also raised for a larger project, which she understood as "an inclusive, flexible, national culture," rather than cultlike obedience.[16]

The American child's potential contributions to democracy were part of the construction of the creative postwar child. Like Mead, Martha Wolfenstein examined official pamphlets on child training, but in the U.S. Children's Bureau publications she noted a shift in the opposite direction, toward what she called a "fun morality" of play, amusement, and gratification.[17] If the child's physical, psychological, and cognitive development would benefit from attitudes toward child rearing that valorized play and curiosity, then it followed that the parent could also endanger a child's creative development. In 1955, Else Frenkel-Brunswik argued, "The intimidating, punitive, and paralyzing influence of an overdisciplined, totalitarian home atmosphere may well exert a decisive influence upon the thinking and creativity of the growing child."[18] To encourage a healthy personality and a democratic culture, experts urged postwar parents to allow children more personal freedom, to moderate their attitudes toward discipline, and to provide toys and amusements that would enhance children's cognitive and social development. The confluence of a dramatic rise in the number of children born, expanding middle-class values, and anxieties about Cold War political tensions all contributed to the formation of a creative child who was as much the darling of pediatricians, psychologists, and anthropologists as he or she was of manufacturers, advertisers, merchants, and parents.

CREATIVITY AND CONSUMPTION

Postwar middle-class parents told to provide amusements and space for developing children increasingly directed their dollars toward children's "needs." These parents were not alone. The rise in wages fueled a national ideology of consumption, which Lizabeth Cohen has called a "consumer's republic."[19] In addition to newly affluent parents, the great numbers of new children gave postwar consumption of household goods a child-centered cast. Yet, as Lisa Jacobson and Daniel Thomas Cook have shown, questions about consumer goods and childhood predate the postwar boom. In the early twentieth century, as the United States became a full-fledged consumer society, advertisers and retailers pitched a wide variety of products to youthful consumers.[20] By the 1920s and 1930s, the figure of the child consumer was well established. Mickey Mouse underwear, Dick Tracy knives, Kewpie dolls, cereals, and other products were sold directly to children through movies, juvenile magazines, and radio spots and clubs. Jacobson, however, has also argued that middle-class families who remained skeptical of mass culture encouraged specifically creative pursuits, including a properly outfitted playroom, as a means of protecting children from the enticements of popular culture.[21] Thus, the discourse of creativity, which was built on an older romantic notion, was recast as the antidote to modern consumer culture already in the early twentieth century.

The consumerist anxieties of prewar middle-class parents shifted in the years after the Second World War.[22] Items for babies and children flooded the market. From new plastic rattles in the mid-1940s to entire floors of children's and teens' clothing in 1960s department stores, the range of children's goods available to the middle-class consumer was unprecedented. The Boater, a cover for diapers that Marion O'Brien Donovan, a mother of two young children, designed and patented exemplifies the new market for children's goods. Donovan's invention was a waterproof nylon shell that held cloth or disposable pads in place and fastened with snaps, eliminating the need for pins (Figure 1.1). The Boater's attraction was its supposedly leakproof quality, but it also promised to save on laundry. To appeal to a wide market, the Boater came in three different sizes, to accommodate a growing baby, and in three pastel colors. Sold in upscale department stores for the relatively expensive price of $1.95, the Boater seemed to meet a market need. Just after the invention was introduced, in July 1949, the department store Saks Fifth Avenue quickly placed another order after the second working day and by the third day had reordered three times the original amount. In 1950, after receiving a patent for the design, Donovan sold her invention for a million dollars.[23]

In the prosperous years after the end of the war, middle-class, predominantly white families interpreted children's "needs" to include not only diapers and covers but also early education, such as nursery school, more personal space, increased opportunities for play, and an unprecedented number of personal belongings such as books and toys.[24] Gesell listed preferred objects for the various stages of childhood in the back of his books, and Spock identified particular types of objects in his section on toys. Amusements for children were household expenses, and as the dwelling became a focus for family life it was also a primary site of consumption. Between 1945 and 1950, consumer spending rose 60 percent, with spending on household items increasing by 240 percent.[25] The middle-class dwelling, both urban and suburban, required washing machines, kitchen appliances, televisions, and other elements of modern decor. Improving the material comforts of the dwelling meant investing in the family unit itself. The acquisition of toys, backyard amusements, and expansions to the house followed this logic, making consumption on behalf of children a forceful dimension of the postwar market.

Figure 1.1. Marion O'Brien Donovan, the Boater, circa 1949. Marion O'Brien Donovan Papers, Archive Center, National Museum of American History, Smithsonian Institution.

Whereas adults purchased most toys for young children, children's own desires shaped consumption. Children themselves were a prized segment of this expanding postwar consumer culture. Vance Packard's best-selling *The Hidden Persuaders* (1957) viewed the creation of child consumers as a "psycho-seduction" and blamed television's undisputed effectiveness. Television provided a direct link with youthful viewers, who sought out novelties such as Davy Crockett's coonskin cap, the hula hoop, the Mattel Burp Gun, and grape juice, potato chips, pudding, and breakfast cereals.[26] The increased market segmentation made children's television a conduit to the child consumer, just as household cleaners were directed toward women and shaving products toward men.[27] Although an early belief that television promoted domestic harmony was spread through industry propaganda and popular magazines, fears about children's vulnerability and potential corruption from exposure to television images intended for adults gained a following.[28] The creation of a genre of wholesome programs for children seemed to assuage parents' and critics' anxieties. Programs that asked children to "finish the story" or submit drawings that would be viewed on air appeared to promote creativity and gained the approval of *Parents' Magazine*.[29] Yet nearly all network children's shows, such as *Captain Kangaroo*, promoted products, in some cases using the host to pitch.

Even the act of shopping was increasingly designed with children in mind. Santa Claus, holiday parades, and special amusements for children had long enticed parents to bring children to the downtown department store.[30] The large regional shopping centers that were developed in the postwar era, instead of the older, more formal downtown establishments, were often designed with space for community and children's activities. Victor Gruen, who became a prominent planner and designer of postwar shopping centers and malls, described the creation of public areas as "done with the express intention of creating an environment which, if properly utilized, will establish the shopping center as the focal point for the life of a community or a number of communities."[31] The provision of meeting rooms, auditoriums, and other venues for activities that had a cultural, educational, and recreational character was part of the suburban shopping experience. Thus, square dancing, art exhibits, and ice skating, as well as flower shows, fashion shows, and entertainments for children, were written into the plan of these new complexes.

The shopping center embraced children's play as commercial logic. Jan Whitaker has shown that by the 1920s children had their own playgrounds, where parents could leave them for two hours to shop, in one-fifth of U.S. department stores. By the mid-1960s, however, downtown department-store playgrounds had dropped significantly, replaced by the entertainment areas at suburban shopping centers.[32] Whereas the Emporium Department Store in downtown San Francisco had a train and merry-go-round on its roof in the late 1940s, at the Stonestown Mall, which opened in 1952 in the Lake Merced area of the city, an entire children's Playland, including a Ferris wheel, was erected on the roof of the complex. Special "Kiddieland" areas became an integral part of shopping-center design across the country. At the Southdale Mall in Edina, Minnesota (1956), one of Gruen's most influential designs, there was a zoo, as well as rides, games, and refreshments, on the lower concourse.[33] The ubiquity of playgrounds and areas for children's amusement in commercial spaces had an unambiguous commercial rationale. By keeping children occupied, parents would be more inclined not only to shop but also to bring along their children, who might use their "pester power" to provoke even more spending.

In the milieu of this well-developed consumer culture, creativity, which had earlier implied a positive alternative to mass culture, was used both to critique the moral values of midcentury and to boost sales. As the following chapters explain, ambitious parents, wanting to maintain a wholesome distance from "lowbrow" mass consumption, favored toys that evoked traditional craftsmanship while also hoping to satisfy their children's desire for entertainment. Manufacturers were also quick to use creativity as an easy selling point. Steven Manufacturing's sledlike Pixie Wacky Rocker, for example, claimed to have "a terrific impact on child imaginations" and all the inventive potential that a "beat-up" cardboard box could offer (Figure 1.2). The commodification and commercial viability of creativity—not merely sold in the form of special toys and amusements but even informing larger

Figure 1.2. Advertisement for Pixie Wacky Rocker, Steven Manufacturing. Warshaw Collection of Business Americana–Toys, Archive Center, National Museum of American History, Smithsonian Institution.

investments such as home playrooms, new schools, and public educational programs—were unprecedented. Creativity, then, was a flexible concept that embodied both the hopes of parents for their children and some of their own anxious longings of the era. One of the most prominent debates was the self-conscious critique of middle-class consumption and its outward manifestation as social conformity.

CONFORMITY AND THE CRITIQUE OF AMERICAN CULTURE

The figure of the middle-class consumer who embraced the tastes and behavior of the group was a motif of postwar critical discourse that identified social conformity as a relatively recent and unflattering phenomenon. As Mark Jancovich has argued, the discourse on conformity was central to the cultural politics of the era.[34] Throughout the 1950s and 1960s, sociologists, political scientists, journalists, and popular writers explained new character types and documented consumption patterns, beliefs, social aspirations, and the physical habitats of the American middle class. These writers, including influential public intellectuals, called attention to the present state of American society as a culture of conformity. Studies on conformity peeked into postwar American public and private life.[35] Describing the pressures to adhere to a set of behavioral prescriptions, this literature elevated the ideal of creativity as conformity's antidote, giving it new prestige in the debates on childhood, consumption, and social values.

Within a decade of its publication, in 1950, David Riesman's *The Lonely Crowd* became a popular best seller so influential that it provoked a widespread discussion about national character.[36] Riesman, along with Nathan Glazer and Reuel Denney, argued that distinct character types corresponded to the shifts in American economic and social change. Riesman's "other-directed" figure was a new social personality that emerged in a dynamic relationship with the cultural and social order to become the dominant type of the mid-twentieth century. The "tradition-directed" type was bound to the social rules of the larger tribe or community, and the ascetic, "inner-directed" type was internally motivated—thanks to his or her strict upbringing—to achieve and improve him- or herself, but the other-directed type experienced social pressure from his or her peers. Riesman was careful to note that these were generalizations rather than real people, who were more complicated and could be blends of each, yet he and his colleagues argued that the other-directed type was typically middle or upper middle class and that he or she lived in or near cities, had fewer children, and aimed for social acceptance above all. Ruled by the anxiety of fitting in, rather than shame or fear, other-directeds embraced the norms of the group and hoped to instill in their offspring these same values. Even if Riesman distanced himself, as James Gilbert has suggested, from preferring one type over another, readers understood *The Lonely Crowd* and the other-directed character as a critique of postwar conformity.[37]

The other-directed character's patterns of parenting, or "child training" in the parlance of the time, were precisely those of the seemingly "permissive" postwar era. Following psychologist Erik Erikson and anthropologist Margaret Mead (to whom he sent the book in manuscript), Riesman depicted young other-directed parents, aware of the potential psychological burden that weighed upon their decisions, as turning to manuals and magazines for advice on raising children.[38] This "weakened" parent was now subjected to the increasing standardization of children's culture and the growing power of a child's peer relationships. The dominance of popular culture for the other-directed type implicated every member of the family in a cycle of consumption. Indeed, Riesman argued that the demarcations between production and consumption, leisure and work, and private and public interaction were blurred in the lives of the other-directed figure.

The consumer-oriented culture that Riesman described extended to all aspects of work and play. The growing anxiety to fit in therefore affected both adults and children, who learned these values from media and the cultural institutions of their time. Education, for Riesman, was a formidable agent in the reinforcement of peer culture among children. He argued that although school walls decorated with children's art appeared to honor creativity and individuality, the school itself was a singular agent in the destruction of imagination.[39] Children's play received special attention for its unpredictability. But, as Riesman noted, play itself had been taken over by school instructors who emphasized adjustment and fairness.[40]

Riesman was far less judgmental of the consumer habits of middle-class midcentury culture than many of his contemporaries, however, and he hoped that individuality could reappear in the consumer framework of the other-directed American. Recapturing autonomy, discernment, and creativity were the "competencies" that Riesman hoped the other-directed person could cultivate through leisure activities such as "taste-exchanging," rather than the pseudoauthentic activities of craftsmanship and folk dancing. To amateur hot-rodders and critics of comics, movies, and jazz—areas that had not yet entered the domain of the elite connoisseur—he ascribed a competence and autonomy within an available consumer culture. Riesman argued that architects and interior designers serving the upper-middle-class client, although in the business of constructing appearances, also helped an individual to define his or her own aesthetic and spatial preferences. He even envisioned a staged consumer economy set up for children, complete with fake money but real goods, in the hope that they could learn "to express themselves through free consumer choice released from ethnic and class and peer-group limitations, [and] might develop into much more imaginative critics of the leisure economy than most adults of today are."[41] In an other-directed society, Riesman's hope for individual expression lay in cultivating an informed opinion and personal consumer choices. Imagination and creativity remained the qualities that he and others admiringly ascribed to the potential for individual self-expression in a capitalist economy.

In popular images and scholarly debates, suburbia was cast as the telling backdrop of middle-class social conformity. Riesman observed, rather neutrally, that the "typical other-directed child grows up in a small family, in close urban quarters, or in a suburb," but others saw the growth of suburbia as a reflection of the state of American middle-class culture.[42] In 1958, Robert C. Wood noted, "The most fashionable definition of suburbia today is that it is a looking glass in which the character, behavior, and culture of middle class America is displayed. When we look at suburbs we see our homes; when we look at suburbanites we see ourselves."[43] If suburbia presented a neat image of middle-class identity, its key signifiers—racial, social, intellectual, and architectural homogeneity—were, and have remained, a persistent trope of the postwar era. Scholars have challenged this narrow view, but the critique of suburban conformity was itself a powerful current in postwar thought and culture. The anxious lives of suburban citizens were evoked in the fictional couples of Jim and Muriel Blandings in Eric Hodgins's *Mr. Blandings Builds His Dream House* (1946), Tom and Betsey Rath in Sloan Wilson's *The Man in the Gray Flannel Suit* (1955), and John and Mary Drone in John Keats's *A Crack in the Picture Window* (1957), who were satirized for acquiescing to the materialist pressures of their neighbors, especially in the appointment of their suburban dwellings.[44]

The vast transformation of outlying farmland into suburban tracts and subdivisions created what Peter Rowe has called a "middle landscape" erected in pursuit of an ideal of leisure and domestic ease as well as racial segregation.[45] This shift was already well under way at the turn of the century, but the speed with which it was realized after 1950 confounded expectation. The proportion of suburban development rose beyond 50 percent, and average population growth in suburban areas of large metropolitan regions expanded 53.9 percent between 1950 and 1960. Government agencies and programs, especially the Federal Housing Administration, the Veterans Administration, and the Home Owners Loan Corporation, hastened home ownership for the working and middle classes through insured mortgages. These same agencies, however, also encouraged the practice of redlining, which assigned real estate value and signaled investment security according to the age and density of a neighborhood and the race and ethnicity of its inhabitants. Although it was developed for rating urban precincts, redlining directly affected residential areas far beyond the metropolis. In practice, redlining privileged neighborhoods of new construction and homogeneously white populations as sound investments. The racial conformity of white suburbia was mirrored in the architectural choices of the new developments, which mass-produced single-family ranch or Cape Cod designs that were repeated with little apparent modification over acres of housing tracts. Whiteness and architectural monotony were the prominent outward signs of conformity, but the differences in social class and ethnicity, as scholars then and since have noted, were considerable.[46]

At the heart of the postwar exodus from big cities was a strong belief that life in the suburbs benefited children. Indeed, the population arc of the baby boom is mirrored in the growth of home ownership, which increased to 66 percent by 1970, and auto sales (a ratio of one car per family was surpassed in 1955).[47] The combination of the baby boom, decentralized housing, and increasing reliance on the automobile gave suburban developments a child-centered reputation and design. Along with housing tracts came the need for new schools, shopping centers, and places for community activities. In the case of Levittown, Long Island, shopping and community pools were part of the Levitts' scheme, but there was no land allotted, and no plan, for new schools.[48] The pattern of roads in subdivisions was deliberately designed to eliminate through traffic, creating the illusion of rusticity and safety. A 1944 traveling exhibition on planning declaimed, "A good neighborhood has an elementary school," and suggested that "the school should be placed in the park so that children may walk there from any house in the neighborhood without crossing traffic streets. It must also be accessible by car."[49] Lawrence Perkins, a prominent postwar school architect and planner, suggested that new elementary schools should not be more than three-fourths of a mile from the farthest dwelling.[50] Keeping children safe and encouraging a picturesque image went hand in hand in the consumer-oriented sales literature of suburbia.

Architectural critics such as Lewis Mumford decried not only the failure of planning and the aesthetics of uniformity but also the social conformity that seemed so pervasive to critics of suburbia in the 1950s and 1960s. Willful naïveté was one of Mumford's stinging critiques: "In the suburb one might live and die without marring the image of an innocent world, except when some shadow of its evil fell over a column in the newspaper. Thus the suburb served as an asylum for the preservation of illusion. Here domesticity could flourish, forgetful of the exploitation on which so much of it was based. Here individuality could prosper oblivious of the pervasive regimentation beyond. This was not merely a child-centered environment; it was based on a childish view of the world, in which reality was sacrificed to the pleasure principle." Mumford charged that in breaking away from the city the phase of childhood "became the pattern for all the seven ages of man."[51] But Paul Goodman, one of the most influential critics of postwar society, argued that the improved "child world," whether in city or suburb, had the benefit of temporarily enabling adults to participate in their communities in a meaningful way, because the aim was to create "the proper atmosphere for growing up."[52] Developers of new housing tracts positioned the suburb as child-centered, and even Mumford agreed that as a place for children's play it was a contribution, but other aspects of postwar domesticity were less reassuring.

Although suburban developments had been designed and sold for the benefit of families with children, critics of suburbia charged that the boredom and conformity of suburban life, along with expendable income and a burgeoning popular culture, could drive children above the age of twelve to explore a life of crime. Whereas working-class urban adolescents were often depicted as vulnerable to the temptations of delinquency, a growing youth culture that embraced images of rebellion transcended social class and geography.[53] Rock 'n' roll, tight or excessively baggy blue jeans, ducktail haircuts, and the popularity of James Dean were the outward symptoms of a cohesive youth culture that constituted what one scholar has called the "counter-suburban imaginary."[54] The estrangement of adolescents from their parents was hardly new in the postwar era—a youth culture of cinema and ragtime had similarly upset adults two generations earlier—yet the extended discussion in both the popular press and popular culture made the generation gap seem more pronounced.[55] Widely publicized statistics claimed that arrests for teenage crimes, from curfew violation to murder, had increased some 58 percent between the late 1940s and the early 1950s.[56] "Broken" homes and mass media were deemed the root causes in the Senate investigations on juvenile delinquency, which Robert C. Hendrickson and Estes Kefauver led in the mid-1950s.[57] The national fixation on the unruly teenager, who was portrayed as a threat to the future of American society, made juvenile delinquency not only a parent's worry but also a sign of cultural weakness. The uncertain cohesiveness of the family unit, a burgeoning mass culture, and an ascendant peer culture in large high schools all fed adult fears of an ominous conformity.[58]

Along with Riesman's *The Lonely Crowd*, William H. Whyte's *The Organization Man* (1956) was one of the most prominent sociological portraits of the postwar era that achieved popular success. For Whyte, whose study of Park Forest, Illinois, resulted in his book, the "organization man" was the quintessential other-directed type, a figure who stood for the transience and mindlessness of the American middle-class employee in all aspects of work, family, and social life. Beholden to the organization, whether a corporation or a government agency, the organization man subordinated his own desires to those of the larger bureaucracy. Instead of striving for individuality or uniqueness, the organization man deferred to the needs of the group, which required its employees to conform. This tautological system produced a culture of sameness that Whyte observed firsthand. In his analysis, the organization man preferred suburbia, which he described as "packaged villages that have become the dormitory of the new generation," but he also argued that the surface appearances of uniformity were not the defining factor. Instead, the culture of conformity was achieved through personality tests, an emphasis on well-roundedness, and the expectations of predetermined social interaction, as well as pretensions of classlessness and inconspicuous consumption.[59]

Creativity was the casualty that Whyte lamented most in the dominance of the organization. He argued that groups were not creative and that those who promoted the group, especially administrators, possessed a "natural distaste of the noncreative man for the creative." The administrator understood neither the creative individual nor what Whyte called the conditions of creativity: "The messiness of intuition, the aimless thoughts, the unpractical questions—all these things that are so often the companion to discovery are anathema to the world of the administrator."[60] A 1958 study, *Creativity and Conformity*, sponsored by the Foundation for Research on Human Behavior, argued that tests could identify creative and conformist employees, and although "original people do conform to group pressures . . . they conform less than unoriginal people."[61] The lack of personal individuality was not limited to business. Even research scientists, Whyte suggested, were steered toward the application of existing ideas, rather than the development of new ones.[62]

The consensus that conformity was a negative, even "dangerous," quality made it something to be assiduously avoided, as Jancovich suggests. Yet, as he also argues, the discourse of conformity lacked cohesion. Political outlook, group dynamics, consumption, and gender were all areas where the critique of conformity pitted the middle class against itself.[63] Children occupied a unique position in this question; as junior consumers and pupils in social adjustment programs, they were expected to conform, yet they also embodied a living promise for national renewal. Because children were understood as both unpredictable and trainable, they gained the spotlight in the national debates on democracy and the future of American culture. Reprising the romantic discourses of childhood innocence and innate insight, midcentury educational and psychological researchers turned their attention to the personal, social, and national promises that might derive from studying creativity more closely.

POSTWAR CREATIVITY RESEARCH

From the 1930s onward, researchers in the field of educational psychology had begun to address the role of creative thinking and imagination, but it was around midcentury that creativity became a widely researched area of investigation. J. P. Guilford, the president of the American Psychological Association (APA), established the terrain that many others would soon follow. Creativity, Guilford argued in his inaugural address to the APA in 1950, was not only difficult to measure and to predict, it seemed not to correlate with intelligence. Moreover, he suggested that creativity, which psychologists had neglected, was quickly becoming a highly desirable economic value and government interest.[64] Guilford's research on aptitude led to his theorizing of what he called the structure-of-intellect (SOI) model.[65] Unhappy with the limitations of the Stanford-Binet IQ test, Guilford attempted to classify and find relationships among abilities and developed a cubic structure that mapped the intersection of mental operations, informational content, and intellectual products. The three-dimensional SOI model argued for the production of 120 different intellectual abilities.[66] Guilford's work stimulated a vast number of important studies on many aspects of the problem of creativity in children and adults.[67]

Breaking with behaviorism, psychologists explored the responses and representations of the mind as one aspect of the so-called cognitive revolution.[68] Instead of measuring stimuli and response, researchers turned their attention to the nature of human (and artificial) knowledge and related epistemological questions. In the late 1950s and early 1960s, numerous books, papers, and conferences, including three sponsored at the University of Utah between 1955 and 1959, made the study of creativity an interest to university researchers, the National Science Foundation, the U.S. Department of Education, the U.S. Air Force, major industrial enterprises, and the general public.[69] The growth of psychological expertise on creativity and its applications gave visibility to a previously private experience. In order to measure and study creativity, experts sought its source.

Following Guilford, many psychologists believed that creativity was an innate human trait. Because children were perceived as closer to creativity's "origin," scholars turned their attention to children's development, schooling, and play activities. In an interdisciplinary symposium at Michigan State University in the late 1950s, Harold H. Anderson argued, "Creativity was in each one of us as a small child. In children creativity is a universal. Among adults it is almost nonexistent. The great question is: What has happened to this enormous and universal human resource? This is the question of the age and the quest of our research."[70] If creativity was as widespread in childhood as researchers believed, then, many argued, with study and encouragement its demise in adulthood might be spared and its full social, political, and intellectual potential realized.

An important avenue of this research emphasized that creativity suffered in a social and educational system that valued conformity and more conventional measures of academic success. Eliciting, capturing, and analyzing "creative" responses in schoolchildren became an ongoing interest of those who studied aptitude.[71] In the late 1950s, psychologist E. Paul Torrance, of the University of Minnesota, developed a series of tests that purported to measure creativity in children. Torrance was interested in abilities such as sensitivity to problems, fluency, flexibility, and originality, and developed verbal, nonverbal, and figural activities to assess these qualities.[72] Some of his test questions involved finding new uses for ordinary objects such as cans, cardboard, or toys, predicting outcomes of stories or situations, and asking questions of drawings presented to a child. The Torrance Tests of Creative Thinking (TTCT) were first administered in the early 1960s and quickly gained widespread attention. Torrance, on behalf of the Bureau of Educational Research at the University of Minnesota, also initiated a longitudinal study involving four hundred Minnesota children in two elementary schools.[73] The original study was conducted between 1958 and 1965, with follow-up questionnaires at the twenty-two-year mark in 1979–80, in 1998, and again in 2010.[74] This fifty-year study traced the fortunes and lives of children who had attended progressive elementary schools and came primarily from middle- and upper-middle-class families. It revealed that as these children grew up, both the school and the home had substantial influence in recognizing and pursuing what they termed creative experiences. It also suggested that for these children creativity's early manifestation was involvement with the fine arts either at home or in the classroom. In later life, the subjects considered their hobbies, career accomplishments, and approaches to problem solving as evidence of their personal creativity.[75]

Guilford, Torrance, and others had noted the divergence between creativity and intelligence, but the obsession with intelligence testing in the 1950s—American children quietly took IQ tests throughout their school years and were tracked according to the results—left little room for assessing other aspects of personality.[76] At the same time that Torrance was developing his creativity tests, two University of Chicago professors, Jacob W. Getzels and Philip W. Jackson, were also conducting studies on intelligence and creativity.[77] Working with pupils at what was originally Dewey's Laboratory School, but which had become the University of Chicago Laboratory Schools, Getzels and Jackson argued that those who did poorly on IQ tests were often successful in school and in life. They found that children with typically high IQ scores, however, were not concomitantly high in creativity. Beyond suggesting that giftedness was not limited to performing well on IQ tests, these researchers stressed the value of creativity in learning and as a lifelong skill and asked, "Why are not our children more intellectually venturesome and creative?"[78] They, like Torrance, argued for the long-term utility of creativity and questioned the values of schools and parents, both of which seemed generally to encourage a narrow definition of academic success to the detriment of the more unconventional thinkers.

Given that creativity was posited, as Anderson suggested, as an "enormous and universal human resource," it gained both professional and popular attention at a moment of cultural anxiety. The scientific, educational, and military applications of isolating creative talents dominated the postwar research and helped to expand a popular investment in the notion.[79] In 1961, the mass-circulation magazine *Look* examined the problem of the creative child, using Torrance's tests to argue that creative children were being overlooked in the conventional classroom and ostracized by their peers. Quoting Torrance, *Look* suggested, "'The future of our civilization— our very survival—depends upon the creative thinking of our next generation.'"[80] Popular writing on creativity was strongly colored with Cold War tension and postwar exceptionalism. Frank Barron, an important psychological researcher at the University of California at Berkeley, observed in

1968, "Perhaps at no other time in all of human history has there been such general recognition that to be creative in one's own everyday activity is a positive good."[81] The Cold War heightened competition and nourished cultural fears, and gave the idea of creativity as an untapped natural resource a special allure.

While Gesell worried that severe discipline might inhibit creativity, others saw complacency as an equal threat. In his 1948 book, *Your Creative Power: How to Use Imagination*, Alex F. Osborn mused on the Soviet mind and worried, "Our basic danger is that liberty will breed laxity and that apathy will sap the creative power of our people. What can be done to offset that danger? This question is a challenge, not only to educators, but to *every* American."[82] Osborn, quite apart from the cadre of university research, made his name in the Barton, Batten, Durstine & Osborn (BBDO) advertising firm, yet his interests lay in stimulating not just new inventions and products but also individual potential. Osborn's *Applied Imagination* (1953), which was revised and reprinted into the early 1970s, promoted creative thinking as a means of solving a variety of problems.[83] He claimed that women and children were more naturally creative than men and that Puritan ancestors first enriched "our national bloodstream with ingenuity," to which later immigrants "added to our inheritance." Portraying the founding and expansion of the United States as a supremely creative act, Osborn also argued that the country (rather than the city) was the site of lasting creativity. Citing Oswald Spengler and others, he claimed that "a most destructive phase of American civilization is our exodus from country to city—with the resultant debilitation of creative power through 'urbanitis.'" (Osborn himself commuted from Buffalo to his job in New York City once a week by train.)[84] The rise of the prosperous city dweller, taxes, and international conflict all contributed, in Osborn's opinion, to the demise of American creativity in the twentieth century.

Yet, in spite of this grim prospect, the "teachability" of creativity was one of Osborn's strongest convictions. Osborn, who coined the term *brainstorming*, developed exercises that implied that anyone could improve his or her own creative ability by challenging his or her routine thinking. Each chapter of *Applied Imagination* ended with a series of questions or assignments designed to stimulate imaginative thinking about local and universal problems. Writing was especially important. Developing headlines and analogies and keeping a list of inventions and improvements were all ways Osborn suggested to keep ideas flowing. Active encouragement, especially of children, to build confidence was one of the ways that an innate imagination might be retained rather than retrained. Osborn, like Riesman, Torrance, and others, was especially critical of schooling, which he believed squashed creativity and was overly concerned with memorization. In 1954, he founded the Creative Education Foundation (CEF) to encourage "a more creative trend in American education."[85] Funded with the royalties from Osborn's books, the CEF produced conferences and initiated a program of "creative problem solving" course offerings at Buffalo State University with Sidney J. Parnes.[86]

As research on creativity abounded in the mid- to late 1960s, the term *creativity* grew in popular usage. Scientific studies increasingly distinguished between levels or types of creativity, with some focusing on the habits or drives of great or prolific figures and others on creativity's psychological or intellectual bases.[87] Popular usage was less specific, although the numerous conferences, books, tests, and studies informed the discourse and use of the term in the popular press. Already in 1950, delegates at the Mid-century White House Conference on Children and Youth emerged with a pledge to American children: "We will help you develop initiative and imagination, so that you may have the opportunity freely to create."[88] Guiding children's imaginations toward creative activity was both teachers' and parents' new responsibility in the making of healthy personalities, the theme of the 1950 White House Conference. *Parents' Magazine* promised both practical and psychological benefits as a result of "creative" play and kept its readers abreast of the latest developments in creativity research, offering reading lists that included the major scientific studies and conference volumes, and even guidelines to facilitate parent-led discussions.[89] Most of these articles also included a practical component that parents could implement. In 1950, the magazine suggested that creative play would relieve parents from the "constant need to amuse and entertain their youngsters. The children gain a precious ability to be happy even in solitude. They develop initiative and ingenuity, and become popular because they can think of things to do 'for fun.'"[90] Assimilating the psychological research of the period, a 1968 *Parents'* article, "How to Encourage Your Child's Natural Creativity," suggested that in allowing children's creativity unfettered expression, "there is every good assurance that they will become skilled and happy people."[91]

Creativity therefore gained acceptance as the actions and thoughts of ordinary people. The psychologist Abraham H. Maslow (who distinguished between the exceptionally and uniquely talented and a more common type of social knowledge) observed that creativity was a key aspect of what he called "self-actualizing" people, those who seemed to have emotionally healthy, productive lives and who were motivated by needs beyond gaining food, shelter, and clothing.[92] This understanding of creativity as life-sustaining, rather than narrowly artistic or intellectual, became the most common popular implication of the concept between the late 1950s and mid-1970s. Saul and Elaine Bass's short animated 1968 film, *Why Man Creates*, which the Kaiser Aluminum Company commissioned to promote itself, recognized the extraordinary accomplishments of artists, scientists, and inventors, and it identified creativity as an act of nonconformity; however, it implied that the reason man creates is fundamentally that he is human.[93]

Both official and general interest in the idea of creativity stimulated the commission of a government-issued pamphlet, *A Creative Life for Your Children*, which was written by Margaret Mead, the anthropologist and curator at the American Museum of Natural History. Appearing in 1962, a banner year for creativity studies, Mead's pamphlet was directed toward the curious parent rather than to an academic audience. Mead interpreted the term *creativity* as a child's way of understanding and contributing to society. She suggested that creativity is "a chance for every child, as he grows and comes to understand the world, to make new a part of the world he sees. It means giving children a chance to do in play, as they grow, the kind of thing that is done by poets and landscape architects, scientists and statesmen to such a superb degree."[94] Rather than defining the concept of creativity as making in general, or as artistic experimentation, Mead saw creativity as both personal and social. The application of creativity toward explicit types of future gains was left open, although it was implied as a national concern. Katherine B. Oettinger, head of the U.S. Children's Bureau, invested the idea of creativity with visionary qualities. In her introduction to Mead's text, she claimed that a child's potential for creativity "makes each day we live with children of such vast importance to us, to them, to our country, and to the world of tomorrow, so dimly seen by us, but so close and vital to our children." Mead herself was careful to state that the American child was recognized as an individual (with his or her own clothes, playthings, and belongings) but that "the whole community—industry, government, the services—can unite in providing space and time and situations in which young people can experiment with an as-if world before they settle down to dignity and freedom in a real world."[95] The notion that the imaginative experiences of childhood could affect the personality, or fortunes, of the adult—and the country—held implications for the satisfaction, ingenuity, and productivity of future generations.

As the cultivation of creativity became a popular and consumable ideal, skeptics pointing to the lack of a sufficient understanding or definition of the concept challenged the idea that it could be simply encouraged without manifold cultural change. The sociologist Manford H. Kuhn, in a review of Anderson's book, argued that "creativity" was merely a slogan and observed that "to the extent that we think of 'excellence' and 'creativity' purely as weapons for use in the Cold War, we will produce, not these qualities, but their counterfeits."[96] The historian Jacques Barzun was even more critical of the popular embrace of "creativity." In a 1960 article in *Harper's*, he suggested that the casual and imprecise use of the word *creativity* was "a device by which we give ourselves easy satisfactions while avoiding necessary judgments."[97] Creativity was thus at once the ideal of researchers hoping to locate its source, assess its fruits, and expand its applications, and a slippery popular term that intellectuals hoped to separate from what they considered the great, truly creative works of the past.[98] Skepticism about the potential cultivation of creativity, however, was far more limited than the rampant expansion of the ideal into a popular construction of postwar childhood.

IMAGING THE CREATIVE CHILD

The creative child was not only a construction of twentieth-century child-rearing advice, midcentury sociology, and the subject of scientific study; the creative child was also a gendered figure whose exploits were captured in postwar picture books and television shows and disseminated across the country. In these media, the imaginative and spontaneous but still innocent young boy (and occasionally girl) became one of the recurring characters of the postwar age. Along with the advent of children's television, the market for children's picture books, which expanded dramatically after World War II, gave the creative child new visibility in the world of commercial entertainment.[99] The creative child is unequivocally an invention of adults. Some have suggested that because adults generally create children's texts, images, and objects, these creations therefore represent adult (usually parental) ideals of childhood. Scholars of literature have gone further, arguing that adults' efforts to court and please the child through special texts and images coexist with our own longing for the same ideal to be realized outside of the book.[100] Like the romantic characters who first inhabited a modern sentimental notion of childhood and who have persisted in literature and visual culture, the postwar creative child was the embodiment of an ideal that offered a counterpoint to the individual and national stresses around abundance, individuality, and international politics.[101]

At first glance, postwar children's literature seems an unlikely place for a figure of imagination and individualism. In his argument that character types were both produced by mass media and symptomatic of shifting values, David Riesman suggested that educational stories such as the Little Golden Book *Tootle*, with its emphasis on obeying rules and staying on track, served the conformist, other-directed character type.[102] But a host of other postwar illustrated children's books offered a vision of child behavior that was openly inquisitive and even defiant. In books that celebrated the figure of the curious child, the adventurous path was mapped not with signals to get back on track but with signs that exploration and even disaster were worthwhile and did not preclude a way back to normative middle-class domesticity. Julia Mickenberg's research on Cold War children's literature has shown how politically radical editors, authors, and publishers were able to transform the industry in ways seemingly at odds with the new attention to "correct" forms of patriotism. Mass-market books by left-leaning authors asked children to contemplate a society of new possibilities. They depicted children as inquisitive and curious, whose excitement about the physical world in science-themed books was "natural."[103] Despite a venerable literary legacy, the imaginative, sometimes defiant, child in postwar children's books was invoked and received as a new, if not always welcome, social reality.[104]

Alison Lurie reminds us that the disobedient child is a long-standing staple of folktales, fairy tales, and subsequent children's literature.[105] After World War II, the dutiful Dick and Jane characters of the 1930s and 1940s, which critics roundly despised, were replaced with more mischievous figures such as Thing One and Thing Two, a boy named Max, a girl named Harriet, and a monkey named George.[106] George, a small monkey who, after being taken from Africa by the Man in the Yellow Hat and escaping from the zoo, lives out a life of adventure in the domestic comfort of the Man's house. Written and drawn by Margret and H. A. Rey, refugees who immigrated to the United States in 1940, the first Curious George book appeared in 1941, but the six that followed were published between 1947 and 1966.[107] Using a monkey as a surrogate child, the Reys' books depict childhood impulsiveness as an uninhibited, "natural" state. Thus, most of George's dilemmas result from his desire to explore or watch the effects of his actions. Letting baby bunnies or pigs out of their cages and pens, flying a kite or grabbing a bunch of balloons, folding a fleet of newspaper boats, doing tricks on a bicycle, using a mop as a fishing pole, eating a piece of a puzzle, playing with a bugle, and using paint to transform a room into a jungle all result from George's insatiable "curiosity." The consistent line "He was a good little monkey and always very curious," which introduced nearly every book, implies that goodness and curiosity are not incompatible. (In the last two books, the ending of the line is changed to read "but he was always curious.") Although the phrase "he was too curious," which occurs repeatedly in *Curious George Takes a Job* (1947), suggests an admonition on behavior, it is George's and others' inventive and divergent thinking that not only stimulates the reader's interest but also saves the day in every story.[108]

Curiosity and imaginative experimentation are George's traits, yet as Daniel Greenstone has suggested, the portrayal of the monkey-as-child shifts significantly over the course of the seven books, reflecting the changing discourses in parenting. The bold adventurousness of the early George is gradually modified as he begins to register both fear and regret.[109] The depiction of adults also conforms more closely with postwar middle-class advice. By the 1952 *Curious George Rides a Bike*, the Man with the Yellow Hat has moved from the city to a low-density suburb near farmland and large parks. The Man, who provides George's balls, toys, books, bicycles, puzzles, and cozy bedroom, is neither constant companion nor disciplinarian. In *Curious George Goes to the Hospital* (1966), written in conjunction with the Boston Children's Hospital as a text to prepare children for a hospital visit, George's out-of-control go-cart crash creates a huge mess for the doctors, nurses, and attendants and embarrasses the director, who is giving the mayor a tour of the hospital. But because this event also cheers up a sad child who is ill, the director absolves George, stating, "You also made our sad little Betsy happy again, and that is more than any of us has done."[110] Contending that a curious, creative, and even reckless child is worth the mess and trouble, the adult figures echo the idealism of postwar social values.

The depiction of children seeking their own fantasy life apart from the controlled adult realm is another evocation of the creative child and a long-standing theme in children's literature. Yet the postwar representation of the inquisitive, independent child required a new cast of unorthodox, quasihuman characters. The Reys' monkey, Bernard Waber's crocodile, Maurice Sendak's boy in a wolf suit, and any of Dr. Seuss's fantastical characters pair the unknown, magical quality of a child's imagination with associations of wildness. This primitivist representation of the intuitive child was also captured in Leo Lionni's short book *Little Blue and Little Yellow* (1959). Using the pure pigments blue and yellow to stand in for wily boys, Lionni, an art director for *Fortune*, devised a tale of two colors who are best friends and like to play with other colors in the neighborhood. One day, after a long search for each other, Little Blue and Little Yellow are so happy they embrace, merge, and become Green. When their parents do not recognize them, they begin to cry and eventually cry themselves back to their unmixed hues. After the parents realize what has happened, they too rejoice in the possibility of becoming Green.[111] Lionni originally created the story with ripped-up pieces of *Life* magazine as a train-ride amusement for his grand-children.[112] *Little Blue and Little Yellow* assumes that children understand colors as representations of themselves; thus, Lionni's basic color theory is also a lesson in human perception and empathy. Anthropomorphizing color (rather than animals or other creatures), Lionni uses abstraction and a parable of tolerance to cast children's discoveries in play as important social contributions that are gained only from granting the child an autonomous and vivid inner life.

   The creative, often male, child who devises a world apart from parents, and even apart from siblings, became a recurring theme in postwar children's picture books. Solitude and boredom enable the creative child, whether at home, outdoors, or at night, to explore and bring the world of his imagination to life. Crockett Johnson's *Harold and the Purple Crayon* (1955) recounts the nighttime adventures of a boy who decides one evening "to go for a walk in the moonlight" (Figure 1.3).[113] Harold's desire to explore leads him to devise an entire world with his purple crayon. Beginning with the moon and something to walk on, Harold then draws a forest, an ocean and a beach, a mountain, and finally a city. The reader follows Harold in and out of these landscapes without losing the awareness of inhabiting the child's drawing. Johnson depicts the act of drawing as a reflection of the child's

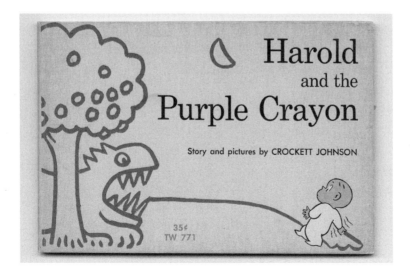

Figure 1.3. Crockett Johnson, *Harold and the Purple Crayon* (1955), 1966 Scholastic edition.

inward desires and anxieties in addition to his creative thinking. Harold's fear, for example, makes his crayon shake, creating the wavy lines that become an ocean. Harold's "wits" and his crayon are the agents of the narrative. Through his drawing, we see Harold's imagination at work, producing scary creatures, such as a dragon guarding an apple tree, and resolving his dilemmas, such as creating a boat in which to sail, a moose to eat leftover pie, and a balloon and basket in which to navigate back to the ground. Harold's creative act ultimately returns him to his own bedroom and his own bed when he remembers the placement of the moon in his window. If the imagination is the source of adventure and resolution to a series of problems, it is also the source of security, as Johnson suggests with a final double entendre: before going to sleep, Harold "[draws] up the covers." Because *Harold and the Purple Crayon* was printed in black and white, with only the purple crayon and its marks appearing in color, the line and the act of drawing are the book's visual and narrative foci. As a representation of the creative act, the drawings' stress on personal exploration and open-ended excursions elevated inward reflection to a universal adventure.

Similarly, Ezra Jack Keats's *The Snowy Day* (1962) suggested that a child alone in a snowy city landscape could create vivid possibilities for the young imagination.[114] When Peter leaves his apartment building on a clear morning after a snowstorm, he encounters a changed city. During his solitary explorations, he makes tracks, angels, and snowballs, the ephemeral results of his imaginary schemes. Even after he has returned home, he is lost in thought about his experience. When it appeared, in 1962, *The Snowy Day* was the first full-color picture book to feature an African American character, and it engendered criticism that focused on the depiction of the boy and his context.[115] Yet *The Snowy Day* shares with other books, such as *Harold and the Purple Crayon* and Maurice Sendak's *Where the Wild Things Are* (1963), a depiction of the child's inner life as a physical transformation of the material world. Keats's collage illustration underscores this as the child's creative act, rendering the textures of the linen sheets, cottony clouds, flat patterns of the tree, plaid dress, and wallpaper as tactile reminders of the everyday and as signs of the transformative power of the imagination. Little Blue and Little Yellow's accidental Greenness, Curious George's experiments with household objects, Harold's purple crayon, and Peter's snowy creations are all ordinary things that enable fantastic adventures. Postwar authors and illustrators envisioned the creative child and his imagination as introspective, curious, and playful, but also sometimes destructive and secretive. Nowhere was this clearer than in Dr. Seuss's *The Cat in the Hat*.

The commercial success of Theodore Geisel's Dr. Seuss books has made his works, especially *The Cat in the Hat,* published with only 236 simple words for beginning readers in 1957, a touchstone of postwar culture. Although earlier writers engaged children with humorous rhyming verse, absurdist situations, and fanciful illustrations, Seuss is continually acknowledged as releasing children from expectations of good behavior while inspiring early literacy.[116] In addition to teaching children to read, Maria Tatar suggests, the book "is also a lesson in using imagination."[117] In *The Cat in the Hat,* two children left alone at home on a rainy day discover new playmates—an adult-sized cat, in a hat, and two child-sized creatures named Thing One and Thing Two—and the play potential of everyday household objects. Like the book's mostly one-syllable vocabulary, everyday things are reanimated and enchanted. Not only do the cat and the pet fish spar, but books, a cake, a cup, and a rake join toy ships and a ball in vertical juxtapositions. Indoor kite flying, like the antic stacking, defies laws of nature and gravity, as well as decorum. Yet once the children and their new playmates explore every space of the household, including the parents' bedroom, the playful fun turns into what the narrator calls "bad tricks." Taking up the position of the admonishing fish, the children face the now-unwelcome intruders, the giant mess, and the moral dilemma of secrecy. In *The Cat in the Hat,* the children's imaginations are therefore also twinned with their consciences.

The representation of the creative child in postwar children's literature depicted and constructed the child as a fantastic explorer and alchemist. However, it also portrayed the inward tensions of a secretive existence. Following Jacqueline Rose's argument that the children's book is in part a seduction that elevates childhood innocence to the status of cultural myth, I suggest that postwar authors who envisioned children as creative, spontaneous, and capable of insight also desired that they pick up their playthings, feel guilt, and atone for their misbehavior. This perspective helped to construct the attractive figure of the creative child. Furthermore, the ascendancy of the creative child not only existed on the page but also penetrated the everyday lives of millions of American families as animated figures on a screen.

VIEWING THE CREATIVE CHILD

Television is perhaps the singular force that defined postwar childhood as an experience apart from childhoods of earlier eras. Television entered American households in a spectacular wave after the end of World War II.

From some one hundred thousand sets in American households at the beginning of 1948, the numbers increased dramatically. In 1949, there were a million televisions in the United States, and by the end of 1959 there were fifty million. As Wilbur Schramm, a prominent critic of the time, observed (along with Jack Lyle and Edwin B. Parker), households with children under twelve were almost twice as likely to have a set than those without any children: "It was in homes with children where television was most eagerly awaited, and most intensively used."[118] The networks did their part to make sure children tuned in. One scholar estimates that between 1948 and 1978 the major commercial broadcasters targeted some 405 series to children.[119] Although scholars have shown that a children's culture developed around media was well defined before the advent of television, the dominating presence of TV accentuated the perception of separating children from their parents.[120] Commercial television was invested in a mass-consuming child and therefore made a direct appeal to children's tastes and, to a lesser extent, parents' approval.

Nevertheless, the television networks developed shows that reflected a cultural acceptance of imaginative and creative children whose curiosity and fantasy were both innocently "natural" and potentially lucrative. Nicholas Sammond, in particular, has argued that values of naturalness expressed in parenting manuals of the era were recast on the screen in Disney's films, television programs, educational guides, and Disneyland itself. For Sammond, Disney evoked a "natural" childhood in its *True-Life Adventures* animal shows and *Davy Crockett* series, which aired on the *Disneyland* program. The figure of the curious explorer and pioneer was intrinsically linked to Davy Crockett coonskin hats and fringed jackets, which brought the company new income in licensed merchandise.[121] Television, therefore, not only perpetuated the figure of the creative child as a romantic innocent on the air but also pitched kits, dolls, and other items that implicated the values of creativity and imagination in an expanding consumer culture.[122]

Imagination also suggested a self-reflective and productive way of watching that countered the image of the passive spectator, which was one of the prominent critiques of television in the 1950s.[123] Parents, psychologists, and network executives immediately noticed the rapt attention children trained on broadcast shows. A few early programs aimed to harness not only attention but also active intellectual participation. Paul Tripp's *Mr. I. Magination*, a thirty-minute show that ran from 1949 to 1952 on CBS, used the pretext of an engineer boarding a diminutive train to "Imagination Land," where children learned about historical and literary figures, explorers, and inventors. Tripp, who wrote the scripts, created the music, and starred as the show's host, used humor and, according to one reviewer, asked the television audience to "bring along its imagination" and a "highly developed sense of make-believe."[124] The relatively simple sets and costumes of *Mr. I. Magination* suggested that the potential for fantasy already lay within each viewer. The show used ordinary props that paired the familiar with the historical— Hercules employed a vacuum to clean up the Augean stables, and in an episode about Christopher Columbus, the *Niña*, *Pinta*, and *Santa Maria* were model ships floating in a galvanized metal tub of water. Asking audiences to accept these imaginative leaps and to valorize the creative achievements of the hero normalized the naturalness of children's fantasy and creativity. Other shows took audience participation much further.

Winky Dink and You was originally aired on CBS between 1953 and 1957, and again for a brief period in the 1960s.[125] In a half-hour cartoon, Winky Dink, a diminutive wide-eyed, buck-toothed boy with spiky hair and a pixie costume drawn minimally in outline, cavorted in a series of adventures. At the beginning of each show, the host, Jack Barry, asked children to affix a special tinted "magic" screen to their sets and use their "magic" crayons and an erasing cloth (Plate 2). The conceit of the cartoon Winky interacting with the live host set up the child to follow. At specific points in the narrative, Barry prompted the television viewer to draw on the screen on top of the cartoon to save Winky from peril by adding bridges, steps, and boats, and by uncovering secret messages. The Winky Dink kits (the screen cost fifty cents, but a deluxe kit consisting of screen, crayons, and eraser was considerably more) were integral to the premise of the show and were advertised prominently along with other Winky Dink toys at the end of each broadcast.[126] When the series was revived, in the late 1960s, the live host was gone, the character was redrawn, and color was added, but the kits remained. Not only did the Winky Dink programs depict the adventures of an imaginative midcentury child but, in demanding a response from the viewer, they also implicated the television audience in this discourse.

Engaging viewers' imaginations was the recommendation of the National Association for Better Radio and Television, which reviewed broadcast shows. In 1965, the organization's editor, Frank Orme, called for increasing "programs which provide wholesome humor, creative entertainment, social values, and use of the imagination."[127] *Winky Dink and You* cast the watching child as Winky's ally. Asking children to "save" or "help" Winky Dink by drawing in some of the cartoon action, the show made the child an active (if dutiful, rather than freely expressive) partner in the execution of each episode. *Winky Dink and You* also answered other critiques of children's television. As scholars have shown, fears that children raised on a visual diet of one-way communication would be susceptible to indoctrination were common in the age of the Cold War. Amid worries of potential brainwashing, *Winky Dink and You* made children into active cartoonists, even though their "action" was entirely predetermined.

Like the nonhuman characters of postwar children's literature, postwar television created some unusual incarnations of the creative child. Amid obedient Mouseketeers and puppets, and zany live hosts and clowns, *The Gumby Show* and its later 1960s version, *A Gumby Adventure*, stood out as series of short animated stories about a green clay boy with a triangular head and mitten hands whose best friend and sidekick, Pokey, was an orange clay pony. Gumby was the work of Art Clokey, who had experimented with clay animation as a film-school student.[128] He developed Gumby at the suggestion of producer Sam Engle and convinced E. Roger Muir of NBC to feature the figure in a children's program. Introduced on *Howdy Doody* in 1956, Gumby received his own show, hosted by Pinky Lee, the following year.[129]

Because he was made out of clay, Gumby possessed unusual powers. He skated from place to place (making efficient use of the stop-action movement), which emphasized his swift, carefree energy. Gumby could stretch or shrink, roll himself into a tight ball, fall apart into miniature Gumbys, and instantly reconstitute himself. Conversely, his weakness was exposure to cool temperatures that would compromise his elasticity or very warm temperatures that would melt him. But Gumby's physical abilities alone were never the premise of the show's plots or main action. Instead, these material qualities reinforced, and symbolized, the unpredictability of his imagination and curiosity. One of the show's main conceits was Gumby and Pokey's ability to disappear into books, making stories literally come to life. Indeed, it was in a book of western stories that Gumby first met Pokey, who was supposedly lost but actually just wanted "to look around." By moving easily in and out of books, Gumby explored a variety of fantasy worlds, including both exotic and historical places, such as the Middle Ages, colonial America, the nest of a triceratops, and the North Pole, and ordinary places, such as a farm with gopher holes.

Other adventures took place in Toyland, the toy shop where Gumby first came to life. Early episodes were shot against a bare set but amid a profusion of toys, often placed in front of their boxes as if on display. "Toy Crazy" (1956) opens with Gumby living with his parents in an open box of Gumbasia clay.[130] As his father, Gumbo, tries to awaken Gumby, the unmolded rectangular block of clay, he tests Gumby's temperature for elasticity and watches amused as the block quickly changes into a series of musical instruments, a toy boat, and a plane. "He's still dreaming," Gumbo announces to Gumby's mother, Gumba, interpreting his son's unconscious consumer desires. Gumby's birthday gift of any toy he wants is the premise for his exploration of the shelves of objects around him. Model cars, trains, and trucks are all the stuff of Gumby's delight. In other episodes, he plays with toy pianos, whistles, and musical instruments (which he reunites with their escaped notes, Too and Loo), as well as telescopes, rockets, roller skates, Erector sets, Lincoln Logs, stuffed plush animals, and many other things that form the ever-changing landscape and props of Gumby's adventures. Even the Blockheads, his archnemeses, have heads fashioned from the toy blocks G and J.

The material world of Gumby is almost entirely made up of playthings, which constitute vital props in episodes beyond those set among the shelves in Toyland. In "Robot Rumpus," which was first aired on *Howdy Doody* in 1956, Gumby lives in a white clapboard house with dollhouse furniture and a yard of model-railroad trees and shrubs. In this episode, Gumby becomes a postwar Tom Sawyer, employing a group of toy robots to do his chores so he can go play with Pokey. Following the older trope of the machine man as cultural threat, the robots wreak havoc upon Gumby's house and yard, much to the dismay of Gumby and his parents (Figure 1.4). Although Michael Frierson has argued that the use of toys for set design reflected Art Clokey's interest in creating a deliberately childlike world of the imagination, it is precisely this attempt to entice viewers with imagery

Figure 1.4. "Robot Rumpus," *The Gumby Show*, 1956. Photograph courtesy of Premavision.

of the "childlike" that actively helped to construct the figure of the creative child.[131] The tautology of the creativity discourse insists that imagination spawns imagination.

Despite the presentation of toys and playthings as animated and desirable in the series, Gumby merchandise was not developed until the mid-1960s, when *Gumby* was in syndication.[132] The bendable Gumby doll quickly became a popular novelty, but it was sold as "delightful, fun, educational."[133] Clokey's company even produced an instructional pamphlet for creating one's own stop-action movies at home with a Gumby doll,

explaining the process, giving hints on positioning Gumby and taking exposures, and implying that the program, together with the merchandise, could inspire genuine creative activities. Whereas *Winky Dink and You* required the aired program and kit to participate, Clokey suggested that "kids like Gumby because all the details aren't filled in for them. Gumby is more sensuous than cell-animated cartoon characters because he appeals to more senses than cartoon characters do. Kids can put themselves into it and imagine all kinds of things with Gumby."[134] Playful experimentation, evident in the program's low production values, minimal backgrounds, surreal gobo lighting, and hand and Claymation lettering gave the show, particularly in its early years, a deliberately homemade quality. Fans wrote to Clokey with their own stories of making Gumby characters and creating their own adventures, from paper projects and cartoons to animated films.[135]

Like other children's shows, *Gumby* was keyed to a TV "norm" of good behavior and domestic peace. Gumby inhabited a fantasy of diminutive middle-class domesticity—a world where a boy can go to the moon and have his father rescue him, hunger is cured with a chemistry experiment, and well-stocked toy-store shelves provide an available playground. Like Winky Dink, Gumby embodied the postwar creative child, an ideal who was plucky, mostly obedient, and kind. Furthermore, Gumby's vast imagination fueled unpredictable experimental play. In postwar middle-class America, these qualities—a good nature and a sunny imagination—became a long-lasting ideal of mass-market publishing and broadcasting.

In 1961, Schramm, Lyle, and Parker argued that television did not by itself stimulate creativity or learning. They were skeptical of the coonskin hats as a fad and saw limited potential in television to teach.[136] In the late 1960s, as the social projects of the Johnson administration gained momentum, the noncommercial corporation Children's Television Workshop developed a program that refuted Schramm's position. When *Sesame Street* first aired, in 1969, it seemed to reveal a new way to adapt television to teach children using the model of preschool education and noncommercial broadcasting. Based on extensive research and the Head Start curriculum of visual comparisons and the repetition of numbers and letters, *Sesame Street* has been consistently associated with a conservative model of drilling—albeit using the innovative visual techniques of commercials—rather than a model of preschool education that values individuality and creativity.[137] Yet the program strongly reinforced the idea that children inhabit a world apart from the unromantic banality of everyday adult life.

Unlike *Winky Dink and You* or *The Gumby Show*, *Sesame Street* had a team of child psychologists behind the program's design. Producer Joan Ganz Cooney hired Gerald S. Lesser, a developmental psychologist from Harvard, to help the producers create a show that could meet and hold the attentions of three- to five-year-olds. A team of researchers continually evaluated the program and tested responses from child viewers before the first programs aired. The role of Jim Henson's monster puppets, or Muppets, was a subject of considerable debate while the show was being developed and tested. Researchers found that children's attentions were stimulated during the sequences when the Muppets were on and began to drop precipitously as soon as the focus returned to the street scenes with live actors.[138] Counter to the prevailing psychological belief, which argued that combining reality and fantasy could mislead children, *Sesame Street*'s developers decided to include Muppets who lived among and interacted with the human inhabitants of Sesame Street.[139] Big Bird, who lived in a giant nest next to a brownstone building on the set, therefore became one of the signature *Sesame Street* characters.

The eight-foot-tall yellow bird was one of the program's most introspective and childlike of the early Muppets. Lesser describes him as "not very bright but charming and lovable," yet Big Bird possesses a vibrant imagination.[140] This was made even clearer in 1971, when Lesser developed an equally gigantic imaginary friend, a woolly mammothlike character named Mr. Snuffleupagus, or "Snuffy," with bulging eyes, long eyelashes, and a shy disposition. Throughout episodes in the early 1970s, Big Bird is frustrated that others cannot see Snuffy, who repeatedly wanders off at strategic moments, thwarting Big Bird's claims that he exists. To viewers, however, he often took up the entire screen. The conflict over whether Snuffy was "real" or "imaginary" placed, and kept, children on Big Bird's side.[141] Casting viewers as Big Bird's peers, *Sesame Street* reinforced the notion that all children, both human and bird, were naturally imaginative. Beyond simply representing the creative child as a figure of wonder or entertainment, *Sesame Street* used this plot to imply that it was precisely imagination that set children apart from adults, even those who inhabited a street where fuzzy monsters were people in the neighborhood.

As Mitzi Myers observes, "The Romantic child is our foundational fiction, our originary myth."[142] In the postwar era, the romantic child was given new life as an imaginative figure whose natural gifts could be developed through correct parenting, studied, quantified, and assessed in new postwar psychological research, and constituted materially in a wide variety of consumer goods and media. This creative figure was an intuitive and independent character who was also natural, artistic, and conscientious. The postwar creative child was the avatar of the well-established myth of the American frontier spirit, repurposed to assuage fears of totalitarianism, delinquency, and conformity. In this postwar "child-centered," middle-class culture of ambition and abundance, this child was not only an image in a book or on a screen but also a consumer of many kinds of educational resources that promised to cultivate and nourish creativity, the most abundant of which were toys.

EDUCATIONAL TOYS AND CREATIVE PLAYTHINGS

THE HEIGHTENED FOCUS on children owing to the baby boom stimulated a national debate over child rearing and encouraged both sharp public interest in education and unprecedented spending on children. In addition to buying new parenting guides and magazines advocating techniques for raising a healthy, well-adjusted child, postwar parents spent record sums on amusements. In 1954, a trade organization estimated that the American toy industry brought in a billion and a quarter dollars annually, and during that Christmas season, families purchased an average of nine toys per household.[1] These numbers increased some 67 percent in the 1960s alone.[2] Toys such as building blocks, beads, wooden trains and cars, and Peg-Boards became standard equipment in the postwar playroom of the young middle-class child. Although seemingly innocent objects, many "educational" toys—toys intended to teach physical skills or develop cognitive abilities— were embedded in changing ideas about early learning, postwar discussions about national image, and new research on the origins and social significance of creativity. The major American educational-toy companies, such as Holgate, Playskool, and especially Creative Playthings, developed and promoted objects that reflected a growing faith in creativity as an authentic value that could encourage a competitive edge in midcentury America.

Although a broad sector of the middle class adopted "good parenting" as both a personal and national obligation and looked to playthings as a means of teaching their children, it was the upper middle classes that most readily embraced the notion that personal creativity could become a source of societal renewal.[3] As a result, many "educational" toys achieved new recognition not only for their pedagogical qualities but also for their design and promises to stimulate invention and train taste. Toys have attracted the attention of scholars from many fields, but educational toys, particularly those of the postwar era, have not.[4] In looking at the ways that the ideal of creativity permeated the educational-toy industry, I argue that what was accepted as a "natural" relationship between creativity and childhood was in fact consciously developed along with postwar discourses on psychology, education, and art.

EDUCATIONAL TOYS

Objects have probably always played a role in educating children, but the concept of an educational device or "toy" that instills specific lessons in children is only about three hundred years old.[5] One of the most celebrated examples of a deliberately educational toy is the set of alphabet blocks that the English philosopher John Locke developed for teaching literacy in the late seventeenth century. Locke's blocks show how teaching objects are historically linked to a specific set of educational ideas and an ambitious, emerging middle class that sought to train—through a solitary, indoor activity—the next generation to preserve or surpass the prevailing social standing of the family, society, or country.[6] Although the concept of the educational toy has shifted over time to encompass a wide variety of objects, it has maintained these emphases on early learning as a form of social and societal improvement.[7]

Like the concept of the toy, notions of play, creativity, and childhood have been knit together as a modern construction. Creativity is embedded in historical and philosophical discussions of play and is closely linked with a belief in the positive effects of the human imagination.[8] Because play is central to the concept of modern Western childhood, it has accumulated associations of imagination and invention. The nineteenth-century writer and art critic Charles Baudelaire observed, "In their games children give evidence of their great capacity for abstraction and their high imaginative power."[9] Since at least the eighteenth century, philosophers and writers have viewed play as liberating and constructive, for both children and adults.[10] By the late 1930s, Johan Huizinga, in his influential study *Homo Ludens* (published in English in 1950), established that play had an important social and spiritual function in the production of art and culture. The French sociologist Roger Caillois, writing in 1958, argued not only that culture derived from play but also that specific aspects of play, especially games, constitute a central means of many kinds of human interaction.[11] The work of the Swiss psychologist Jean Piaget, who promoted the fundamental importance of play for the developing child, was the touchstone for postwar theories of play and cognitive development. In his landmark book *La formation du symbole chez l'enfant* (1945), translated in English as *Play, Dreams, and Imitation in Childhood* (1962), Piaget explored the sequential development of children's play and argued that through play children acquired not only motor skills but also cognitive ability. Having already defined his notion of childhood stages, Piaget examined children's processes of accommodation and assimilation, arguing that play constituted a critical moment of a child's comprehension of reality, "while at the same time it has something of the creative imagination which will be the motor of all future thought and even of reason."[12] Play, naturalized and admired as a free experimental activity that was the special province of children, was also, however, bound up historically with the somewhat paradoxical belief that certain, often quite rigid methods of training could have a liberating effect.

The design of specifically educational playthings has, therefore, been closely tied to a context of ideas and ideologies about enhancing the physical, intellectual, social, and emotional development of children. Whereas Jean-Jacques Rousseau's Émile was offered a branch with leaves and fruit as an edifying amusement, later pedagogues have favored more abstract forms for teaching objects. Throughout the nineteenth century, as theories of education became increasingly codified into teaching systems, the best-known educational toys were instruments of reform and specific programs of learning.

Friedrich Fröbel and Maria Montessori each developed teaching objects as part of a particular, integrated curriculum. Fröbel's program of graduated tasks of arranging spheres, blocks, paper, and other materials was developed from the Enlightenment legacy of understanding the forces of nature through experimentation but was joined to a romantic quest for spiritual harmony with God, nature, and humanity. His "gifts" and "occupations" (he did not use the term *toys*) were symbolic elements that formed part of a complete system (Figure 2.1). Although developed in Germany around the 1830s, Fröbel's *Kindergarten* (literally a children's garden) had widespread influence in late nineteenth-century America. Reformers such as Elizabeth Peabody advocated the kindergarten model for all children, whether rich or poor, urban or rural, as a means of improving society through the training of both children and their mothers.[13] Although later American educators criticized Fröbel's theory as limiting creativity and imagination, his designs were produced in large quantities, and some established types outlived his specific kindergarten pedagogy.[14] Moreover, the term *kindergarten* became a way of selling products, especially toys, even those that had no relevance to the Fröbel system.[15]

Figure 2.1. Bradley's Occupation Material for the Kindergarten, gift no. 5, 1880. Milton Bradley and Company, Springfield, Massachusetts. Photograph from Collection Centre Canadien d'Architecture/Canadian Centre for Architecture, Montreal.

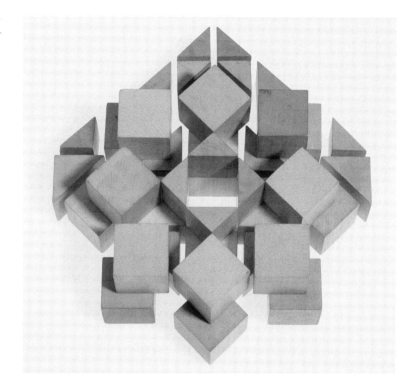

Objects that might instill lessons for life at an early age have often resembled, in both abstract and literal form, the things of everyday life. For Montessori, objects taught real skills as well as abstract values. In addition to teaching self-discipline and self-reliance through cooking, washing, and cleaning, the Montessori method included the apprehension of principles of mathematics, writing, and color theory through things. Child-sized furniture and small-scale glass, ceramic dishes, and real tools (such as knives and scissors), as well as colored rods, counting beads, letters, and sandpaper, taught concrete lessons that required the child to modify or train his or her body to accomplish tasks. Objects required a physical response, thereby awakening the child's sensory faculties. Like Montessori, the American educator and philosopher John Dewey linked learning with doing meaningful activities. Although Dewey did not rely on specific sets of objects to teach (and rejected the Fröbel kindergarten model at his Laboratory School at the University of Chicago), he embraced the idea that toys and play could expand a child's consciousness and appetite for learning. The strongly practical activities of American progressive schools in the late nineteenth century (such as sewing, weaving, cooking, and woodworking) suited reformers'

goals of reconciling craft labor and industrial society. Dewey's emphasis on the importance of experience in learning was taken up by one of his most influential students, William Heard Kilpatrick, who suggested that democratic America required alternative models for educating young children. Moreover, Kilpatrick's 1914 critique of Montessori's program, which rested on, among other things, the design of her teaching toys, diminished her influence on American preschool education until the postwar era.[16]

Whereas nineteenth-century reformers sought to teach through tangible lessons, ambitious twentieth-century parents adopted the idea of the educational toy to provide early opportunities for their children. Like the kindergarten, the nursery school, which reformers established in the 1920s, followed European models. But unlike the American kindergarten, which was employed as a means of transforming the lives and habits of poor families, the nursery school in interwar America remained firmly associated with privilege.[17] The importance of play with objects was a central aspect of the early nursery school idea. In the 1920s, Caroline Pratt called her Play School philosophy "creative pedagogy" and considered both children and teachers "artists."[18] A series of "Do-Withs" that Pratt designed in the first years of the twentieth century were not successful. However, the Unit Blocks she developed with Harriet Johnson, a series of differentiated wooden building forms, became the basis of Pratt's curriculum at the City and Country School in New York City. Moreover, these were widely adapted for use in nursery schools around the country, and remained continuously in production.[19]

Two of the major American producers of educational toys, Playskool and Holgate, were established during the interwar period as nursery schools first gained social acceptance.[20] Many educational toys were developed specially for these institutions, but with the onset of the Depression, toy makers also sought a market in the middle-class home. Like the nursery school, which emphasized "scientific" approaches for raising children, toy makers seized on the advice of the expert to develop and then legitimize their products. The Holgate Brothers Company derived from a manufacturer of brush handles, baskets, and rolling pins founded in 1789.[21] In 1929, the company turned its experience with hardwood objects to the making of toys at the suggestion of Mary Frank (the wife of Lawrence K. Frank, a prominent advocate of nursery school programs), who conducted her own research projects in the emerging field of early childhood education.[22]

This close link between the design of teaching toys and the needs of the nursery school was evident in Holgate's earliest products. A hammering set and a construction-block set were each developed by nursery school teachers who sought direct means of developing basic motor skills and hand–eye coordination in young children.[23] By the early 1930s, however, the company had appointed an in-house designer who worked with teachers to develop and test products. Although he had little training in design, Jarvis Rockwell, the brother of the painter Norman Rockwell, turned to woodworking after a career in finance and became the company's sole toy designer.[24] Many of the maple toys that Holgate produced in the 1930s and well after the Second World War were Rockwell's adaptations after established types. These included pull toys, variations on the Peg-Board, and sorting toys, such as the Old Woman of the Lacing Shoe, a solid wooden shoe form that offered places for inserting colored pegs, carved to suggest human forms, and the opportunity to practice lacing and tying (Figure 2.2). The combination of play with the repeated movements of placing figures in holes and handling string instilled habit into a child's bodily knowledge. The nursery-rhyme theme, one of Rockwell's hallmarks, was not a central part of the nursery school pedagogy and was probably added to give the toys commercial appeal.

Yet Holgate products, the company claimed, were developed in consultation with experts on child behavior and tested in real-life situations.[25] Lawrence K. Frank, an administrator at the Laura Spelman Rockefeller Memorial Foundation (LSRM), exemplified the role of the expert in Holgate's toy production and in the expansion of the child study movement during the interwar years. Frank's advocacy for the popularization of child development in the 1920s led to the establishment of child study centers at major universities and the growing acceptance of child development as a field of scientific study.[26] Frank, with grants from the LSRM, also promoted the foundation of *Parents' Magazine,* a popular monthly magazine that, like the toy companies of the period, relied on esteemed scientists as advisors and editors.[27]

Playskool, Inc., also claimed to have pioneered the use of experts in developmental psychology and education, and its toys promised improved intelligence, school readiness, and character building. The Playskool Institute, established in 1928, developed objects such as desks, dollhouses, and nail boards to stimulate physical and social development

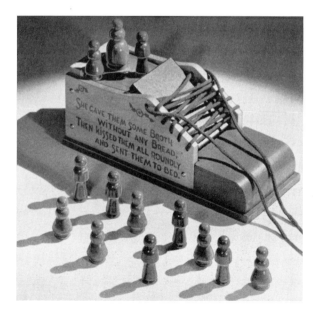

Figure 2.2. Old Woman of the Lacing Shoe, circa 1943. Holgate Brothers Company, Holgate Toys, catalog no. 19 (Kane, Penn.: Holgate Brothers Company, 1943), 10. Courtesy of Holgate Toys.

in young children. Like Holgate, Playskool produced toys according to the needs of the nursery school curriculum, including some of the most ubiquitous designs for educational toys such as a pounding bench and a linked train. An early 1930s Playskool Floor Train had a bright blue locomotive and tender, three open cars of orange, green, and yellow, and a red caboose, all linked together with oversize tabs (Figure 2.3). The smooth shapes were designed for small hands, and the sloping curve of the "streamlined" locomotive deliberately evoked the form of contemporary trains. Toys such as these emphasized manual coordination and also the visual skills of arranging shapes and creating lines. Using colored forms to denote the individual parts of the multicolored whole, these Playskool toys—like those that Holgate produced—were designed both as entertainment and as educational equipment for young children. The headline across the Playskool catalog, "Learning While Playing, an Idea and an Ideal," reinforced the link with progressive theory, but the company's mottoes, "Playthings with a purpose" and "Not just toys," underscored how scientists, manufacturers, and parents viewed the seriousness of children's play.

Educational toys were expensive and appealed to parents who put their faith in the next generation. Yet, despite the apparent elitism of the educational toy, a two-page spread in a 1935 Butler Brothers catalog, a wholesaler to five-and-dime stores, also advertised "educational playthings." Traditional learning toys such as embroidery sets and building toys were joined with nursery school hammer and nail sets and sold to middle- and working-class parents even during the Great Depression. The progressive ideals formed in the 1920s and 1930s remained central in American edu-

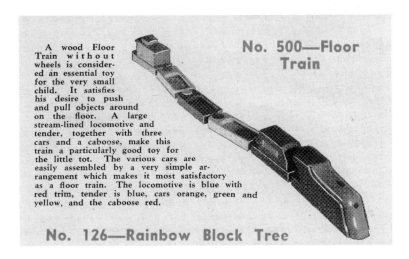

A wood Floor Train without wheels is considered an essential toy for the very small child. It satisfies his desire to push and pull objects around on the floor. A large stream-lined locomotive and tender, together with three cars and a caboose, make this train a particularly good toy for the little tot. The various cars are easily assembled by a very simple arrangement which makes it most satisfactory as a floor train. The locomotive is blue with red trim, tender is blue, cars orange, green and yellow, and the caboose red.

No. 500—Floor Train

No. 126—Rainbow Block Tree

Figure 2.3. Playskool Floor Train, circa 1930s. From Playskool Institute, *Playskool Playthings* (New York: Playskool Institute, n.d. [circa 1930s]). Courtesy of Hagley Museum and Library.

cation in the early postwar period. Indeed, this pre–World War II context, which emphasized personal improvement and "scientific" methods of raising children, set the tone for the postwar obsession with providing early, "correct," and "creative" stimulation for the first baby boom generation.

RAISING CREATIVE CHILDREN

The promises of the educational toy reemerged in new and particularly forceful ways in the postwar era. Changes in American society, especially the swelling birthrate, meant new commercial opportunities for toy makers. As an article for *Playthings*, the trade journal of the American toy industry, proclaimed in 1945, "Millions of War Babies Should Have Educational Toys."[28] Toy companies themselves had to adapt to new conditions, materials, and markets. During the early 1940s, most toy manufacturers were refitted to suit the needs of the war effort, producing munitions primarily, and toys only on a limited basis. Once companies returned to normal production, in the mid-1940s, they also returned to competition with foreign imports, largely from Germany and Japan.[29] With the steady growth in the number of American births and merchants' desire to sell year-round, toy makers, pediatricians, and education experts redoubled their efforts to promote the domestically produced educational toy as equipment fundamental to a healthy child's development.

Psychological research reached a wide audience in the postwar period as discussions about raising "emotionally healthy" children attracted national attention. At the 1950 Midcentury White House Conference on Children and Youth, delegates agreed that adults should recognize and develop leisure and play for the positive psychological effects those activities would have on their children.[30] As theories of child development became increasingly familiar, and acceptable, to American parents, they were readily assimilated into the selling and promotion of playthings. Piaget's theory of developmental stages and a child's need for hands-on experiential learning was known among prewar American nursery school teachers, but it was widely adopted in postwar pedagogy and fit neatly with educational-toy manufacturers' aim to sell toys continuously during infancy and youth. Erik H. Erikson's conception of ego development also relied on successive stages. With his 1950 book, *Childhood and Society,* Erikson became one of the most celebrated figures among the many postwar child-development experts. His view of the significance of play for children, who were testing and mastering their new world, and its effects on the psyche of the human adult lent new urgency to the importance of toys in the making of a healthy personality. For Erikson, like Piaget, play and toys held symbolic meaning for the child. The "creative ritualization" that the play-stage child practiced through his or her toys had direct implications for the later adult, whose own ritualizations affirmed these early accomplishments in what Erikson called the "unity of culture."[31] Toy makers' catalogs offered psychological advice and adhered to these models to sell products. Playskool and Holgate, for example, both divided their catalogs into sections for different ages and advised retail merchants to suggest age-appropriate goods. An early postwar Playskool catalog included a short essay, "What Toys Shall I Buy for My Child?" by University of Chicago child-development expert Ethel Kawin, who exclaimed, "It is not enough that toys are educational—they must be correctly educational so that they teach the right things at the *right time* in the *right way*!"[32] Adopting a similarly rationalizing approach to selling toys, Holgate produced a wheel-shaped "toy selector" to aid parents in identifying the most suitable items for the ages of their children (Plate 3). The whimsical, animal-shaped Holgate logo made the ubiquitous wheel-shaped form used for calculating mileage, proportion, simple recipes, and cooking times into a playful activity for choosing developmentally correct toys.[33]

The shift in attitude toward the toy as an everyday object, rather than just a holiday or birthday gift, also reflected social changes since the Depression. Educational toys were essential equipment in the day cares and nursery schools that became common institutions of twentieth-century childhood. Although the nursery school of the 1920s was the exclusive province of the wealthy, Depression-era programs had reduced the stigma of day care and increased the number of federally funded nursery schools. During wartime, nursery, day-care, and play-school programs took on an increasingly educational mission for the families who used them.[34] Although most mothers with children under six years old did not seek work outside the home even during the war, many women who took factory jobs, especially in the West, used federally subsidized day-care centers that were established, albeit belatedly, both to care for and also to educate children.[35] After the war, as the government money for day care dwindled and many parents returned to more seemingly traditional gender roles, the private home again became the primary locus of middle-class early childhood.[36] Even mothers who did not put their children in an organized day care or nursery school sought opportunities to share child-rearing responsibilities. Robyn Muncy has shown how cooperative child care and nursery schools flourished in the postwar suburbs, creating a culture of what she calls "cooperative motherhood."[37] Organizing community playgroups and play spaces was the mission of the

Play School Association, which offered recreational diversions such as block building, painting, and construction for part of the day or after school.[38] Articles on sharing child care, which abounded in *Parents' Magazine* in the 1940s and into the 1950s, suggested that parents provide activities akin to those of the nursery school. Postwar families increasingly believed in the educational benefits of nursery schools. By the early 1960s, Congress passed far-reaching federal legislation to establish Head Start programs that would provide nursery school education for the poor.[39]

For middle-class families, toys were also an expression of material abundance, and providing developmental aids for young children was often discussed as a parent's "responsibility." As parents' incomes rose and pressure to provide "appropriate" stimulation—recommended in the wildly popular parenting magazines and guides—increased, toys were bountiful in the postwar middle-class home. Mothers and fathers were encouraged to give their children materials and toys identical to those encountered in the day care, nursery, or play school; blocks, modeling clay, paints, hammering tools, and stringing beads were recommended as basic home equipment. While nursery schools evoked a homelike atmosphere, home itself was supposed to accommodate early learning, especially through objects. As one designer proposed, "For a good object lesson in what to buy preschool children for their daily play every parent should take a trip to a good nursery school while his child is still in the cradle to observe what the children use there."[40] Toy companies reinforced the idea that children would benefit with promises that their products would develop skills and raise IQ.[41] Holgate argued that "baby learns quicker" with a smooth set of colorful stringing beads, and Playskool claimed its toys would "develop your child earlier."[42] In a 1955 *Ladies' Home Journal* cartoon by Al Kaufman, women mob a display of "Toys for Very Bright Children," playing up the faddishness of educational toys, the effectiveness of retailing strategies, and postwar parents' obsession with achievement.[43]

Consensus about the importance of basic learning toys such as beads and blocks is perhaps also evident in children's furniture of the postwar period. Mass-market playpens, cribs, and rockers from the late 1940s and 1950s were embellished with turning beads or discs that children could manipulate from inside, whereas the decals that also ornamented these items remained on the exterior. The red and blue moving discs on two sides of a collapsible wooden Abbott and Company playpen simultaneously offered amusement to children and a sign of educational value to adults (Figure 2.4). Although the beadlike shapes on the playpen's legs were symbolic, the

Figure 2.4. Abbott & Company, playpen, mid-1950s. Courtesy of the Strong Museum, Rochester, New York.

flattened, movable discs signified manipulation and figured the curious child who might attempt to stand up in order to reach the bright, spinning forms. The playthings that many parents, especially those who perceived themselves as educated, chose for their children represented their desire for wholesome, constructive entertainment. But they often opted for objects that evoked a discourse of refinement in addition to that of achievement.

TOY MATERIALS AND TYPES

The postwar years saw a wide variety of new materials used in the production of toys. The availability of pressed, lithographed tin for toy cars and other vehicles was extremely limited during the war years, as toy manufacturers shifted their energies and materials to produce munitions. When factories were reconverted, in the mid-1940s, mechanical toys flooded onto the American market. Plastic, the quintessential postwar material, had been adapted for the production of toys even before the war. Although early plastic proved fragile and useful only for small objects, it would eventually become one of the most important factors of postwar toy production.[44] Yet in the educational rhetoric of the era, plain wooden toys emerged as solid, unpretentious reminders of simpler times of the past and as seemingly blank objects upon which children's imaginations might be given free rein. Gary Cross has discussed how prewar toys that stressed making and building dovetailed with the Arts and Crafts movement in America.[45] This preference for wood remained laden with vitalist associations of handicraft in the postwar period—even if the toys themselves were mass-produced—and was in line with the consumer habits of upper-middle-class American parents who bought Scandinavian furniture for its evocation of craftsmanship and sophisticated design. The person who purchased educational toys probably resembled Russell Lynes's "upper middlebrow" consumer or midcentury *New Yorker* magazine readers who, Louis Menand has noted, valued craftsmanship and eschewed commercialism in domestic goods, even if commerce was a means of making a living.[46]

Although many postwar consumers explored the possibilities of a new world of synthetics for domestic goods, among the educated middle and upper-middle classes, wood became the material symbol of timelessness, authenticity, and refinement in the modern educational toy. In France in the mid-1950s, Roland Barthes condemned plastic and metal as "graceless" and "chemical in substance and color" and mused upon his fondness for wooden toys:

> A sign which fills one with consternation is the gradual disappearance of wood, in spite of its being an ideal material because of its firmness and its softness, and the natural warmth of its touch. Wood removes, from all forms which it supports, the wounding quality of angles which are too sharp, the chemical coldness of metal. . . . It is a familiar and poetic substance, which does not sever the child from close contact with the tree, the table, the floor. Wood does not wound or break down; it does not shatter, it wears out, it can last a long time, live with the child, alter little by little the relations between the object and the hand.[47]

Barthes's evocation of images of the past, sensuous pleasure, and artistry shows how the symbolic qualities of wood were perceived as antithetical to the technological associations of plastic and metal.

Whereas Barthes emphasized the "poetic" properties of wood, others saw in wood the antithesis to the "realistic" qualities of metal and plastic. (Realism was a selling point for metal and plastic toys and was emphasized in advertisements that stressed their appearance.) The veneration of wooden playthings was also a comment on the proliferation of mass-market toys, such as Louis Marx's tin-plated wind-up toys, which aimed to please without an "educational" program.[48] Many of Marx's dime-store tin toys and plastic play sets were manufactured in Japan with colorful graphics (some based on television and movie characters) and moving parts that a turn of a key activated. Educators and parents who were dedicated to the progressive notion that children should learn and discover by doing rejected these amusements as hindering development. In 1947, shortly after Frank Caplan founded his company Creative Playthings, he commented, "There is a huge flood of mechanical toys from abroad for the first time in years. Many of them are devoid of real toy value. Young children don't need gadgets. Their imaginations are enough."[49]

Sturdy hardwood toys in abstract shapes, such as the Playskool Floor Train, became the dominant aesthetic for postwar educational toys. A Playskool catalog from about 1950 shows how the design of the train was adjusted to reflect reigning theories. Instead of the streamlined curves of the earlier 1930s locomotive, which mimicked contemporary industrial design, the 1950 train was reduced to its most cubic elements (Figure 2.5). The cars were still brightly colored, but the forms themselves had been made deliberately abstract. Suggesting visually the form of the child's block, the train's geometry declared not only its manipulative ease but also a growing belief that the young child's own imagination could—and should be allowed to—provide the details. The venerable Dr. Spock commented at length on the importance of abstract form and secondarily on toy materials in his best-selling postwar manual, *Baby and Child Care*:

> There are two very different kinds of toy trains. One is made of metal painted to look real. . . . The other is made of plain, flat wooden blocks that link together easily. All the *young* child can do with the realistic train is push one car along the floor. It's too hard to put the cars on the track or hitch them together. . . . The wooden block cars are different. He can link a string of them together and admire his long train. Two make a trailer truck. He can pile small blocks on top, call it a freight train and make deliveries. When he is bored with dry land, the blocks become separate boats or a string of barges with a tug. He can go on like this forever.[50]

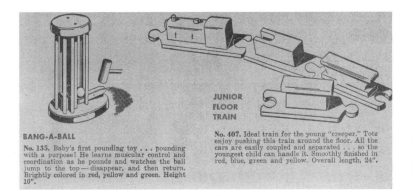

BANG-A-BALL

No. 135. Baby's first pounding toy . . . pounding with a purpose! He learns muscular control and coordination as he pounds and watches the ball jump to the top—disappear, and then return. Brightly colored in red, yellow and green. Height 10″.

JUNIOR FLOOR TRAIN

No. 407. Ideal train for the young "creeper." Tots enjoy pushing this train around the floor. All the cars are easily coupled and separated . . . so the youngest child can handle it. Smoothly finished in red, blue, green and yellow. Overall length, 24″.

Figure 2.5. Playskool, Junior Floor Train no. 407, from *Playskool Toy Catalog: The Right Toy for Every Age* (1950). Donald Wallance Collection. Photograph by Matt Flynn. Cooper-Hewitt, National Design Museum, Smithsonian Institution/Art Resource, New York.

Although Spock is ostensibly discussing the suitability of forms for manipulation, he suggests that the versatility of this *wooden* train enhances a child's experimentation and inventiveness. In Spock's scenario, the easy transformation of train into truck and boat suggests that representational forms and imagery of the "real" adult world are unnecessary and perhaps even inhibiting. To the equation of wooden and wholesome was added the emphasis on plainness as a means of fostering a child's imagination.

Despite the growth of the market, the design of many postwar toys did not differ markedly from earlier models. Holgate and Playskool, for example, continued to produce prewar designs. Even nineteenth-century educational toys, which had come to define progressive educational values in their own time, lingered in postwar playthings. For example, parquetry sets (Fröbel's seventh gift) were manufactured and sold throughout the mid-twentieth century by Playskool. When Montessori theory returned to the United States, in the 1960s, American toy makers produced objects for the Montessori curriculum but also sold variations to parents. A system of "tangible arithmetic" that Creative Playthings produced in the late 1950s was directly based on the Montessori counting beads.[51] Moreover, Caroline Pratt's hardwood Unit Blocks remained a fixture in nursery schools but also entered the home. Although toy sellers continued to stock embroidery and chemistry sets, the cultivation of imagination, artistic expression, and private fantasy became a consistent theme in the selling of educational toys to schools and parents.

SELLING CREATIVITY

Playskool, which became the largest producer of educational toys in America by the late 1950s, had always relied on the promise of raising "better" children, but the tone of its assurances changed from practical manipulation in the 1920s to a new emphasis on personality, citizenship, and creativity in the years after World War II.[52] Ads from the 1950s stressed a parent's responsibility to provide for the future: "Today—*you* make their tomorrow! You can help build a better, happier future for your children—by the wise selection of educational toys. . . . Playskool Toys stimulate earlier, sounder development—help build valuable skills, healthy attitudes and good habit patterns."[53] In addition to promoting early intellectual and social development, and a "better, happier future," Playskool also sponsored ads promising "creative play" with wooden blocks, and advertised a hammer-and-nail set with the slogan "creative pounding" (Figure 2.6).

Holgate, too, claimed that its toys were "scientifically designed to put the 'create' in re*creat*ion."[54]

Playskool's 1956 announcement for the unpainted Skaneateles wooden train, track, and block sets, advertised in *Playthings* (the magazine of the toy industry), proclaimed to retailers, "When a toy is designed to make the most of a child's natural creativeness . . . you gain an unlimited selling market" (Figure 2.7). While emphasizing the commercial viability of "creativeness," Playskool pushed the manufactured quality of the Skaneateles sets. Like the Junior Floor Trains, the differentiation between the engine, caboose, and tanker in the Skaneateles set was indicated in generalized forms, but unlike the colorful floor trains, the Skaneateles train set was produced from Vermont maple, sanded, and waxed for a natural finish and ran on track that was also unpainted and grooved to hold the small wheels (Figure 2.8). Playskool argued it would "put no adult limits on a child's imagination."[55] In the ad, two children of different ages and genders are shown kneeling and surrounded by track. As they handle the small shapes, moving them around and over the tracks, their entire bodies are engaged. Sensory stimulation, the ad implies, is not a passive activity but rather a productively absorbing one.

Educators seeking to train parents in the importance of play and advertising copywriters for educational-toy makers often emphasized that play should be considered a child's work. One result was that educational toys were often perceived as inappropriately serious and even unimaginative. What was sold as "educational" for older, school-aged children included science kits, construction toys, anatomical kits, and encyclopedias, whereas pounding benches, Peg-Boards, and plain blocks were intended for younger ones. Lawrence K. Frank addressed this problem in his introduction to a 1957 handbook of children's play: "Some people have been so impressed by the importance of play that they want all the child's playthings to be 'educational,' that is, to be limited to those toys and games which are designed to teach some specific skill or to convey some definite meaning." Frank continued: "But if we do this we deprive the child of a large area of experience equally essential to his development as a well-rounded personality. It is as if we say that everything in life must be usable and practicable and reject everything that is esthetically desirable, that gives tone, color, and richness to living."[56] In contrast to "educational," the modifier "creative" was posed to indicate something more durable and desirable.

Figure 2.6. "Creative Pounding," Playskool advertisement, *Parents' Magazine*, October 1949, 152.

What does a child's imagination mean for you?

When a toy is designed to make the most of a child's natural creativeness . . . you gain an unlimited selling market.

The new Playskool-Skaneateles train, track and block sets put no adult limits on a child's imagination.

No more durable toy piece is cut square and exact from Northern Vermont hard maple, then smoothly sanded and waxed to a natural finish that's completely scrubbable and safe. Wheels and couplings stand

up even under the heaviest use they might receive.

And consider how perfectly these train sets meet the needs of the 2-to-8 year old . . . how many hours of fun they provide for boys and girls. The precision-cut tracks can be fitted firmly together in any number of ways, rearranged countless times without showing signs of wear.

There are extra profits waiting when customers come back for accessories and advanced sets. Write for illustrated catalog of sets and accessories, Playskool Mfg. Co., 1750 No. Lawndale Ave., Chicago 47, Ill.

Playskool
educational toys

Skaneateles train, track and block sets . . . now in the famous blue and white Playskool box

Figure 2.7. Playskool Skaneateles train advertisement, *Playthings* 54, no. 4 (April 1956): 76. Photograph from Science, Industry, and Business Library, the New York Public Library, Astor, Lenox and Tilden Foundations.

The University of Chicago creativity researchers Jacob Getzels and Philip Jackson pointed to the heavy emphasis on what they called "factualism and usefulness" at the expense of play and imagination, particularly in the early years of childhood. Getzels and Jackson identified the child's toy box as critical in the formation of children's thinking. They suggested, moreover, that the promises of the "educational toy" bore some of the blame for encouraging academic lessons at the expense of free imagination:

Even that last bastion of the child's private world—his box of toys—is being taken over by the press of practicality. Here too the key adjectives are "realistic" and "educational" or at the very least "readiness-producing," instead of "imaginative" or "exciting" or even just plain "enjoyable." The floppy rag doll that did nothing and yet everything as the malleable companion of the child's dreams has given way to the true-to-life human replica that leaves nothing to the imagination—it "really talks" and takes in and oozes at all the appropriate orifices. The ancient lead soldier in his frozen posture, which the child could transmute into anything his play required, is no match for the modern Transparent Man whose removable vital organs form an educational jigsaw puzzle for mother's little, successful doctor-to-be. . . . Even the preverbal child's toys are now sold not just as playthings but as Play-School, the pitch being that these toys are not "just toys" but carefully designed to train the infant in "appropriate" motor, intellectual, and problem-solving skills, presumably appropriate for gaining early admission to pre-nursery school.[57]

From educators' and psychologists' perspectives, therefore, the "educational" toys that proliferated on the postwar market had become mindlessly didactic tools of social competition rather than open-ended objects that might stimulate original thinking. A 1960 article on creativity in *Parents' Maga-*

Figure 2.8. Skaneateles train set, circa 1950s. Collection of Dave Pecota; photograph courtesy of Dave Pecota.

zine urged parents to "enrich [the child's] opportunities to dream up activities of his own and discover his own materials for play. When selecting
toys and games, include some which provide free self-expression as well
as those which come with rules and instructions."[58] Toy makers, especially
those most active in marketing the promise of improvement, developed
research departments that closely followed academic literature. An early
1970s Playskool catalog, for example, argued for the importance of "playtools" in the "creative environment of the home," citing a bibliography that
included Getzels and Jackson's 1962 study.[59] The Swedish scholar Birgitta
Almqvist has suggested that the "educational" toy was reborn as an open-
ended "creative" toy in the late 1960s. In the United States, however, the
creative toy genre was established earlier, and among its promoters were
not only psychologists and educators but also other, more unlikely sources:
designers, architects, and the modern art museum.[60]

The vogue for "creativity" among child-development experts, along
with the critique of the pedantic "educational" toy and a growing audience
for modern art and design, are some of the reasons that a genre of aestheti-
cally sophisticated toys flourished in the two decades after World War II. In
1948, the Walker Art Center in Minneapolis developed a toy called the Magnet Master, a kit of brightly painted steel plates in the shapes of circles, tri-
angles, rectangles, and squares, with long and short rods, compact colorful
magnets, and a base plate, all packaged in a lemon-yellow box emblazoned
with the slogan "a new creative toy" (Figure 2.9). Arthur A. Carrara, the
young Chicago architect who designed Magnet Master, had experimented
before the war with the use of magnets for structural joints but had little
success. In the late 1940s, he found that the
stronger alnico magnets, developed for wartime use, improved the structure and aesthetics of the product. Carrara approached
several manufacturers about a magnetic toy
and eventually secured the participation of
the Walker Art Center. Carrara, together with
his brother Reno and Daniel S. Defenbacher,
the museum's director and also an architect,
founded Carradan Associates to manufacture Magnet Master with financial support
from Walker Art Center trustees.[61]

Magnet Master's planes were perforated for building with the rods and magnets, offering easy construction of what its

Figure 2.9. Arthur A. Carrara, Magnet Master
box set no. 900, circa 1948. Photograph from
Collection Centre Canadien d'Architecture/
Canadian Centre for Architecture, Montreal.

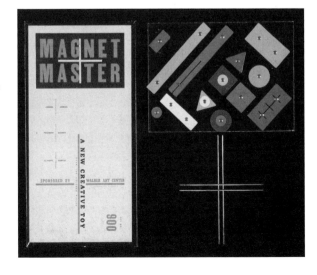

promoters called "objects or arrangements having either a utilitarian or abstract 'work of art' appearance."[62] The Walker Art Center advertised this "new creative toy" as a "playtool" that taught principles of construction and expressive play, and urged parents to allow the child to experiment by him- or herself (Figure 2.10). There were no diagrams for children to follow because, the enclosed pamphlet argued, "children are naturally imaginative and will derive greater pleasure and benefit when left to their own images and devices."[63]

The discourse of creativity was prominent in the toy's advertising. An article in *Look* magazine showed the painter Max Weber playing alongside an eleven-year-old named Johnny, suggesting that through play children could develop authentically creative skills akin to those of the professional artist.[64] Initially, Magnet Master was sold through the Walker Art Center and other museums and at select design shops, but it was advertised widely and distributed nationally with a complicated cardboard counter display that emphasized the *Look* profile as well as the properties of magnetism (Figure 2.11).[65] Although the kit came in two sizes, with different prices, it was relatively expensive.[66] According to a list of suggested sales techniques, counter staff were encouraged to stress that "Magnet Master is a piece of playroom equipment. It is not merely a short lived toy."[67]

As well-designed "equipment" for the home, Magnet Master grew out of the Walker Art Center's commitment to a program of good design in "everyday art," which the museum demonstrated in a series of exhibitions and publications in the late 1940s and early 1950s.[68] Although the toy was also used in museum test-studies on children at a local Minneapolis elementary school to adapt the product for use in a program of art education, and a supplier expressed interest in handling it for the school market, Magnet Master was aimed at a sophisticated consumer who favored modern art and design.[69] Despite substantial promotion and strong interest in the concept,

Figure 2.10. Cover from Magnet Master playtool, 1949. Photograph from Collection Centre Canadien d'Architecture/Canadian Centre for Architecture, Montreal.

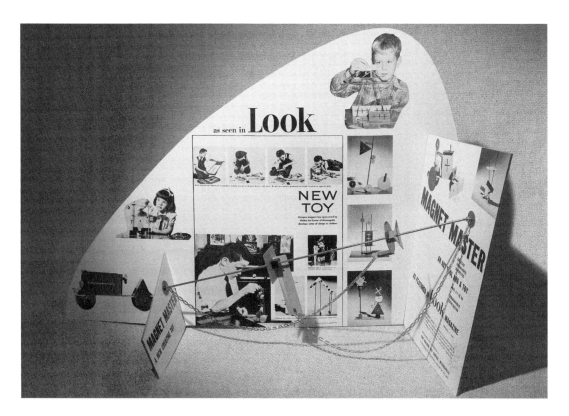

Magnet Master was not commercially viable, and the remaining sets that Carradan Associates owned were liquidated in 1950.

At around the same time, the designers Charles and Ray Eames developed a number of paper toys, such as the Toy (1950) and the Little Toy (1951), the House of Cards (1952), the Giant House of Cards (1953), and the Coloring Toy (1955), all of which were simple kits that allowed the child to experiment with construction, arrangement, and building.[70] The Toy was a set of rigid wires and panels rolled into a long, octagonal box that sold for around $3.50. These pieces could be transformed into many different forms and spaces, including places for play and hiding.[71] In promotional texts, the Eameses emphasized that the Toy created spaces "large enough to play in and around."[72] The numerous photographs, some of which were used for advertising, show the Toy erected as an airplane, a playhouse, a lemonade stand, and other spaces. *Interiors* magazine argued that it offered children and their parents a means of experimenting and hoped it would give "commercial toy design a healthy nudge along a new and more imaginative path."[73]

Figure 2.11. Magnet Master counter display. Photograph from Walker Art Center Archives, Minneapolis.

Unlike the Toy, which was intended for all ages, a smaller version, the Little Toy, was intended for children and was scaled accordingly (Figure 2.12).

The designers of Magnet Master eschewed examples for children to follow, but the Eameses' toys included explicit instructions for building tents, airplanes, tunnels, towers, and other forms. Yet the instructions also implied that children themselves were designers: "We know you can create your own objects with the Little Toy."[74] The Eameses' toys married modernist design and aesthetics to what they considered the child's own play instincts. The Coloring Toy included cutout cards and shapes, crayons, and a note to parents: "The Coloring Toy does not presume to make artists out of children or to teach them how to play (children are far ahead of us on both counts). But we do hope that the contents of this box and the clues it offers will stimulate the use of these and other materials in an ever expanding variety of ways."[75]

The most successful and long-lived of the Eameses' toys was the House of Cards, which was produced in three sizes.[76] Like the Toy, it was designed for both adults and school-aged children, who could assemble it easily. The cards, each with a photograph or abstract image on one side and a starlike office logo on the other, were slit in six places, allowing the user to create an infinite number of interlocking combinations and forms (Figure 2.13). The stiff cardboard rectangles asked the child to exercise patience in fitting the slots into each other and discernment in selecting the images. One critic ar-

Figure 2.12. Charles and Ray Eames, the Little Toy, 1951. Photograph copyright Eames Office, LLC (www.eamesoffice.com).

Figure 2.13. Charles and Ray Eames, House of Cards, 1952. Photograph copyright Eames Office, LLC (www.eamesoffice.com).

gued, "These cards are starting points only—the rest is up to the boy or girl (or man or woman) whose active participation is essential if the toy is to have meaning."[77] The images on the cards' surfaces evoked a playful variety of associations, and when assembled they juxtaposed antique toy cars, marbles, crayons, vegetables, pins, and other ordinary household objects, as well as exotic things such as a kachina doll, an abacus, and Chinese firecrackers. These toys, like many others, inverted an earlier notion of training children to become proper adults. Instead, they encouraged play as a suitable occupation for all ages. As the value of creativity gained currency, playful adults were understood not as regressive but rather as productive.

The cultural ethos of play pervaded experimental architectural circles, especially after the 1950 translation into English of Huizinga's *Homo Ludens*, and other designers also began to design toys both for their own children and for manufacture. In the mid-1950s, Seattle architect Fred Bassetti, experimenting with a way to make a cardboard playhouse, created a paper toy based on the mathematical concept of the flexagon, folded strips of paper that could show multiple faces. Bassetti's cardboard set, Flexagons, which his own Førde Corporation originally produced, consisted of small, colorful triangular and square cardboard panels that were bent and could be assembled with rubber bands to create an infinite variety of three-dimensional shapes and structures.[78] In a printed sheet enclosed with the set, Bassetti encouraged users to experiment and learn about geometry, and to send in pictures of their projects. The Flexagons box, which depicted children manipulating the cardboard pieces, bore the sustaining promise of postwar educational toys: "develops creative ability" (Figure 2.14).

Colorforms, another educational toy that claimed it taught children to "build, play and learn," consisted of a simple kit of colorful vinyl shapes that adhered to a smooth surface. Harry and Patricia Kislevitz, two New York art students, developed the concept by experimenting with cutting thin sheets of vinyl and sticking the shapes to their bathroom wall.[79] Like Magnet Master, Flexagons began as an architect's idea, but unlike Magnet Master it achieved moderate commercial success. And Colorforms has endured ever since its boxed sets began appearing in the early 1950s.[80]

The Eameses' toys, Bassetti's Flexagons, and the Walker Art Center's Magnet Master privileged design and aesthetic experimentation over a specific educational theory. Unlike the pedantic educational toy, these objects emphasized the pleasures of arrangement and assembly and the cognitive

Figure 2.14. Fred Bassetti, Flexagons, Førde Corporation, circa 1960. Photograph from Collection Centre Canadien d'Architecture/ Canadian Centre for Architecture, Montreal.

benefits of play. Designers, artists, and corporations embraced play as a means of sharpening ingenuity. In 1966, a writer for *Progressive Architecture* theorized that toys might affect the next generation of professionals and clients, asking, "Is creativity in these matters being sufficiently developed in the important and impressionable years, no matter what the future occupation of the child? Is sensitivity to material, form, structure, connection, and modularity a byproduct of these toys?"[81] Although many important postwar artists designed toys and children's furniture, anonymously produced toys also gained attention for their educational promises and the quality of their design.

CREATIVE PLAYTHINGS, INC.

In contrast to Holgate's and Playskool's established businesses, Creative Playthings was begun in the mid-1940s and perhaps best embodies how the idea of creativity was associated with toy design and merchandising after World War II. Frank and Theresa Caplan began Creative Playthings as a small shop, originally called the Playhouse, in New York City in 1945.[82] Frank Caplan, who once worked under Caroline Pratt, had experience with both educating children and making goods for their use. Creative Playthings was expanded in 1950, when Caplan and Bernard Barenholtz, who also ran a toy shop with his wife in St. Louis, entered into an informal partnership. Unlike most figures in the trade, both Caplan and Barenholtz held graduate degrees in education and designed items themselves, in addition to running the business.[83] Creativity was emphasized in the company's name, and its products combined educational theory, older toy traditions, and sophisticated design.

In a 1946 prospectus for manufacturers at the New York Toy Fair, Frank Caplan announced that the firm had been established to promote the ideas of pioneering educators to parents, retailers, manufacturers, and designers through a central buying service. With the advice of experts (including Lawrence Frank) in psychology, education, and art education, Creative Playthings developed and sold carefully selected objects. Caplan proposed "approved play centers" where parents could "shop 'with confidence' in the knowledge that their selections contribute[d] to the wholesome development and happiness of their children."[84] From this beginning, Creative Playthings continually handled the designs of other manufacturers, including Holgate, Playskool, and Tigrett Enterprises (which produced the Eameses' toys). Creative Playthings aligned itself with progressive educational values, producing and reviving designs developed for earlier nursery school models, which they sold through shops and catalogs to schools and parents.[85]

Creative Playthings' own early designs were indebted to the company's spiritual predecessors. In the late 1940s, the company developed hardwood building forms called Hollow Block, designed by Caplan, who also helped to build them, and Martha New (Figure 2.15). Plain maple cubes that were open on one side, Hollow Block seemed little more than a sturdier version of a wooden crate or a larger, hollow version of nursery school blocks.[86] The regularity of the cubes when paired or stacked enhanced the flexibility of these large blocks, which were light enough that a three-year-old child could arrange them him- or herself. With the addition of cushions or casters, the forms could be transformed into practical furniture (such as desks or storage units) or left to the child to create his or her own private world. In early catalogs, these units were configured as a pretend store, a fort, and a boat, complete with planks and a pine barrel, which the company also sold. Even in the mid-1960s, Creative Playthings' leaders echoed Pratt's position, maintaining that "the block still is, and probably always will be, the most important toy . . . a child can build and create. It's an unlimited activity."[87]

Other objects also embodied current notions of "unstructured play," in which the games, objects, or fantasies were left to the child instead of being determined by the manufacturer. Creative Playthings' lacquered birch planes, boats, cars, and trains were deliberately unpainted and freely defined, and some were large enough for a child to ride. In addition to child-sized household implements, such as sweepers, doll beds, kitchens, costumes, and playhouses, the company sold carpentry sets, easels, and art materials. Toys with social studies and science themes were also developed for both home and school use. A set of See-Inside puzzles, for example, revealed the workings of a dairy barn, post office, circus, airport, city street, firehouse, and television station. In the early 1960s, the company developed a large, three-legged birch magnifying glass that offered opportunities to investigate the scientific properties of unusually large objects, and it doubled as a stool. Yet, in addition to pursuing a progressive educational mission of exploratory and dramatic play, the company's toys grew increasingly abstract, acquiring the cast of artistic modernism. A puzzle of abstract yellow and orange birds in a tree could be positioned flat or arranged upright,

Figure 2.15. Frank Caplan and Martha New, Hollow Block, Creative Playthings, Inc., circa 1950. From School Interiors Co., Inc., and Creative Playthings, Inc., *A Guide to Equipment and Materials for Early Childhood* (1957).

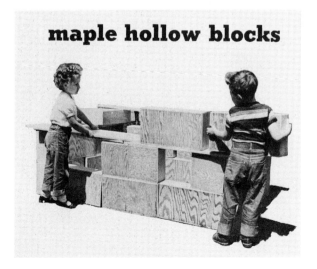

maple hollow blocks

according to the child's ability to balance the pieces (Plate 4). And, a rocking toy, called the Rocking Beauty, consisting of two pieces of bent plywood and a large orange knob, eliminated suggestions of any animal form (Figure 2.16).[88] Caplan and Barenholtz, following psychologists and pediatricians of the era, believed that providing children with unpainted and vague forms would stimulate their imaginations.[89] Therefore, these "representational" objects emphasized shape and natural textures and colors rather than realistic details.

Creative Playthings was invested in quality design and manufacture and a European tradition of solid wooden toys. In 1954, the company hired the Swiss sculptor and toy maker Antonio Vitali to design a series of wooden Playforms. Vitali worked with Caplan and Barenholtz to adapt the aesthetics of his hand-carved toys and sculptures to a specially designed mechanical lathe that could produce the small animals, vehicles, and figures in sufficient quantities (Figure 2.17).[90] Smooth, undulating, unpainted surfaces that formed to a child's hand, Vitali's toys embodied the association between visual abstraction, tactile appeal, and imaginative development. By eliminating details, such as facial features, doors, and separate parts, Vitali's designs put the visual and intellectual emphasis on the form and the natural grain of the wood, reinforcing the company's ideal of freeing the child's imagination through abstraction. Creative Playthings was one of several postwar toy companies that emphasized natural materials and forms, but the sculptural qualities of the Vitali designs gained the attention of professional designers, who embraced both the artistic qualities and the theory behind them. Art and design periodicals, such as *Interiors* and *Arts and Architecture*, promoted the Vitali toys, largely paraphrasing the company literature, as a "bold experiment in art education. These toys embody good design, sturdiness, and play value."[91]

Creative Playthings not only sought the liberation of the child's imagination but relied on contemporary artists and an

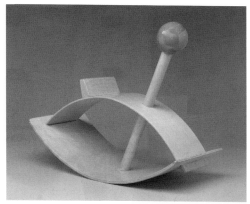

Figure 2.16. Gloria Caranica (American, born 1931), Rocking Beauty hobbyhorse, designed 1964–66. Plywood, solid wood, pigment, 20¼ × 25¼ × 11¾ inches (51.4 × 64.1 × 29.8 cm). Brooklyn Museum, Bequest of Laura L. Barnes and gift of Mrs. James F. Bechtold, by exchange, 2007.38.

Figure 2.17. Antonio Vitali, Playform family, Creative Playthings, circa 1954.

association with the Museum of Modern Art (MoMA) in New York City. Through a series of collaborations with MoMA, Creative Playthings became linked with sophisticated taste and modern aesthetics.[92] Like Walker's commitment to Magnet Master as "everyday art," the alliance between Creative Playthings' products and MoMA's "good design" standards was carried further, as Creative Playthings began to hire artists, in addition to its in-house staff, to design for them. In addition to Vitali, Isamu Noguchi, Louis Kahn, Robert Winston, and Henry Moore all agreed to collaborate with Creative Playthings, although many of their schemes were not realized.[93]

In addition to household toys and furniture for schools, Creative Playthings also took on the outdoor environment of the playground. The company had always sold toys for active play, including rockers, wagons, slides, a platform that could be reversed into a rocking boat, and eventually outdoor climbing structures. Yet in 1953, the company added Play Sculptures as an independent division of the company. Play Sculptures produced playground equipment designed by artists and industrial designers in an effort to expand and refresh ideas about playground planning. Long interested in urbanistic questions and the landscape of play, Creative Playthings' directors launched Play Sculptures to redefine the conventional Junglegym through art. The Danish Swedish sculptor Egøn Moeller-Nielsen's cast stone helical slide, which Creative Playthings sold in America, was held up as a model for modern playground equipment, because it encouraged both exercise and fantasy (Figure 2.18). Unlike conventional playground slides, the rounded, mountainlike structure with an internal ladder and a molded ridge for sliding was a large-scale evocation of the free forms that the company championed. At once plainly utilitarian and daringly sculptural, Moeller-Nielsen's design became a signature of the company's aspirations to reform children's playgrounds. One of the company's quieter but most successful designs was Milton Hebald's Turtle Tent and Baby Turtle, a large cast concrete form with smaller versions placed in close proximity (Figure 2.19). The solid sculptural presence of the mother turtle was molded with indentations to imply a shell-like pattern and also to hold small feet and hands attempting to scale the animal's back. Because it was often situated in sandboxes, the turtle set also pro-

Figure 2.18. Egøn Moeller-Nielsen, slide, circa 1950. From Play Sculptures, Inc., *Play Sculptures: A New World of Play* (1957).

Figure 2.19. Milton Hebald, Turtle Tent and Baby Turtle, Creative Playthings, circa 1953. From Play Sculptures, Inc., *Play Sculptures: A New World of Play* (1957).

vided places to dig, crawl, and hide beneath the large form, and, owing to a variety in scale, it accommodated children of various ages.[94] The company's catalog text underscored the turtle's tactile qualities and exhorted the child to "touch it . . . hug it . . . sit on it . . . make cakes on its back . . . step from one to another."[95]

To promote its new venture, Creative Playthings sponsored, with MoMA and *Parents' Magazine*, a competition for new playground structures in the fall of 1953. The Play Sculpture competition emphasized inventive sculptural designs that promised not only to enliven the conventional playground but also to stimulate children's imaginations, exercise their bodies, and adhere to safety requirements. Of the 360 submissions, the jury (which included Caplan; Philip Johnson, then curator of Architecture and Design; education director Victor D'Amico; and Greta Daniel, from Architecture and Design, who chaired the committee) chose three designs that Creative Playthings produced in full-size models, exhibited at MoMA, and sold through catalogs.[96]

The first-prize winner, Virginia Dortch Dorazio, a twenty-eight-year-old painter, created Fantastic Village, four concrete playhouses with pierced panels and a trellis of metal rods (Figure 2.20). Robert J. Gargiule's second-prize design, Stalagmite Cave, used spool-shaped upright forms that could serve as low tables or provide narrow hiding places. Sidney Gordin, a sculptor, created Tunnel Maze, consisting of five bridgelike forms that could be staggered in an undulating landscape, offering places to crawl or hide beneath (Figure 2.21). The museum exhibited the models and full-size reproductions, allowing child visitors to test the designs. All of the winning entries

Figure 2.20. Virginia Dortch Dorazio, Fantastic Village, Creative Playthings, 1954. From Play Sculptures, Inc., *Play Sculptures: A New World of Play* (1957).

relied on a single unit that could be repeated to create a striking visual environment, and all emphasized how children could explore shapes and textures while creating their own fantasy scenarios in the recessed and hidden spaces. Just as Caplan advocated for plain wooden toys that might free the child's imagination, he also claimed that Play Sculpture designs might liberate the mind when exercised in concert with the child's body and the wider context of the city, school, or park. Given that "sculptured" playgrounds let many children play simultaneously (rather than waiting for turns), they were sold as a practical and social improvement. Unlike the playgrounds of the early twentieth century that employed an instructor to enable correct recreation and coordinated movement, Play Sculpture was designed to chal-

Figure 2.21. Sidney Gordin, Tunnel Maze, Creative Playthings, 1954. From Play Sculptures, Inc., *Play Sculptures: A New World of Play* (1957).

lenge the child's body physically and to prompt invention in its use. Yet, in addition to issuing claims of educational soundness, the company advertised that in Play Sculpture "there emerges a play environment which is a spot of good design—harmonious with today's architecture."[97]

The "creative" playground was widely discussed after World War II as cities and suburban towns sought new ways to deal with both children's play needs and perceived crises of American life, such as juvenile delinquency and diminished physical capability.[98] Susan G. Solomon has analyzed how attitudes toward playgrounds shifted in the mid-twentieth century as European notions of city play areas were revived in American discussions of urban planning.[99] The mid-1960s playgrounds of Richard Dattner and M. Paul Friedberg embodied some of the aesthetic ideals of the Play Sculpture program, but instead of using individual sculptural objects, they aimed for a total environment that would stimulate children to explore, learn, and create (Figure 2.22). The complex topography of Friedberg's and Dattner's New York City playgrounds used the different textures of wood and granite, concrete and water for tree houses, mounds, tunnels, and slides. Evoking the natural landscape for city children playing in public areas, these playgrounds adhered to an organic ideal. The ability to transform some aspect of the environment or to move around and through it, which both designers, paraphrasing Piaget, argued gave the child a sense of control and mastery, required a more complex space than the predictable asphalt yards and swing

Figure 2.22. Richard Dattner, Adventure Playground, Central Park, 1966. Photograph courtesy of Richard Dattner.

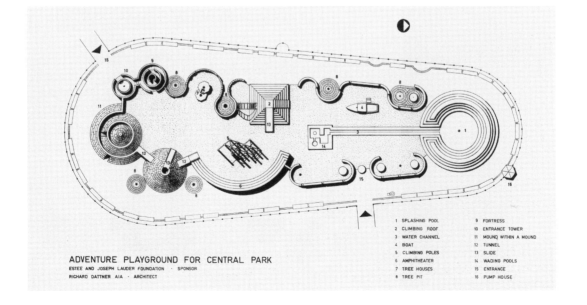

ADVENTURE PLAYGROUND FOR CENTRAL PARK
ESTÉE AND JOSEPH LAUDER FOUNDATION · SPONSOR
RICHARD DATTNER AIA · ARCHITECT

1 SPLASHING POOL	9 FORTRESS
2 CLIMBING ROOF	10 ENTRANCE TOWER
3 WATER CHANNEL	11 MOUND WITHIN A MOUND
4 BOAT	12 TUNNEL
5 CLIMBING POLES	13 SLIDE
6 AMPHITHEATER	14 WADING POOLS
7 TREE HOUSES	15 ENTRANCE
8 TREE PIT	16 PUMP HOUSE

sets. For Dattner, the natural world was a ready source for creative stimulation: "The child who plays with real sticks and leaves transforms them in his imagination into whatever he wants and creates another, more personal reality not bounded by the real and commonplace."[100] Conversant with the psychological implications of play, Dattner, like Caplan and Barenholtz, envisioned a higher cognitive function, such as creativity, as the desired, even expected, outcome of his design.

Critics such as Aline Saarinen hoped that sensitizing children to form, color, and texture through play might enrich and help shape a national culture, but others argued that play itself was the answer.[101] In 1965, David Aaron, a former designer of Creative Playthings' Play Sculpture, proposed that "child's play should continually stimulate and strengthen creative inclinations until they are capable of adult direction. Yet something in our environment, in the climate of play in this country, seems to inhibit creativity and to destroy the potential for inventiveness with which most children are born. Our problem, then, is not so much how many creative people we can give birth to, but how many of the creative people who are born we can keep."[102]

Although developing creativity in children through play was an ideal of the educational theory that proliferated during the interwar period, Cold War tensions reinforced associations between the idea of creativity and the values that seemed to embody democracy.[103] Many scholars have suggested that postwar artistic and popular culture was used to serve an American political project, especially in Europe.[104] Behind the theory that abstraction could enhance creativity was the example of American modern art and design, which were achieving new heights of prestige at home and abroad.[105] The image of the creative American child, who owned numerous playthings, was a central theme in the international exhibitions of the period.[106] At the Brussels World's Fair of 1958, the Islands of Living, a section of the American Pavilion devoted to consumables for the home, showed a large selection of children's furniture and toys, including a wind-up robot, wooden trucks, and an abstract geodesic climbing structure (Figure 2.23). At the American National Exhibition held in Sokolniki Park in Moscow in the summer of 1959, Creative Playthings provided a three-thousand-square-foot playground placed adjacent to the free Pepsi-Cola stand and the Model Home.[107] The juxtaposition of a playground, which included the winning Play Sculpture designs in addition to the concrete Turtle Tent and other abstract climbing forms, in close proximity to consumer products such as soft drinks and kitchens reinforced the carefully designed impression that future Americans would perpetuate this vision of invention and abundance.[108]

While exhibition propaganda put new emphasis on children's goods and theories of art making in selling a wholesome image of America abroad, political tensions between the United States and the Soviet Union enhanced the worries of postwar parents at home. Postwar toy companies therefore relied not only on the ambition of middle-class parents but also on their anxieties. In the 1962 Creative Playthings holiday catalog, under the heading "A Parent's Responsibility," the directors exhorted: "Parents and teachers everywhere face an unusual challenge. They are being called upon to prepare children for a world so radically new that we dare not forecast its direction, its technology and its social organization. Certainly rote text book learning or preconceived ideas cannot suffice for children facing such complexities. A bold approach to education in the home and in the school is indicated!"[109]

After the Soviet Union launched the Sputnik space satellites, in 1957, educational-toy companies such as Creative Playthings

Figure 2.23. Islands of Living, American Pavilion, Brussels World's Fair, 1958. Photograph by Casali and Vogel. From *Interiors* 18, no. 2 (September 1958): 117.

adapted their stock to suit the times. Creative Playthings, which had long catered to preschool and kindergarten ages, now entered the school and science areas directly, developing furniture systems for new buildings and pedagogy and a variety of science materials, from live animals to child-sized working stethoscopes and inexpensive cardboard kits. Under Roland Glenn, an educational expert whom the company hired to develop science materials, Creative Playthings began a home-science "discovery of the month" subscription series in 1964. Projects involving gears, shadows, a projector, mirrors, and a seed garden were suitable for children from six to ten years old. Another series, tailored for older children, included building paper structures, constructing a model of the solar system, a simple telescope and other optical machines, and a pendulum and musical instruments. A series of animals—newts, frogs, and fish—came with appropriate cages and instructions on care and observation to encourage children's understanding of conservation and ecology.[110] In 1965, Creative Playthings announced the availability of Mongolian gerbils for Christmas, and more than two thousand parents throughout the United States ordered them.[111]

As Creative Playthings expanded its business, it attracted attention for objects that were unusual in the United States. Dolls were a staple of the toy industry, but Creative Playthings sold them only selectively and sometimes controversially. In 1965, it began importing Sasha and Gregor dolls, developed in Switzerland by Sasha Morganthaler and produced in Germany and England. These dolls were sixteen-inch vinyl forms with honey-colored skin and a wistful expression. In a 1969 catalog, the company argued, "In the child's imagination a doll lives, laughs and cries, and shares his life. For this reason it is very important that the expression of the doll's face is only suggested. No grotesque caricature can awaken a child's true feelings. A piece of wood, barely carved, is far superior to a conventional doll with an exaggerated smile."[112] The dolls' complexions, which were designed to be "universal" and therefore welcome in any household, created a stir. Two years later, the company introduced anatomically correct dolls, Little Brother and Little Sister. Little Brother, who was modeled on a Florentine Renaissance sculpture, was designed in France with the genitalia of a four-month-old. Although Caplan argued that Little Brother had a valid educational use, charges of obscenity made it a cause that gained momentum in the press and polarized store owners.[113]

In 1966, the Columbia Broadcasting System (CBS) acquired a controlling interest in Creative Playthings, along with Wonder, Gym Dandy, and Ideal Toys toy companies and educational publishing concerns such as Holt, Reinhart & Winston. CBS's interest in consolidating a foothold in the educational-materials and -media market points to the large audience it anticipated among middle-class parents. Creative Playthings catalogs were redesigned with a new logo, printed entirely in color, and grew thicker. Around 1970, the company added even more toys by European designers, including British designer Patrick Rylands's sculptural molded plastic fish and bird bath toys and a jewel-colored acrylic building toy called Playplax, Swiss designer Kurt Naef's Naef Spiel wooden building forms, and unpainted wooden playthings by Finnish designers Pekka Korpijaakko and Jorma Vennola.[114] Creative Playthings expanded dramatically in the late 1960s, adding stores and seasonal shops in major department stores, and increasing the variety of items available through the mail-order business. In 1967, the company sent three million catalogs to parents and forty-three thousand schools, and by 1971, it included an eight-page catalog insert along with a two-page advertisement in an issue of *Life* magazine, which had a circulation of around 8.5 million.

By this time Creative Playthings' objects were widely available in department stores and in baby shops around the country.[115] Yet in 1969, the firm opened a new store in New York City, adjacent to Paley Park and near Eero Saarinen's CBS building on Fifty-Third Street. The store, designed by Studio Works, aimed to bring the child into the act of shopping and used design to entice young consumers. The long, narrow plan, dictated by the existing structure, was arranged around themes such as Community Play, Science and Space, and Active Play, with interlocking shelving units that not only held merchandise but also included working levers to activate lights and places to create electronic music (Figure 2.24). Acting as a kind of toy in itself, the space was pitched directly to a child's scale and interests, encouraging a young visitor to play with merchandise in a carpeted area at the back and enjoy him- or herself throughout the store (Figure 2.25). An oversize marble run and two-story castle of Pratt's Unit Blocks placed near the stairways beckoned children and parents to ascend to the second floor, where the company held changing exhibitions of children's art. Creative Playthings consistently cultivated a strong association between firm educational ideals and good design in its products. The new store framed these values and tethered the company to CBS's own reputation for sophisticated design.[116]

Figure 2.24. Studio Works (Lester Walker, Craig Hodgetts, Robert Mangurian, and Keith Godard), Creative Playthings Store, New York, 1969. Photograph by Lester Walker.

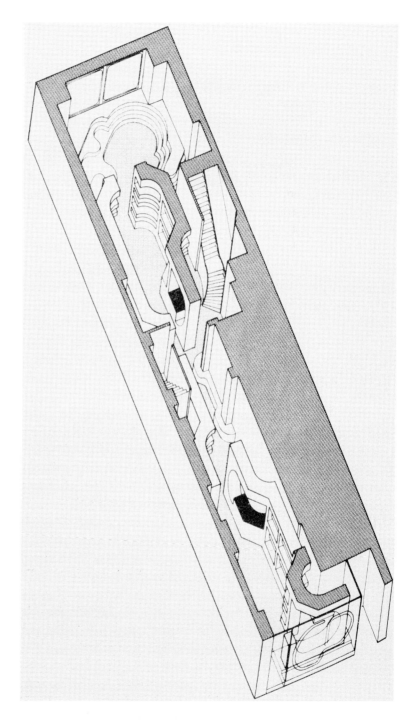

Figure 2.25. Studio Works (Lester Walker, Craig Hodgetts, Robert Mangurian, and Keith Godard) plan, Creative Playthings Store, New York, 1969.

The educational toy that promised to boost cognition and stimulate creativity was directed toward adults rather than children. In urging parents to prepare a "richly rewarding ego building environment" for their children and arguing that its toys could help them "brainstorm ideas in independent play," Creative Playthings rephrased the long-standing promises of educational-toy manufacturers and adopted the rhetoric of current creativity research.[117] But as the company grew and tastes changed, it also gained its share of criticism. In the 1970s, mass-market toy manufacturers relied heavily on realism in design and on television advertising to appeal to a children's culture of action, fantasy, and novelty. Creative Playthings went in the opposite direction, suggesting to parents that children actually needed fewer toys of higher quality and better design.[118] In 1971, the company produced an elaborate *Guide to Good Toys,* which aimed to educate and cultivate consumers. This attitude, and the psychological tone of its catalogs, made it a target of critics who claimed its expensive products and its approach were hopelessly elitist.[119]

Broader shifts within the toy industry affected the fortunes of the postwar educational toy. Mergers with Lincoln Logs and, in 1958, with Holgate Toys made Playskool the major producer of educational toys until it was absorbed into Milton Bradley and later into Hasbro, which continues to manufacture educational toys under the Playskool name. Creative Playthings as a wing of CBS grew increasingly distanced from its original model. Caplan and Barenholtz remained as consulting directors for a period but also took on other educational projects at CBS, and eventually they resigned.[120] In the late 1970s, Creative Playthings, under new management, radically decreased the number of objects it sold, canceled its mail-order division, and joined the prevailing trend of plastic toys, even producing some using popular cartoon characters, which would have been anathema for the company's founders.[121]

The benefits of educational toys have always been hard to measure. As Brian Sutton-Smith observes, "We have little compelling evidence of a connection between toys, all by themselves, and achievement. . . . What is more obvious is that, since the appearance of toys in the seventeenth century, we have steadily and progressively developed a belief that there is a connection between toys and achievement."[122] Playskool, Holgate, and Creative Playthings relied on this well-established belief to sell their toys to midcentury American parents. Like their predecessors, these firms depended on an adult culture that valorized achievement and competition, and in middle-class parents of the baby boom they found a healthy market for their products and promises of improvement. These firms, museums, and designers manufactured a wide variety of items in unprecedented quantities, advertising them in new ways and to new consumers, making educational toys a fixture of the postwar nursery. Postwar educational toys therefore reflect not only a long history of teaching objects but also their specifically twentieth-century American context. Similarly, the construction of creativity as a transcendent force of personal liberation was indebted to earlier ideas, but the circumstances of the postwar period gave the idea of creativity new appeal and a newly material expression. As researchers, toy makers, and parenting experts encouraged the idea that a generation raised to think "creatively" could ensure American interests in the future, they helped to sustain a market for consumable goods. The educational toy, after all, was right at home in the postwar playroom.

3

CREATIVE LIVING AT HOME

THE EDUCATIONAL-TOY INDUSTRY emphasized the creative potential of playing with blocks, cards, and other construction toys. Although these were age-old favorites of the middle-class toy box, in the years after World War II the act of building itself acquired new relevance. One of the biggest problems facing postwar reconstruction was housing. A severe shortage throughout the Depression and limited wartime building made housing a pressing social and architectural issue. Returning GIs, a rising birthrate, and an increasing demand led to the Housing Act of 1949, which promised a decent home for all Americans but disproportionately benefited middle-class suburban families with children.[1] Depression-era legislation, such as that which the Federal Housing Administration created to stimulate construction of moderate-cost housing, had made the single-family dwelling a national cause. Although housing starts were low throughout World War II, families anticipated and planned their postwar dwellings, clipping out pictures and collecting ideas for plans, materials, and products as the home became a singular image of patriotic hopefulness.[2] A March 1945 ad for building materials in *American Home* magazine showed a small child wearing Uncle Sam's hat, sitting on a globe and holding a straightedge. The text declared, "In the years ahead we'll build millions of *new* homes! Beautiful, livable, economical homes—the kind Mummy and Daddy dream of for *you*!" (Plate 5).[3] Given the ingrained belief that families with children belonged in nonurban settings and federal financing policies that reinforced it, the smaller, single-family house with its combined living-dining room, picture window, and gleaming kitchen, became a reigning symbol of the ambitions of white middle-class postwar America.[4]

The preoccupation with housing and domestic life was a particular motif of postwar culture, and the design and furnishing of household spaces for children's use gained new importance as a measure of national self-image. The anthropologist Margaret Mead argued, "Americans show their consciousness that each age has its own distinctive character by all the things that are fitted to the child's size, not only the crib and the cradle gym and the bathinette, but the small chair and table, too, and the special bowl and cup and spoon which together make a child-sized world out of a corner of the room."[5] Mead's vision of American childhood was fundamentally bound to material goods; the making of a "child-sized world" in the postwar family house was, therefore, a discourse not only of spatial planning but also of consumer culture.

Although the social and political dynamics of postwar domestic architecture have been well documented, the design and decoration of children's spaces has received little scholarly attention, even though these areas became a new focus of household planning in the increasingly informal middle-class houses built after the war.[6] The organization and decoration of the children's playroom, bedroom, and outdoor play areas, which were widely discussed in popular magazines, advice literature, and housing exhibits, reflect not only parents' increased buying power and child-centered attitudes but also a more subtle discourse of personal improvement. For designers such as Norman Cherner, the presence of children in the household required a new outlook: "A child-conscious home should have a casual atmosphere; yet it should be clean and esthetic. It should be an example for Peter and help him develop positive attitudes and standards for neatness and good taste. Peter can very well serve as an incentive for Parent to plan a more effective home for all those who live in it, a home conducive to well-balanced and creative living."[7]

The moral discourse of providing a clean, well-appointed environment recalled nineteenth-century prescriptive literature, but the desire for wholesome "creative living" was a singularly postwar obsession. In the debates on housing and parenting, an important and consistent theme was the provision of play space to encourage a child's inner life. Children's playrooms, nurseries, and bedrooms in postwar housing reveal how parents, designers, and psychologists envisioned and idealized creativity and imagination. If areas in the single-family house seemed to offer cognitive benefits for developing children, they also appeared to satisfy parents who labored to meet expectations of "well-balanced and creative living."

PLAY SPACE AT HOME

The compact housing of the 1920s and 1930s set an example of modern efficiency that became widely accepted in the rush to expand housing for the middle class after World War II.[8] The ubiquitous open plan, often sold in the name of informality and efficiency, meant that postwar parents in new housing shared more space with their children.[9] Whereas nineteenth-century children were assigned nurseries in the attic, or large upstairs bedrooms, postwar kids took their place at the center of the dwelling, in family rooms, playrooms, and patios or terraces. L. Morgan Yost, a Chicago architect and an editor of the Homebuilders of America's *Small Homes Guide*, created several ideal dwellings that were configured specifically around the perceived needs of children. In a design published in 1944, Yost provided zones of active and quiet spaces, clustering the bedrooms together as a means of preserving peace, and placing the kitchen and "activity room" around an open "play court" with swings, a sandpit, and a playhouse (Figure 3.1). In Yost's scheme, the children's play spaces are ample, clearly defined, and contiguous to the kitchen. Moreover, in renaming rooms he erased the convention of separating by gender and age, so that all members of the family share together the "active" and "quiet" zones. Seizing on parents' worries and paraphrasing a widely held belief, Yost claimed that a rise in juvenile delinquency was directly tied to lack of an adequate home life. He cautioned, "Even your home, which you thought so well ordered, may not be giving the child that environment, opportunity and peace that is so necessary to growing children."[10]

Enhancing family togetherness with special spaces for play was the prominent theme in the discourse on family housing after the war. The Walker Art Center's 1947 Idea House II, created on a lot near the Minneapolis museum, was a completely furnished, inhabitable demonstration of the latest ideas in modern housing. As the second iteration of the Walker's original 1941 Idea House, Idea House II offered a clearly *postwar* vision of domesticity. Along with the split-level floor plan, large living room window, and sloping roof, one of the significant contrasts to the earlier Idea House was the addition of a children's playroom or study area near the compact bedrooms. Alexandra Griffith Winton has noted that the Walker projects were never intended as models but rather were designed as a three-dimensional demonstration of the latest ideas in the debates on housing.[11] To promote the project, the museum sought out local families to live

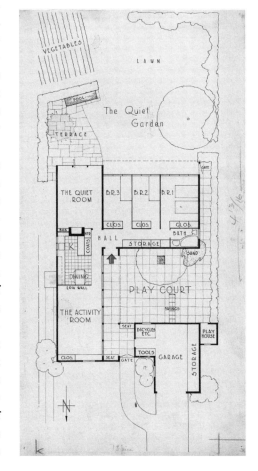

Figure 3.1. Lloyd Morgan Yost, *House Studies Published in Small Homes Guide: Homes for Our Children*, 1943–44. Ink and colored pencil on tracing paper and ink on drawing paper, 31.8 × 45.6 cm (38 × 20.4 inches). Gift of L. Morgan Yost, 1985.577b, The Art Institute of Chicago. Photography copyright The Art Institute of Chicago.

in the house for short periods of time. Idea House II gained national attention when *Life* magazine arranged for the Stensrud family of Minneapolis to spend a week in it and documented their experience in a series of comparisons with the family's own World War I–era stucco house. The parents admired the informality of the plan but disliked the modernist furnishings. The children, however, according to the magazine, thought the house was "swell." The playroom, which the Stensrud children did not have in their own house, was especially appealing, but *Life* emphasized that for the children "every room was a play room."[12] Giving children their own play space in the smaller middle-class dwelling was one of the key ideas that took hold in postwar housing, yet the central location of this area meant that postwar children—like Sally and the narrator in Dr. Seuss's *Cat in the Hat*—turned the entire house into a house for play.

Family housing was a consistent theme in popular family magazines such as *Ladies' Home Journal, American Home*, and *Parents' Magazine*. The *Parents' Magazine* "Expandable House" series, begun in 1945, offered plans for dwellings deemed ideal for a growing family. Like major merchant builders and other publications, *Parents'* developed a series of prototype dwellings that combined economical building with current ideas about family life. The magazine sponsored a survey polling architects, builders, contractors, and parents on trends in postwar housing. In addition to fewer basements, fewer architect-designed houses, and more one-story houses, respondents concurred that there would be fewer rooms in the postwar house and more dual-purpose rooms.[13]

A scheme similar to Idea House II was depicted in *Parents' Magazine*'s Expandable House number 9, designed by Marvin Fitch and published in 1949. Between the children's bedrooms and the kitchen and dining areas was the designated playroom, an open space that could be combined with, or separated from, the dining area with a folding wall (Figure 3.2). This arrangement, which allowed for small private bedrooms and a larger open playroom with supervision from the kitchen, became a familiar configuration in suburban postwar houses. Combining rooms was a key means of economizing on floor space. A "Build It Yourself" house by Edward Durrell Stone, one of a series of widely emulated small dwellings published in the *Ladies' Home Journal,* put the children's "playroom"—a corridor between the children's bedrooms and the kitchen—at the center of the house. Although it was defined as a playroom on the plan, only the presence of toys and children's furniture gave material evidence that the space was specifically intended for children's use (Plate 6).[14] This arrangement was practical,

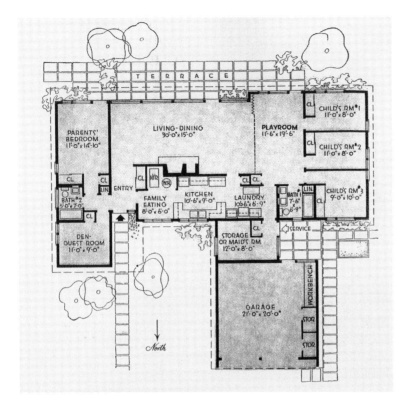

Figure 3.2. Marvin Fitch, Expandable House no. 9, *Parents' Magazine*, 1949.

but it also had therapeutic implications. In popular literature, the returning veteran could make up for time lost with his children by playing with them; thus, "every room in his house should be a place where the children are always welcome."[15]

Keeping an area adjacent to the kitchen for children shows the geography of gender at work in the postwar dwelling. In her 1946 book, *If You Want to Build a House*, published by the Museum of Modern Art, Elizabeth B. Mock noted, "Since small children need attention and the mother or maid will be spending a great part of her time in the kitchen, it seems reasonable to provide play space nearby."[16] The juxtaposition of a mother's, or maid's, work area and a children's play area was often couched in the promotional language of "flexibility." An Armstrong Linoleum advertisement from 1950 suggested transforming a dining area near the kitchen with a four-stage movable table that would descend flush into the floor to create a play-pen for baby, rise slightly to a kindergarten child's height for play, rise higher to become a kitchen table, or extend fully upward for evening entertaining (Figure 3.3).[17] It is unlikely that many middle-class families implemented

this complex scheme, but in a 1949 textbook on family housing, intended for high school and college home-economics courses, the authors suggested that families preferred having space for play near the kitchen.[18] In addition to addressing practicality, postwar theories of child development also informed the relationship between the kitchen and children's play. Annmarie Adams has argued that this arrangement in houses that the California builder Joseph Eichler erected was tied to the child-rearing theories of Dr. Benjamin Spock, who suggested that proximity between mother and child reinforced an "instinctual" means of learning and mothering.[19]

The well-informed postwar parent who consulted the popular parenting guides and magazines of the era encountered a consistent refrain that it was through play and exploration that children learned the social skills that would make them happy, well-adjusted adults. Arnold Gesell and Frances Ilg's *Infant and Child in the Culture of Today* (1943) emphasized the role of play, exploration, and parental guidance in developing children for a democratic society. Gesell and Ilg's concept of finding equilibrium between "self-activity" and society as the child developed was highly dependent on material goods, such as age-appropriate toys, playpens, and playrooms.[20] In Gesell and Ilg's theories, time alone with toys and other playthings was essential for developing autonomy. Furthermore, the mother had a prominent role in observing her child's development in the dispassionate and calm way of a well-trained researcher.[21] Before a young child could be left alone in his or her room, the playpen, a collapsible enclosure that could be moved around the house or placed in the backyard, offered a conveniently portable solution to the spatial problem of keeping young children contained and nearby. One designer even noted, "A play pen is really an almost essential part of a kitchen."[22] Yet beyond its utility for containment, the playpen was sold to parents as a means of encouraging physical and intellectual development. With its built-in turning beads and disks for a child to manipulate, the playpen offered an early opportunity to train the child. A 1949 article in *Baby Talk* magazine advised that the playpen should be "more than a parking lot—it must be a playground."[23]

Gesell and Ilg argued that respect for individuality was essential in cultivating democracy and predicted that postwar housing could affect both children and American society: "It is the intimate architecture of the home which ceaselessly impinges on the growing child. The postwar period is bound to bring about far-reaching alterations in domestic housing. There will be need of a new technology which will create more than shelter and physical comfort. It will plan for psychological and educational values, particularly in behalf of the infant and young child."[24] Thus, ideal planning for "psychological and educational values" enhanced both space for independence and proximity between mother and child in the family dwelling. In Spock's best-selling *Common Sense Book of Baby and Child Care* (first published in 1946), it was not only proximity to family members but also solitary entertainment akin to Gesell and Ilg's "self-activity" that stimulated learning and motor development.[25] The children's spaces in the postwar house that encouraged both proximity and independence were built around the belief that play had beneficial effects on physical, psychological, and cognitive development.

EXHIBITING PLAYROOMS

Creating children's play space in the postwar American house extended beyond using a portable playpen or carving out a corner of the kitchen. The specially designated playroom, outfitted with appropriately stimulating toys and furniture, was a recurring ideal in the housing and decoration schemes of middle-class magazines and especially in the architect-designed dwellings erected and furnished for public consumption. In Marcel Breuer's 1949 exhibition house (developed two years after the Walker's Idea House II) for MoMA in New York, built on a lot adjacent to the Museum Garden, the playroom was one of the house's most admired aspects. Conceived as a "moderately priced house . . . fitted to the requirements of a typical American family," Breuer's three-bedroom dwelling was an idealistic model of middle-class living furnished with examples of "good design," such as Charles and Ray Eames's plywood chairs, Eero Saarinen's fiberglass Womb Chair, and Breuer's own Isokon furniture. At the center of the Breuer house was the kitchen, which allowed for the surveillance of other areas, especially the children's playroom and adjoining bedroom. The playroom was an open area at the back of the house furnished with Creative Playthings' Hollow Block—maple plywood building forms—arranged as a desk and shelves, exemplifying the progressive belief that children should be allowed to create and modify their own spaces (Figure 3.4). David Snyder has suggested that the triumph of the playroom in the postwar suburban house reflected conventional gender roles and the new social value put on play and leisure.[26] Extending this idea, I would argue that the playroom—along with other spaces in the dwelling, such as the bedroom and the playhouse—reflected not only the belief in the beneficence of play but also confidence that a dedicated space might cultivate specific qualities.

In addition to the Hollow Block, the playthings in the Breuer house show that the fictional children of the House in the Museum Garden were expected to spend their playtime productively. All of the amusements in this model playroom, which Creative Playthings and New Design lent, reinforced the idea that children should have toys that could enhance and develop their creativity. The toys in this room included a child-sized loom, a carpentry set mounted on the wall, plain Skaneateles wooden trains, and a brightly colored Magnet Master set assembled on the playroom table. Like the playpen, with its built-in entertainment, the playroom's specially appointed furnishings implied that the children of Breuer's house were contained and under the watchful eye of Mother. Thus, the creative and autonomous inner life that the playroom presupposed was one that was carefully prescribed.

The House in the Museum Garden was widely publicized and received nearly one hundred thousand visitors in the six months that it was open. A questionnaire survey conducted at the time revealed that visitors' favorite rooms were the central kitchen and the children's playroom, each receiving an 84 percent approval. Of those polled, 76 percent showed interest in the furniture in the children's rooms.[27] Even Eleanor Roosevelt approved of the flexibility of the children's furniture: "I particularly like the children's playroom with nothing but those hollow blocks which could be made into furniture and still remain toys."[28]

Including a room for children's play remained an ideal even in more modest exhibition houses. In 1950, MoMA erected Gregory Ain's House in the Museum Garden, which was cosponsored with the mass-market publication *Women's Home Companion* to counter charges that Breuer's house was too expensive for most middle-class families. (The Ain House was designed to meet a $15,000 price range, whereas the Breuer house was estimated at

$27,000.) In Ain's design, the shared children's bedroom was adjacent to the playroom and separated with a movable partition (Figure 3.5). A more compact space than the lavish Breuer playroom, Ain's playroom nonetheless retained the modernist stamp of "good design" and reflected a similar faith in a child's individuality and creativity. Along with practical plywood paneling, lamps that could be pulled up and down on retractable cords, an Eames cabinet with open shelves, Creative Playthings' Hollow Block, and a wooden Skaneateles train set, the museum's education department provided children's drawings that were tacked on the wall.[29] Like the loom and tools in the Breuer house, the children's drawings in the Ain dwelling (developed in a MoMA art class) signified the creativity of the house's inhabitants.

The animating impulse of the playroom was giving children space to explore and develop a creative inner life. Although the child's capacity for imagination was theorized as innate, in postwar rhetoric this quality could also be fostered through consumption. Lisa Jacobson has discussed how the growth of playrooms was one response to the anticonsumerist debates of the interwar years. She has shown that educators and parents believed that wholesome educational occupations and amusements redirected the child from the position of a mere spectator—one of the fears that accompanied the rise of popular cinema—to that of an active creator of his or her own world.[30] Similar fears and hopes characterized the postwar television

Figure 3.5. Gregory Ain, Joseph Johnson, and Alfred Day, *Women's Home Companion* Exhibition House, Museum of Modern Art, New York, 1950. Photograph from Gregory Ain Collection, Architecture and Design Collection, University Art Museum, University of California at Santa Barbara.

era, but in regard to housing there were fewer anxieties around consumerism and even greater, more widespread, hopes for producing authentically creative children.

Consensus about children's "need" for play and playrooms also dovetailed with the booming toy industry's desire to sell more toys to parents. Between 1947 and 1951, Joseph Aronson, an architect and writer, was commissioned to design three playrooms for the American Toy Institute, a research wing of the Toy Manufacturers of the U.S.A. Aronson's first model playroom, which was on view in New York in June 1947, was billed as a "practical, low-cost play space" in which some one hundred toys could be sensibly stored (Figure 3.6). The room included built-in shelves, a climbing stair, a play table, a desk, and a pull-down cabinet for storing model train sets. Aronson's design, which was intended for parents to build at home, made the ordinary room into a multilevel indoor playground with places to hide, draw on walls, and hang up artwork. (The room was conceived as 12 feet by 18 feet, which was considered average.) A small door beneath

Figure 3.6. Joseph Aronson, "So You're Going to Build a Playroom!" American Toy Institute, New York, 1947. Photograph from Walker Art Center Archives, Minneapolis.

the desk provided what a *New York Times* reviewer called "an escape exit, a neat hideaway or a 'cave' vital to imaginative games."[31] By creating elevated spaces in the play area, Aronson attempted to give variation to the conventional playroom, both to encourage varied kinds of play activities and to create space for storing large objects.

The palette of the decor was also intended to stimulate a child's imagination. Instead of the pastels that adults often chose for juvenile spaces in the late 1940s, Aronson used vivid colors for yellow walls, a saturated blue ceiling, and speckled red linoleum floors, and he featured little ornament. He argued, "Whatever pattern a child sees every day he will tend to copy—to the detriment of his own creative development. If you must have some decorative design, let it be strictly abstract, or something the child has drawn himself."[32] Aronson's interest in designing a space suitable to current theories of child development reinforced the toy industry's ob-

So you're going to
Build a Playroom!

Here's how to make the most of your playroom space. A series of interesting and unusual plans designed by Joseph Aronson, distinguished American architect.

Featuring a Model Playroom on exhibit at the American Toy Institute, Research Division of the Toy Manufacturers of the U. S. A., 200 Fifth Ave., New York City

jective in making large numbers of toys seem desirable and easy to store. Aronson's later designs, in 1949 and 1951, were even more elaborate schemes that included a playhouse, a puppet theater, a revolving bookcase, a stage, and tree-house bunk beds. These exhibitions, all popular events that attracted thousands of visitors, were carefully designed to encourage parents to invest in their homes and their children. They portrayed an idealized vision of well-adjusted, self-sufficient, and creative children who lived in domestic harmony with their parents. At once reassuring and persuasive, the interiors on view encouraged parents to spend money on toys and playrooms not only to nurture their offspring but also to realize "creative living" for themselves.

Housing designed for middle-class tracts or developments also included unique provisions for children's play. Levittown houses were appealing to young families and sold as beneficial to children.[33] Compact and inexpensive, these dwellings were not spacious enough for separate playrooms, but they offered large expanses of common lawn area, and eventually many owners remodeled attics as children's spaces.[34] In builder houses that were slightly more upscale, however, playrooms were more common. Three-bedroom houses erected by Cecil E. Jennings after designs by Donald H. Honn, in Lubbock, Texas, divided the dwellings into separate areas for children and adults. The playroom, which was contiguous to the children's bedrooms and the kitchen, also had access to the rear yard, keeping dirt and noise far from the living room and parents' bedroom. *Parents' Magazine*'s annual builder's competition recognized both regional and national builder designs, highlighting houses, such as a Fox and Jacobs "Flair for Living" model in the Park Forest subdivision of Dallas, Texas, that included separate play spaces for children in their plans. (Fox and Jacobs's "Flair" houses were top-of-the-line models, costing about $29,420 for house and land in 1959.)

Robert Billsbrough Price's 1954 design for Tacoma Master Builders in Washington included special provisions for children's privacy and play.[35] In Price's scheme, which was furnished for the annual Tacoma Home Show, bright folding doors separated two small bedrooms that could be combined to create one large play space (Plate 7). The bedrooms were appointed with built-in dressers, closets, desks, and shelves, thus maximizing the usable floor area when the separating curtains were retracted. The amount of private space was minimal, but the symmetrical arrangement of beds, built-ins, and patterned curtains on the upper third of the bedroom walls enhanced the illusion of spaciousness in the combined area. Furthermore, the larger play area expanded play opportunities with chalkboards and additional furniture. Price's aim in predetermining so much of the children's space was both to contain the activities of young children and to anticipate their need for privacy as they grew up.

The playroom was a luxury of a solidly middle-class childhood, but creating space for play was widely advocated for all children. In this discourse, a properly designed play space not only promoted a child's intellectual, physical, and social development but also held implications for the future health of the country. The widespread Cold War belief that an American education would not prepare school-age children for future demands led to a broadly voiced call for stimulating an interest in science in young children.[36] After the Soviet Union launched the Sputnik space satellites, in 1957, the federal government stepped up science education in public schools, but some advocates argued that scientific curiosity should also be nourished at home. Marianne Besser, who examined the bedrooms of the teenage national precollegiate Science Talent Search winners in the late 1950s, posed the issue in stark terms: "How many children lose interest in science or in other creative fields because of overly tidy mothers or noise hating fathers? We will never know, but we do know that when curiosity and enthusiasm are hampered by an unfriendly environment, inspiration withers."[37] At stake was not only personal fulfillment and intellectual development but also a larger preoccupation with both the image of America and democracy. By providing a bedroom or play area in which to experiment, parents seemed to invest in the future of both their growing children and their country.

THE BEDROOM-PLAYROOM

The expansion of suburban housing gave many middle-class children their own room away from adults, even if they shared it with a brother or sister.[38] Margaret Mead suggested that children needed space to make things, yet she also believed that "children need . . . privacy even when they are not doing anything that seems a bit creative—when they are growing or just wondering about what they have learned. Children need a place to be alone in."[39] Because it often had to fulfill requirements for play, experimentation, and reflection over a period of changing needs, the child's bedroom was one of the most self-consciously decorated rooms of the middle-class house.[40] This "private" space was expected to serve many functions.

For younger children, solitary, imaginative play was the aim of the playroom-bedroom. A 1957 handbook of children's play, written by child-development experts Ruth Hartley and Robert Goldenson, urged parents to set aside half or three-quarters of a child's bedroom for play. Building bunk beds or using space dividers to separate sleeping areas, they argued, could maximize play space.[41] Throughout the postwar period, *Parents' Magazine* regularly featured a "Rooms to Grow In" section, recommending that children would feel a greater sense of emotional security and aesthetic appreciation in spaces devised with their interests and personalities in mind.[42] In its checklist of "every child's needs," *Parents'* listed "space for free play," as well as "a wall to mark and pin," "creative play equipment to stimulate his physical and mental growth," and "colorful surroundings that suit his temperament."[43] The magazine showed how, in addition to space for toys, guest beds, and built-in furniture, decoration might enhance a child's room and sense of self. Whereas railroad and nautical themes were intended for boys, a dressing table was used in a girl's room as a "psychological antidote for pronounced symptoms of tomboyism."[44] Other, less gendered themes, such as a circus motif or tree house, were recommended for both boys and girls, especially those who shared a room. Like the playroom, the child's bedroom was given new attention for its spatial and psychological potential as an incubator of the child's fragile ego and gender identity, and a place where creative energy might originate.

Maurice Sendak's *Where the Wild Things Are* (1963) vividly depicted the creative possibilities of being alone in one's room. Max builds a tentlike playhouse with books, sheets, and a length of rope nailed to the wall of the living room. When he threatens the dog and speaks sharply to his mother, he is sent to bed without his supper. Once alone, his vivid imagination transforms his bedroom into a land of vast oceans and jungles that exotic beasts inhabit. The practical bed and table disappear as Max's fantasy redefines the contours of his room. In this cycle of defiance, escape, and reassurance—he returns from where the wild things are to find his supper "still hot"—Max's imaginative journey takes place entirely at home. His solitary creative acts of constructing his own play space and the parallel transformation of his bedroom draw attention to the potential of childhood imagination in this best-selling Newbery Award book. Although Max manipulates his own ordinary bed and table, postwar parents faced new choices in decorating their children's bedrooms.

FURNISHING CHILDREN'S SPACES

To serve as a reassuring and stimulating environment, children's spaces required careful thought and planning. In his book of children's furniture and toy designs, Cherner advised, "If Peter's room is unorganized and drab, it can hardly invite use—or cultivate a respect for its furnishings. However, if it is properly planned, it can encourage a sense of order, self-discipline, and creative growth."[45] Aside from its organization, the decoration of the child's room was central to his or her aesthetic formation: "Color, line, and pattern are important factors in giving Peter's room a crisp, airy appearance. The decorative treatment should give support to his creative development."[46] The choice of furniture, pictures, rugs, and wallpaper in the child's room was therefore laden with the larger social responsibilities of cultivating imagination and individuality.

Unlike the sparsely furnished urban nursery of the nineteenth century, later nurseries were increasingly elaborate. Karin Calvert has shown how nurseries and special furniture, especially the crib, gained popularity through the nineteenth century as a means of containing and protecting the innocent baby.[47] The changing importance of sleep may also have encouraged the growth of nurseries.[48] By the end of the nineteenth century, British and European schemes set the ideological and artistic tone for nursery design.[49] Rooms with matching furniture, illustrative friezes, and embroidered curtains were shown in major exhibitions, drawing attention to the importance of children's rooms for consumers of means.[50] The emphasis on providing "correct" decoration for children's developing tastes was tied to a discourse of innocence and a strong belief in the educational potential of the child's first surroundings. Thus, providing children with "appropriate" decoration in order to train their tastes and behavior was a long-standing concern for upper-middle-class and elite households. If the nursery, which separated children from their parents but not from governesses or nurses, had elite associations, then the bedroom-playroom embodied the child-centered culture of middle-class postwar America. "Nursery" was still a designation that lingered in descriptions of babies' and pre-school-aged children's spaces, and these spaces were still designed to cocoon the innocent, but beyond safety and hygiene, they were also created to amuse and stimulate.

In 1949, the artist and designer György Kepes and his wife, Juliet, a designer and illustrator, developed a space for their five-year-old daughter, Julie, at their house in Cambridge, Massachusetts. Designed to provoke their daughter's imagination and to develop both her muscles and her senses, the Kepes room included a bed with a large piece of driftwood and plywood cutouts for climbing, a table that could be raised, a wire mobile, a large clock of cork balls, a Peg-Board wall on which to create compositions, and a ceiling mapped with glowing moons and stars (Figure 3.7). In addition, Juliet Kepes painted a mural of animals, silk-screened curtains with

Figure 3.7. Julie Kepes climbs the Nursery Tree, 1949. Photograph by Ralph Morse, *Life*, August 22, 1949. Time & Life Pictures/Getty Images.

playful monkeys, and made a shaggy rug featuring the body of a lion.[51]

György Kepes, a Hungarian émigré associated with both the European and American avant-garde, became a professor at MIT in 1946 after working with László Moholy-Nagy in London and at the New Bauhaus, in Chicago. Juliet Kepes designed wallpapers and fabrics and illustrated children's books. Reflecting both modernist interests in childhood and psychological research on early visual and intellectual stimulation in developing and enhancing creativity, the Kepeses claimed, "The first years are a time of concentrated learning and development. They should also be a time of wonder and delight. They should be spent in a room that has a variety of cheerful colors, beautiful lines and shapes; the room should contain materials with which to color, mold, and make things; larger playthings to carry and structures to climb; space to run, jump, skip, and dance; child-proof and child-sized furniture and finishes; light, air, warmth, and quiet."[52]

The Kepes nursery was featured in popular publications and design periodicals. Photographs taken for *Life* magazine show Julie Kepes exploring her space, jumping from her headboard onto her bed, painting, arranging forms on her Peg-Board wall, and playing with other children.[53] Her movements suggest not only that she was curious about her room, which was still new at the time the images were taken, but also that her enjoyment and occupation of the space was active.

Around the same time, György and Juliet Kepes produced a line of wallpaper and fabrics for Laverne Originals, the New York firm known for employing painters and other artists to create wallpaper and textiles (Figure 3.8).[54] The pattern of smiling lion faces derived from a print Kepes created specifically for children, which was also exhibited in the Ain house playroom at MoMA in 1950.[55]

The Kepeses' designs made the child's bedroom into a space of personal amusement and sensory exploration. At once avant-garde and beholden to a tradition of social training, the space reflected the sincere admiration for childhood creativity that European modernist artists and designers professed. Jonathan Fineberg's research has shown how modernist painters venerated the child as an innocent "primitive" with a unique and abstract vision.[56] In addition to collecting children's drawings, many artists and designers were preoccupied with creating material goods for children's spaces.[57] Kepes, a student of Bauhaus master Moholy-Nagy, who favored the technological expressions of photography and film, was also well acquainted with Walter Gropius and Marcel Breuer, who were both teaching at Harvard in the mid-1940s. Breuer, first as a student and later as a master, constructed children's furniture in the Weimar and Dessau workshops. Breuer's first cubic children's chairs were on display at the Haus am Horn, a full-scale dwelling fitted out with the school's products for textiles, ceramics, metalwork, and furniture created for the 1923 Weimar Bauhaus exhibition. For the Haus am Horn, Alma Siedhoff-Buscher, another Bauhaus student from the woodworking workshop, designed a large room spacious enough for two beds and a play area. In addition to a changing table and a blackboard close to the floor, the children's room had a

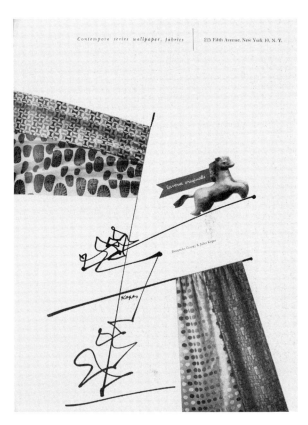

Figure 3.8. Advertisement for György and Juliet Kepes, Contempora Series, Laverne Originals, 1950. From *Interiors* (April 1950): 21.

large, colorful wooden cabinet, which dominated one corner. With shelves and knobs that a child could reach, the cabinet provided practical storage of clothes and toys that implied a built-in program of good behavior. But the wardrobe was also designed to encourage imagination. The brightly colored nesting boxes were as much for play as for storage, and a cutout window in the door doubled as a puppet theater (Figure 3.9).[58] The toylike quality of Siedhoff-Buscher's furniture was deliberate. She argued, "Whenever possible, children should have a room of their own where they can be whatever they wish to be, in which they rule. Every object in it should belong to them and their fantasy will give it shape."[59] Play embodied the Bauhaus's attitude toward art making, and toys were a commercially successful aspect of prewar Bauhaus production.[60] Siedhoff-Buscher deliberately rejected the imagery of conventional fairy tales in favor of abstract forms and strong colors.[61] This emphasis on play and experimentation as a means of discovery was fundamental to the Bauhaus curriculum. The *Vorkurs* (or Preliminary Course) embraced the childlike activities of playing with materials and self-

Figure 3.9. Alma Siedhoff-Buscher, children's room, Bauhaus Haus am Horn, Weimar, Germany, 1923. Photograph from Bauhaus-Archiv Berlin. Copyright 2012 Artists Rights Society (ARS), New York/VG Bild-Kunst, Bonn.

discovery. In 1924, after he had begun teaching the *Vorkurs*, Moholy-Nagy noted of Siedhoff-Buscher's designs, "[Her] toys and toy cabinet clearly exemplify the pedagogical principles of the Bauhaus: self-affirming creativity as a basis for primary forms of personal expression."[62]

Children's furniture, sold with new psychological theories about child development, was also an expanding area for commercial manufacturers in the United States during the Great Depression.[63] In the 1930s, the American designers Russel Wright and Gilbert Rhode produced lines of nursery furniture intended for middle-class families. Rhode's suite, initially developed for his own children following the ideas of the Child Study Association, brought modernist forms into the American child's room.[64] Like Siedhoff-Buscher, Rhode emphasized durable, easy-to-clean surfaces and playful shapes, including colorful, open blocklike boxes, which could be adjusted and rearranged as the child grew. Kristina Wilson has argued that modernist designers working for mass manufacturers, such as Ilonka Karasz (who created children's furniture for Donald Deskey's Amodec series), adhered to both contemporary and established notions of moral and aesthetic hygiene, and believed the simplicity of their designs could enhance a child's imagination.[65] At the 1940 extension of the New York World's Fair, a model playroom by Theodor Carl Muller, part of the America at Home exhibits, was praised for its blackboard and color scheme but criticized for not leaving more of the decoration "to the whim of the youthful tenant."[66] The growing belief in a child's uniqueness and the importance of personal expression encouraged parents and designers, even during the Depression, to provide both space and special furniture that the child could transform at will.

The Kepeses' 1949 designs for Laverne Originals were part of the growth in products intended for the baby boom bedroom-playroom. Child-sized dressers, wardrobes, and other furniture, such as small chairs and tables, proliferated as parents turned their postwar incomes toward their children's spaces. A postwar child's room retained the crib or bed and dresser of earlier periods, but added newer items, such as the bathinette, a folding, rubber-coated canvas hammock that could be filled for bathing or drained with a tube and used for changing. Mass-produced playpens, feeding chairs, rockers, and rocking chairs were sold to parents to keep children occupied at home. A small rocking chair with a decal of the freckled face of Howdy Doody on the back splat shows how furniture makers adapted their products to the television era and to ideals of self-entertainment (Figure 3.10). The child's rocker, a longtime staple of juvenile furniture, was updated with the

Figure 3.10. Howdy Doody rocking chair, circa 1950s. Photograph courtesy of the Strong Museum, Rochester, New York.

imagery of the show's star and a movement-activated music box that played the show's theme song. No longer just a means of displaying the child in the nineteenth-century family parlor, the child's rocker had become a toy.[67]

Along with the rapid growth of media-related domestic consumables in the postwar era, there was a counterresponse. For parents skeptical of popular imagery, juvenile furniture that played up values of "good design," which gained admiration among the cosmopolitan upper middle class in postwar America, also expanded. The "good design" programs that MoMA and other institutions developed in the late 1940s and 1950s raised the profile of everyday goods, including things created for children. These items were often more expensive and were sometimes available only through the design trades, but they promised both aesthetic sophistication and educational play value. An article in the *New Yorker*, for example, praised the abstract and practical qualities of Creative Playthings' Hollow Block on view at the MoMA House in the Museum Garden as a refreshing change from mass-market design. The writer even jestingly linked the aesthetics of children's furniture to broader social effects: "If the present kindergarten generation develops, when it has grown up, some rather horrid mass psychosis, I shall certainly be the first to blame it on the general insipidity, if not downright vulgarity, of the nursery decoration that our young are exposed to. Parents who share my mistrust of cloying pink or blue color schemes, of the ubiquitous Donald Duck motif, and of the sort of furniture that looks like stunted examples of humdrum pieces should by all means investigate the nursery paraphernalia to be found at Creative Playthings."[68] The educated *New Yorker* reader was the ideal consumer of a new spate of stylish toylike furniture for the playroom or bedroom.

One of Charles and Ray Eames's earliest designs in molded plywood was their 1945 children's furniture, which Evans Plywood produced and distributed. The Eameses' chair, stool, and table were diminutive in scale and dyed in saturated hues of red, blue, yellow, black, and magenta (Figure 3.11). Unlike their designs for the family living or dining room, the Eameses' children's chairs were created out of two pieces of molded plywood.[69] Like other modernist bentwood designs, the children's furniture exemplified efficient modern technology and rational production. Pat Kirkham has also suggested that the cutout heart on the small child's chair, a vernacular motif revived around the turn of the twentieth century, "humanizes" the design and reveals the vital importance of love for the Eameses.[70] I would argue that the heart shape signifies not only these personal sentiments but also the toylike quality of the chair's design, which (like Hollow Block) is light enough for a child to move. Indeed, one of the Stensrud children staying at the Walker Art Center's Idea House II in 1948 was photographed having turned the Eameses' chairs and stools into "a train I can sleep on" (Figure 3.12).

Henry P. Glass's 1952 Swingline series of children's furniture, produced by the Fleetwood Furniture Company of

Figure 3.11. Charles and Ray Eames, plywood chairs, Evans Plywood, 1945. Photograph copyright Eames Office, LLC (www.eamesoffice.com).

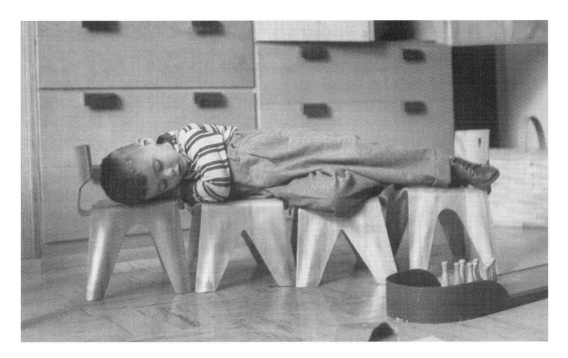

Figure 3.12. Rocky Stensrud Jr. uses children's chairs in a modern home to make a train on which he can sleep. Idea House II, *Life*, October 18, 1948. Photograph by Joseph Scherschel, Time & Life Pictures/Getty Images.

Grand Haven, Michigan, were similarly toylike. Glass's Swingline designs for a child's wardrobe, table, toy chest, easel, bookcase, and other pieces were lightweight, durable, and intensely colorful (Figure 3.13). Glass, who emigrated to the United States from Vienna in 1939, worked in Gilbert Rhode's office before establishing his own industrial design firm in 1945.[71] Like Rhode's prewar children's furniture, Glass's designs were modular and used inexpensive but durable materials. Yet, unlike other juvenile furniture of the period, Glass's Swingline designs relied on a pivoting action that children could easily manipulate and use without the help of adults. Instead of cumbersome chairs, a circular table had four circular stools that pivoted out from each leg. The Swingline toy chest swung open to enable easy access rather than using heavy sliding drawers or deep spaces (Plate 8). As a means of encouraging exploration, the Swingline designs featured individual compartments in different colors. Instead of conventional doors, the Swingline wardrobe had two long cavities that swung open to reveal a three-part space with a bar for hanging clothes. A similar notion of playfulness animated Richard Neagle's Bamboozler (1953), a child's clothes tree, which was manufactured for the Gimbels department store.[72] Like Siedhoff-Buscher's and Rhode's designs, Glass's ideals of self-sufficiency, practical storage, and playful discovery gave his furniture a strongly toylike character that beckoned play.

Figure 3.13. Henry P. Glass (American, born Austria, 1911–2003), Child's Wardrobe, 1952. Painted Masonite and wood, 107.6 × 80.7 × 44.5 cm (42 ⅜ × 31 × 17 ½ inches). Gift of Henry P. Glass, 2000.133, The Art Institute of Chicago. Photography copyright The Art Institute of Chicago.

Despite receiving critical praise for their designs, neither the Eameses' children's furniture nor Glass's Swingline designs reached a mass audience.[73] Yet the limited success of these designs in the early postwar years did not deter major manufacturers from adding children's furniture to their lines. In the mid-1950s, Knoll Associates introduced several designs for children's use. Smaller-sized editions of adult-sized furniture included Isamu Noguchi's cyclone table and Harry Bertoia's wire side-chair design, available in eleven- and fourteen-inch models and intended for use at home, in schools, and in other spaces such as libraries and lunchrooms. Knoll underscored the sturdiness of the enameled wire chairs on black runners, but also their playful qualities. In an advertisement by Herbert Matter, the Bertoia children's chairs were paired with toys (Figure 3.14).[74] On a blank white field, a Bertoia chair is suspended from two of the Danish designer Kay Bojesen's clasping wooden monkeys, and a plush Jocko monkey is posed as if examining a different, stationary chair. Using toy monkeys as stand-ins for exuberant children (who were included in other ads), Matter depicted these Knoll products as both solid furniture and sound playthings.[75]

Figure 3.14. Herbert Matter, poster for Knoll Associates furniture. From *Architectural Forum* 102 (February 1955): 227.

Self-consciously "designed" children's furniture gained new attention among upper-middle-class parents in the 1960s and 1970s. While American designers created novel products for children's spaces, European, especially Nordic, designers—whose products were imported into the United States in large quantities—gained equal visibility on the American market. The Bojesen wooden monkeys, ride-on toys, and other designs were especially popular.[76] Another Dane, Kristian Vedel, devised a thin plywood chair (1956), which could be transformed into a table, tunnel, or cradle.[77] Like the bentwood birch furniture by Finnish designer Alvar Aalto for Artek, which was continually produced in adult- and child-sized versions from the mid-1930s, other Scandinavian designs, such as Nanna and Jørgen Ditzel's baby chair (1955) and Nanna Ditzel's series of graduated wooden spool-like Trisserne (1962), offered solid construction, sophisticated design, and playful qualities. The plastic and fiberglass designs that Walter Papst designed for the German company Wilkhahn, and Marco Zanuso and Richard Sapper's K1340 Bambini chair (1963) for the Italian furniture firm Kartell, were even more toylike.[78] Papst's Kinderschale (1955), a polypropylene shell, fit into a rocking base or could be used and stacked separately. A similar shell form could be suspended on cords, and was also part of the brightly colored sculptural forms that Wilkhahn produced. The fine line between furniture and toys was further blurred as both toys and furniture became increasingly abstract in the 1960s. Even the cardboard box, an old favorite of children's play, reentered the child's room. British designer Peter Murdoch's Spotty children's chair (1963) was a hollow seat with a low back, created from one sheet of plastic-coated fiberboard for International Paper.

The diversity of the designs on the market, however, had not changed the central impetus of providing places to sleep and sit. Rather, wholesome decoration and sturdy play value had gained even more importance. In 1963, *Design Quarterly* (a publication of the Walker Art Center) published a special issue on children's furniture. Incorporating both a comparison with historical examples of high chairs, sleeping furniture, and a promotion of "good design" for children from European and American firms, the issue suggested continuity with the past while simultaneously demanding greater abstraction in juvenile furniture. In her introduction, Anna Campbell Bliss argued, "Furniture can also be elements for creative play, offering a greater challenge for the imagination than the too specific toy that is soon discarded."[79]

The decoration of children's spaces encompassed more than choosing furniture and wallpaper. In the 1950s, architects and designers of children's rooms recommended plywood walls, cork or linoleum flooring, and corduroy upholstery to meet needs of durability. Built-in furniture, especially closets and bookshelves, some argued, were needs that would not be outgrown, and built-ins could keep a small room tidy and cohesive.[80] By the late 1970s, children's playrooms and bedrooms were often combined and designed in new and inventive ways. The toylike furniture of the 1950s and 1960s gave way to systems for entertainment. Like Max's environment in *Where the Wild Things Are*, conventional "furniture"—even measured against the playful forms of the early 1950s and elegant abstract designs of the 1960s—was transformed into unique habitats in the 1970s. Often referred to as "environments," the hideouts, jungles, and capsules of the era combined the bedroom and playroom with the backyard.[81] Norman and Molly McGrath's book *Children's Spaces* (1978) documented the increasingly elaborate areas designed not only for sleep and play but also for exploration. The McGraths' project rephrased in sumptuous photographs and short texts much of the earlier popular advice. In his foreword, designer Ivan Chermayeff proposed:

> **There must be places for heroes and heroines.**
> **Space to foul; room to move; soft corners to fall asleep in.**
> **Storage, lots of it, for incredible accumulations.**
> **Color and light.**
> **Not a classroom.**
> **No images that won't erase.**
> **No one wants to live in somebody else's personal expression.**
> **No invasions of privacy.**
> **A *tabula rasa*, because children don't have to be reinvented.**[82]

Given that Norman McGrath was an architectural photographer and Molly McGrath was a writer, they collaborated to describe projects of professional architects and interior designers, which offered a variety of possibilities, from adding a new room to remodeling part of an old one, "to find new ways to bring fantasy and fun as well as practical solutions to everyday problems into the spaces where children live."[83] In these projects, many of which were fairly inexpensive to build, beds could become forts, puppet theaters, platforms, cars, or giant sneakers. Storage for collections was integrated unobtrusively into the ensembles, and supergraphics (the use of huge painted motifs on walls and ceilings) made an ordinary room into a page from a picture book.[84] Many of the spaces were architects' designs for their own children's rooms. Hugh Hardy, Malcolm Holzman, Charles Gwathmey, Myron Goldfinger, and Robert A. M. Stern all discussed the rooms they had designed for their children. Hardy observed that children's imaginations, using bunk beds and other level changes, could transform their own spaces: "Upper levels can become fortresses and ships; low levels become tunnels, houses, and secret hiding places. But there is no need to be specific about this. Children have such a visual imagination of their own that the efforts of adults to give rooms a 'ship motif' or a 'garden atmosphere' probably go by unnoticed. These are the artifices of the literal-minded 'decorator,' not the child."[85] Just as Frank Caplan insisted that children's imaginations could provide the details and color of his deliberately abstract Creative Playthings, Hardy expressed a similar faith in a child's inner ability to animate the spaces of his or her own room.

Projects by Owen Beenhouwer and Henry Smith-Miller were unusual alternatives to mass-manufactured furniture, making it difficult to distinguish between furniture and toys or even furniture and architecture. Beenhouwer's ensembles of plywood or laminates seemed to emulate the spare geometry of the homemade fort. Smith-Miller's elaborate, self-contained construction, which he called the Box, also implied a link with cardboard constructions of castles and lookouts.[86] Smith-Miller's cubelike "room within a playroom" provided three beds on multiple levels, storage, and a fold-down table to meet the needs of a child for ten years (Plate 9). A giant circular window pierced the plywood walls, letting light into the private sleeping spaces. Designed for an urban child's room, the compact intersecting structure, Smith-Miller explained, "is essentially a giant toy to be lived in and on, and played with."[87] Instead of mimicking toylike qualities on the smaller scale of individual chairs or tables, the 1970s environments made a child's entire room toylike.

CREATIVE LIVING

If enhancing creativity or building imagination was seemingly the prized outcome of children's rooms, it also promised parents an additional sense of personal fulfillment. The postwar notion of "creative living" was expansive. In 1955, the influential Unitarian minister Preston Bradley argued that "creative living" was a "practical system of living that enables people to meet the complexities of life—and not only to survive these complexities, but to survive them as stronger, more potent personalities."[88] Bradley's notion encompassed coping with life and devising enterprising solutions to everyday problems, with optimism and faith as chief attributes. Given that themes of improvisation and ingenuity were embedded in the concept of creative living, making things for the family or household was one of the most tangible and material ways to realize the ideal. Alex F. Osborn, who wrote several popular books on creativity, advocated manual hobbies as a means of stimulating creativity. In his view, "handicrafts do more for us creatively if and when we think up the designs as well as carry them out."[89] Those who did not have a budget for Knoll furniture or lavish, architect-designed bedrooms but who believed that their children would benefit from specially designed play objects could make their own furniture, toys, dollhouses, playrooms, and playhouses. If they could not "think up the designs" themselves, then the ubiquitous plans, books, and guides were a ready and inexpensive means of carrying them out.

The do-it-yourself movement flourished in postwar middle-class America.[90] As weekend hobbies proliferated with the desire for productive leisure, the dwelling became a focus for creative energy.[91] The guides and kits that flooded onto the market implied that modeling creative activity was also a parent's responsibility. In Levittown and other postwar suburban developments around the country, the "easy creativity" of paint sets and needlework fulfilled this expectation.[92] Popular magazines regularly issued designs for bedspreads, curtains, and matching pillow shams, as well as playhouses and toys that could be sewn or built at home. Plans for building Aronson's model playrooms were included in a free pamphlet available by mail from the Toy Institute of America.[93] By the mid-1970s, handbooks and guides offered endless ideas for making playthings and other entertaining domestic projects.[94] The encyclopedic *Family Creative Workshop* series, a twenty-three-volume set that proposed a range of craft projects and experiments, was envisioned "as a school-in-the-home, teaching useful and rewarding skills that people would take pride in, giving them the means of expressing their own creative imaginations."[95] Observing household economy and enhancing play were therefore bound together with personal satisfaction in making things for children's amusement. As parents invested in the family, the dwelling, and their children, they embraced the ideal of "creative living."

Furniture and toys that enabled play and exploration and that could be made inexpensively at home were the objective of Norman Cherner's 1954 book, *How to Build Children's Furniture and Toys*. Cherner, who taught industrial arts at Teachers College and later became a well-known designer, argued that in addition to a well-designed home, sturdy, useful furniture and toys could enhance a child's development: "Good play calls into action Peter's full power of concentration and creative energy. It should be directed toward developing his sense of independence, imagination, and taste."[96] Although Cherner maintained separate sections for toys and furniture, his designs overlapped significantly. He included drawings for small and large toys, playhouses, oversize building blocks, and puzzles, as well as desks, chairs, storage cabinets, and play equipment. He emphasized that a child's own desires and developmental age should be taken into account, but he stressed that "the most important toys for Peter are those with which he can create and explore—toys which are generously scaled and which can be regrouped, assembled, disassembled, added to, which can hold things, can be moved, and have multiple application."[97] The same principle of flexible interlocking parts was evident in his slatted building forms and in his designs for plywood chairs with flat, boomerang-shaped legs (Figure 3.15). Many of Cherner's designs had a discernibly modernist sensibility. In addition to a pitched-roof single-family dollhouse design, he also created a modular flat-roofed dwelling that could be made into apartment towers.

Figure 3.15. Norman Cherner, *How to Build Children's Furniture and Toys* (1954), 90. Photograph by Thomas Yee.

Cherner's line drawings of children's rooms implied that a parent's industriousness could directly affect a child's play. One room, presumably for younger children, included a climbing structure and slide, a mobile, a wall for tacking up drawings, and a long surface for the creation of artwork, on which also lay a small toy saw (Figure 3.16). In another picture, of a space intended for two older children, a kite took the place of the mobile, and a train set occupied the center of the room, along with a free-standing easel (Figure 3.17). In the foreground, however, was space for drawing, a T square, and the same small saw, along with a mallet and a vise. In these images, Cherner took pains to depict his furniture designs in the child's room. But the presence of the child's drawings, paintings, and tools also implied that a room a parent had properly designed for play would, in turn, stimulate its young occupants to become creative on their own. In other words, a parent's industriousness would encourage similar values in his or her children.

Cherner's book provided advice and designs for a variety of toys and furniture that "any parent should be able to build." Although he suggested that the designs were simple, he included a section on basic woodworking techniques. Thus, if one was not already a skilled home carpenter, being a parent meant becoming one. Hobbies became an "expected leisure" for both

Figure 3.16. Norman Cherner, *How to Build Children's Furniture and Toys*, 126. Produced with permission of The McGraw-Hill Companies.

Figure 3.17. Norman Cherner, *How to Build Children's Furniture and Toys*, 74. Produced with permission of The McGraw-Hill Companies.

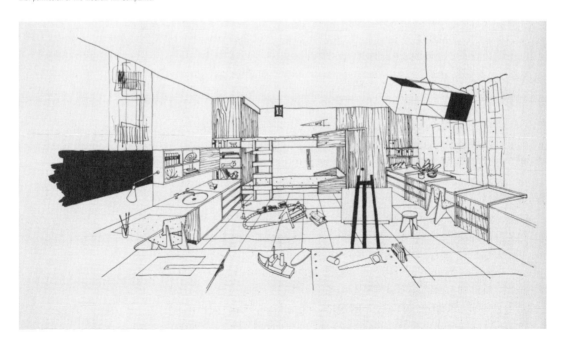

men and women after World War II. Provisional home workshops, created in other areas of the small suburban dwelling, made do-it-yourself home repair, construction of furniture, and creating children's amusements the expectation of middle-class homeowners. Seeking fulfillment in handiwork, middle-class men and women embraced the ethos of personal satisfaction in creative activities.[98]

Mass-circulation magazines reinforced the appeal of do-it-yourself projects, giving tips on planning, building, and providing numerous images of happy children enjoying their new play spaces. *Sunset: The Magazine of Western Living*, a home-decoration publication targeted at middle-class homeowners with modernist sensibilities in the West, published home-improvement guides with projects culled from the magazine's pages. *Children's Rooms and Play Yards* (1960), fully revised in 1970, depicted numerous projects for children's indoor and outdoor amusement. In addition to photographs and plans for children's play and sleeping areas, the *Sunset* guides included designs for building shelves, toy storage, bulletin boards, dollhouses, train tables, modular boxes similar to Hollow Block, and detailed instructions for creating outdoor playhouses, which remained a consistent theme in the California magazine from the 1950s through the 1970s.

At the same time that middle-class children gained space in the general living areas of the family house and their bedrooms were decorated to enhance self-esteem and creativity, they also acquired their own miniature dwellings. The profusion of designs for indoor and backyard playhouses transformed a formerly elite amusement into a middle-class toy that parents could assemble or make themselves, reinforcing the image of the dwelling and its attendant ideal of "creative living" as an emblem of postwar family life. Although children have probably always sought out spaces removed from adults, the wherewithal to present them with their own separate houses for play was once the exclusive pleasure of the rich.[99] In the nineteenth century, diminutive playhouses erected for children, such as Queen Victoria's 1854 Swiss Cottage, built for her children at Osborne House, and the Peabody and Stearns structure that Cornelius Vanderbilt II commissioned for his children, especially his daughters Gertrude and Gladys, in Newport, Rhode Island, were princely additions to large estates.[100] These examples, which had working kitchens, their own china and glassware, and seating for guests, taught practical skills—which these children would probably never need to use—as a form of play. Emulating the practices of the aristocracy, wealthy British children also enjoyed their own private domestic spaces, especially in the garden. The Arts and Crafts garden designer Gertrude Jekyll recommended a separate, two-room playhouse with a working stove and surrounding gardens, claiming children would "look back on its lessons of play-work with thankfulness, both for joyful memories and for the abiding usefulness of all that it had taught them."[101] In Jekyll's descriptions, the child's house and garden were physically removed from the adult sphere, but their practical lessons in the arts of domesticity were training for adulthood.

Just before and after World War I, wealthy Americans began building or buying playhouses for their children, but, unlike those with working appliances, these dwellings were uniquely for pretend. Under the banner heading "To Develop Creativeness," playhouses and educational toys were recommended to readers of *Vogue* magazine in 1915, and a prefabricated playhouse was available through *House and Garden* the following year.[102] By the late 1930s, playhouses for middle-class children were described as educational amusements, especially for summer months.[103] It was after World War II, however, that the playhouse became thoroughly middle-class, and its construction or assembly a family hobby. In addition to *Sunset*, magazines such as *American Home, Women's Home Companion, Ladies' Home Journal, Popular Science,* and *Parents' Magazine* published plans and hints for do-it-yourself playhouses and championed the playhouse's potential for stimulating imagination. Whereas the playhouse was compared in 1950 to "magic carpets on which children are transplanted to the land of make-believe," *Parents'* described the playhouse in 1962 as "a house full of play, a room full of imagination for any child."[104] The playhouse offered the same attractions that the playpen, playroom, and bedroom play space did: keeping children occupied with minimal supervision, and space to develop autonomy and encourage creativity. The expectation of creative behavior therefore governed the postwar child's playhouse.

Parents assumed children would create their own world in the playhouse, but because they chose or erected the playhouse, its architectural cues often reflected the tastes of adults. One of the most common and inexpensive playhouse designs was a draped card table that was easy to set up inside or out.[105] A plastic structure by Doughboy Industries came in the form of large and small "ranch" houses, allowing the child to inhabit his or her own suburban dream (Figure 3.18). Another model, a simple cotton cover produced by Bemis Brothers, a maker of grain sacks, and sold through FAO Schwarz and other shops, gave girls a chance to live in a colonial while boys played in a firehouse. A similar pattern available from *Ladies' Home Journal* transformed a card table into a sew-it-yourself circus tent (Plate 10). Larger free-standing structures also mimicked the architecture of the past. A complex gingerbread house portrayed in *Parents' Magazine* required "above average craftsmanship," custom-cut pine siding, and leaded windows. FAO Schwarz sold a deluxe Log Cabin, which it promised was "without an equal for active, creative and social play."[106] Combining climbing equipment with space for domestic play, a model published by the *Ladies' Home Journal* in 1964 made reference to *Alice in Wonderland*, with oversized keyholes and giant cards. *Sunset* showed parents how to build structures with shingled roofs and Dutch doors, as well as designs with sloping corrugated roofs and redwood siding. With input from nursery school teachers, *Sunset* argued that play equipment must "appeal to the unpredictable imagination of the child" and suggested that children preferred big things that were "non-representational," which they could adapt and transform.[107]

Dr. Spock's advice to a parent who "can't buy a shiny automobile to pedal or a playhouse" was to provide the child with "a packing box. By turns it's a bed, a house, a truck, a tank, a fort, a doll's house, a garage."[108] A cardboard appliance box that the child could make into a castle or fort was the reigning ideal. The architect Fred Bassetti developed his Flexagons toy in the mid-1950s while experimenting with designs for a cardboard playhouse he hoped to sell nationally, and by the early 1970s Creative Playthings developed a ready-made cardboard house with a pitched roof and movable doors and windows (Figure 3.19). Even *Sunset* concurred that a cardboard box, or other inexpensive materials, often "scores the greatest success."[109]

For older children, building a play- or clubhouse was itself a creative activity. Like Beverly Cleary's character Henry Huggins in *Henry and the Clubhouse* (1962), the process of imagining and building a structure, and inhabiting the space, was a practical learning experience in self-sufficiency and problem solving. From the late nineteenth century onward, the process

Figure 3.18. Advertisement for Doughboy playhouses, circa 1951. *Playthings* 49 (August 1951): 79. Photograph from Science, Industry, and Business Library, the New York Public Library, Astor, Lenox and Tilden Foundations.

of having children build a small structure was believed to impart valuable practical knowledge and character building. Campers, for example, in the 1920s, erected tents and then their own cabins. But the child-made club-house was also associated with imagination. In J. M. Barrie's play *Peter Pan*, the Lost Boys build Wendy a small house on their island of Neverland to pretend she is their mother. In Walt Disney's 1953 animated version, the Lost Boys already have a fanciful dwelling, a playgroundlike hideout they have carved from a tree.

This belief that children might construct their own playhouses in-formed both construction toys and experimental kits for inside or backyard building. Like Charles and Ray Eames's the Toy, which came with directions for making a playhouse, many building toys were sold with the promise of small-scale construction. One developed by Yale architecture professor Gil-bert Switzer, and retailed through Creative Playthings around 1957, required children to assemble rods and Masonite panels. A project for notched planks cut from standard-sized lumber was another do-it-yourself project that the parent could initiate and the children could complete. The large size of these sets demanded cooperation among children and suggested that creativity could be a group activity, rather than just a solitary one.

Aside from the cardboard box and covered card table, many of these projects required substantial building and expense. Thus, even more than the playroom, the backyard miniature dwelling reflected the dreams of adults. In a 1957 book, Robert Paul Smith drily described a playhouse visible from the road: "I passed a house that had a yard, and in the yard there was a tree, and in the tree there was a tree house. And that tree house was built by a carpenter. It had a floor, made of tongue-and-groove boarding, it had sides built of siding, it had a roof made of a new tent. It was probably built from a plan by a carpenter. It probably has wrought-iron furniture in it, and a Rouault print on the wall. There were not kids in it."[110] A 1962 *Parents' Magazine* article began, "Remember, dad, your Fort Apache from which you and the neighborhood children fought the Injuns to a standstill? Or your clubhouse, mom, in which your private tea parties were held? Not really a fight. Not really tea—but how you could imagine!"[111]

In addition to evoking nostalgia for middle-class parents' own childhoods, their firm belief that special goods and spaces could enhance their children's childhoods motivated them to invest their time and energy. In a 1958 article, "Playhouse for the Kids," published in *Parents' Magazine,* Suzanne Hart Strait described her and her husband's summertime project to build and outfit a playhouse for their children, who were away visiting grandparents. At the end of the laborious, twelve-day construction effort, she recounts, "I honestly felt that Tom and I had achieved a major goal for our children: a gift to them of privacy, beauty and space of their own." When the children return home and she asks with anticipation whether they would like a playhouse, the children respond that they already have them—one apiece, in fact, carved out of a forsythia bush, an apple tree, and a pine grove. Realizing that "those houses are better than the one we built," Strait and her husband recognize that the playhouse was actually their own dream, born of childhoods spent in small city apartments.[112] Instead of a specially designed miniature house, three acres of land had achieved the same goal. This story underscores the paradox of affluent postwar parenting, which made a child's imagination both an innate quality and one that could seemingly be enhanced with consumer goods. Magazines and guides repeatedly emphasized the "play value" of playhouses, whether they were made from leftover cardboard boxes or permanent additions to the family house. The story also suggests that although children's desires may have directed some spending and parental effort, adults also consumed children's goods to please themselves.

The psychological and educational rhetoric that encouraged parents to give children unstructured playtime and educational toys in order to cultivate imagination and fantasy was extended to the design of the single-family house. Playrooms, bedrooms, and toy playhouses were some of the special areas designated for children both inside and outside of the family dwelling. In these carefully designed spaces, outfitted with surfaces to draw and paint upon, toylike furniture to encourage active play, and a decor that would stimulate imagination, postwar children were offered the material embodiment of their parents' values. Yet "creative living" was not only an ideal for young children; it became an ongoing project for postwar middle-class families who aimed to meet the social expectations of a popular culture obsessed with family life.[113] For middle-class families, buying and decorating a house after World War II was both a personal exercise of consumer or aesthetic gratification and part of a broader national project. In addition to ranch houses, toasters, and craft kits, families invested in children's spaces and amusements because they believed their children—and, by extension, the future of the country—could better compete in a chilly, uncertain world *if* they prepared at home. Once these children reached school age, the ideal of creativity became an ever more public discourse in the newly erected schoolhouses designed to educate a growing generation of American citizens.

4

BUILDING CREATIVITY IN POSTWAR SCHOOLS

THE RISING POPULATION of young American children made school build-ing, together with housing, the most widely discussed architectural chal-lenge after World War II. High prices and scarcity of materials during the Depression and wartime had left few possibilities for renovating or even maintaining older structures, much less constructing new schools. Fur-thermore, the population migration to areas in the West and to developing suburban towns created a need where there was little existing provision for school-age children and nothing that could match their ever-growing numbers.[1] Enrollment in U.S. elementary and secondary schools was 25.1 million during the 1949–50 school year. By 1959–60, it had increased by almost 11 million, and it peaked in 1970 at 51.3 million.[2] The surge of new births that began during wartime meant that at the end of the war the de-mand for new classrooms collided with an outdated, limited stock of school buildings.[3] In 1955, editors at the *Architectural Forum* worried, "Every 15 minutes enough babies are born to fill another classroom and we are already 250,000 classrooms behind."[4] To deal with the shortage of school seats, chil-dren often attended school in split sessions using overcrowded classrooms, rundown buildings, or hastily built temporary quarters. Even a small dis-trict estimated that a new classroom had to be ready for occupancy every third day of the year just to keep up with fresh enrollments.[5] Thousands of public schools were built to meet postwar needs. The designs, plans, ma-terials, and furnishings of these buildings reflect the endurance of debates on creativity and imagination at a time of growing concern over the state of American education.[6]

The public school, as an agent for national renewal and the cultiva-tion of democracy, has long been a cultural symbol of American aspiration. After World War II, the implications of public education gained increased significance with the rising birthrate and the growing specter of a communist threat. As the Cold War enhanced nationalist anxieties, it placed new attention on education and creating a competitive edge in American children. These forces, together with shifting educational ideals that emphasized personality, creativity, and citizenship, had a profound effect on the mission and design of postwar schools. Behind the architectural changes to the school plant and classroom lay the increasing acceptance of modern design and methods of "modern teaching" as means of helping children learn in ways that might stimulate their attention and their imagination. Architects and educators argued that young children should be offered ways of expressing their own desires in order to develop the creative impulses that, they reasoned, would provide a firm basis for academic skills at a later stage. As pedagogical theory and architectural design became closely intertwined, debates on the role of the school and its design made discussions about space, materials, and pedagogy the business of thousands of school board members, local elected officials, architects, designers, and parents.

The modern American public school, as a cultural and architectural form, emerged from a complex interaction of technical concerns, educational theory, and the larger historical forces of postwar expansion and Cold War tension. I argue that the material qualities of the new schools— from the plan and materials to decoration and furnishings—were devised in dialogue with educational progressivism that was resurgent in American school-building campaigns after World War II. This evidence counters a popular belief that progressivism collapsed in the face of Cold War conformity. Instead, the discourse of creativity was written into the programs and plans of both elementary and high schools. These buildings achieved notoriety as a set of ideas. They were created primarily for white, middle-class children, yet they were promoted as model solutions to a nationwide crisis. Architects, educators, and manufacturers, together with local school board members, created a popularly disseminated image of school bound to ideal methods of building and learning, and a persistently romantic notion of the creative child.

PREWAR SCHOOLS AND THE PROGRESSIVE IDEAL

As architects faced the problem of designing new school buildings, they quickly rejected the multistory structures from earlier school-building campaigns. Nineteenth-century American schoolhouses already constituted a distinct architectural type closely tied to educational theory.[7] The relatively

Figure 4.1. R. W. Shaw, public school,
Watonga, Oklahoma, circa 1914–25. From
William C. Bruce, *Grade School Buildings*
(Milwaukee: Bruce Publishing, 1914–25),
223. Avery Architectural and Fine Arts Library,
Columbia University.

standardized plans of these monumental four- or five-story brick buildings usually had a central entrance, symmetrically planned classrooms on either side of a long corridor, and a large auditorium (Figure 4.1).[8] These designs reflected modern notions of capturing daylight and enhancing ventilation, as well as principles of aesthetic refinement.[9] Yet, whether in urban areas or rural towns, the school was often a monumental edifice embellished with references to the past, such as Greek pediments, neo-Gothic parapets, or colonial-revival urns, signifying a Progressive Era investment in civic and national identity. As beacons of American citizenship, prewar schools embodied both venerable traditions of learning and a modern system of American public education. In these buildings, the plan of the classroom was predictably rectangular (Figure 4.2). With blackboards on one or two walls, a bank of windows on one long side, desks in rows, and the teacher's desk located in the front, these classrooms emphasized order, desk work, and the teacher's authority.[10]

Although postwar school architects rebuked monumental facades and masonry construction, they did not reject the entire model. Just as the postwar educational toy had its roots in the interwar nursery school, the postwar school developed from the spatial and pedagogical model of a prewar institution. After the First World War, kindergarten schoolrooms were designed as well-lit open spaces often decorated with murals or special edifying pictures. The classrooms were larger than most others, even though they held fewer pupils, and were often located near an exit on the ground floor. Because the modern kindergarten classroom was intended for multiple

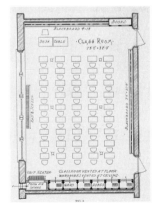

Figure 4.2. Plan of a schoolhouse, circa
1925. From Walter W. LaChance, *Schoolhouses
and Their Equipment* (Niagara Falls, N.Y.:
White & LaChance, 1925), Figure 6. Collection
Centre Canadien d'Architecture/Canadian Centre
for Architecture, Montreal.

activities, from playing circle games to folding paper, it required small-sized movable furniture, spaces for storage and equipment such as sand tables, and separate toilets. These elements, which were devised to make the child feel welcome and to enhance his or her exploration, became the signature forms of the postwar elementary schoolhouse.

European-trained architects working in the United States during the late 1930s and early 1940s designed schools based on the kindergarten model. These were small, one-story, pavilion-type buildings with expansive windows and access to outdoor space just beyond the classroom.[11] The Oak Lane Country Day School of 1929 and the Hessian Hills School (1931–32), by the Philadelphia firm of Howe and Lescaze, were both well-publicized single-story buildings with large corner windows to bring light into the classroom area. The experimental schools that Richard Neutra designed in Los Angeles also favored open classrooms with extensive windows and access to the outdoors. From the 1930s onward, Neutra had developed an ideal school plan of one-story buildings that led to adjacent gardens through a large sliding-glass door. Modeled in part on contemporary architectural ideas about access to air and light, as was Johannes Duiker's Open Air School, in Amsterdam (1928–30), Neutra's Corona Avenue School, in Bell, California, was also a response to the California climate and the experimental schools built in the state.[12] Called a "test tube" school, Neutra's Bell school had large, well-lit L-shaped classrooms outfitted with movable chairs and tables, and was equipped for an indoor-outdoor curriculum.[13] Neutra's later schools, especially the Kester Avenue School, in Sherman Oaks (1949), restated his earlier forms but, by the postwar era, shared the spotlight with many similar school projects (Figure 4.3).

These conspicuously avant-garde buildings gave a formal and spatial identity to progressive educational ideas. Deriving in part from John Dewey's emphasis on cultivating democracy and learning both abstract concepts and real skills through projects, progressivism at the elementary school level was always imprecise. It implied a child-centered (rather than teacher-centered) classroom, where children could move freely around the room, use materials other than textbooks, sit in movable furniture that could be easily rearranged, and explore the physical world through hands-on projects. Historians of education are still divided on the real impact of progressivism on American education, but its effect on the architectural discourse was profound and enduring.[14]

The Crow Island School, in Winnetka, Illinois, a wealthy suburb of Chicago, was indebted to these earlier projects but provided an even more

Figure 4.3. Richard Neutra, Kester Avenue School, Sherman Oaks, California, 1949. Copyright J. Paul Getty Trust. Printed with permission. Julius Schulman Photograph Archive, Research Library at the Getty Research Institute (2004.R.10).

influential model, which legions of architects and school designers adapted after the war (Figure 4.4). Designed by Eliel and Eero Saarinen, the father-and-son firm based in Bloomfield Hills, Michigan, along with the young Chicago designers Lawrence B. Perkins, E. Todd Wheeler, and Philip Will Jr., between 1939 and 1940, Crow Island evoked experimentalism in curricular ideals and architectural form.[15] Nursery, elementary, and intermediate school-age children were arranged in a pinwheel plan that provided access to the central block (containing the auditorium and basement workshops) with its monumental chimney (Figure 4.5). The kindergarten and nursery classrooms were located toward the front entrance and paired with gardens and separate play areas. A wing of classrooms for the primary grades along one side of a corridor and the upper grades along two sides of another corridor reached into the wooded site. A low-rise brick structure, the building's widely discussed features were the long corridors connecting L-shaped

Figure 4.4. Eliel Saarinen, Eero Saarinen, Lawrence B. Perkins, E. Todd Wheeler, and Philip Will Jr., Crow Island School, Winnetka, Illinois, 1939–40. Photograph by Ken Hedrich, Hedrich-Blessing HB-06184-F2, Chicago History Museum.

classrooms, the individual gardens between classrooms, the expansive use of windows on two exposures, and ceilings lowered to a height common in residential architecture.

Crow Island reflected the pedagogy of Carleton Washburne, superintendent of the Winnetka schools, and teachers who collaborated with the architects on the plan. The design developed from a belief that large schools and big spaces often overwhelmed young children. The classroom was a self-contained, L-shaped unit including a workroom with storage, long counters, and a sink for messy projects, as well as a small toilet (Figure 4.6). Draperies, colorful shelves, built-in seating under the large plate-glass windows, and plywood chairs and tables that could be easily rearranged were designed to make each classroom seem friendly to young children. The autonomy of the classroom, comfortable sofas in the entrance hall, a fireplace in the library, and the individual gardens between each classroom reinforced a strongly

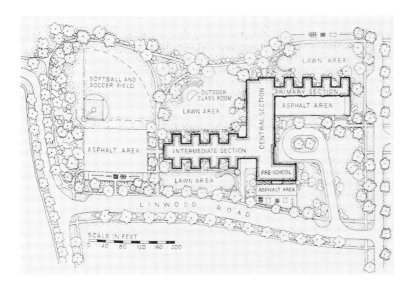

Figure 4.5. Crow Island School plan, 1941. From *Architectural Forum* 75 (August 1941). Courtesy of Perkins + Will. Photograph from Avery Architectural and Fine Arts Library, Columbia University.

Figure 4.6. Crow Island School, Winnetka, Illinois, 1939–40. Hedrich-Blessing, HB-06184-K, Chicago History Museum.

domestic ideal. In a letter to the architects, Frances Pressler, the director of activities, hoped the classrooms would "give [a] feeling of security. These are especially the places of living together and should give feeling of inviting home-likeness, settings in which constant, confident realization of self and others together can take place."

The interior decoration of the school was also part of the designers' vision and curricular aims. The capabilities of the Saarinen family were evident in the abstract-patterned draperies that Eero designed with his mother, the weaver Loja Saarinen. Eero also designed the pale bent-plywood classroom furniture, and Lillian Swann (his fiancée) made brightly glazed ceramic reliefs. Yet Pressler stressed from the outset that the building should not be entirely finished. Instead, she asked that "there be no illustrative frieze decoration as the means of *presenting* the place to children, lest such illustration be not the fanciful picture of the children who behold it, and lest it designate too definite a form of creation thereby inhibiting instead of encouraging child expression."[16] This emphasis on an active emotional and imaginative life of young children was therefore part of both the curriculum and the design of the school.

Washburne was nationally known for his Winnetka program, which championed the individuality of each child and paid careful attention to his or her emotional needs.[17] This fundamentally progressive outlook on nurturing the individual, rather than adhering to a predetermined rate of progress, was augmented with practical experience through hands-on projects. The design of the school structure and its curriculum were thoroughly considered before construction began. The architects observed the Winnetka pedagogy firsthand and created prototypes to present to the community.[18] Amy S. Weisser has argued that the Crow Island project advanced a local planning concern of the Village of Winnetka that it be kept homogeneous and serve as a beacon of good citizenship. By carefully managing the town plan and maintaining a rural character, as well as a solid social and physical infrastructure, the village leaders hoped to attract upper-middle-class families and to protect their property values.[19] The Crow Island School promoted citizenship, character, and creativity as its contribution to the community and in so doing helped to polish the reputation of the village.

Crow Island was widely published and became a model for postwar architects who designed spaces with progressive ideals in mind. Throughout the late 1940s and 1950s, hundreds of adaptations of the Crow Island idea were built around the country.[20] For example, the firm Robinson, Stanhope, and Manning built two nearly identical schools modeled on Crow Island in northern Delaware in 1947–48.[21] In addition to emulating the plan, these schools also adapted the colorful and friendly interior design as a means of enhancing learning.[22] One of the most influential interpretations came from the architect William Wayne Caudill, who conducted a study on the state of schools in Texas and showed how the Crow Island idea might be adapted in the Southwest. In *Space for Teaching* (1941), Caudill interpreted the signature features of Crow Island in his illustrations of schools he predicted the state would need to build. The usable "space for teaching," such as the L-shaped classroom, fenestration, and access to the garden, rather than the structural materials of the Crow Island design, was most significant. Caudill admired the integral relationship between curriculum and design exemplified in Crow Island. For him, "the architect should interpret the curriculum in terms of architecture."[23]

Schools like Crow Island gained the attention of architects and educators, but they were also in the public eye. Because the burden of building, outfitting, and running schools fell on local communities, the concept and design of educational facilities became a highly public project. The primary source of funding for school building came from local budgets, and especially from property taxes. Between 1951 and 1957, 79 percent of total funds came from local district resources.[24] To publicize new ideas in school architecture, MoMA, in New York, sent a traveling exhibition, "Modern Architecture for the Modern School," to universities, museums, and community centers across the country between 1942 and 1946.[25] Arguing that schools, especially at the elementary level, could answer a child's psychological needs through planning, materials, and new methods of teaching, curator Elizabeth Mock pressed for changes in American school design. She included Crow Island and two California schools, Neutra's Corona Avenue School (1934), in Bell, and C. H. Franklin and Ernest J. Kump's Acalanes Union High School (1939–40), in Lafayette, praising the "unpretentious," one-story structures with bilateral lighting and access to the outdoors.[26]

The dissemination of a low-rise school plant with single- or double-loaded corridors and bilaterally lit, self-contained classrooms with lowered ceilings was the result of ongoing critical praise of Crow Island and other similar schools, as well as the availability of inexpensive building technology and new ideas about lighting and furnishing. Another traveling exhibition, "Schoolroom Progress USA," sponsored by the Henry Ford Museum and Greenfield Village and the *Encyclopedia Americana* nearly ten years after MoMA's exhibition, cast the modern elementary school as an institution sensitive to the psychological needs of young pupils. "Schoolroom Progress USA" toured the country in two railroad cars in the mid- to late 1950s. Five prominent architectural firms created model classrooms that showed the newest ideas in plan and design. The up-to-date classrooms were exhibited along with displays of historical rooms from a frontier school, a rural school of the 1870s, and a city school of the 1890s. The rough seats, slates, dunce caps, switches for punishment, and folded-paper kindergarten projects showed the material conditions and artifacts of schoolrooms of the past.[27] In contrast, the newly designed spaces depicted in architects' renderings were brightly lit, and the latest products and materials, donated from major suppliers, were displayed as a vignette in the railroad cars. The Los Angeles firm Smith, Powell, Morgridge, for example, designed an elementary schoolroom with direct proximity to nature through a sliding-glass door, outfitted with movable furniture and even a television set (Figure 4.7).

Although MoMA and the Henry Ford Museum were very different institutions, they shared a similar vision of postwar school design and a common aim of transforming the iconic nineteenth-century schoolroom into a modern learning environment. Mock emphasized avant-garde forms and new building techniques, but she was careful to note how "the latest development in elementary school architecture embodies the intimate and

Figure 4.7. Smith, Powell, Morgridge, classroom, "Schoolroom Progress USA." From the collections of The Henry Ford.

personal qualities of the little red school-house of our forefathers."[28] The sentimental image of the one-room school dovetailed with the congenial environment that progressive educators envisioned, even as the schoolhouse underwent dramatic physical changes in the postwar period. Firms such as Perkins and Will of Chicago, Caudill Rowlett Scott of Texas, John Lyon Reid of San Francisco, the Architects Collaborative of Cambridge, and others that embraced these formal and pedagogical values became leading school designers of the era.[29]

POSTWAR ECONOMY AND "FLEXIBILITY"

Many postwar architects emulated aspects of the Crow Island idea, but they adapted it to economical construction. The methods of building and the profile of the elementary school changed significantly in the postwar period. Architects across the country used poured concrete slab for low-rise structures, lightweight steel frames with exposed trusses and joists, radiant heat floors, and expanses of glass. The desire for "flexibility," a key term of postwar building, enhanced the popularity of new materials and finger or cluster plans for school plants. As Andrew Shanken has suggested, the rhetoric of flexibility reflected a sense of uncertain anticipation and seemed at the same time to affirm democratic values.[30] In discussions of school building, flexibility was a desirable quality for the physical aspects of the building, embodied in open corridors, non-load-bearing partitions, and zoned ventilation and heating systems, but it also included the provision of folding walls for small groups, movable cabinets, and lightweight furniture deemed vital to new methods of instruction.

Low-rise schools became common in postwar suburban and rural locations. The lasting anxieties of wartime and newer Cold War fears led many to suggest that one-story schools were safer for evacuation.[31] In the mid-1940s, the National Council on Schoolhouse Construction proclaimed the staircases required in multiple-story buildings hazardous and unnecessarily expensive.[32] Another benefit of one-story schools was expansibility. Administrators embraced low-rise, rigid-frame construction and continuous fenestration in the hope of building the much-needed schools quickly while allowing for modifications in the future.[33] The output of the government-supported war industries made materials such as steel ubiquitous in postwar school building.[34] The steel industry, moreover, promoted one-story, steel-framed schools as cost-effective, able to be rapidly built, and flexible.

John Lyon Reid's northern California elementary schools from the late 1940s and early 1950s show how architects modified innovative prewar forms to suit postwar conditions. Reid's single-story Montecito School (1949), in Martinez, maximized space and access to light.[35] Unlike the Crow Island pinwheel, the Montecito plan was designed with parallel rows of classrooms and open corridors. This arrangement derived from an established tradition of in-line corridors,[36] but it also made reference to Franklin and Kump's Acalanes Union High School in nearby Lafayette, California.[37] Built contemporaneously with Crow Island, Acalanes was noted for its economical, one-story classrooms, openness to light and air through the large windows, and especially for the long corridors of its "finger plan," a scheme that became closely associated with postwar school planning in California (Figure 4.8). Reid's Montecito School, built with H-shaped concrete columns and open-web steel joists that were erected in two and a half days, demonstrated that a low-cost building could also embrace the architectural and pedagogical innovations of more expensive models.

Like Crow Island, Montecito featured L-shaped classrooms for the lower grades that created sheltered gardens or yards for indoor-outdoor instruction. At the John Muir School, built for the same district in 1951, Reid

Figure 4.8. View of Acalanes Union High School, Lafayette, California, circa 1956. Photograph by Roger Sturtevant. Ernest Kump Collection, Environmental Design Archives, University of California, Berkeley.

used a similar plan of long, open corridors and extensive bilateral lighting, but modified the L shape so that the work alcoves were slanted for better supervision. In both schools, the long, parallel outdoor corridors maximized space, traffic flow, and light, and provided integrated areas for indoor and outdoor teaching for kindergarten to third grade. Instead of a large auditorium, as at Crow Island and other prewar schools, Reid created an "all-purpose" room for meetings, lunches, and play, which looked onto a central courtyard through large, sharply angled windows (Figure 4.9). Seeking to use space pedagogically, Reid placed the large heating plant at the John Muir School prominently along a corridor and made it visible to the children through a plate-glass window.[38]

This emphasis on the school as not only the site but also the means of instruction stressed the child's experience, and particularly his or her sensory encounter. The concept of an object lesson was fundamentally pedagogical and was well established in the United States by the turn of the twentieth century. The nineteenth-century scientist and Smithsonian administrator George Brown Goode stated in 1889, "In the schoolroom the diagram, the

Figure 4.9. John Lyon Reid, John Muir School, Martinez, California, 1951. Photograph by Roger Sturtevant. Collection of the Oakland Museum of California.

blackboard, and the object-lesson, unknown thirty years ago, are universally employed."[39] Teaching objects such as maps, primers, pictures, and plaster casts of Greek sculpture and notable thinkers were also used for instruction; however, these items privileged literacy rather than introspective wonder or tactile interest.[40] In the postwar school, at the elementary and secondary level, the building itself was designed as a Pestalozzian object lesson to awaken a readiness toward learning.

Greater attention to the school plan, materials, and their psychological implications informed a number of new technical improvements in postwar school design. Nineteenth-century schoolhouses were devised to maximize daylight, but experiments carried out during World War II raised the technical standard for new postwar classrooms.[41] In addition to measuring luminosity and air movement, other material concerns for optimal learning, such as the shape, paint colors, textures, and furniture of the classroom, were widely discussed.[42] Yet the science of postwar school architecture was often secondary to psychological considerations. In a 1947 handbook for school building, Reid and Charles Wesley Bursch, chief of the division of schoolhouse planning for the California Department of Education, described the material and psychological qualities of the new educational environment:

> School plant architecture must start off with its basic conception in terms of the child occupants; it must recognize that its forms, dimensions, color, materials, and texture are capable of creating an environment which either attracts or repels the child; which can influence his attitude and stimulate him. The school plant designed for the child is unpretentious, open, colorful; spread out planning permits him to blow off steam and breathe fresh air; doors can be opened without a major struggle against the strength of the door checks; the walls are built to be surreptitiously kicked; the general environment is not forbidding and monumental but as informal and devoid of affectation as the child himself.[43]

The child, constituted in relation to these physical aspects of the school plant, was both a physical body who might "blow off steam and breathe fresh air" and open doors without a "struggle against the strength of the door checks," and a psychological being sensitive to attraction, repulsion, and stimulation.

The experience of the larger school plant and the smaller unit of the individual classroom constituted the "environment" that architects, landscape architects, designers, and "schoolmen"—a designation given to consultant planners, as well as education experts and school superintendents—now considered. In an attempt to show their fluency in the latest scientific research on schoolhouse design and prevailing educational theory, manufacturers and researchers developed model classrooms. In a Westinghouse Lighting advertisement from 1952, two schoolmen contemplate a dollhouse-sized "Progressive Classroom" (Figure 4.10). Moving the miniature desks into curved rows and pointing approvingly to the colored walls that gleam under the bright incandescent fixtures, the two figures frame the technological and aesthetic changes in the postwar school environment and embody the eagerness of manufacturers to sell materials that met the new standards.[44]

A life-sized model classroom built with donated products at the University of Michigan in 1954 was also created to demonstrate the new research (Plate 11).[45] In addition to providing filtered light from the glass block, clear "vision strip," and luminous ceiling panels, the model featured reflective floor and desk surfaces that enhanced the brightness of the environment. The use of contrasting color—greens for the side walls and chalkboard, red for the end walls—was another aspect of postwar schoolroom research. Although many emphasized the importance of color for regulating temperature, designers and architects argued that the social, psychological, and aesthetic aspects of the classroom were equally important.[46] William

Figure 4.10. "Progressive Classroom," Westinghouse Lighting advertisement, circa 1952. From *Progressive Architecture* 33 (August 1952). Avery Architectural and Fine Arts Library, Columbia University

Caudill and William Peña cautioned against exaggerating scientific principles and argued, in 1951, "The sensation of colour may create feelings of pleasantness and harmony, of drabness and depression, or of stimulation and excitability. It is just this factor which causes colour to be of such importance in the classroom, for the classroom is the home—the environment—of the learning process."[47] Whereas color in furniture and toys was used for similar reasons—to attract the child's attention and also to heighten consumer appeal—in schools color served to give a sense of positive cheeriness. Peña, in particular, believed that vivid colors could produce happy, well-behaved children receptive to their environment and suggested that color could re-create "the warm, informal atmosphere of the home."[48]

The materials, colors, and arrangement of the Michigan Research Laboratory classroom derived from practical concerns for reflectivity and flexibility, but they also underscore this widespread interest in making the elementary classroom appear homelike.[49] The patterned fiberglass curtains, for example, could be pulled into place to create smaller, or darker, spaces for the use of audiovisual equipment while adding color and an evocation of domesticity. As a transitional institution between family life and formal schooling, postwar elementary schools embraced the progressive idea of encouraging autonomy within a protective space.[50] Perkins and Will and Caudill Rowlett Scott, which were among the most renowned school designers in the postwar era, incorporated fireplaces, casual seating, large windows, and lower ceilings to make the elementary school deliberately resemble the postwar dwelling. "Homelike" schools were distinguished as an innovation in the postwar era: "The modern elementary schools are becoming more child-like and more similar to home, if we understand the term 'home' correctly in contemporary terms."[51] Prewar school architects had also emulated "the spirit, quietness, and refinement of a good home."[52] Yet by the postwar era, the notion of home had shifted from a moralizing sense of shelter as a model for civic or national cohesion, to modernist values of domestic informality and openness as a means of enhancing the individual potential of each family member. Postwar schools therefore enacted "home" because it underscored democratic citizenship as the outcome of a carefully nourished individuality.

LIVING ROOMS FOR LEARNING

Not only were parents and households considered children's earliest educators, but the school expanded the homelike metaphor in material terms, with curtains, televisions, and comfortable furniture. Any number of critics, designers, and educators pointed to the image of the oak desk bolted to the floor as the measure of how much American schools had changed in the course of the twentieth century. The old rows of iron-and-wood desks were looked upon as a rigid and heartless arrangement compared to the living room–classroom ideal. The grouping of tables for grades above kindergarten reflected newer attitudes about pedagogy.[53] The progressive ideas of John Dewey were subsumed into the more generalized practice known as modern teaching. In traditional, prewar schools, the teacher was the authority, and his or her desk was placed at the front of the room facing the rows of students. New, or "modern," methods that were widely adopted after World War II cast the teacher as a guide who constantly moved around the room and, in theory, kept a desk at the back or side of the classroom and used it only for recording marks.[54] Just as "flexibility" became the byword among school architects and planners, the flexible classroom was promoted as a fundamental aspect of modern school design and modern pedagogy.

Movable and stackable chairs, large worktables, informal seating, and open storage were hallmarks of the flexible classroom.[55] Eero Saarinen's plywood chairs and tables were an important feature of the Winnetka pedagogy at Crow Island. (However, older children at Crow Island used individual desks with attached seats, which were common in upper-grade classrooms throughout the country.) A number of studies examining the arrangement of the classroom concluded that modern teaching methods required different kinds of furniture in the classroom. Instead of providing a desk for each pupil, planning experts theorized that small groups, group projects, and less formal seat work would require different kinds of work surfaces.[56]

Although an architect could design or specify furniture that was built-in, most loose furniture was the responsibility of the superintendent or district supply department. American Seating's Universal Desk was probably the most widely used combination of pedestal desk and chair for older elementary grades (Figure 4.11).[57] A wooden writing surface and seat were bolted to an adjustable steel frame that held the sitter upright. Although it did not meet the ideal of flexibility that education experts called for (and was the target of considerable criticism), the linked desk-chair combination remained popular because it maximized space.[58] Mary Crowley and David Medd, prominent British architects studying American schools, observed that "only since 1955 has school furniture been made in the quantity, and of the kind, needed to meet the requirements of modern education."[59] Art-education historian Diana Korzenik also observed this shift: "I started first grade with my knees under desks, bolted to the floor, seated on a smooth

Figure 4.11. Universal Desk, American Seating Company advertisement, circa 1948.

narrow bench attached to the desk behind me. Row after row of children sat so. Then in 1954 came new moveable desks. Tables could be grouped. We children could look at each others' faces, all the better to defy the teacher. This moment marked a change in the school environment and in the authority of the teacher."[60]

The furniture of the Brunswick Corporation epitomized the ideal of movable furniture. When Brunswick-Balke-Collender, a manufacturer of billiards and other sporting equipment, decided to enter the school market, in the early 1950s, it invested heavily in research and design. (The company was called the Brunswick-Balke-Collender Company until it officially changed its name to the Brunswick Corporation in 1960.) Brunswick promoted ergonomically designed seats and backs made of lightweight materials such as plywood, fiberglass, and hard plastic that could be stacked and moved, following the changing formation of the classroom (Plate 12). A molded chair from 1953 that came in colorful hues was sold as resilient, comfortable, "scientifically" designed, and flexible.[61] The company promised that its designs could "[turn] your classrooms into *living rooms for learning*" and developed a model schoolroom in Kalamazoo, Michigan, where prospective clients could try out different arrangements.[62] In developing and promoting designs that were easily rearranged and stored, the company (like other materials manufacturers of the period) displayed a mastery of the generalized rhetoric of progressive pedagogy. The analogy drawn between the private living room and the space of the classroom, which extended the cozy image of the kindergarten into spaces for older children, also shows how the discourse of informality and domesticity in public schools aligned individual goals with institutional desires.

NURTURING THE INDIVIDUAL

The ideals of flexibility, domesticity, and economy encouraged clusters as an alternative to the long corridors of Crow Island or Acalanes. Schools built according to a cluster plan, with classrooms in semi-isolated "age-neighborhoods," strongly evoked the postwar house.[63] Although designed to maximize space, many cluster-planned schools claimed both economy and a meaningful spatial experience. In organization and details, the prominent cluster schools of the early and mid-1950s reflected a new sensitivity to a child's perception.

Perkins and Will's Heathcote Elementary School (1953), in Scarsdale, New York, exemplified the educational benefits of the cluster plan. One-story classrooms were grouped in fours around a central space, giving each six-sided classroom four window walls set at sixty-degree angles. Superintendent Archibald B. Shaw and Lawrence B. Perkins described Scarsdale's educational approach as "concern with the pupil—both as an individual and a member of a group."[64] The classroom's nearly circular shape reflected a desire to bring children together in a circle and to allow for small group instruction (Figure 4.12).[65] The wide, continuous windows looking onto the rambling hillside also evoked the postwar suburban house with its ubiquitous plate-glass window.[66]

Heathcote was designed to enhance the relationship between children and the natural beauty of the wooded site. With its clusters of hexagonal classrooms, the architects likened the plan to an image of "children under a tree" (Figure 4.13).[67] As at Crow Island, the firm designed built-in seats next to windows to increase the children's proximity to nature. Heathcote's long, glazed corridors had no classrooms strung along them. Instead, they were

Figure 4.12. Perkins and Will, Heathcote Elementary School, Scarsdale, New York, 1953. View of a classroom. Hedrich-Blessing, HB-16711-L, Chicago History Museum.

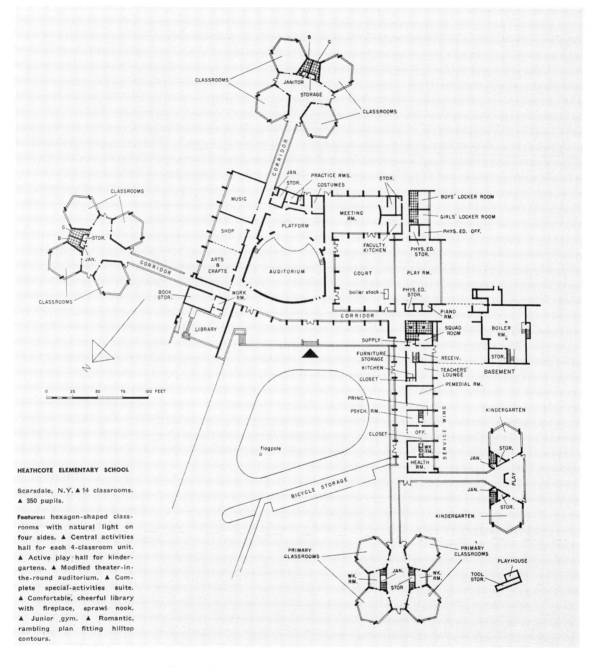

CLASSROOMS

JANITOR
STORAGE

CLASSROOMS

B G

CLASSROOMS

G
B STOR.
JAN.

CLASSROOMS

CORRIDOR

CORRIDOR

MUSIC

SHOP

ARTS & CRAFTS

BOOK STOR.

WORK RM.

LIBRARY

JAN. STOR.

PRACTICE RMS.
COSTUMES

PLATFORM

AUDITORIUM

STOR.

MEETING RM.

FACULTY KITCHEN

COURT

boiler stock

BOYS' LOCKER ROOM

GIRLS' LOCKER ROOM

PHYS. ED. OFF.

PHYS. ED. STOR.

PLAY RM.

PHYS. ED. STOR.

PIANO RM.

M W

SQUAD ROOM

BOILER RM.

CORRIDOR

SUPPLY

FURNITURE STORAGE

KITCHEN

CLOSET

PRINC.

PSYCH. RM.

CLOSET

OFF.

WK RM.

HEALTH RM.

RECEIV.

TEACHERS' LOUNGE

REMEDIAL RM.

SERVICE WING

STOR.

BASEMENT

KINDERGARTEN

STOR.

JAN.

JAN.

STOR.

PLAY

KINDERGARTEN

flagpole

BICYCLE STORAGE

N

0   25   50   75   100 FEET

HEATHCOTE ELEMENTARY SCHOOL

Scarsdale, N.Y. ▲ 14 classrooms.
▲ 350 pupils.

Features: hexagon-shaped classrooms with natural light on
four sides. ▲ Central activities
hall for each 4-classroom unit.
▲ Active play hall for kindergartens. ▲ Modified theater-in-
the-round auditorium. ▲ Complete special-activities suite.
▲ Comfortable, cheerful library
with fireplace, sprawl nook.
▲ Junior gym. ▲ Romantic,
rambling plan fitting hilltop
contours.

PRIMARY CLASSROOMS

WK RM.

JAN.

STOR.

WK RM.

PRIMARY CLASSROOMS

PLAYHOUSE

TOOL STOR.

Figure 4.13. Perkins and Will, Heathcote School
Plan. From *Architectural Forum* 101 (July 1954).
Courtesy of Perkins + Will. Photograph from Avery
Architectural and Fine Arts Library, Columbia
University.

transparent and followed the rolling topography, connecting each cluster to the administrative center and auditorium. The jewel-colored panes set into the glass walls of the corridors cast bright reflections on the floor and provided contrast to the natural palette of wood, stone, and earth.[68] Placed at two heights, they invited children and adults, as they made their way down the corridor, to peer out and rediscover the surrounding landscape in red, blue, orange, or green (Plate 13). This direct appeal to the senses called out the building's agency in grasping the child's attention. The panes asked the child to pause on his or her way and stand on tiptoe or crouch to reflect on the perceptual experience. The extensive use of plate glass and pleasurable details—even the gymnasium had expansive windows that looked onto a secluded, landscaped rock garden—suggested that individual aesthetic appreciation was as important as reading and writing. Indeed, Perkins valued the child's subjective experience over technical formulas. He described Heathcote as a rebellion against "the current concentration on how to pour air over a child, throw light on his book, fit his contours to the seats. This building is not an exercise in lighting and ventilation." Instead, he claimed to focus on the "in'ards of the child" and those intangible aspects of the child's sensory experience.[69]

Expensive and lavishly outfitted, Heathcote reflected the esteem that progressive education held in suburban Scarsdale, one of the richest towns in the country at the time. Heathcote gained national attention, and images of the school were printed in full color in popular magazines. An article in *McCall's*, "What's Happened to the Little Red Schoolhouse?" praised the effect of the school environment, with its flexible classroom clusters and elegant details, upon the behavior of the children.[70]

Although Heathcote's cost per pupil was notoriously high, one point made frequently during the period was how economical modern design was compared to "traditional" prewar schools with their masonry construction, multiple stories, large auditoriums, and architectural ornamentation.[71] The cluster plan was especially noted for its economy. Donald Barthelme's West Columbia Elementary School (1952), in Brazoria County, Texas, built around the same time as Heathcote but for a much poorer school district, won an award from school administrators and was featured in MoMA's 1952 "Built in USA" exhibition.[72] Planned around open-air courts, Barthelme's school embraced the metaphor of the neighborhood using a modular grid to save the expense of corridors (Figure 4.14). The exposed steel frame and expansive plate-glass windows allowed children to see each other across the open space. The classrooms were skylighted, with a system of louvers

to control glare and temperature. Instead of an auditorium, the school featured a common room, which could be used for lunch hours, performances,
and community needs. Additional clusters of classrooms around this central space were eventually added. Exposed beams and pipes were left un-
concealed in classrooms and public areas as a measure of economy, but
bright Vermont marble slabs mounted on the steel frame and open bar joists
served as deliberate adornment.[73] The long, vaulted concrete canopy that
sheltered students who arrived on buses was, likewise, an embellishment
aimed at making school enticing. Although praised for its economy and
forthright structure, West Columbia also gained attention for its sensitivity
to the child's experience.

Both Heathcote and West Columbia were admired in the professional
press, which covered school building with avid interest and produced special
annual issues on schools throughout the period. Popular magazines, such as
Life, *Parents' Magazine*, and *Collier's*, also devoted entire issues to education, drawing national attention to physical problems of overcrowding and
schoolhouse design, as well as questions of curricular content and the future implications for democracy.[74] Writers for *Ladies' Home Journal* and
Reader's Digest, suspicious of the rising cost of these buildings, charged
that taxpayers were being duped into paying for lavish facilities by haughty
architects and educators "preying on school boards in thousands of communities."[75] Yet the ongoing preoccupation with the nationwide dilemma

of building more classrooms encouraged popular publications to commission their own solutions.[76]

One of these was published in *Collier's* in 1954. The Architects Collaborative (TAC), the Cambridge, Massachusetts, firm that Walter Gropius founded, designed a model school that could be quickly and economically built, allowing for future modification.[77] The prototype TAC school featured a cluster plan of individual, one-story classrooms grouped around a central administrative structure (Figure 4.15). A syncopated grid of square classrooms created intimate gardens and "outdoor classrooms" that were interspersed throughout the school grounds. Clusters of four classrooms hugged

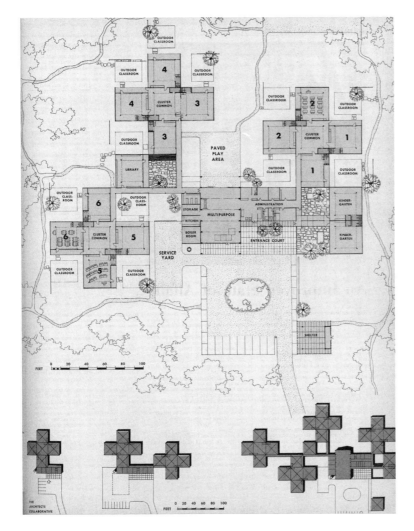

Figure 4.15. The Architects Collaborative, model school plan, 1954. *Collier's,* April 30, 1954.

a common area where group activities could take place. In each classroom, the architects designed movable, self-contained spaces for projects and storage, as well as toilets, skylights, and clerestory windows. Because the building was constructed with steel columns set in concrete piers, the rooms' walls, freed from load-bearing and windows, could be made of inexpensive materials and provide space for exhibiting children's work.[78] The TAC design promised expansion in any direction and according to any topography. It also offered the internal flexibility that purported to make each classroom unique.[79] Although dedicated to economical building using prefabricated materials, TAC also underscored the importance of color and aesthetics. The *Collier's* project featured colorful tile murals on the school's facades. For John C. Harkness, who designed many of TAC's schools, art was essential to the larger project of developing young minds: "The will to understand and appreciate beauty and order must be generated within people. And this must be done during the formative years, which correspond generally to the years of public school education."[80]

ARCHITECTURE AND THE CURRICULUM

The notion of school as an enchanted experience of discovery, a core belief of progressive education, had implications for both pedagogy and architecture. The progressive values that expanded in the postwar era, especially at the primary school level, endowed the material and spatial qualities of the postwar schoolhouse with social and psychological importance. In a 1957 advertisement for Libbey-Owens-Ford glass, one architect observed: "The environmental influence of a school building blends into the entire landscape. As a child approaches, he feels a kind of structural welcome. The transparent features of the entrance and rooms seem to beckon. He sees what and who are within, a perception that becomes more interesting with each step. There is an unconscious transition as the child's personality merges psychologically with the school and its visible activities. He suddenly is within, yet he has no recollection of a physical threshold."[81]

The use of glass as a psychological tool to enhance—and govern— the child's subjectivity went far beyond the technical questions of daylight and airflow. Giving pedagogy a fundamental role in the design of schools, postwar architects made formal choices, such as self-contained classrooms, indoor-outdoor teaching areas, glass walls, and colorful, homelike spaces, because of their educational implications. As Caudill remarked, "The good school is more than a legally constructed shell around a certain amount of space and equipment. It is also a second home for the school child for a good part of his time—an enclosed little world managed by teachers but designed, built, and operated for the child."[82]

Caudill had been interested in educational architecture even before wartime. In *Space for Teaching*, he showed that rural Texas schools generally lacked electricity and modern toilets, and were housed in outdated structures. Besides the evident need for physical modernization, he argued, many newly built schools exhibited a lack of suitability to modern methods of teaching: "Education has changed profoundly. More changes are expected in the future. No longer is the schoolhouse a mere shelter for the three R's. The scope of the curriculum has broadened. 'Learning by doing' is replacing 'Learning by listening.' Now the school building envelops many and varied activities. Traditional school structures cannot be satisfactorily used. Educators need modern structures, structures that are flexible enough to conform with the changing needs of education."[83]

To meet the curricular demands of modern educational methods, Caudill developed a series of architectural requirements for the design of new schools. In the classroom, he pressed for space that could be partitioned, semiprivate areas for individual instruction, large, open areas for projects such as a model grocery store, movable furniture for creating informal reading circles, space for drama and painting, bookshelves and bulletin boards, and rooms designed for film, radio, and phonograph technology. Looking beyond the individual classroom, he also called for conference rooms, health clinics, gymnasiums, and gardens.

After the war, the Caudill Rowlett Scott firm (CRS) put many of these ideas to work in two schools built in Blackwell, Oklahoma, a small, conservative, wheat-growing town. Caudill rejected the monumental forms of an existing school in favor of a concrete slab with radiant heating and a sloping roof to maximize breezes and keep out the sun's glare.[84] If residents thought the Huston School (1948) in Blackwell resembled a "cowshed" or a "chicken coop" and puzzled over the open corridor, as was reported at the time, they seemed to embrace the logic of economy and the large, bilaterally lit classrooms (Figure 4.16).[85] They also liked CRS's covered play shed, a concrete slab with a roof but no walls, which enabled outdoor play during rainy months and community use in the evenings.[86] Huston's self-contained classrooms could be transformed with minimal effort. To create differentiated space, the firm developed the Teaching Center, a large, free-standing unit that combined a blackboard, a tackboard, a Peg-Board with dowels, and a perforated panel (Figure 4.17). Designed to replace the traditional wall, the Teaching Center divider could be used for teaching, exhibition, dramatic

uses, and storage. Making the classroom larger, well lit, and hospitable to different activities that could be carried on simultaneously was an overriding concern in CRS's numerous elementary schools of the 1950s and 1960s.

The flat roof and thin columns of CRS's 1955 Belaire Elementary School, in San Angelo, Texas, created a deep overhang sheltering a polygonal plan that eliminated the need for corridors and focused the classroom inward (Figure 4.18).[87] Compressing the cluster plan into a single structure, CRS combined economy, technology, and the curricular possibilities of the circular plan.[88] The school was built on a reinforced concrete slab,

Figure 4.17. Caudill Rowlett Scott, the Teaching Center, Huston School, Blackwell, Oklahoma, circa 1948.

Figure 4.18. Caudill Rowlett Scott, Belaire Elementary School, San Angelo, Texas, 1955. Photograph by Dewey G. Mears. Courtesy of CRS Center Archives, College of Architecture, Texas A&M University.

and thirty-four slim steel columns supported the long-span steel joists of the roof. The large, flat, insulated roof provided solar protection while also creating covered outdoor play areas. Belaire was also the first elementary school designed for air-conditioning in the United States. The air-conditioned environment meant fewer windows and few that opened, a strategy that climate control, as well as the school's location near Goodfellow Air Force Base, dictated. In a reversal of school-building norms and the firm's earlier work, Belaire's pie-slice-shaped classrooms had one half-glazed external wall and relied primarily on artificial lighting.

Belaire's small scale, unusual plan, and use of air-conditioning reflected Caudill's technological interests and commitment to a progressive educational model. Designed to hold only 240 pupils, the school was divided into ten equal wedges. A central elevated platform, which could be used for a lunchroom or a stage, was built over the half-sunken heating and cooling plant. This area opened onto three classrooms with movable partitions that could form another multipurpose room. In diagrams and photographs, the classroom space was divided into different areas for individual and group work (Figure 4.19). Furniture, then, determined the classroom

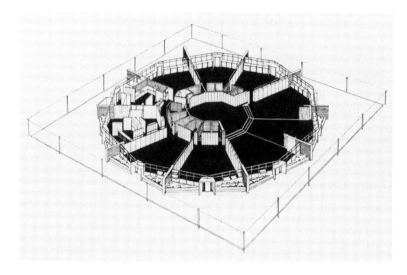

layout; desks at Belaire were designed for two students to sit side by side
with shared storage between them, maximizing the surface area yet maintaining mobility.[89]

A "COLD WAR OF CLASSROOMS"

Long-standing debates over the federal role in funding American schools
had left the question of paying for the desperately needed new buildings
up to local communities, which raised money through bonds and taxes.
Successive attempts to direct revenue to poor states with large school-age
populations were introduced throughout the early 1950s. After the *Brown v.
Board of Education of Topeka* decision, in 1954, which ruled that state laws
providing separate schools for black and white children were illegal, this
question became even more urgent. Yet, despite a major government survey
indicating that existing school facilities were inadequate, federal investment
was limited because of suspicion of government control.[90] After the Soviet
launch of Sputnik I and II, in October 1957, however, the U.S. government
passed far-reaching legislation in the form of the National Defense Education Act (1958), which provided unprecedented funds for school buildings
and equipment, as well as curriculum development in science, mathematics, and foreign languages. The public examination of the state of American
education gained urgency in this intense climate, putting new emphasis on
domestic policies to win what Sen. William Benton of Connecticut had already called a "cold war of classrooms."[91]

Even before Sputnik, nervous questions about the quality of American education and its role in fostering democracy sustained an ongoing debate about the effectiveness of progressive methods. David Riesman argued in *The Lonely Crowd* (1950) that the original aim of progressive education, to foster individuality, was ironically self-defeating. For Riesman, "Educational methods that were once liberating may even tend to thwart individuality rather than advance and protect it."[92] He acknowledged that the physical changes in the classroom had a social purpose. Movable chairs, open shelves, and children's work on the walls all seemed to reflect an encouragement of the child's agency. However, he maintained, this was paradoxical: "It often happens that those schools that insist most strongly that the child be original and creative by this very demand make it difficult for him to be so."[93] Although individual creativity was an important aim of the progressive ideal, the progressive classroom could act, unwittingly, as a tool of conformity. The more popular critique of progressive education—that it emphasized social adjustment over "the basics"—erupted in the press during the Korean War and again after the launches of Sputnik. Arthur Bestor's *Educational Wastelands* (1953), a scathing and widely read book, questioned the curricular content of American education and its usefulness in cultivating a democratic ideal. Bestor, a professor of history at the University of Illinois, charged that educators were preoccupied with the learning process at the expense of teaching the disciplines.[94] At stake for Bestor and others who extended his argument was a loss of potential intellectual skill, which he believed would be vital to American interests.[95]

The widespread fearfulness regarding the American ability to prepare school-age children for future needs led to a Senate investigation, in the spring of 1956, into the future shortage of scientists and engineers. Led by Melvin Price, the Subcommittee for Research and Development of the Joint Committee on Atomic Energy listened to the testimony of esteemed scientists, heads of research institutions, and independent experts on the state of the American educational system in preparing students for careers in engineering and science. The statements pointed to problems such as too few and ill-paid teachers, a curriculum that did not encourage students to pursue science or provide encouragement for especially talented children, and little research money for scientific inquiry. Comparisons with Soviet schools were especially worrisome, yet British schools also seemed to outpace American ones. As Price stated in his preface to the published transcript, "We are in a battle for brainpower. Are we to lose it by default?"[96]

One of the witnesses at the Senate hearing was Hyman G. Rickover, an admiral in the U.S. Navy and creator of the atomic submarine, who charged that American education was mediocre and frivolous compared to European models and would not prepare citizens to meet the demands of the complex postwar world. In a series of essays collected as *Education and Freedom* (1959), Rickover insisted that "education in a democracy need not only be democratic, it must also be education."[97] Like Bestor, Rickover objected to the move away from college-preparatory curriculum, such as foreign languages and mathematics, and toward classes that emphasized functional knowledge about everyday life, such as personal and social development. Moreover, he called for the cultivation of intellectually talented and "creative" students as the only hope for future innovation: "Somehow every organization must make room for inner-directed, obstreperous, creative people; sworn enemies of routine and the *status quo*, always ready to upset the applecart by thinking up new and better ways of doing things. They are troublesome mavericks, unloved by the administrator who cannot forgive their contempt for conventions. However, unless these people are permitted to lead the way, there will be stagnation."[98]

Postwar idealism had renewed an older belief that the public schools could nourish democracy, but Cold War anxieties about the ability of Americans to meet future challenges made discourses over all aspects of schooling especially fraught. Arthur Zilversmit has shown that in some areas of the country progressivism was viewed as subversive and in others as an unnecessary extra. Yet he concludes that the rhetoric of progressivism—more than the practice of it—was highly successful, especially among the educated middle class.[99] Architects and consultant planners envisioned modern, well-lit classrooms appointed with suitable furniture that would optimize both teaching and learning, instill an aesthetic sense, and stimulate individual agency and creativity. To this degree, progressive rhetoric was readily assimilated into postwar architectural discourse.[100] In the debates around the planning and design of elementary schools, skepticism about progressive methods similar to that articulated in the popular media was virtually absent. Instead, faith in design and in building systems to create spaces to educate and improve postwar citizens became even more visible, and more closely tied to pedagogical models, in the succeeding decades.

The scientific research on creativity was central to national discussions on education and curriculum. Many educational psychologists wrote short articles for publications that reached school administrators and teachers, in addition to guides and pamphlets synthesizing research that appeared in the late 1950s and throughout the 1960s. One 1959 guide for teachers warned of the danger of suppressing children's creative impulses: "Years of disuse of [a child's] imaginative faculties dull the growing edges. Memoriter learning, complete domination, unquestioning submission convert the bubbling, effervescent, spontaneous four-year-old into the compliant, conforming, unimaginative ten-year-old."[101] Given that research consistently showed that teachers were more apt to favor the well-behaved, conformist pupil over the impulsive, imaginative one, the national teachers' unions published pamphlets that digested the voluminous research on creativity and offered teachers hints for identifying creativity and ideas for encouraging it in their classrooms. E. Paul Torrance's 1963 pamphlet for the National Education Association advised that "many things can be learned in creative ways more economically and effectively than by authority."[102] He argued that exploration, manipulation, experimentation, and questioning stimulated productive thinking and that when teachers rewarded and respected unusual questions and abilities, provided opportunities for reflection, and withheld immediate evaluation, students and teachers could reap the personal and pedagogical benefits. *Creativity and the Teacher*, which the American Federation of Teachers issued in 1966, similarly parsed the literature to present a case for the teacher's key role. It argued emphatically, "Creativity, if not smothered, will be a precious asset to the child as he grows to adulthood. It will serve him, and serve the nation."[103] Anthologies of short articles, popular guides for teachers, and special workshops on recognizing and building creativity all supported the increasingly mainstream belief that creativity could and should be cultivated in the classroom, and not only at the elementary school level.[104] Even stated generally, this curricular emphasis played directly to the ideals of the designers and planners who were remaking the American school plant. Torrance claimed that the results from creativity studies had persuaded school leaders to initiate "a demand for truly revolutionary changes in educational objectives, curriculums, instruments for assessing mental growth and educational achievement, instructional procedures, counseling and guidance procedures, supervisory and administrative practices, and even in school building planning."[105]

EDUCATIONAL FACILITIES LABORATORIES

In the 1960s and 1970s, Educational Facilities Laboratories, a nonprofit corporation funded by the Ford Foundation's Fund for the Advancement of Education, brought together educators, architects, manufacturers, and government officials responsible for school building to encourage new ideas about both curriculum and architecture.[106] In response to the extreme need for new schools, the American Institute of Architects had formed a Committee on School Buildings in 1953. In 1956, this committee joined a group at Teachers College and, with funds from the Ford Foundation, became Educational Facilities Laboratories (EFL) in 1958. Between 1958 and 1976, under the direction of Harold B. Gores, EFL spent $25.5 million toward redesigning American education.[107] EFL hosted conferences, funded studies, and collaborated on building projects around the country, but the organization's main interest was the design of the school as a complete environment that responded to the needs of teachers, students, and shifting social conditions. Following the ideas of cognitive psychologist Jerome Bruner (who rephrased progressivism by arguing that a child's curiosity was a vital part of the process of education), and facing the reality of a teacher shortage, reformers of the 1960s emphasized team teaching, nongraded levels, flexible schedules, and classroom use of media such as television, which seemed to require another complete reconfiguration of the school plant.[108]

In 1959, Gores observed, in an essay entitled "Educational Change and Architectural Consequence," that the experimental classroom designs of the early postwar period were no longer useful for current notions about pedagogy. Working with the ideas put forward by J. Lloyd Trump, whose report *Images of the Future* advocated multiple forms of instruction and use of technology such as television, Gores argued, "As instruction turns more and more to the individual, as children are grouped across class and grade lines according to their academic pace, the desire for space that can be divided or multiplied at will and at once increases accordingly. The time is fast approaching when not just a few, but many clients will ask that the design of an elementary school be more than the ingenious arrangement of fixed and uniform quadrilateral boxes."[109] The once-daring school plants with long corridors and classrooms located on one or both sides were now dismissed as hopelessly dull "egg-crates." Even the self-contained classroom, which many believed would bring the school closer to a domestic ideal, was rejected as inflexible and formulaic.

One of EFL's first events was a workshop conducted at the University of Michigan in October 1959 to design new proposals for high schools—which were then experiencing the first stresses of the baby boom—that were inspired by Trump's report.[110] EFL invited ten school architects, including John C. Harkness of TAC, William Brubaker of Perkins and Will, William Caudill of CRS, Donald Barthelme, and John Lyon Reid, to explore and adapt Trump's ideas for reorganizing instruction, class schedules, staffing, and use of technological aids. The other participants, educators, school administrators, deans, doctors, and psychologists, from the University of Michigan and elsewhere, debated the forms and ideas that the architects introduced. Caudill's presentation at this "New Schools for New Education" conference was a graphic narrative of a teacher breaking out of a box to embrace a large, loftlike space that could accommodate a variety of smaller areas. Caudill's ideal was the barn (Figure 4.20). In the final drawing, he envisioned a space that was economical, adaptable, and "creative": "The last drawing suggests a new kind of learning space, at least new to the public schools, but certainly familiar to boys and girls who have a nook in their attic, garage, or barn which they can call their own and in which they can pursue creative learning activities. It advocates the use of an enormous barn; good, cheap space that provides a large number of nooks, crannies, and cubicles for independent research projects. In essence, this barn for learning is a place in which to exercise creativity."[111]

The large, comprehensive high schools of the postwar era, although built according to some of the same principles of psychological engagement and using many of the same materials as primary schools, required increasing numbers of specialized rooms for science and subjects that were no longer considered purely vocational, such as shop and home economics. The complex needs of the secondary schools posed significant problems to the architect who aimed, as Reid stated, "to provide a framework in which

Figure 4.20. William W. Caudill, "The Busted Box," *New Schools for New Education* (1959), 21.

all learning experiences can be synthesized in a meaningful whole."[112] The most current embodiment of the new thinking about flexible schedules and decentralized planning, which EFL promoted, was TAC's Wayland Senior High School, in Wayland, Massachusetts, designed in 1958–59 and opened in 1960.[113] Built on more than ninety acres of open farmland sixteen miles from Boston for around 850 students, Wayland High School was planned to absorb the dramatic population increase the town experienced after World War II. In 1950 the town's population was 4,400, and by 1960 it was 10,000, having drawn new, mostly upper-middle-class residents to settle near growing missile and electronics industries, which proximity to Harvard and MIT propelled.[114]

Wayland Senior High School was the result of a yearlong examination and reconsideration of the relationship between educational process and architectural form.[115] To accommodate large- and small-group meetings, team teaching, independent study, and the use of media in the classroom, TAC created six clusters of subject areas with sets of classrooms grouped around a reference center (Figure 4.21). Instead of uniform classrooms strung along a corridor, which they dismissed as the "cells and bells" approach, TAC designed a variety of classroom spaces—from large lecture halls to small conference rooms—and relegated circulation to the exterior. With the reference center as the focal point of each cluster, the school more closely resembled a college campus with its varied disciplinary centers.[116] This, it was thought, would enhance identification with particular subjects and teachers. Small conference rooms grouped together with specialized lab or media spaces (the school had a closed-circuit TV system) and lecture rooms would, the designers and educators believed, not only enable but insist on individualized instruction. The smaller scale of each subject cluster and the building's nonmonumental, mostly one-story construction, arranged around landscaped courtyards and open corridors, also played an active role in engaging the students and teachers in a collaborative relationship. The ideal of student participation in the process of learning was at the heart of the TAC design. Harkness, the TAC partner in charge of the project noted, "Above all, [the design] attempts to create a sense of involvement. The students and others using these buildings not only observe them from a distance, but are brought in and through them and are thus forced to become involved with the design. After all, is not this the key to education, to get the students really involved in what they are studying, not merely in the passive memorization of facts?"[117] Benjamin Thompson, another TAC

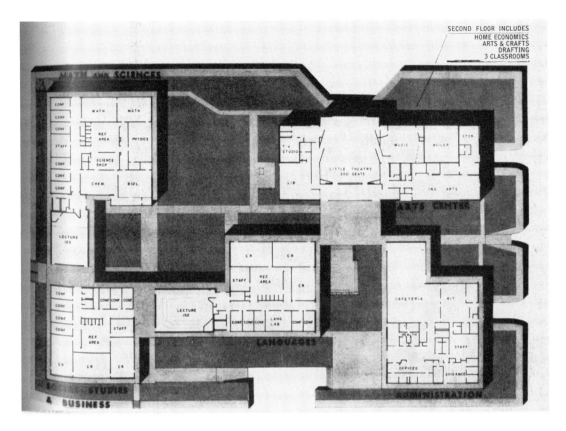

Figure 4.21. The Architects Collaborative, Wayland Senior High School, plan, circa 1960. Photo courtesy of The Architects Collaborative.

architect, stressed that both teachers and students must be engaged in discovering what he called "creative teaching": "Experience plus live information, and feeling plus intellect, are the building blocks of untried creative ideas. Neither talking nor analyzing, nor theorizing, nor reading about it will suffice alone: the teaching and learning of creativity is in the doing of things creatively. The teacher must do it and the student must do it too."[118]

Openness and the aim to encourage the effective use of space were also indicated in the provision for rooms that might meet the needs of the larger community. Yet TAC omitted a standard feature of high school design, the general auditorium that could seat the entire school for special occasions. Instead, Wayland had only a small theater that could seat 350, which was built into the Arts Center. For bigger groups, such as town meetings, the school used a large, circular field house devoted to the physical-education facilities. The laminated wood domed space had a peripheral track and could accommodate a variety of sporting and public events. Wayland embodied an open ideal that educators hoped would stimulate a variety of teaching methods and community activities and therefore give form to EFL's ideal of spatial and curricular "flexibility."[119]

THE OPEN SCHOOL

Encouraging individual discovery and intellectual freedom was the pedagogical aim of the open-plan schools. Instead of comprising boxy classrooms with bilateral lighting, open schools were large spaces with few walls or windows, partitioned with folding panels and lit from the ceiling.[120] The ideal of team teaching, mixing grade levels, and providing individualized instruction required temporarily larger or smaller areas that could be reconfigured quickly. The underlying points of postwar creativity studies supported a growing belief that children could learn most effectively if allowed to explore at their own pace and in differentiated spaces, an idea that inspired this new openness. Organized into pods, units, areas, and suites, the open-school classrooms were loosely defined and easily transformed. Earlier buildings had used glass walls and transoms and movable, or freestanding, walls to maximize space, but the open schools prized few, if any, walls. According to Ronald Gross and Judith Murphy, "Old walls should not stifle new ideas. Identical boxes must not enforce the same program on all students and teachers; each is a unique individual. Fixed furnishings must not quash spontaneous inquiry. Dismal, spiritless, and uniform decors must not blight a child's creativity."[121]

EFL argued that developing self-motivation and "giving the child more opportunity for creative work" would build independence.[122] In theory, the open spaces maximized the potential for continually changing arrangements, whether among a small reading group or a large homeroom. EFL invoked the nineteenth-century one-room schoolhouse as the open-plan school's ancestor while stressing that the pedagogical aims to differentiate instruction and provide a responsive environment were innovative. The physical design and appointment of the classroom were a reflection of the social principles of the open classroom. Herbert R. Kohl's influential book *The Open Classroom: A Practical Guide to a New Way of Teaching* (1969) urged teachers to consider how the spatial and material qualities of their rooms minimized an authoritarian role and maximized a democratic one. Even in the "confined and boxlike" rooms of older buildings, he suggested that teachers might redefine their classrooms away from the conventions of the "front," where the chalkboard was located and toward which the desks all faced, and the "back" of the classroom, possibly even allowing pupils to arrange their own places, to make free use of the class-room resource center, and to reassign the teacher's desk to some other use. Confronting the "spatial malaise," Kohl argued, went far in encouraging "an environment where many people can discover themselves."[123] In the open-plan school with large rooms, few doors or windows, central air-conditioning, and carpeting, these values of flexibility, independence, and informality were the starting point.

The open-plan school ideal relied on long spans and systems of low or demountable walls for internal flexibility. Eager to promote the adoption of the open system, EFL awarded a large grant to develop an economical, standardized building system they called School Construction Systems Development, or SCSD (Figure 4.22).[124] SCSD comprised standardized components that could be largely prefabricated and quickly installed. A team led by architect Ezra D. Ehrenkrantz, with researchers from the Stanford School Planning Laboratory and the Department of Architecture of the University of California at Berkeley, devised the project. Begun in 1962, SCSD secured the commitment of thirteen California school districts to develop and build schools worth $25 million.[125] SCSD aimed to save costs through the large-scale purchasing of modular systems that could be erected in many different interchangeable configurations depending on the specific site requirements.[126] In addition to implementing economical construction, the designers of SCSD hoped to create schools to meet the needs of a rapidly changing curriculum with open spans of sixty to seventy feet that could be easily partitioned and modified, without a monotonous row of classrooms along a corridor.

Figure 4.22. School Construction Systems Development (SCSD), component parts, circa 1967.

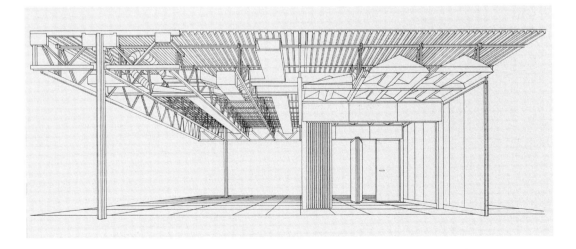

The SCSD project was directly modeled on the British Infant Schools built after World War II.[127] Ehrenkrantz spent two years on Fulbright fellowships in the mid-1950s at Britain's Building Research Station studying modular building and the mathematical patterns that might become the basis of a far-reaching system. The postwar English school-building program enjoyed widespread renown for its economical system of building from component parts. In the urgent push to replace war-damaged schools and meet their own booming population needs, British architects and educators, especially those at the Hertfordshire County Council, worked to develop low-cost solutions for specific educational requirements.[128] The centralized national system of education differed significantly from the local administration of American schools. Unlike the British architects, who created the entire design, SCSD hired individual manufacturers to develop the products. And, instead of giving a single manufacturer a contract for all schools built, SCSD solicited open bids.

One of the popular fears about the standardized, prefabricated structures was that they would lead to monotonous design. Although SCSD schools were constructed of identical components, individual architects designed the schools, and local contractors, which each district hired, built them. SCSD did not specify any materials or designs for walls, so the schools' external character varied, from glass to cast concrete and brick. Furthermore, the schools were arranged according to the needs of each institution. Unlike the British postwar schools, the SCSD system allowed for internal flexibility and variety of room configurations. The structures built (all of which were in California) encompassed small elementary schools as well as large high schools.[129]

One of the most adventurous examples of the open school was CRS's Paul Klapper School, Public School 219 (1966), in Queens, New York (Figure 4.23). With money from EFL, CRS had developed for a school system in Port Arthur, Texas, a huge dome floating on glass walls with no fixed interior walls.[130] When a bond issue for the Texas school failed, this model, which the firm called the Dome School, was adapted for several locations, including New York City.[131] As a demonstration school for the City University of New York's Queens College, P.S. 219 was an example of how open schools might work in an urban context. The school was designed for 150 children at kindergarten through second grade, who would be able to move freely with a team of five teachers. CRS believed that the circular form could better enhance the practice of team teaching. According to Caudill, "The uniqueness is that there will be a CONTINUOUS movement of children."[132] Under

Figure 4.23. Caudill Rowlett Scott, Paul Klapper School, Public School 219, Queens, New York, 1966. Courtesy of CRS Center Archives, College of Architecture, Texas A&M University.

the dome, the low dividers created four classrooms that could be combined into a single space (Figure 4.24). A freestanding mezzanine placed just off center made use of the vertical space for a second-story research center and created a curtained assembly area beneath. Beyond the dome were four outdoor courts for natural science, gardening, arts and crafts, and math and social science. The sophisticated shell structure, although technologically and pedagogically innovative, reprised the romantic image of the nineteenth-century one-room school.

Throughout the 1960s and early 1970s, examples of open schools along the lines EFL recommended were erected around the country. Limited studies suggested that students in open classrooms performed better on Torrance's creativity tests.[133] Yet the open schools faced problems of practicality and perception. Poor acoustics, the most notorious area of

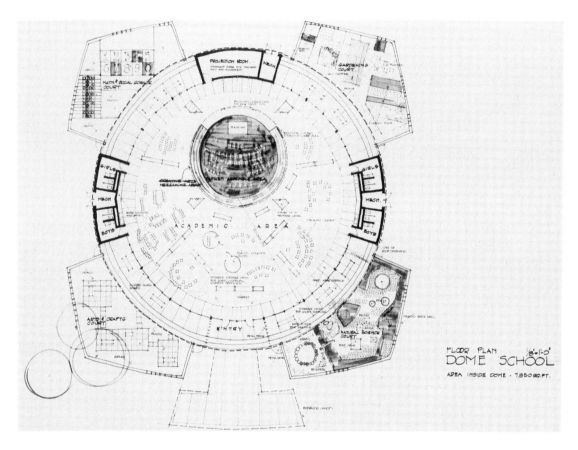

Figure 4.24. Paul Klapper School, Public School 219, plan. Courtesy of CRS Center Archives, College of Architecture, Texas A&M University.

criticism of the SCSD buildings, also plagued other open-plan schools.[134] Open-plan schools, which deliberately omitted the conventional walls and doors of older buildings, were theorized as vibrant spaces where individual concentration and wall-to-wall carpeting would make up for ambient noise. However, the acoustical problems from using television and film in rooms without doors, or separated only by thin panels or folding walls, were considerable. Furthermore, the physical openness did not by itself condition teachers to adopt the pedagogical techniques developed for these spaces. Larry Cuban has argued that the spread of the movement to use open classrooms with movable furniture, to teach using individualized instruction and research centers, and to allow students to move freely about the classroom was probably limited, although reliable national data was not collected at the time. This pointed to a larger gap between theory and practice. A study by John Goodlad in the late 1960s revealed that although teachers expressed enthusiasm for reforms such as individualized instruction, observers found that they actually geared their lessons to the existing norm, using primarily textbooks and seat work.[135] Although researchers recommended tables and chairs that could be easily rearranged and suggested that pupils preferred variety in the classroom, they noted that even in classrooms with "flexible" furniture, the furniture was seldom actually rearranged.[136]

Unlike the domestic analogy of the 1950s elementary schoolhouse, the closest model to the open schools of the late 1960s was the corporate office. Similar ideas about opening up the office with long-span steel frames preoccupied specialists in organizational behavior and interior design. In the interest of raising productivity and streamlining the flow of paper, businesses expanded offices, took down walls, and changed the arrangement of desks to form clusters rather than rectilinear rows. The idea of the open office, or *Bürolandschaft* (office landscape), that the Quickbörner Team of Eberhard and Wolfgang Schnelle of Hamburg, Germany, developed had far-reaching influence in the United States in the 1960s and 1970s. In order to heighten the efficiency of office work, to address changes the computer had hastened, and to reduce emphasis on management authority, Quickbörner and manufacturers such as Herman Miller proposed that the open office could be easily reconfigured to meet the rapid pace of change and to encourage a democratic style in which individual initiative was valued over corporate hierarchy. The same principles of flexibility, democracy, and individualism in the open schools were implied in the arrangement of the open office. But, also like the open school, the open office experienced acoustical problems, a lack of practical commitment to the system, and difficulty finding an objective means to evaluate the success of the open plan, leaving the effectiveness of the design uncertain.[137]

Postwar educators, architects, psychologists, parents, and community leaders all participated in the lively and public conversation about school and schooling, and all contributed to the recognition of the postwar school as an architectural and cultural type akin to the historical Little Red Schoolhouse.[138] Yet postwar American schools shared many formal similarities with English, Swiss, Danish, German, Mexican, and French schools of the era.[139] Shifts in planning from large, multistory buildings toward single-story structures arranged in long, fingerlike rows or clusters, and self-contained homelike spaces or open environments that embraced the very idea of change, were attempts to answer both an unprecedented demand for seats and educational strategies devised to enhance learning.[140] In this sense, the school participated in a wider postwar embrace of the romantic image of childhood and a desire to re-enchant the process of learning after

World War II. Yet the specific forms and materials of postwar American schools reveal a national preoccupation with making schools active tools for teaching and learning, and a means of fortifying the nation. Although larger social questions were interpreted and debated in built form, school buildings were never a pure reflection of either educational theory or policy. Instead, they reveal how their designers wrestled with creating optimal plans, how they explored the possibilities of materials and technology, and how they aimed to integrate the child's physical and psychological experience in the process of learning. They show how a wide constituency of designers, planners, psychologists, and local citizens believed that architecture, together with pedagogy, could affect and improve creativity. The discourse on childhood creativity informed the shape and design of the school and the classroom. Moreover, it was also evident in the materials used to teach art and science, and in programs and other public institutions that exemplified the ideal of learning through the senses.

5

LEARNING IMAGINATION IN ART AND SCIENCE

THE DISCOURSE OF CREATIVITY rephrased the progressive ideal of teaching through hands-on projects, which was written into the postwar public elementary schools through outdoor yards and self-contained classrooms with long counters and sinks. In these newly built institutions, special rooms for art, science, and shop put spatial and educational emphasis on teaching children to become productively creative. Yet if new elementary school architecture only appeared to reinforce creativity as an educational value, shifts in art instruction after World War II fully assimilated childhood creativity into the curriculum. Champions of manual training and progressive education who believed that firsthand experience gave vital meaning to abstract subjects incorporated the arts into their pedagogy in the late nineteenth century. Art education was a relatively elite practice before World War II, but it became an ordinary expectation of modern childhood in the postwar years. As the cultural value of the arts rose, the increasingly affluent postwar middle classes enrolled their children in special courses, bought crayons and finger paints for home use, and attended museums that were attracting and accommodating the bulge of the baby boom. Moreover, the postwar critique of American education, which the Cold War and the baby boom precipitated, brought attention to the methods and means of teaching both art and science to young children. In this chapter, I discuss how school arts, manufacturers of art supplies, and new programs and facilities for children in museums disseminated the educational values of creativity to children across the country. Because creativity implied individual thought and action, it was upheld as a fundamentally humanistic ideal and the epitome of a democratic personality. These institutions and commodities show how postwar approaches to teaching both art and science relied on personal experience, free play, and experimentation as means of stimulating children's curiosity and awakening their "natural" creativity.

CREATIVITY AND POSTWAR ART EDUCATION

The belief that children, especially young children, have unique access to unfettered expression was a consistent theme in Beverly Cleary's books about ordinary children who live in a middle-class neighborhood in Portland, Oregon, in the 1950s and 1960s. The two Quimby sisters, Beezus (short for Beatrice) and her younger sister, the indefatigable Ramona, are a study in personality contrasts. Whereas Ramona is continually praised and sometimes punished for her hearty imagination, Beezus, the responsible, well-behaved older sibling, is not. In a chapter called "Beezus and Her Imagination" from *Beezus and Ramona* (1955), it is Beezus who learns how to unleash her imagination while attending an afternoon art class at a local recreation center. Young Ramona, who drags a string tethering an imaginary green lizard she names Ralph behind her, immediately gains the teacher's attention and approval. In the chapter, as Beezus struggles to create a picture of her own imaginary animal, she learns that trying too hard to be creative can have the opposite effect, for "real imagination"—which her teacher assures her everyone possesses—comes in moments of unselfconsciousness. (In later books, Beezus and Ramona's father aspires to become an art teacher.) The dragon Beezus creates is a whimsical version of Ramona's invisible Ralph, with lollipops (she had earlier wrestled a lollipop away from Ramona) protruding from his back. In Cleary's story, it is the gentle coaxing of her teacher that provokes Beezus to make creative use of the day's trials. If imagination could be taught or could reveal itself at the suggestion of a teacher versed in both art and psychology, then art education had the potential to transform not only the individual but also society more broadly. The postwar union of art and psychology entered children's lives in forceful ways, therefore making creativity an ordinary expectation of childhood.

The desire to tap the deep well of children's creativity was the aim of art education in schools and community programs between the early 1940s and the 1970s. "Creative expression" and "creative art education" were two of the names given to a pedagogical emphasis on cultivating children's skills at depicting and describing their own feelings and experiences using art materials. Instead of following prescribed steps, copying historical sources, or learning or replicating artistic conventions, creative art education prized children's emotions and natural abilities at expressing them. Like progressive school design, creative art education had its roots in the progressive educational practices of the interwar era but achieved greater prominence after World War II. Creative art education was so dominant that it became the general name of art activities.[1]

In the late eighteenth and early nineteenth centuries, the romantic construction of the child as an unselfconscious "primitive" whose "naturalness" was increasingly admired instead of suppressed laid a foundation for the twentieth-century veneration of childhood creativity.[2] In the late nineteenth century, as children's drawings and paintings became the material evidence of a child's insight, artists, educators, and psychologists collected them. Jonathan Fineberg's studies of children's artwork have shown how modern artists who valued abstraction and the representation of emotion revered the naive qualities of children's drawings and paintings, and in some cases used them as a direct inspiration for their own work.[3] The frankness of children's art also appealed to psychologists. Children's drawings, paintings, and modeled or assembled objects thus constituted the serious evidence of their cognitive abilities, social relationships, and mental health. Aside from the diagnostic utility of children's expressions, children's art gained recognition and admiration for its unique qualities. As the cultural value of creativity grew, which these artistic shifts in the history of the modern era reinforced, widespread acceptance of a primitivist view of authentic childhood expression as a vital innate force was coupled with a notion that it could also be unleashed through careful direction.

Art education's romantic outlook gained force in the twentieth century. Franz Cižek, a Viennese pedagogue who established art classes for children in 1897, is often seen as the father of creative art education, although his influence in the United States was diffused.[4] Cižek's proposition that children should be taught to unleash their emotions and thoughts through art stood in opposition to organized drawing classes. Yet, although he intrinsically valued children's work as art, Cižek had clear expectations of how children's art should look. As scholars have shown, Cižek's instruction emphasized the values of flat, bold, deliberately crude imagery of contemporary folk art, which he "taught" to children.[5] Cižek's followers embraced his belief in children's art as a unique artistic product, but they also substantially modified his ideas and practices to meet the needs of their own time.

One of the figures most closely associated with creative art education in postwar America was Viktor Lowenfeld, a Viennese refugee from Nazi Europe, who was once Cižek's student.[6] Lowenfeld brought together the progressive ideal of childhood exploration through art and a psychological attitude that saw a developmental and therapeutic value in children's work.[7]

His 1947 book, *Creative and Mental Growth,* was forthright in addressing itself to teachers "who want not only to appreciate the creative production of children merely from an aesthetic viewpoint but would like to look behind the doors to see the sources from which their creative activity springs. It is written for those who want to understand the mental and emotional development of children."[8] In this book, Lowenfeld argued that children's art developed over successive stages that corresponded generally to cognitive and physical growth. From a child's first scribbles to teenage realism, Lowenfeld mapped the shifts in artistic representation and motivation. Although he rejected Cižek's emphasis on the aesthetic outcome, seeking instead to understand children through art making, he remained tied to an established ideal of children's creativity as pure and innate:

> If children developed without any interference from the outside world, no special stimulation for their creative work would be necessary. Every child would use his deeply rooted creative impulse without inhibition, confident in his own kind of expression. We find this creative confidence clearly demonstrated by those people who live in the remote sections of our country and who have not been inhibited by the influences of advertisements, funny books, and "education." Among these folk are found the most beautiful, natural and clearest examples of children's art. What civilization has buried we must try to regain by recreating the natural base necessary for such free creation.[9]

Childhood creativity as it was understood in postwar art education was therefore both "natural" and malleable.

Creative and Mental Growth was continually reprinted and revised, becoming the most important text of the period to inscribe the values of creative art education into the postwar school curriculum.[10] In somewhat dogmatic terms, Lowenfeld spoke directly to teachers, offering them a "tool" for understanding child growth. He told teachers to encourage children to express their experiences and feelings, and to avoid suggesting preference of one child's work over another. He also assured them that creative expression contributed to a positive integration of abilities in other areas, such as reading. Lowenfeld insisted that children be allowed to use their own modes of expression in order to keep their creativity "free," yet his book also included charts for noting a child's progress in self-expression and emotional maturation. In 1954, he published a similar book for families interested in cultivating happiness in their children through the practice of creative art at home.[11] Scholars have argued that *Creative and Mental Growth* found a positive reception because of the acceptance of progressive educational ideas during and after World War II, the presence of earlier studies, and the expanding interest in the arts at this time.[12] The book also invoked the particular postwar obsession with cultivating a healthy personality as a means of contributing to a positive future society.

The embrace of children's art as both an outlet for emotions and a window into their psychological state marked a significant shift from earlier rationales for incorporating art into the curriculum. Formal art education was first introduced in American public schools to support a post–Civil War economy in the 1870s. Whereas drawing for industrial or artisanal uses dominated in nineteenth-century school arts, using art therapeutically to examine and develop a healthy, democratic personality was one of Lowenfeld's main concerns. For Lowenfeld, independent creative work not only allowed emotional release, it also developed self-confidence and fostered what he saw as natural democratic tendencies in children.[13] Copying exercises and coloring books were examples of damaging conformity and submissiveness, whereas free drawings or paintings from the imagination or authentic experience were a healthy outlet for a child's emotions. Lowenfeld's book was primarily a guide to analyzing children's artwork, although he included summaries of growth analysis along with exercises and "laboratory work" in several media at the end of each chapter.

As others warmly received and repeated Lowenfeld's ideas, expressive creativity became the most prominent objective of art education, especially that of elementary school children from the 1940s until the late 1960s.[14] A curriculum guide called *Creative Art for Elementary Schools*, produced for the Denver Public Schools in 1949, rephrased Lowenfeld's notion that "art is visual and personal. It never copies nor repeats. It reorganizes ideas so they express the feelings, understanding, and maturity of the child artist." Moreover, it emphasized, "the democratic way respects the child's contribution."[15] Another handbook argued that the advantages of creative expression included developing individuality, organizing ideas into an acceptable form, and striving for satisfaction, which prepared children for American culture at large: "Our American system of private enterprise needs persons who have ideas, who can think creatively, and who can not only present new ideas but improve existing ones."[16] Creative expression in children therefore implicated much broader social concerns. The emphasis on a therapeutic art pedagogy that would release the child's emotions and experiences, reintegrating his personality in a "healthy" way, was given as the basis of a sound, inventive, and democratic society. Art education therefore had benefits well beyond the immediate artwork itself. At once a means to train a confident and democratic citizen, Lowenfeld saw art as a way to develop creativity that would be useful in other aspects of daily life. He noted, "If Johnny grows up and through his aesthetic experiences has become a more creative person who will apply it to his living and to his profession, one of the main aims of art education will have been fulfilled."[17] Abraham Maslow, echoing the civic benefits of creativity, ventured that creative art education "may be especially important not so much for turning out artists or art products, as for turning out better people."[18]

THE COMMITTEE ON ART EDUCATION

Lowenfeld's research for *Creative and Mental Growth* was taken from his experiences working with blind children in Austria, with African Americans at Hampton University, as a visual consultant with the U.S. Air Force during World War II, and through his contact with Victor D'Amico and Dorothy Knowles of the Committee on Art Education, a program based at MoMA, where D'Amico had worked as director of the Educational Project since the late 1930s. Formed at the end of World War II, the Committee on Art Education grew from MoMA's Veterans' Art Center, which D'Amico established to provide a therapeutic outlet and training for returning veterans. The Committee on Art Education championed the role of the artist-teacher; challenged what it saw as threats to expressive creativity, such as children's art contests and paint-by-numbers kits; and advocated for new research. Under D'Amico's direction, the annual conferences held at MoMA and various universities brought distinguished artists, architects and designers, philosophers, and critics, in addition to leading figures in art education, together in keynote lectures and discussion groups.[19] Lowenfeld attended regularly, gave formal lectures, and hosted the committee's annual meeting at Penn State in 1956.

Formed earlier than the National Art Education Association, which was founded in 1947 and eventually became the main professional organization for art teachers, the Committee on Art Education was concerned with the larger relationship between art and the public. It was founded to support the benefits of creativity to American society and was philosophically devoted to the transformative power of art education. At the committee's first meeting, in 1943, D'Amico stated, "Today, with our aim of art for all for the purpose of fuller living, education becomes a more complex matter. We cannot scrap art or the art teacher in the curriculum without scrapping America's creative power, the creative youth of our schools."[20] In 1960, when the committee issued a comprehensive statement on art education in the United States, it suggested that, in the face of profound social and political problems, including nuclear devastation, "the way to a positive solution and enduring peace lies in the development of the security of people, the increased respect for the brotherhood of man and the growth of the creativity of the individual which we believe is a sound basis for human understanding."[21] The committee maintained that creativity, cultivated by sensitive professional art teachers, could improve not only the individual student but American life and society at large.

The committee and other professional art teachers saw the role of arts education as increasingly removed from the technical applications that might benefit an industrial economy. Instead, the group stressed that stimulating creativity could have broader social relevance. International figures such as the critic Herbert Read, the poet Archibald MacLeish, and the psychologist Bruno Bettelheim gave addresses at the annual meeting that explored the social, political, and personal implications of creativity.[22] Each argued, in his own terms, that creativity was less a skill that could be taught than a deeply personal expression, which, with cultivation and release, revealed the promises of humanity.

A firm champion of the principles of creative arts education, the committee spoke out against popular efforts to diminish the meaning of the term *creativity*. In 1955, Milton Bradley raised the ire of the committee, which objected to an advertisement in *School Arts*: "We are shocked beyond words to see the device, a step-by-step method in making a turkey, under the title 'Creative Art Ideas.'"[23] The committee's response indicates that "creative art" was already widely used to describe many kinds of arts activities. As the popular embrace of the idea of creativity reached new heights in the early 1960s, divisions within the group and the growth of other organizations led to a restructuring, and then the demise, of the committee. Always an elite group primarily from the Northeast, the museum leaders, academics, and educators who comprised the committee voiced positions that largely reflected the interests of D'Amico and MoMA. Yet there is no doubt these views were widely held among arts professionals of the time.

ART IN THE SCHOOL AND AT HOME: BINNEY & SMITH

Lowenfeld cultivated teachers to encourage children's personal creativity, and the Committee on Art Education aimed to professionalize school arts instructors and to promote the social relevance of creativity. The Binney & Smith Company manufactured and sold arts materials and actively disseminated the image of creative education. As the maker of Crayola crayons and other products, Binney & Smith courted both the home and school markets.

The company, founded in the nineteenth century, originally produced pigments and then slate pencils, but its best-selling product was the wax crayon, which it introduced in 1903. By the 1970s, Binney & Smith claimed some 70 percent of the American crayon market. In the postwar era, a series of publications and free guided workshops for teachers gave the company a firm foothold in American schools, where the increasingly accepted values of creative art education helped to sell its products. Binney & Smith also appealed to parents to purchase crayons and other art materials for both school and home use. In both these markets, the company employed the rhetoric of childhood creativity to encourage the consumption of its crayons, paints, clay, and other items.

The wide reach of this company, and others, into the American school market shows how creative art education was put into practice along with advertising of art products and projects to elementary school teachers. In the 1930s, *The Drawing Teacher,* a folded newsletter for art teachers with art lessons using Binney & Smith products, reflected both traditional practices, such as drawing, rendering geometric shapes, and applied uses of art, and more progressive currents in art education, especially the growing value of free expression.[24] By the end of the war, *The Drawing Teacher* more thoroughly paraphrased the values of creative art education to build character and appraise the child's emotional development. A 1946 editorial with the title "Post-war Art Education" urged teachers to plan art experiences around the child "with the thought of developing in him an awareness of the fact that he possesses certain creative powers."[25] Binney & Smith's competitor, the American Crayon Company of Sandusky, Ohio, which manufactured Prang products, also cultivated school art teachers with a promotional publication, *Everyday Art: News and Comment on the Trend of School and Industrial Arts*.[26] The perspective of the company's designer and art director, Emmy Zweybruck, who had studied with Cižek and Josef Hoffmann at the Kunstgewerbeschule and ran her own school for painting and applied arts in Vienna, was evident in several articles on Cižek and other central European artists and stressed the importance of the teacher to the cultivation of the child.[27]

In addition to *The Drawing Teacher*, Binney & Smith provided art consultants whose expertise in art instruction supplemented general classroom teachers' limited training. Its art workshops were free classes that demonstrated art projects to teachers using Binney & Smith products. Although this marketing was indirect—the teaching staff did no selling—the

Plate 1. Philipp Otto Runge, *The Hülsenbeck Children*, 1805–6. Bildarchiv Preußischer Kulturbesitz, Hamburger Kunsthalle/Art Resource, New York.

Plate 2. *Winky Dink and You* "magic" screen, circa 1957. Photograph courtesy of The Strong Museum, Rochester, New York.

Plate 3. Holgate Toy Selector, circa 1952. Courtesy of Holgate Toys. Photograph courtesy of Jessica Helfand.

Plate 4. Bird puzzle, Creative Playthings, Inc., circa 1968. Photograph by James Goldwasser.

"What's ahead for Me?"

Plenty, little feller. Plenty. For you're a young American . . . and America itself is *young*. Young in years! Young in vigor! Young and strong in determinations! It's going places. And so are *you!*

That's why, in this land of yours, there's a great future for you. But we mustn't waste time! Once we've won the war—*and* the peace—we've got to start building!

Yes, sir . . . *building!* You know, that's the way our forefathers started this country. They *built homes!* That's the way they began to make America grow.

And we've been building and growing ever since. But along side what we're going to build in *your* day we've hardly begun!

In the years ahead we'll build millions of *new* homes! Beautiful, livable, economical homes—the kind Mummy and Daddy dream of for *you!* There's work to do—young man! Millions of homes to be repaired, remodeled, made new! Millions of wonderful *new* homes to be built!

And why do we Americans believe so in building? Because we want every youngster in our democracy to grow up in the healthy environment of a home of his own! But that's not all! We want you—our children—to know the blessings of American progress and prosperity. And both depend so much upon the building of these homes.

All over our land home building can be the sparkplug of our peacetime prosperity . . . the foundation of our country's growth.

Young America—that is what's ahead for you! A greater country, a greater future, a greater opportunity—because yours is the land of "Home, Sweet Home!" Certain-teed Products Corporation, Chicago 3, Illinois.

*C*ERTAIN-TEED

BUILDING   PRODUCTS

Plate 5. "What's Ahead for Me?" Certain-Teed Building Products advertisement, *American Home,* March 1945.

Plate 6. Edward Durrell Stone, playroom of the Stech House, Armonk, New York. Published as "Build It Yourself,"
Ladies' Home Journal, April 1950. Photograph by Ezra Stoller. Copyright ESTO. All rights reserved.

Plate 7. Robert Billsbrough Price, playroom in the Tacoma Home Show House, Tacoma Master Builders, 1954. Photograph by Dearborn-Massar. University of Washington Libraries, Special Collections, DM 6209.

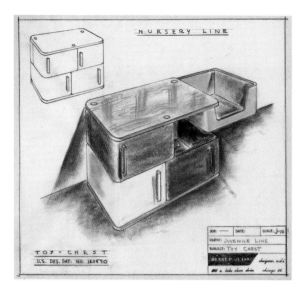

Plate 8. Henry P. Glass, Swingline Juvenile Furniture, Fleetwood Furniture Company, circa 1952. Colored pencil, pastel, and graphite on tracing paper, 33 cm × 35.3 cm (13 × 13¼ inches). Gift of Henry P. Glass, 1999.543.1, The Art Institute of Chicago. Photography copyright The Art Institute of Chicago.

Plate 9. Henry Smith-Miller Project, the Boxer Box, circa 1970. Courtesy of Henry Smith-Miller, architect. Photograph by Norman McGrath.

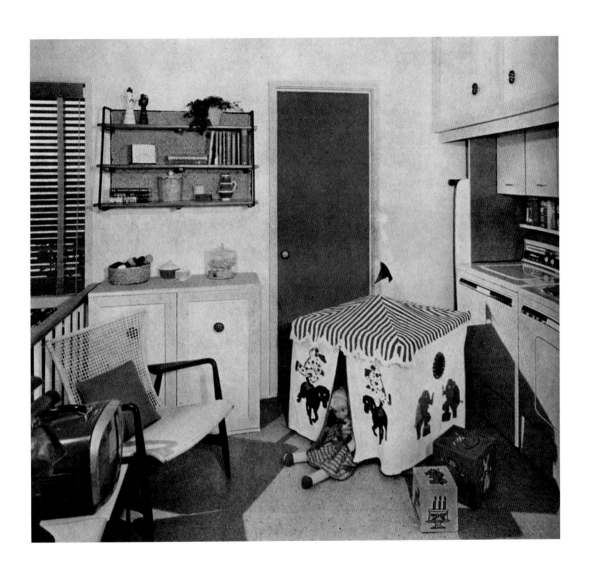

Plate 10. Circus tent playhouse, *Ladies' Home Journal,* March 1958, 94.

Plate 11. University of Michigan model classroom, 1954. Gold Seal Rubber Tile advertisement, from *Progressive Architecture* 35 (February 1954). Collection Centre Canadien d'Architecture/Canadian Centre for Architecture, Montreal.

Plate 12. School furniture, Brunswick-Balke-Collender Company catalog, circa 1954.

Plate 13. Perkins and Will, Heathcote School, view of a corridor. Hedrich-Blessing, H-16711-X, Chicago History Museum.

Here kitty, here kitty, kitty, kitty. Looks live doesn't it? It is to the youngster coloring it. His cat meows. He can [   ] it. Play with it. Make it drink milk. Sit on a fence. Or [   ] twitch his whiskers at people. Cats and things really [c]ome alive with CRAYOLA® crayons.

Imagination is as free to roam as old Tom. And there [ar]e certainly plenty of colors to choose from. Up to 64. [Unu]sual colors like silver for shining cat eyes. Blue gray [fo]r twitchy whiskers.

And besides all the great fun children have with crayons, these colors in a box make colors in the world a little easier to understand.

So why don't you give your child his very own box of brand new, pointy CRAYOLA crayons. Only pennies for thoughts. And cats of the most remarkable colors.

CRAYOLA is a trademark of Binney & Smith Inc. Reg. U.S. Pat. Off. © 1965 Binney & Smith Inc.

Plate 14. "Here Kitty, Kitty, Kitty," Binney & Smith advertisement, 1966.

Plate 15. Amy Kasai, *Jungle Gym*, circa 1940. Courtesy of the Estate of Amy Kasai.

Plate 16. Hardy Holzman Pfeiffer Associates and Peter J. Pearce, Curved Space, Brooklyn Children's Museum, 1975. Photograph by Norman McGrath.

company provided a service that had clear commercial benefits.[28] Begun in 1934, the consultant program grew rapidly in the postwar era. In 1948, Binney & Smith added five new members of the workshop staff and estimated that it conducted twelve workshops a week, with fifty teachers in each, who would in turn conduct art projects with an average of thirty-five students each, thereby reaching an estimated twenty-one thousand schoolchildren in a week. By 1956, the company estimated it reached more than half a million children in one year. When a workshop was held in Garwood, New Jersey, that year, the superintendent closed the town's schools early so that all thirty-five teachers could attend the fifteen-hour, three-day sequence of lessons on using crayon, tempera, watercolor and ink, finger paint, papier-mâché, and plaster of Paris.[29]

The Binney & Smith consultants, all trained artists, designers, and teachers (and all women), traveled around the country giving demonstrations and lessons that had been developed in a central studio in New York City. More than an effective means of encouraging sales of products, the workshops were a forum for teaching teachers how to explore their own creative potential. The company summed up the role of the workshop consultants as a "contribution to the increasingly widespread enjoyment of art by the masses."[30] The desire for training in creative arts and the commercial willingness to provide these services created a symbiotic relationship between for-profit companies and public schools. The American Crayon Company also held regular educational programs on the East and West Coasts, as well as an annual holiday exhibition in New York.[31]

Finger paint, which became a quintessential expressive medium for young postwar children, was popularized as a Binney & Smith product. Ruth Faison Shaw originally developed finger paint for the experimental school she ran in Rome in the 1920s, and by 1936 Binney & Smith was manufacturing nontoxic finger paints in the United States under the name Shaw Finger-Paints and Paper. (By the late 1950s, the Shaw name had been dropped when all products were subsumed under the Crayola brand name.) As her fame grew, Shaw sought out psychologists and increasingly promoted finger paints as a therapeutic material and finger painting as a therapeutic activity. A Binney & Smith pamphlet argued, "It is the experience of the individual, rather than the result, that has value. Naming a painting, or telling a story about it is optional and should not be dictated by the instructor."[32] Shaw traveled for Binney & Smith, giving demonstrations that were the basis of the art workshops. In each session, she recalled or read a story and taught specific techniques for using the fingers, hands, and forearms to render predetermined, largely pictorial scenes. Although she hoped to persuade teachers that finger painting was a "stimulus to the imagination," scholars have shown that Shaw's method largely directed the limited imagery and techniques of manipulating the materials.[33] Lowenfeld advocated and praised finger paint as a material with useful applications for younger and older children, but he warned that finger paint should not be used pictorially or to imitate nature.[34] Shaw and Binney & Smith's directions for using finger paint, although hitched to the values of creative art education, were therefore at odds with Lowenfeld's belief in the primacy of the child's experience as the source for all creative expression.

Binney & Smith, nonetheless, embraced the associations of creative release and promoted finger-paint products explicitly. A 1958 print advertisement for finger paint depicted a hovering butterfly shape cut from finger-painted paper and a single word: "Imagination" (Figure 5.1).[35] In a brochure aimed at teachers, the company illustrated a painting by a ten-year-old and suggested that finger painting "is relaxing and develops imagination. It helps children develop their senses . . . feeling, seeing, moving."[36] Other products, such as Clayola modeling clay, were similarly presented to educators as both play and a means of achieving cognitive and emotional growth.[37] As creativity became a ubiquitous (if not always measurable) goal of school art, the consumption of art supplies became big business in and outside of school.

Binney & Smith's foothold in the schools gave it recognition in the home market. In the late 1950s, the company added new products to its series of small packages of crayons for the young child at home (Figure 5.2). Crayons packaged in twelve-, forty-two-, or sixty-four-stick boxes were "designed to compete with other crayon items on the toy counters of the major variety chains."[38] Crayola had already produced packages of washable crayons, jumbo-sized crayons, and other items for home use. The Playtime box of chalk included an image of a smiling figure drawn in a deliberately naïve, childlike style, and the name emphasized that the product was

Figure 5.1. "Imagination," Binney & Smith advertisement for finger paint, 1958, Binney & Smith, Inc., Records, Archive Center, National Museum of American History, Smithsonian Institution.

aimed at hours outside of school. Binney & Smith products were, however, closely tied to the school-year rhythms and purchases of supplies. In September 1957, the company introduced the sixty-four-crayon box with a built-in sharpener, and advertised it as a gift or toy. At around the same time, it also spent increasingly large amounts of money on print and radio ads to entice parents of young children to purchase its products.

In 1956, Binney & Smith determined that children from two to ten years old primarily used crayons and thereafter concentrated its attempts to reach mothers and children in this market.[39] Two-color print ads called "Crayola Corner" appeared in *Parents' Magazine* and *Family Circle,* featuring art projects and ideas for different seasons and upcoming holidays. Advocating "quiet, constructive play" that used many Crayola products, not just crayons, the commentary fit in with the educational tone of these publications. Moreover, Binney & Smith also sought advice from parents and paid five dollars for

Figure 5.2. Advertisement, Binney & Smith, circa 1958. Binney & Smith, Inc., Records, Archive Center, National Museum of American History, Smithsonian Institution.

every tip published. Aiming for back-to-school and Christmas buyers, Binney & Smith put its money on print, rather than television, advertising until the early 1960s and even then maintained print ads.[40] These advertisements idealized childhood creativity and a rich inner life by using children's drawings and paintings as a signifier of innocent, imaginative play. A series of ads from 1966, which were placed in *Ladies' Home Journal* and *Parents' Magazine*, featured full-color, three-quarter-page images of either children drawing or their pictures. "Here Kitty, Kitty, Kitty" showed an oversize head of a cat, with copy declaring that the "imagination is as free to roam as old Tom" (Plate 14). Another, from 1964, bore the heading "I colored my pony green" and suggested that crayons accelerated learning and thinking. The question the copy then posed to parents—"Has your child the keys to open a door and explore?"—implied that crayons were a household necessity not only to be ready for school but also to develop the highly valued and abstract notions of imagination and creativity.

Parental anxiety about providing correct stimulation was the theme of several print advertisements. A four-color ad from the "Remember" series, which appeared in *Parents' Magazine* in 1961, showed a young girl coloring intently and urged the parent to "inspire the secret dreams and bold accomplishments that only children know. Give them the means to explore and relight your own glad memories. Act soon . . . before the dreams of youth escape, beyond recapture." Positioning crayons as an old standby in the wildly expanding postwar toy market, Binney & Smith described childhood creativity as precious and fleeting, and as an inward, imaginative activity. Nostalgia for a parent's own lost childhood and growing skepticism about the conditions of modern American childhood also reinforced the image of crayons as a refreshingly simple toy and an inexpensive investment in a child's future.

In the late 1960s, Binney & Smith mounted a campaign to promote crayons as "the quiet toy." Along with Lego, which advertised similar advantages, Binney & Smith promoted a vision of childhood that appealed to parents who were increasingly skeptical of battery-operated playthings.[41] The company continued this idea in the early 1970s in a television ad that announced, "Crayola crayons. They work on brains, not batteries." The themes of solitude, imagination, and invention were reused into the 1980s. A print ad reading, "Our toys run on imagination," which advertised kits for designing vehicles and interiors, implied that childhood dreams could have lasting effects upon personal ingenuity.

When Crayola turned to television advertising, in the early 1960s, it bought spots on children's television shows, especially *Captain Kangaroo*. Seeking a direct link to children who were viewing the program, Binney & Smith invested in commercials that appeared integral to the show. The company shot commercials on "how to make things," hiring Bob Keeshan, Captain Kangaroo himself, to narrate the spots, which would then air seamlessly during breaks of the program.[42] In seeking audiences of young children and mothers at home, Binney & Smith encountered a television market crowded with advertisements for toys and food. By the early 1970s, the company moved out of print advertising altogether. Promising both respite from noise and productive playtime, Crayola TV commercials from the late 1970s and early 1980s also used the themes of quiet amusement. "Circus" was a wordless commercial that showed a child absorbed in coloring, and in "Rainbows," a commercial for Crayola markers, two children worked side by side on their own projects. The tagline declared, "Crayola means creativity." In the mid-1970s, Binney & Smith produced a trio of commercials addressing parents with a developmental plea, babysitters with an argument for keeping children occupied, and teachers with the belief that crayons helped a child's dexterity, "but mainly," the commercial argued, "it's the exploring that personal world each child enters when he colors."[43]

The values of creative art education—exploring a "personal world"—boosted the fortunes of companies such as Binney & Smith. Yet, beyond the training of teachers and enhancing school-supply orders, Binney & Smith sought the lucrative market of family households. Putting its products in toy aisles, packaging sets for playtime and gift giving, and increasing advertising during the Christmas season and eventually on children's television programs, the company emphasized that play and leisure time could enhance a child's personal development. As a middle-class public willingly consumed art materials and the ideals of creative art education, it also turned to other forms of leisure-time education, especially in public museums.

MUSEUMS

Museums, especially art museums, participated in the important professional debates around children's art education and the discourse on creativity. Lynn Spigel has indicated that postwar audiences for the arts and art museums expanded rapidly in the 1950s and 1960s.[44] Museums enjoyed record numbers of new members and visitors, which also included a large contingent of baby boom children. The physical and educational changes in two major museums, the Metropolitan Museum of Art in New York and the Art Institute of Chicago, show how the postwar demographic swing affected institutions of high culture.

The Metropolitan Museum of Art and the Art Institute of Chicago each redeveloped "junior museums" that put lavish quarters outfitted with touchable exhibits, spaces for art making, and special libraries and lunchrooms at children's disposal. A junior museum was first opened at the Met in 1941 on the first floor, near the park entrance.[45] This plan included special galleries, a library, and a lunchroom designed to appeal to children and to "stimulate young imaginations and give the children some part in the life of the Museum."[46] In 1957, a major renovation more than doubled the children's area, to sixteen thousand square feet, which now covered much of the south wing on the first floor, including a special entrance for children (Figure 5.3).[47] The New Junior Museum, as it was called, contained expanded exhibition space, an auditorium, library, classrooms, a lunchroom, and a snack bar, and was placed adjacent to the Gallery of Models, a selection of diminutive forms of the great monuments. When Claudia and Jamie

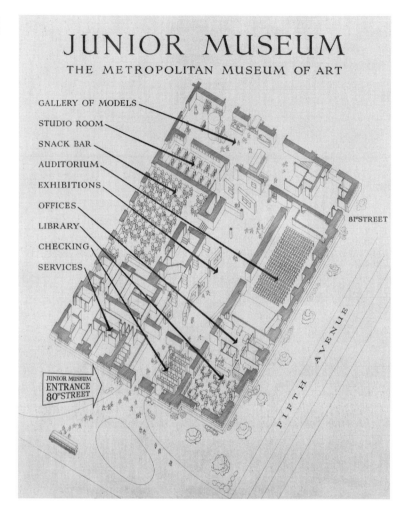

Kincaid hide out in the Metropolitan Museum in E. L. Konigsburg's novel *From the Mixed-Up Files of Mrs. Basil E. Frankweiler* (1967), they use the children's entrance, eat at the snack bar, and bathe in the restaurant fountain, all created in the recent transformations to the museum's plan.

The first exhibition to open with the New Junior Museum, in October 1957, was the "Age of Discovery," dovetailing with the New York City public schools curriculum. (The exhibition closed in June 1958.) In addition to displaying more than one hundred objects from the museum's collection, the exhibition made use of recordings, peepholes, push buttons, an interactive map, spices to smell, and touchable objects, such as a morion, a sari, and a delft tile (Figure 5.4).[48] Successive exhibitions of painting and sculpture also

Figure 5.4. "Age of Discovery—by Caravan and Caravel," October 11, 1957–June 29, 1958. The Metropolitan Museum of Art. Image copyright The Metropolitan Museum of Art.

featured audio recordings and push buttons, and included with the school tour was a film and a studio session of drawing with Cray-Pas, an oil pastel crayon.[49] Making the art museum a place that welcomed children with new spaces that suited their needs, tastes, and attention was increasingly the responsibility of venerable institutions.

The Art Institute of Chicago also made significant changes to its art-education programs after World War II. Although there had been a children's museum within the Art Institute, it was dismantled in the late 1930s.[50] In response to the Metropolitan Museum's elaborate example, the Art Institute sought to create its own space for children, to encourage and increase young visitors and their adult companions.[51] With the hope that exhibitions designed specifically for children might result in "a feeling of security and a desire to learn more," the Junior Museum was opened in February 1964, in a basement area the museum's kitchens once occupied.[52] The main space, designed by Arthur Myhrum around a fountain sculpture by Women's Board member Sylvia Shaw Judson, with flanking benches made of tree trunks, showed exhibits designed for children, such as one of children's furniture and toys in 1969. In the Little Library, under large George Nelson lamps, Eero Saarinen's tables were sunk into carpeted wells that provided ample seating for children examining books on art and artists (Figure 5.5). Even the lunchroom was used as an exhibition space.

Although the Metropolitan Museum and the Art Institute of Chicago dedicated unprecedented and lavishly outfitted space to children, their notion of exploration and learning was bound to conventions of art education that emphasized art-historical periods, libraries, and docents. The Metropolitan Museum was clear in its distinction that its Junior Museum was "not, be it understood, a children's museum," but rather a place where a child might find objects and subjects to interest him or her.[53] One official,

Figure 5.5. Junior Museum Library, children seated at tables, 1964 (E07258). The Art Institute of Chicago. Photography copyright The Art Institute of Chicago.

objecting to a list of talks and activities in the Junior Museum, noted, "This is not an amusement center. It is first and last an art museum."[54] In contrast, museums of modern art offered a vision of art education that emphasized learning about art as a form of free play.

THE MUSEUM OF MODERN ART

Under Victor D'Amico's direction, art education at the Museum of Modern Art expanded to reach visitors from the age of three to adult, and the program gained wide prominence internationally. The critical mission of the educational programs was to tap and guide personal creativity. D'Amico's experience as a teacher at progressive educational institutions during the height of the child study movement informed the kinds of programs he eventually developed at MoMA. Eschewing color wheels and perspective charts, he worked with settlement-house children in Brooklyn to explore imagery of their neighborhood and their own personal experiences. During wartime, D'Amico expanded educational programming and created the Veterans' Art Center as a therapeutic outlet. The People's Art Center, established in 1949, grew out of these programs and offered weekly instruction for both adults and children. Already in 1939, D'Amico had established the Young People's Gallery to give children a place in the museum. This space was devoted to the work and interests of children and occupied its own quarters in the new museum buildings of the 1950s. D'Amico created art classes for children who were once thought to be too young for artistic expression and developed festive annual art-making carnivals for children, nationally televised programs, and traveling exhibitions and slide talks that were circulated in cities and small towns across the country.[55] D'Amico, like Lowenfeld, held that drawing on personal experience, rather than copying existing models, encouraged children to explore materials, textures, and their own imaginations in works of art.[56]

MoMA's program of art education stressed that everyone could be creative if exposed to art as a freeing, rather than a rigid, experience. The programs that the education department developed focused on the relationship between experience and expression. Jane Cooper Bland, an instructor, argued, "Creative activity can be a vivid language through which a young child can tell about his experiences. Everyone needs some outlet for his feelings. Sometimes these may be so vague and diffused that the child has not been able to put them into words. The fact is becoming recognized that the more ways we have to express our feelings, the happier and healthier we are apt to be."[57] Talking about places, people, and feelings and having children paint to music were means of exploring ideas and materials that did not presuppose a formal outcome. For D'Amico and Bland, as for Lowenfeld, the rigidity and precision of copying images or using coloring books was especially danger- ous: "Coloring books at their worst may . . . destroy natural creative expres- sion, induce imitation, and injure the child's taste."[58] Liberating creativity and freeing imagination were thus at the heart of MoMA's educational po- sition, which was put into practice in the museum's regular art-education classes and in the exhibitions mounted in the Young People's Art Center.[59]

In the years during and after World War II, the educational program produced and circulated many exhibitions that carried the explicit message of Lowenfeld and the Committee on Art Education. "Understanding the Child through Art," an exhibition that circulated in various forms between 1944 and 1954, stressed that physical, psychological, and personal growth could be enhanced through art making. One panel stated, "Self-expression in the arts develops the individual, builds emotional stability, helps the child adjust to his environment." In the 1955 exhibition "Developing Creativeness in Children," the museum repeated the notion that children's individual dis- covery in art should be encouraged rather than hampered, and went further with panels that superimposed images of prescribed children's drawings (following a teacher's instruction) onto a photograph of Hitler Youth march- ing in unison.[60] Furthermore, MoMA mounted several special exhibitions that showed children's art, toys, furniture, and amusements, as well as ex- hibitions of artwork by European, Soviet, and Japanese children, which were held in the Young People's Gallery, on the second floor of the museum.

Although less elaborate than the museum's regular art exhibitions, the small exhibitions held in the Young People's Art Center suggest that in- stilling creativity had distinctly material and commercial implications. One of the earliest exhibitions was a show called "Pictures for Children," which was presented at the museum in 1941 and then circulated between 1942 and 1946. The exhibition was a collection of original silk-screen prints, including the work of prominent figures in the New York social-justice movement at the time, such as Mervin Jules, Elizabeth Olds, Harry Sternberg, and Sylvia Wald, as well as Juliet Kepes and Amy Kasai, a young Japanese American woman whose *Jungle Gym,* a serigraph on blue paper, depicted three young girls wearing strawberry-red dresses determinedly climbing the iron bars of a play structure (Plate 15).[61] The Progressive Era picture-study movement had also put an emphasis on didactic mass culture suitable for school and home. MoMA, as one of the first museums dedicated to modern art, em- braced its mission to educate the general public about modernism and the work of living artists.[62] The museum therefore promoted prints as original art affordable within the means of the middle-class family.

In 1946, D'Amico curated an exhibition called "Designed for Children," featuring prints from "Pictures for Children" as well as toys, furniture, and specially designed art equipment. In addition to the Eameses' plywood children's furniture, serigraph prints, puzzles, and art sets for painting, pastel work, sculpture, and collage were D'Amico's own designs for worktables and easels (Figure 5.6). A freestanding easel in either a red, blue, or yellow finish was devised for the child's playroom and came in three sizes to accommodate children from age three to twelve. With surfaces for working and display, the easel also had storage compartments for paper and a drawer for paints. D'Amico's design for a standard art table had a maple frame with a linoleum top. The jigsaw puzzles, created from color reproductions, were created to suit each age and psychological stage. These items had been developed for use with the museum's educational programs and its children's holiday festival. Thus, in addition to proper art instruction, correct materials played an important role in the creative work of young children. As D'Amico remarked in the press release for the exhibition, "While this [equipment] may be considered less important than the philosophy of teaching, or the creative activity itself, it is important because much of the misdirection in

Figure 5.6. Installation view of the exhibition "Designed for Children," June 11–October 6, 1946. The Museum of Modern Art, New York. Photographic Archive. The Museum of Modern Art Archives, New York. Photograph by Soichi Sunami. Digital image copyright The Museum of Modern Art. Licensed by SCALA/Art Resource, New York.

creative teaching can be laid to wrong materials introduced by the parent or teacher. For example, many young children get a bad start because their parents give them hard pencils or crayons and meager watercolors when they need equipment that is large and tools that are flexible."[63] By calling attention to the materials needed to stimulate creative activity, D'Amico also hoped the exhibition would encourage a higher aesthetic and utilitarian standard in children's furniture. Unlike other exhibits in the Young People's Gallery, many of the goods on display in "Designed for Children" were for sale, because the museum said it frequently received requests for these materials.[64] Although the exhibition was aimed at bringing art materials into the home, the museum also mounted a model school art room with bilateral lighting, wall easels, and storage. Like the progressive educational architecture that MoMA was concurrently promoting, the school art room adhered to the new ideas of school-building design and educational psychology. After its debut at MoMA, "Designed for Children" traveled to regional art centers and university galleries until 1948.

D'Amico's convictions that all children had creative capacity and that artwork should be the product of personal experience informed his creation of a series of holiday art fairs for children held at the museum, in a local New York City art center, and in a traveling international version. The Children's Festival of Modern Art, an annual event at the museum, began in 1942 as a way of demonstrating that children were capable of creative work when they were given motivation and proper tools. Renamed the Children's Holiday Circus, and eventually the Children's Holiday Carnival, D'Amico's concept emphasized the enjoyable and playful aspects of making and learning about art. In fifty-minute sessions, children entered a gallery to explore works of art, were able to touch objects and play with special toys, and then created their own paintings and collages. As the program became standardized, children entered through a specially contoured gate to allow only those from ages four to twelve (in early years it was four to eight) and no adults. Next, the children began a two-step process of motivation and production. To stimulate the senses and the imagination, D'Amico arranged a semidarkened room with special toys bathed in deep jewel-like colored light, while musical recordings enhanced the mysteriousness of the space. The forms and toys included a "color player," a pianolike instrument on which children created rhythmic patterns; a piece of shaped metal covered with fur that responded to the child's touch; a magnetic board for arranging designs; and a large-scale building toy with cantilevered projections and abstracted geometries (Figure 5.7). A large vehicle took children through space and time with a series of changing colored disks that were operated by steering, pedals, and push buttons. After experiencing the "Gallery of Toys," the children entered a studio area, where they could paint, produce collages, and work independently (Figure 5.8).

The Holiday Art Carnival was repackaged and sent along to trade fairs in Italy and Spain, and it became the Children's Creative Center at the Brussels World's Fair in 1958.[65] Indira Gandhi observed the carnival in Brussels, and in 1962 First Lady Jacqueline Kennedy presented the Children's Art Carnival to the National Children's Museum of New Delhi as a gift of the International Council of the Museum of Modern Art and the Asia Society.[66] D'Amico's belief in the universality of childhood creativity animated the carnival projects. Just as play was perceived as a means of developing coordination and social skills in children, artistic exploration was linked to the liberating experience of discovery, which gained considerable acceptance by the 1960s. The Canadian Government Pavilion at Expo 67 in Montreal included an elaborate Children's Creative Centre that consisted of a model nursery school, studios for music, art, and drama, and a landscaped play-

Figure 5.7. Participant at the exhibition "Children's Holiday Carnival of Modern Art," December 5, 1950–January 7, 1951. The Museum of Modern Art, New York. Photographic Archive. The Museum of Modern Art Archives, New York. Photograph by Soichi Sunami. Digital image copyright The Museum of Modern Art. Licensed by SCALA/Art Resource, New York.

Figure 5.8. Participants at the exhibition "Children's Holiday Carnival," December 10, 1956–January 13, 1957. The Museum of Modern Art, New York. Photographic Archive. The Museum of Modern Art Archives, New York. Photograph by Soichi Sunami. Digital image copyright The Museum of Modern Art. Licensed by SCALA/Art Resource, New York.

ground.[67] And in 1968, MoMA began operating the Children's Art Carnival at the Harlem School of the Arts, which served a largely African American and Hispanic population in northern Manhattan, at first during summer only and, after 1969, year-round.

Although the MoMA carnival embodied an optimistic view of universal creativity, it was a diplomatic gift that came with overt political implications. Scholars have noted how the museum, under the direction of wealthy Americans such as John D. Rockefeller, used modern art as a form of international propaganda against the Soviet Union.[68] Furthermore, Robert Haddow has argued that the Children's Art Carnival served an openly propagandistic role and gave the idea of creativity a political character, especially as part of the American Pavilion at the Brussels World's Fair in 1958.[69] D'Amico insisted that creativity in children depended on the quality of art instruction: "Italian children . . . are neither more nor less creative than American. Creative children are the result of an education that develops creativeness; uncreative children are the victims of indoctrinary teaching. It is that simple."[70] The image of the creative child that the museum envisioned was therefore developed against the image of indoctrination, social and aesthetic conformity, and other critiques of both American and Soviet culture.

The sustained efforts of MoMA to transform the way that art was taught to young people transcended national boundaries, but it was limited within the United States. The museum adapted the carnival idea for a television show, called *Through the Enchanted Gate*, which aired on a New York City NBC affiliate in thirteen segments between 1952 and 1953. In each program, children entered through a gate similar to the one created for the carnival, and viewers observed children, who had taken museum classes, making things under the guidance of two art teachers. At the end, D'Amico himself spoke to parents and the television audience, encouraging them to become surrogate art teachers with good listening skills. Although the program was relatively successful (one parent wrote to say that it was "the first meaningful show for children since the inception of television"), it was not repeated.[71] Within New York City, MoMA embraced school programs, especially at the high school level. According to high school art teacher Louise Kainz, "We were always closer to MoMA [than the Metropolitan Museum of Art,] because it gave materials to work with in the schools."[72] These supplies, 130 teaching sets by 1960, circulated each month. Despite such efforts at outreach, MoMA was criticized, even by those who benefited from D'Amico's young people's courses (such as Architecture and Design curator Arthur Drexler, who attended as a child), for its relatively elite audience of upper-middle-class children.[73] MoMA's programs, however, were emulated at other modern-art museums, which were equally invested in building imagination through the figure of the playful, creative child.

THE CHILDREN'S FAIR, WALKER ART CENTER, 1948

In May 1948, the Walker Art Center in Minneapolis, Minnesota, gave over the entire museum to an unprecedented "children's fair" (Figure 5.9). Five boxes from MoMA's "Designed for Children" exhibition constituted one part of this lavish event, which included exhibits of toys, games, books, and furniture that children could touch and use, paintings from the permanent collection, and films and exhibits of children's art from all over the world, hung low on the wall.[74] The museum also held art classes for young children to explore their own expressive potential. Through play and experimentation the Walker Art Center believed a child could find aesthetic stimulation that would encourage and nourish an inborn creativity.

The Children's Fair drew five thousand children during the first week (triple the normal attendance figures) and twenty thousand children throughout the month. The Gallery of Everyday Art, which the museum used to promote "good design," was filled with things that the visitors could purchase or order. Alvar Aalto's and Charles and Ray Eames's children's furniture, Babee-Tenda's Masonite feeding chair, and Dowcraft's tubular steel tables and chairs were displayed in the Walker galleries, along with outdoor

Figure 5.9. Children's Fair, Walker Art Center, 1948. Photograph Rolphe Dauphin for Walker Art Center, Minneapolis.

amusements (Figure 5.10). Toys from major American manufacturers such as Skaneateles, Holgate, and Playskool, well as toys and vehicles from the Danish designer Kay Bojesen, were arranged on low cases for children to handle.

The museum also showed experimental designs. Magnet Master, the Walker Art Center's "new creative toy," debuted at the 1948 Children's Fair. Hugo Weber's set of colored wooden balls and base was available only through the Chicago and Minneapolis design shop Baldwin Kingery.[75] Moving the nine large-, medium-, and small-sized spheres around on a base with seventy holes could become a homemade game or an exercise in pattern making. A similarly open-ended toy was Philadelphia architect Anne Tyng's transformable plywood Tyng Toy. The toy's twenty pieces, including dowels, washers, and pegs, fit together to create a rocking horse, a car, a blackboard and desk, a chair, or other constructions, with enough pieces for two or three simultaneous constructions (Figure 5.11). Tyng had already introduced the toy to young children in progressive schools but was working on selling it

Figure 5.10. Furniture, Children's Fair, Walker Art Center, 1948. Photograph Rolphe Dauphin for Walker Art Center, Minneapolis.

as a domestic amusement for the home.[76] In the promotional text, she claimed that with the Tyng Toy a "young sculptor or architect may create abstract constructions in three dimensions," and that the toy would develop, as Tyng said, "ingenuity and resourcefulness and [stimulate] the imagination to create life-size equipment for work and play."[77] Like Magnet Master, Tyng's design exemplified the small-scale, artfully designed toy that promised to enhance a child's creativity through play. When the Walker returned the exhibition set to Tyng, it estimated that some twenty thousand children had played with it, a fact she included in the toy's promotional brochure.

Figure 5.11. Anne Tyng, Tyng Toy, circa 1948. The Architectural Archives, University of Pennsylvania.

The Walker Art Center's Children's Fair paralleled MoMA's interest in selling "good design" to an ever-growing number of middle-class parents. The two museums also shared a similar practice of creative art education, which asked children to explore materials rather than to follow prescribed steps. A highlight of the Children's Fair was a demonstration called "Making Pictures," an art-education project that Walker's Carol Kottke had developed. "Making Pictures" emphasized sensory knowledge in creating pictures "that are good to touch as well as look at," using materials such as rubber bands, sandpaper, yarn, colored scraps, and toothpicks, as well as paint, chalk, and crayons (Figure 5.12).[78] By creating three-dimensional structures and activating the child's other senses, Kottke adapted the ideals of MoMA's Children's Art Carnival for Minneapolis children.[79]

The Walker's Children's Fair, however, reached beyond the immediate Minneapolis and St. Paul region. It required the collaboration of Chicago and New York businesses, and the event was covered in the museum's publication, *Everyday Art Quarterly*. Other museums, aware of MoMA's and Walker's projects, organized their own children's exhibits. The Contemporary Arts Museum of Houston, for example, planned a similar fair with art, toys, and books in 1950. In correspondence with Kottke, a codirector of the Houston's Children's Festival described it in terms evoking those in New York and Minneapolis: "Our prime goal in this exhibition is to create an atmosphere in which the child is given the opportunity to express himself creatively through the use of toys, books, etc."[80] As modern art museums readily

Figure 5.12. "Making Pictures," Children's Fair, Walker Art Center, 1948. Photograph Rolphe Dauphin for Walker Art Center, Minneapolis.

adopted the pedagogy of creative art education, they downplayed its therapeutic dimensions. Playing with materials and goods made the notion of creativity at once intensely personal and eminently consumable. Embracing the modernist ideal of individual expression through free creativity, MoMA, the Walker Art Center, and others cultivated a new generation of citizens who understood that learning required playful experimentation, that their artwork did not have to reflect anything beyond their own experiences and thoughts, and that creativity was a birthright. While art museums sought to accommodate children through special programs and classes, other museums already dedicated to children's interests redefined themselves in the postwar period to embrace the notion of learning through play.

"HANDS-ON" MUSEUMS

Although creativity gained status in modern art museums during the postwar period, children's museums had already been practicing this pedagogical aim. At the first International Council on Museums Biennial Conference, in 1948, Margaret Brayton, director of the Detroit Children's Museum, presented a report stating that the aim of children's museums was "*aesthetic, intellectual* and *social development* of children."[81] In an article published in the same year, she observed that "child-centered museums use craft classes, museum games, dramatics, music and story hours, laboratory demonstrations and experiments, field trips, and even archaeological expeditions on a simple scale . . . to provide a chance to learn by doing and to give the individual a means of self-expression."[82] Brayton's stress on the ideal of learning "by doing" to stimulate the creative development of the youthful individual became widely accepted after World War II. Even though children's museums were already designed and dedicated exclusively to children's interests, they expanded in the postwar era, both gaining in numbers and shifting in emphasis toward learning through play.[83] As institutions dedicated primarily to education rather than the preservation of collections, children's museums closely mirrored the broader value changes in education, and arts education in particular, toward firsthand experience. In this context, "hands-on" learning—with the emphasis on exploration—offered seemingly more direct access to the child's social and emotional development, because it yoked learning to the child's curiosity. The creative child was therefore constructed and embodied in the aims of public museums that encouraged autonomous exploration through play.

The origins of the children's museum lay in the Progressive Era, when Brooklyn, Boston, Detroit, and Indianapolis children's museums were founded to teach principles of natural history.[84] After the war, even these venerable older institutions were redesigned around the ideal of learning about science and art through discovery and play. The Brooklyn Children's Museum was founded in 1899 as an extension of the Brooklyn Institute of Arts and Sciences (later called the Brooklyn Museum). Scientific specimens from the larger institution were the children's museum's first objects, and other collections and models of insects and animals, as well as plants, shells, and minerals, were soon added. Anna Billings Gallup, who arrived in 1902, developed a program of firsthand exploration in the gallery and off-site field trips. In the 1950s, the museum remained closely tied to study of the natural world, sponsoring after-school hobby and science clubs.[85] Margaret DeWolf Tullock, then the museum's director, emphasized that it was practical application of sciences to everyday life that was the main purpose of the museum.[86] And this had explicitly Cold War overtones. Tullock stated, "It is the aim of the Brooklyn Children's Museum to be a vital, inspiring institution, where children will be given the opportunity to achieve an understanding which will take the place of unsteady thinking and will learn a patriotism which will defeat revolutionary doctrine."[87] Like Brooklyn, the Boston Children's Museum was closely involved with local children and local schools, sending exhibits into the classrooms.[88] The emphasis on seeing, touching, and exploring was already a fundamental aspect of the early children's museum concept, but it did not reach wider acceptance until the mid-twentieth century, when political, social, and educational shifts made engaging children's curiosity and interest in science a new priority.

Federal money for innovative educational projects that made science and learning appealing to children encouraged the growth of children's museums and science centers. In the mid- to late 1950s, substantial funds were directed toward improving science education, especially at the high school level. Although intended as a temporary, "emergency" program, the National Defense Education Act issued appropriations that rose from $115 million in 1959 to $459 million by 1968.[89] The push to develop programs to enhance students' interest in science was felt throughout the educational spectrum. John Rudolph has shown how, through the 1950s, research scientists, supported by the National Science Foundation, developed a vision of scientific education that emphasized the broad goals of improving general knowledge of scientific ideas and rational thought. In the reformist school curriculum materials they produced, science education was reoriented away from technological conveniences of modern life to the fundamentals of the scientific disciplines, which were increasingly portrayed as creative and humanistic.[90]

The Cold War tensions that touched every aspect of education joined larger social concerns that stimulated innovative new means of teaching arts and sciences to young children. At the 1965 White House Conference on Education, President Johnson commented that "exploitation of the challenges and escape from the perils of modern life demand new leaps of imagination and creativity."[91] Johnson's belief that education and culture could create a "great society" was implicit in his Elementary and Secondary Education Act of 1965. This legislation's most well-known program, Title I Head Start, proposed early childhood education for underprivileged children. Similarly, another program created in this act, Title III, Projects to Advance Creativity in Education (PACE), awarded money through individual grants to nurture innovative educational, scientific, and cultural resources in schools and communities. In its first year, PACE money supported an artmobile bus in Indiana, an outdoor school in Oregon, rural education in upstate New York, theater education in Northern California, and an educational TV program in Utah, among many other projects.[92] Placing cultural activities within a vision of educational and community enrichment, the Johnson administration hoped the cultivation of creativity would not only become a means of uplifting those at the bottom of the social spectrum but also contribute to the vitality of all kinds of institutions. Unprecedented government funds were spent on programs that employed interaction as a way of teaching. Together with a more general and ongoing shift in educational theory and practice, hands-on exhibits and lessons gained new support.

Michael Spock, the son of Dr. Benjamin Spock, became the director of the Boston Children's Museum in 1963. One of Spock's earliest decisions was to mount an exhibition exploring the insides of everyday objects, from a baseball to a city street. "What's Inside?" attempted to "move . . . away from displays in exhibit cases."[93] Spock also wanted to move away from pushing buttons. Asking the child to explore the exhibit and encourage firsthand contact with real things was, for Spock, "the only medium where all the senses may be excited."[94] The exhibit lasted five years and became a model for other institutions and for the concept of a hands-on or "interactive" program.

The call for hands-on learning was, therefore, an expansive ideal for museums in the postwar era. A 1975 report called *Hands-On Museums: Partners in Learning,* from the Educational Facilities Laboratories (EFL), the nonprofit corporation funded by the Ford Foundation, documented the growing phenomenon of "creative," "hands-on" museology in fifteen institutions.[95] EFL, which had promoted new designs for American schools through grants and influential publications, acted as an advocate for engaging children in learning through firsthand experience in museums and directed public attention to the educational mission and unique design requirements of these institutions. It pointed out that the spatial needs of hands-on museums followed a general pattern, from a house to a temporary structure to a new building (which was the case for Boston and Brooklyn), but argued that keeping a modest, child-friendly scale through use of zoned areas preserved intimacy and enhanced experience-oriented exhibits.

THE EXPLORATORIUM

The Exploratorium, founded by physicist Frank Oppenheimer in 1969, made play and exploration a means of learning about the forces of nature and human perception. Housed in the open loft spaces of the architect Bernard Maybeck's Palace of Fine Arts, originally built for San Francisco's Panama-Pacific International Exhibition in 1915, the Exploratorium was dedicated to understanding scientific and technical knowledge through the senses.[96] Its full name, the Exploratorium: A Museum of Art, Science, and Perception, suggests that "science" was never narrowly the focus; instead, play, perception, and experimentation were the museum's concern. Oppenheimer belonged to the generation of research scientists who aimed to change the public image of science and scientists during the Cold War. Although he had worked on prized government projects during the war, he was ostracized from university-level research by McCarthy-era accusations of Communist Party allegiances; he had taught high school and college science in Colorado before developing the Exploratorium in 1968. As the brother of J. Robert Oppenheimer, with whom he worked closely on the development of the United States' first atomic bomb, Frank Oppenheimer was well connected and had a personal stake in shifting sinister perceptions of science.[97] Oppenheimer's unique personal history and his background as a teacher informed both his vision of a museum that would teach the general public basic principles of science and his idea that experimentation was a vital aspect of human cognition and experience. In some of the earliest promotional literature, Oppenheimer characterized the museum as a means toward overcoming a fear of science and technology: "Today, science is so important and technology so complex and ubiquitous, that the public needs an environment in which these aspects of our society can be appreciated, understood and related to other creative aspects of our culture."[98] The image of science and technological invention as creative rather than destructive fields paralleled National Science Foundation–supported research on creativity and the reform of American school science curricula. Through personal experience and experimentation, along with straightforward explanations of phenomena, the Exploratorium temporarily transformed visitors of all ages into creative scientists.

The openness of the building gave the institution an unfettered space for exhibition (Figure 5.13). The museum was laid out in groupings that examined the human senses but without a predetermined path for visitors to follow. Clusters of exhibits explored perception and vision, sound, touch and dexterity, and smell, as well as mechanics, atoms, molecules, rays, environment, electricity, maps, and seismographic measurement. Early exhibits such as a forty-foot section of the Stanford linear accelerator and spark chamber made specialist materials available to the general public, but the staff also devised many of the exhibits using donated and scavenged materials.[99] Oppenheimer's model for the museum's exhibits was the genre of homemade science-fair displays. Thus, most of the exhibits were constructed on site in a workshop that was open and visible to visitors. Using ordinary objects and everyday materials to demonstrate and explain com-

Figure 5.13. The Exploratorium, circa 1975.
Copyright Exploratorium, www.exploratorium.edu.

plex ideas, exhibit designers reinforced the notion that anyone could explore the wonder of science.[100] The homemade qualities of these displays gave the museum the allure of a large-scale laboratory. The collaborative culture of the institution extended to the high school students it employed and trained as Explainers, who would perform such diverse tasks as informally guiding a visitor's encounter with an exhibit or dissecting a cow's eye.[101] Although it was never intended as a children's museum, and internal studies showed that half of the visitors were adults, the Exploratorium cultivated a youthful reputation and aimed to show that a childlike experience of wonder and play could make natural phenomena and human perception accessible to the general public. As a museum for adults and children to learn and play in together, the Exploratorium embodied the encompassing vision of creativity as a project of self-discovery and improvement that transcended age.

Artists as well as scientists devised Exploratorium exhibits to show a playful interpretation of natural phenomena. Artists designed some of the most popular exhibits at the Exploratorium, including a temporary exhibition called "Cybernetic Serendipity" (1969–71), a display of computer-generated graphics and kinetic and electronic exhibits;[102] and August Coppola's Tactile Dome (1971), a geodesic space that was darkened to enhance the nonvisual senses.[103] The Tactile Dome stimulated the kinesthetic experience by requiring the visitor to move through spaces of varying sizes, touching smooth and rough surfaces, experiencing chambers that were warm and cold, and crawling, climbing, and falling from one area to the next. Bob Miller, an artist, was hired to work at the Exploratorium developing exhibits. His *Sun Painting*, a series of abstract spectral patterns of color, was created by projecting a beam of sunlight through a rack of prisms inside the museum and onto Mylar mirrors that visitors could walk around and touch. Although the Exploratorium had included art exhibits when it opened, the museum began to sponsor artist residencies only in the mid-1970s.[104] The residencies encouraged collaboration between the museum's staff and visiting artists, who produced site-specific works. San Francisco artist Ruth Asawa, already known for her work with children, collaborated with visitors to create a variety of spheres and domes using milk cartons (Figure 5.14).[105] William Parker created a large tube in which drops of glowing argon gas rained. Richard Register created the large cement Tactile Tree, and the poet Muriel Rukeyser developed graphic exhibits on the role of perception in language. An aeolian harp by Doug Hollis on the Exploratorium's roof captured and magnified the natural resonance of the wind. Showing natural phenomena through the work of artists, the Exploratorium challenged the visitor to understand his or her environment in creative terms. Moreover, the art experiments lent weight to the museum's position that the exhibits should not have a predetermined lesson that the viewer then "discovered."

Oppenheimer was outspoken in his belief that museums could play a distinctive role in American education. He argued that objects—or props, as he called them—installed in a welcoming public space offered a kind of engagement that the classroom could not. In striving to make visitors understand science and technology as the outgrowth of deeply human values, Oppenheimer stressed that museums did not involve "work" but were places of pleasure or "sightseeing," where a casual encounter with an object could transform a visitor's understanding. In a 1970 report on precollege science, he stated:

> **But museums should be playful. Animals learn about their culture through play, and so do humans. Children become familiar with both the tools and customs of society through play. Play involves using the forms and instruments of society out of context and can thus reduce fear. Acculturation is apparently universally achieved by play. In our era of incessant and rapid cultural change, legitimizing play in the appropriate kind of educational institution is essential for adults as well as children. This aspect of museums, the fact that they appear more as play than as work, should therefore add rather than detract from their value.[106]**

Instead of dismissing entertainment, Oppenheimer used it pedagogically. Play, he argued, and manipulation of exhibits, engaged the visitor's curiosity and made learning fun. In 1974, the comic book character and neighborhood terror Dennis the Menace visited the Exploratorium (Figure 5.15). In "Visit to the Exploratorium," Dennis makes a "Design-o-gram" with a colored pen and a pendulum motion, explores optical illusions and the principle of momentum, and investigates the Ames Room with its distorted, sloping floor, and the museum's strobe room. Even in a space that

Figure 5.15. *Dennis the Menace*, "Visit to the Exploratorium," 1974. *Dennis the Menace*® printed by permission of Hank Ketcham Enterprises, Inc., 2012.

was designed for experimentation, Dennis, in his exuberance, re-interprets the exhibits' open-ended lessons. When an Explainer asks him to say something into a microphone to make a voice-print, Dennis yells to his beleaguered neighbor, Mr. Wilson, "Hi, Mr. Wilson! We're havin' fun here!"[107]

Children's letters to the museum expressed the same sentiment. In one from 1970, a fourth-grader observed laconically, "I don't have much to say, except that I liked the exploratorium very much. I learned many many things in a fun way."[108] By making science approachable and fun, the Exploratorium's hands-on position put agency and engagement in the visitor's experience. The Exploratorium transcended the established science museum and children's museum genres. It stressed the physical manipulation of exhibits and the interaction between art and science in human sensory perception. With an emphasis on manipulation and experimentation, the Exploratorium became known for its unorthodox approach to museum pedagogy and exhibit design. As the designers Edwin Schlossberg and Brent Saville were planning the exhibits for the new Brooklyn Children's Museum, in the early 1970s, they visited the Exploratorium, and Schlossberg wrote to Oppenheimer, "Without exaggeration, the Exploratorium is the most interesting place for children that I have seen in the United States."[109]

THE BROOKLYN CHILDREN'S MUSEUM

Large residential structures were the early locations of both the Brooklyn and Boston children's museums, with space allocated for collections, projects, libraries, and auditoriums. In the case of the Brooklyn Children's Museum, limited space and the unstable condition of the museum's two dwellings required a new building in the 1960s.[110] The long-discussed new home of the Brooklyn Children's Museum was finally begun in 1968 and was very nearly finished in 1975 when last-minute construction problems and the New York City financial crisis halted the opening, which was delayed until May 1977.[111] Both a temporary structure called Project MUSE (located nearby in a former automobile showroom and pool hall) and the rebuilt permanent space put new emphasis on learning through free play and exploration.

In reports developed in the early and mid-1960s, the trustees of the Brooklyn Children's Museum stressed that the new museum would not only house museum collections but also "provide facilities for the child to

participate creatively in his own developing awareness of self and environment."[112] The architectural firm Hardy Holzman Pfeiffer Associates, which
designed both MUSE and the new museum, made discovery the buildings'
parti.[113] By situating the museum, whose construction finally began in 1972,
partially belowground, with one corner of the museum exposed in a sunken
courtyard, it was an extension of the public play space in Brower Park. Thus,
the new museum was sited to engage the public park rather than disrupt
it. Partially burying the museum's boxlike concrete structure opened up the
space to many levels that were not readily apparent from the street but were
gradually revealed inside (Figure 5.16). Echoing the trustees, the architects
advanced the idea that children, and society, would benefit from self-discovery. In a preliminary program analysis, Hardy Holzman Pfeiffer Associates
put special emphasis on urban children, implying the increasingly African
American and Hispanic surrounding neighborhood that lobbied hard to
keep the museum in its original location: "If they are to make a constructive
contribution to society, these children must also learn more of the world of
people. Their quick response and keen observation can be joined with self-
teaching activities to assist the development of individual identity."[114] To this
end, the firm deliberately exposed the building's structure and mechanicals

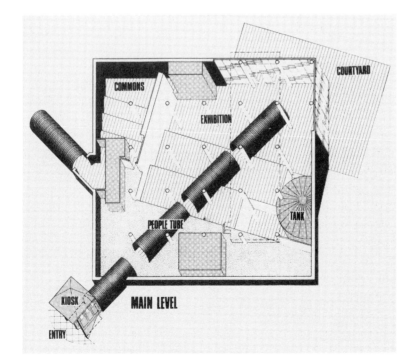

Figure 5.16. Hardy Holzman Pfeiffer
Associates, Brooklyn Children's Museum,
1975, plan. Courtesy of Holzman Moss Bottino
Architecture (HHPA).

to show visitors that the building itself was a working machine.[115] In the open space, the three floors encouraged simultaneous activity and allowed children to see each other. The architects also included playfully repurposed everyday objects. A former bridge kiosk, interstate highway sign, grain silo, and steel gas tank were given new uses as the building's front entrance, signage, emergency exit, and theater. An outdoor amphitheater on the sod roof had bleacher seats and an undulating poured-concrete wall that was designed expressly for graffiti, according to Norman Pfeiffer, to give "children a chance to express their artistic feelings, which is in keeping with the free spirit of the museum" (Figure 5.17).[116]

As it had done at the temporary MUSE building, Hardy Holzman Pfeiffer placed the axis of the Brooklyn Children's Museum on the diagonal to create numerous small-scale residual spaces around a series of corrugated steel culverts they called a "People Tube," which bisected the three floors (Figure 5.18). The People Tube enclosed a 180-foot ramp and a flowing stream where children could play and learn how water generates power

Figure 5.17. Hardy Holzman Pfeiffer Associates, Brooklyn Children's Museum, 1975, view. Photograph by Norman McGrath.

and nourishes plant and animal life. A 320-foot neon helix showing the light spectrum illuminated the darkened ramp. Displays for children from ages six to fourteen addressing sound, power, visual perception, science, and art were tucked into the interlocking spaces on each level. Edwin Schlossberg, who devised the exhibits as a "participatory learning environment" (the individual exhibits were designed by Brent Saville), included a greenhouse with a soil-preparation station, a ripple tank that allowed children to experiment with waves and light, a refurbished 1924 calliope powered by a blower, and an operable hydraulic lift. Other power-generating devices, such as a Nebraska windmill and a grinding stone attached to a waterwheel in the People Tube stream, gave children the opportunity to experiment with simple machines. Grain grown in the museum's greenhouse, for example, could be milled into flour in the People Tube.

Creating an awareness of how and why things work was the motivation of the participatory learning environment. In a program statement, Schlossberg noted that he aimed to move away from the button or lever

Figure 5.18. Hardy Holzman Pfeiffer Associates, People Tube, Brooklyn Children's Museum, 1975. Photograph by Norman McGrath.

experience and the static display case: "If we supported the static display case method we would be contributing to the disassociation of people from their environment. We would be telling children that things as they are in the world today are all they can expect to have. We would be accepting the world of inevitability and passive relationship. We cannot do this."[117] Nonetheless, the museum maintained a large permanent collection, aspects of which were visible in glass-fronted storage cabinets and in a series of "Occurrences," objects or vignettes installed in unusual places throughout the museum, which children could discover on their own.[118]

One of the most striking exhibits was a series of three huge, labyrinthine plastic models of molecules that children could tunnel into and climb. Called "Curved Space," developed by Peter J. Pearce, the structures of a diamond and protein molecules were expanded several billion times and rendered in a polycarbonate plastic on an aluminum frame (Plate 16).[119] The largest section of Curved Space was twenty feet high and more than twenty feet long, and accommodated both children and adults. Beyond the entertainment value of the structure, the designers likened a child climbing through the space to a free electron moving within a diamond's molecular structure.[120] Molecules and ripple tanks were subjects that formed part of a broad and reformist vision of the post-Sputnik high school science curriculum.[121] Encountering these instruments in a children's museum setting therefore emphasized the free exploration of patterns and structures. Like the physicists and biologists who devised the new curriculum and the Exploratorium, the aim of the Brooklyn Children's Museum was not to put children on an early path to a science profession but rather to encourage play, experimentation, and curiosity as means of building a knowledgeable general public.

Because the Brooklyn Children's Museum was the world's first children's museum, its radical transformation was widely noted, but it was hardly alone. In the 1970s, several children's museums expanded or remodeled their buildings to enhance the hands-on quality of their exhibits. The Indianapolis Children's Museum, for example, opened a large new facility in 1976 with touchable exhibits, a ride-on fire engine, a Conestoga wagon, a limestone cavern, an Egyptian tomb, and a nineteenth-century train car. The Boston Children's Museum also received a new building with elaborate exhibits and resource centers in a renovated warehouse structure on the Boston waterfront in 1979. The "hands-on" discourse in children's education and museum pedagogy was widely accepted by the late 1970s. It had begun decades earlier in Progressive Era programs that stressed the sense of awe and discovery, but by the 1970s it depended upon an increasingly complex museum apparatus that had expanded to meet the demands of the postwar era.[122] If stimulating wonder was still an abiding desire of educators, it now intersected with problems the baby boom and the Cold War had hastened. As the discourse of creativity enveloped science as well as art, hands-on projects and exhibits placed agency in the child's desire to know and to create, rather than in the teacher's desire for him or her to acquire a predetermined set of facts. The ethos of learning through entertainment and revelation was, nonetheless, a carefully designed object lesson.

The forms of creative art education for home and school and the hands-on techniques for teaching science that I have discussed imagined a postwar psychological being whose latent creativity could be revealed under the guidance of correct methods. At the same time, however, these objects and spaces rephrased the romantic doctrine of sensory training. The powerful combination of these two notions made the promise of children's creativity at once novel and natural. If the creativity discourse was a useful means of selling art supplies to parents and teachers, it was also a guiding belief that changed not only mass consumption but also public-education programs and the ways in which museums that served children understood and approached their mission. Through the seemingly unremarkable acts of drawing with crayons, finger painting, or visiting a museum with parents or on a school trip, the creative child embodied a vision of postwar hopefulness.

In 1946, Leonard S. Kenworthy, who had worked in Berlin under the American Friends Service Committee in the early 1940s, described the postwar child in war-devastated countries as a person with the right to happiness, education, and individual development. "There is a greater awareness than ever before," he wrote,

> **that such happiness and growth depend upon the child's physical and mental health; upon the exercise of discipline developed from within rather than imposed from without; upon the encouragement of individual abilities as well as the acquisition of the skills needed by all; upon an appreciation of beauty and a chance to develop self-expression through some form of creative art; upon the ability to communicate with others; upon an understanding of the scientific age in which we live and an ability to adjust to it and make use of it for worthy ends; and upon an intelligent participation in the life of society or societies of which one is a member.**[123]

Kenworthy's vision of postwar childhood as an opportunity both to understand and to contribute to society as an informed and creative individual was equally a statement on the possibilities for humanity in the aftermath of wartime destruction. In the years that followed, these ideals were increasingly the ordinary expectations of American, and European, children and their parents. As a force for individual development and national regeneration, the pursuit of creativity gained increasing acceptance in children's early training at home, at their schools, and in their leisure time. Encouraging children to explore art and science to liberate their individuality and develop their own subjectivity was an attempt to mold a new generation to accept the complex demands of citizenship in the era of the Cold War. Investment in children's creativity, then, was an expression of faith in this postwar future.

CREATIVITY, IN THE POSTWAR IMAGINATION, implied individual thought and action, and was widely considered a fundamentally human and democratic quality. If, as many suggested, childhood creativity was an untapped natural resource, then it could be cultivated, harvested, and consumed, making the creative child both a sentimental and a strategic figure. The project of the creative child was, and still is, the dream and the work of adults.[1] As a group of educational psychologists observed in 1967, "We are all potentially creative, but only those who have become creative realize it. One of the best ways to cultivate our own creativity is to help children cultivate theirs."[2] Parents, then, desired creativity for their children and for themselves. Creativity was embedded in an ambitious postwar, middle-class ideal of raising exceptional children, but it also played a broader and more nationalistic role in attempting to ensure competitiveness. At an ideological level, creativity provided a foil for the preoccupations of the age. Positioned against the critique of social conformity, creativity stood for an admirable individuality. In contrast to rote learning, it embodied pleasure and curiosity. In the face of rising political tensions and fears of weakness, creativity was a useful myth of revitalized and endless national ingenuity.

I have argued that material goods participated actively in the dissemination and consumption of creativity at a quotidian level. The construction toys, playrooms, classrooms, stacking school furniture, and working experiments at the Brooklyn Children's Museum and the Exploratorium each in their own way contributed to the growth and cultural acceptance of childhood creativity. While psychological research advanced the social acceptance of these things, their own material properties animated the discourse and, through manipulation, realized the figure of the creative child. The six slots in stiff cardboard rectangles or alnico magnets created play possibilities from industrial materials; lightweight plywood or polypropylene seats made school furniture reasonably easy to move; open plans made possible the idea of dedicated play areas even in small houses; and a long stream of cool water in a dark tunnel enticed touch. Undoubtedly, of course, postwar children devised other, darker schemes for their toys. Children played without playrooms, teachers did not transform their classrooms into living rooms for learning, and both children and adults may well have found even the most open museums stifling. Nonetheless, the design of these objects and spaces, and other forms of the proliferating material culture of postwar childhood, engendered in the idea of childhood creativity a strongly sensory engagement. These object lessons redefined the cultural mythology around creativity away from an elite concern of the interwar years to a fully consumable and aspirational notion that has not yet abated.

The cultural myth of creativity has roots in the discourses around individuality and invention that flourished in the eighteenth and nineteenth centuries and has been continually reenvisioned to suit our needs. Exceptionalist notions of American culture devised well before the postwar era persist, especially around the idea of innovation and inventiveness, which are often synonyms for creativity. In business, in education, and in playthings, the rhetoric of creativity is ubiquitous. It promotes a vast range of goods and services for children and adults, corporate self-image, pedagogical theory, and individual output. The pervasiveness of the creativity discourse suggests that we remain heavily invested in its promises. As an advertisement for Mega Bloks (2006) suggests, creativity—in the form of children's construction toys—will grow up and "save the world" (Figure E.1).

The importance of play in stimulating children's creativity and imagination is still a central theme for research psychologists, educators, and designers. The belief that children no longer have the time to play because of academic preschools and kindergartens, a screen culture of video games, an epidemic of childhood obesity, and a fear that children do not have the same freedom that earlier generations experienced has informed efforts to create opportunities for free play in schools and communities. A push to build "creative playgrounds," such as the Rockwell Group's Imagination Playground at Burling Slip (2010), in Lower Manhattan, is under way, although the expense of the nonstandardized equipment and a trained play associate may inhibit its expansion.[3] The popular psychological literature behind this movement maintains that more unstructured time is beneficial for children's mental and cognitive health, but the precise benefits of imaginative play remain relatively difficult to prove objectively.[4] Yale researchers

Once upon a time, there lived a creature named Creativity.

When Creativity was young, he was allowed to explore
the farthest reaches of his imagination.

No one told him what noise his train was supposed to make.
So he made it sound like a cockatoo.

And nobody told him that his dragon was scary.
So he had it over for pizza.

Then one day, when Creativity was all grown up,
people throughout the land turned to him for inspiration
in good times and bad.

All the world rallied around Creativity to solve their
most confounding problems.

And that's how Creativity saved the world.

Creativity to the Rescue.™ MEGA™
We believe creative toys can make the world a better place. If you agree, visit megabloks.com
© 2006 MEGA Brands Inc.

Figure E.1. Mega Bloks advertisement, 2006.

Dorothy and Jerome Singer, leading voices for the cognitive benefits of play, stress that they "assume that early imaginative play *is* a precursor of later fanciful thought, and we propose that such play has particular adaptive features. When children engage in symbolic games they are practicing mental skills that will later stand them in good stead, just as practice in walking, balancing, or swimming aids the development of motor skills."[5]

Play in childhood, and its relationship to creativity in adulthood, is part of this position, although it, too, remains hard to measure. Brian Sutton-Smith and others have suggested that we tend to idealize play and have assumed its benefits.[6] Furthermore, he charges that the idealization of imagination encompasses the sentimental preferences for wooden or homemade toys over plastic, and nonviolent imagery over fantasy or phantasmagoria.[7] The sacralization of creativity in the twenty-first century now allows for plastic toys and even video games, but it remains steadfast, in part because of the adult investment in creativity's promises.[8]

Since the 1950s, the psychological research on creativity has grown and diversified in ways that reflect an even stronger interest in applied creativity's dividends. Mark A. Runco, a leading researcher, estimates that ten thousand research articles on creativity have appeared since 1960, and some six hundred books just in the 1990s.[9] Business and management, early promoters of creativity research in the 1950s and 1960s, have become some of its biggest consumers. The late twentieth-century business cliché "Think outside the box" has become management doctrine. In 2002, Richard Florida identified a highly educated, mobile, and influential workforce that he called the "creative class," who, he suggests, are the key not only to new economic expansion but also to a transformation of the labor market and a re-definition of social class.[10] These "no-collar" knowledge workers—scientists and engineers, as well as professional artists, musicians, and writers—are, in Florida's vision, transforming business culture. Similarly, the ideas of Alex F. Osborn and other postwar businesspeople who stressed the economics of creativity continue to live on not only in advertising and entrepreneurship but also in the realm of management. For example, a 2010 IBM survey of 1,500 global chief executive officers in sixty countries and thirty-three fields found that creativity was the most important leadership characteristic for managing a complex future.[11]

Just as echoes of the postwar era's faith in creativity linger, so do a host of anxieties around its perceived loss. In 1996, the Alliance of Artists Communities, with funding from major American arts foundations, held a symposium called "American Creativity at Risk." The conference aimed to "[restore] creativity as a priority in public policy, cultural philanthropy, and education," taking the particular view that creativity was an underlying principle of an esteemed history of American arts, science, and political thought and action. The conditions that put it at risk as the millennium approached were a diminished government investment in the arts and public schools, the growth of the prison system, and a lack of corporate commitment to long-term research. The group's "blueprint for action" consisted of seven points that broadly advocated collaboration across disciplines, cultures, communities, and countries; openness to risk; and experimental educational models that promoted innovation, excellence, and social responsibility.[12]

These ideals and concomitant fears, once phrased in the Cold War language of containment, have been adapted to suit a now-globalized economy. And if creativity has ascended to the canon of American values, it has also been continuously deemed in jeopardy. The fear that Americans might be losing a creative edge in international competition has been asserted repeatedly. As a 2010 *Newsweek* magazine cover story, "The Creativity Crisis," pronounced, "American creativity scores are falling."[13] Using results from E. Paul

Torrance's tests for creativity, which have been renormed several times since 1966 but are still given to quantify divergent and convergent thinking in American children, researchers claim that scores show American children are less creative than earlier generations. Contrary to predictable models of gradual improvement, these data suggest that American creativity may have already peaked. It is not difficult to make the alarmist leap from these results to broader assumptions about American educational models, prosperity, and ingenuity, which is precisely what the authors of the *Newsweek* article claimed: "While our creativity scores decline unchecked, the current national strategy for creativity consists of little more than praying for a Greek muse to drop by our houses. The problems we face now, and in the future, simply demand that we do more than just hope for inspiration to strike."[14]

Postwar educational reformers argued that nourishing creativity in the classroom could create a more responsive and talented workforce. This dimension remains a primary motivator of educational reform. The developmental psychologist and historian Howard Gardner, a student of Jerome Bruner and best known for his theory of multiple intelligences, has continually pursued questions about creativity, children, and education. Gardner's work on creativity has centered on questions of artistry and cognition, and increasingly on the applied benefits of creativity for schools and organizations.[15] Between 1972 and 2000, Gardner was a director of Project Zero, a program of the Harvard Graduate School of Education that was established in 1967 to study education in the arts and to promote the study of cognition to enhance learning and "creative thinking" in the arts, humanities, and sciences. Sir Ken Robinson, a British educational reformer now living in the United States, has become a leading voice for international educational reform in the name of creativity. Robinson is known for accusing schools of "educating out creativity" with their overwhelming emphasis on skills in math and literacy. He argues a familiar position, that every child possesses creative abilities and that developing them will enhance the appetite for discovery, and adds the practical promise that these gains in self-confidence will result in high academic achievement and skilled employees ready for a knowledge-based economy. Robinson chaired the National Advisory Committee on Creative and Cultural Education's 1999 report to the British secretary of state for education and employment, which stated emphatically that the committee's proposal was *not* a "return to the progressive teaching ideas of the 1960s."[16] Robinson's subsequent book, *Out of Our Minds: Learning to Be Creative* (2001; rev. ed., 2011), his Internet TED Talks, and other publications make him one of the most popular promoters of the belief that recognizing and cultivating creativity in schools can rescue a system that has indeed left children behind.

The rhetoric of creativity in education is strongly tied to expectations from the marketplace and managers, along with the fear that insufficiently creative Americans will lose out in a global economy. The specter of the Cold War haunts discussions of national competition and education. In late 2010, the president of the United States, Barack Obama, revived the educational discourse of the postwar era in his reference to a "Sputnik moment" during a visit to a community college science class, and again, more prominently, in the State of the Union address in January 2011. Sputnik, Obama argued, provoked an American investment in education and "unleashed a wave of innovation."[17] Redoubling efforts to improve American education in strategic areas implies precisely the applied results of creativity and imagination that Admiral Rickover and others lionized. Indeed, the quest for creativity is tied to promises of profitable results of idea generation and innovation. Universities, playing up this applied dimension, have founded multidisciplinary centers or hubs for creative activities, have created degree programs in creative studies, and have positioned themselves as "creative campuses."[18]

Creativity still holds enormous cultural value, and the word *creativity* is used colloquially with only positive connotations. But *creativity*, as Brendan Gill has described it, "is a word as light and wayward and almost as untetherable as milkweed down."[19] That is, it is often too personal, too easy, and too empty. Creative toys, creative growth, creative development, creative living, and creative thinking: these innocuous, sloganlike designations imply a value-added dimension to ordinary life. Who, after all, does not want his or her children, pupils, or future workers and leaders deemed "creative"? If we believe the advertisers, both children and adults can buy their way to creativity through consumable goods and direct downloads. Anyone can be "creative" with the right courses, tools, kits, books, apps, or apparel. Creativity sells products to an uneasy consumer wary that globalization may eventually submerge individuality. Creativity, in other words, is tied to a stalwart belief in authenticity, originality, and innovation. It is this persistent assumption of the authenticity of creativity that carves out what Nikolas Rose calls a "psy-shaped space" within ourselves. The psychological "truth" of childhood creativity is the work of scientists, doctors, architects and designers, editors, advertisers, teachers, and parents. Together they have assembled and transmitted the cultural implications of the word *creativity*.

The everyday "little-c" creativity of the mass market also implies democratic potential, just as it did after World War II. And this is where the

creativity discourse is most problematic. The rhetoric of creativity over-
looks differences and inequality. It assumes a universalizing position that,
although innate, is operational only in those who have actively cultivated
it. In Florida's schema, the elite "creative class" is economically and morally
bound to cultivate the individuality of service workers and laborers: "This
vision must reflect the very principles of the Creative Age: that creativity is
the fundamental source of economic growth, and that it is an essential part
of everyone's humanity that needs to be cultivated."[20] This paternalistic outlook—similar to the notion that parents can become creative by cultivating
creativity in their children—restates, if unconsciously, the language of postwar self-improvement as a method of cultural renewal.

   Creativity is an elastic term. It can imply great works of art and
science, or the humble insights of daily life. It is difficult to define and to
measure with any precision, but it is easily commodified. If creativity is so
abstract, so intangible, why, then, do we insist on its importance? Creativity
appeals, I think, because it promises hope. It describes our longings rather
than our certainties. Creativity was the subliminal desire of postwar middle-
class culture, the optimistic view of a new generation's social and cultural
potential after the atom bomb, and a reassurance at a moment of growing
insecurities about geopolitics, social conformity, and economic abundance.
Constructed and represented in material forms for both children and adults,
the national, psychological, and educational discourse on creativity reawak-
ened a radiant image of individuality that has continued to haunt us well
past the end of the Cold War.

ACKNOWLEDGMENTS

I AM GRATEFUL for the financial support of the American Association of University Women, the Canadian Centre for Architecture, the Lemelson Center at the Smithsonian Institution, the CRS Archive Center at Texas A&M University, and the Spencer Foundation. I thank Pieter Martin for taking on this project and Kristian Tvedten for expert guidance at the University of Minnesota Press.

There are many scholars whose work on the history of art, architecture, design, and material culture has affected my thinking. Abigail A. Van Slyck, Kate Solomonson, and Marta Gutman helped shape this manuscript, and I am indebted to their insights, generosity, and kindness. I also signal my gratitude to Ning de Coninck Smith, Ned Cooke, Maarten Delbeke, Gabrielle Esperdy, Alice Friedman, Michael Golec, Carma Gorman, Elizabeth Guffey, Dale Allen Gyure, Mimi Hellman, Juliet Kinchin, Medina Lasansky, Barksdale Maynard, Caroline Maniaque, Victor Margolin, Jennifer Milam, Wallis Miller, Jacki Musacchio, Aidan O'Connor, Jacqueline Reid-Walsh, Kirsi Saarikangas, Ezra Shales, Andy Shanken, Susan G. Solomon, and Gennifer Weisenfeld.

I thank Susan Weber for her sustaining commitment to the serious study of design, decorative arts, and material culture that the Bard Graduate Center represents. My colleagues at the Bard Graduate Center are inspiring models and intellectual partners. They have made many years on West Eighty-Sixth Street a constantly enriching experience. I owe a special debt to Ken Ames and Pat Kirkham, whose advice and recommendations helped sustain my research and writing. The title of the book was suggested by Catherine Whalen. Many students, especially Alexa Griffith Winton, Sarah Lichtman, and Marie Warsh, generously fed me tidbits from their own research. I especially appreciate contributions to my initial research from my former student assistants Monica Obniski and Sonya Topolnisky Abrego. Colin Fanning helped heroically with editing and the production of illustrations and the index.

I owe a huge debt to the staffs of the archives, museums, and libraries I visited, especially the Museum of Modern Art, the Cooper-Hewitt National Design Museum, the Strong Museum, the Canadian Centre for Architecture, the Archives Center at the National Museum of American History, the Architectural Archive at the University of Pennsylvania, the Walker Art Center, the Metropolitan Museum of Art, the Art Institute of Chicago, the CRS Archives Center at Texas A&M University, the Bancroft Library at the University of California at Berkeley, Beth Alberty (formerly of the Brooklyn Children's Museum), the National Education Library, the Library of Congress, the Bobst Library at New York University, and the Avery Library at Columbia University. I owe much more to several generations of Bard Graduate Center library staff, especially Heather Topcik, Janis Ekdahl, Greta Earnest, Erin Elliott, Cheryl Costello, and Karyn Hinkle, whose intelligence and effectiveness have been invaluable.

My thanks go to Joan Barenholtz, Fred Bassetti, Theresa Caplan, Malcolm Holzman, Philip W. Jackson, Amy Kasai, Diana Korzenik, Norman McGrath, David Sprafkin, and Lester Walker, who shared personal experiences and private archives.

Elizabeth J. Moodey, Pippa White, and Michèle Majer deserve special notice for their friendship, intellectual insights, and exquisite gifts of vintage toys and ephemera. I am also grateful to many friends and neighbors, especially Kati Koerner, Paule Moureaux-Néry, Catherine Mulcahy and John Curry, Alexandra Neuber, and Sharon Silber, whose company on the benches at Bennett Park has given me new perspective on the project that is childhood.

My gratitude and love go to my parents, who bought Creative Playthings toys and the House of Cards (and then saved them) and spent their lives toiling creatively. Eugene Goldwasser, my father-in-law, died as the manuscript was nearing completion. I am in awe of his contributions to science and humanity and his generous and humble spirit, and feel grateful to have known him. Matthew Goldwasser helped me pick through the education debates. My biggest debt and deepest thanks go to James Goldwasser, whose presence is everywhere in this project. I am the grateful recipient of his love and creativity, which have taken manifold forms: well-edited texts, full bookcases and walls, fine family dinners, and good music. Finally, this book owes much to the children in my family: my two sisters, Piet and Miye, who were the most important actors in my own childhood; my nephews, Jonah and Caleb; and most of all my son, Felix, who has accompanied me on trips to libraries, museums, schools, toy stores, and academic conferences, and has lent his expertise on Web sites, play, and parents. He has made the prolonged research and writing of this book both real and joyful.

NOTES

INTRODUCTION

1   Gesell and Ilg, in collaboration with Learned and Ames, *Infant and Child in the Culture of Today*, 65.

2   Nadel, *Containment Culture*; May, *Homeward Bound*; Stephens, "Nationalism, Nuclear Policy and Children in Cold War America"; and Castillo, *Cold War on the Home Front*.

3   Mintz, *Huck's Raft*; Henriksen, *Dr. Strangelove's America*, 88–91; Gilbert, *Another Chance*, 54–75; and Strickland and Ambrose, "Baby Boom, Prosperity, and the Changing Worlds of Children, 1945–1963," 533–38.

4   Coontz, *Way We Never Were*; May, *Homeward Bound*; Meyerowitz, *Not June Cleaver*; Hayden, *Building Suburbia*; and Harris, *Second Suburb*.

5   *Webster's Third New International Dictionary*, rev. 1961, s.v. "creativity." Psychologists have, however, tried to define this word empirically. Jonathan A. Plucker, for example, suggests a relatively open definition: "Creativity is the interplay between ability and process by which an individual or group produces an outcome or product that is both novel and useful as defined within some social context." See Plucker and Beghetto, "Why Creativity Is Domain General, Why It Looks Domain Specific, and Why the Distinction Does Not Matter," 156.

6   Frank, *Conquest of Cool*.

7   Csikszentmihalyi, *Creativity*.

8   See Ariès, *Centuries of Childhood*; and Cunningham, *Children and Childhood in Western Society since 1500*.

9   Locke, *Some Thoughts concerning Education*, 79 (emphasis in original).

10 Rousseau, *Émile*, 79.

11 Milam, *Fragonard's Playful Paintings*.

12 Sutton-Smith, *Ambiguity of Play*, 129–33.

13 Cooke, preface to Pestalozzi, *How Gertrude Teaches Her Children*, 2.

14 Silber, *Pestalozzi*; and Ashwin, "Pestalozzi and the Origins of Pedagogical Drawing."

15 Fröbel, *Friedrich Froebel's Pedagogics of the Kindergarten*, 9.

16 As Anne Higonnet has shown, pictorial representations of the innocent child are the deliberate work of adults. See Higonnet, *Pictures of Innocence*, 27–28.

17 Rosenblum, *Romantic Child*; and Higonnet, ibid., 15.

18 See Connelly, *Sleep of Reason*; Evett, *Critical Reception of Japanese Art in Late Nineteenth-Century Europe*; and Ogata, *Art Nouveau and the Social Vision of Modern Living*.

19 Fineberg, *Innocent Eye*.

20 Goode, *Museums of the Future*, 427.

21 Lienhard, *Inventing Modern*, 190–203.

22 See Latour, *Reassembling the Social*, 88–93. See also Turmel, *Historical Sociology of Childhood*.

23 Rose, *Governing the Soul*, 123.   .

24 See the work of Ariès and Cunningham, as well as Brewer, "Childhood Revisited"; Mintz, *Huck's Raft*; Cross, *Kids' Stuff*; and Cross, *Cute and the Cool*.

25 Important exceptions are Schlereth, "Material Culture of Childhood"; and Calvert, *Children in the House*.

26 Highmore, "Sideboard Manifesto."

27 Attfield, *Wild Things*.

28 Solomon, *American Playgrounds*; Gutman and de Coninck-Smith, *Designing Modern Childhoods*; Van Slyck, *Manufactured Wilderness*; and Colomina, Brennen, and Kim, *Cold War Hothouses*.

29 Cross, *Kids' Stuff*; Jacobson, *Raising Consumers*; Cook, *Commodification of Childhood*; Mickenberg, *Learning from the Left*; Nel, *Dr. Seuss*; and op de Beeck, *Suspended Animation*.

30 Kline, *Out of the Garden*; Sammond, *Babes in Tomorrowland*; Seiter, *Sold Separately*; and Spigel, *Welcome to the Dreamhouse*.

31 Pugh, *Longing and Belonging*; and Buckingham, *Material Child*, 32–42.

32 Cohen, *Consumer's Republic*.

1. CONSTRUCTING CREATIVITY IN POSTWAR AMERICA

1 Elaine Tyler May argues that the reasons for the baby boom have to do with an ideology that pervaded many aspects of American culture. See May, *Homeward Bound*, 142.

2 Harvey, *Fifties*, 105. Scholars have shown that concern for children's cognitive abilities grew at the end of the nineteenth century to become a veritable obsession by the postwar era. See, for example, Wrigley, "Do Young Children Need Intellectual Stimulation?"; and Stearns, *Anxious Parents*, 100–101. Wini Breines, however, argues that mothers had relatively little academic ambition for their children, preferring them to be "normal" and "well adjusted." See Breines, *Young, White, and Miserable*, 68–69.

3 Church, "Parents," 18–19. See also Harvey, *Fifties*, 91–92.

4 Grant, *Raising Baby by the Book*. Peter Stearns argues this attitude toward parenting advice "spilled over" to other parts of the world; see Stearns, *Childhood in World History*, 104.

5 See Patterson, *Grand Expectations*, 362.

6   See Grant, *Raising Baby by the Book*, 215–18.

7   Smith, *"Where Did You Go?" "Out" "What Did You Do?" "Nothing,"* 8.

8   Midcentury White House Conference on Children and Youth, *Personality in the Making*, 7.

9   Ibid., 16. The report also suggested that if enterprise and imagination were restricted too greatly, the personality could become overconstricted and might never realize its "inner capacities for imagination, feeling, and performance" (16).

10 Genter, *Late Modernism*, 13–16.

11 Gesell and Ilg, *Infant and Child in the Culture of Today*, 9–10.

12 Sammond, *Babes in Tomorrowland*.

13 Mead and Calas, "Child-Training Ideals in a Postrevolutionary Context," 190–91.

14 Bronfenbrenner, *Two Worlds of Childhood*, 81.

15 Mead and Calas, "Child-Training Ideals in a Postrevolutionary Context," 200.

16 Ibid.

17 Wolfenstein, "Fun Morality."

18 Frenkel-Brunswik, "Differential Patterns of Social Outlook and Personality in Family and Children," 383.

19 Cohen, *Consumer's Republic*.

20 Jacobson, *Raising Consumers*; and Cook, *Commodification of Childhood*.

21 Jacobson, *Raising Consumers*, chap 5.

22 Cross, *All-Consuming Century*, 140.

23 Marion O'Brien Donovan Papers, 1949–1996, Archives Center, National Museum of American History, Smithsonian Institution.

24 Strickland and Ambrose, "Baby Boom, Prosperity, and the Changing Worlds of Children, 1945–1963."

25 May, *Homeward Bound*, 147.

26 Cohen, *Consumer's Republic*, 303. See also Cross, *Kids' Stuff*, 162–71; and Mintz, *Huck's Raft*, 275.

27 Cohen, *Consumer's Republic*, 304.

28 Spigel, *Welcome to the Dreamhouse*, 190–95.

29 Ibid., 200.

30 As William Leach has shown, this was common practice at the turn of the twentieth century. See Leach, *Land of Desire*, 85–90.

31 Gruen and Smith, *Shopping Towns USA*, 257.

32 Whitaker, *Service and Style*.

33 Gruen and Smith, *Shopping Towns USA*, 261.

34 Jancovich, "Othering Conformity in Post-war America."

35 Stouffer, *Communism, Conformity, and Civil Liberties*, 89–97. Opinions on the relative role of age and education on conformist outlook varied in these studies.

36 Gitlin, foreword to Riesman, *Lonely Crowd* (rev. ed.). See also Gilbert, *Men in the Middle*.

37 Gilbert, *Men in the Middle*, 35–37.

38 Ibid., 42.

39 Riesman, *Lonely Crowd* (rev. ed.), 62.

40 Riesman claimed that "play, which in the earlier epoch is often an extracurricular

and private hobby, shared at most with a small group, now becomes part of the school enterprise itself, serving a 'realistic' purpose." Ibid., 63.

41 Ibid., 302.

42 Ibid., 48.

43 Wood, *Suburbia*, 4. As a political scientist, Wood emphasized the statistical data and political organization of suburban life, arguing that instead of a modern society distinct from historical precedent, suburbia reflected old suspicions and a rejection of cosmopolitan values.

44 Long, *American Dream and the Popular Novel*.

45 Rowe, *Making a Middle Landscape*.

46 See, for example, Kimmel, "Re-reading the History of Levittown, One Voice at a Time," 30. Barbara M. Kelly, however, argues for relative homogeneity on Long Island; see Kelly, *Expanding the American Dream*, 59–60.

47 Rowe, *Making a Middle Landscape*, 4–6.

48 Hayden, *Building Suburbia*, 135–36.

49 Press release 44328-12, March 21, 1944, The Museum of Modern Art, New York.

50 Perkins and Cocking, *Schools*, 19. Perkins estimated that ideally elementary schools should be no farther than three-fourths of a mile from the farthest dwelling, intermediate schools should stretch no farther than a mile and a half, and high schools should be a maximum of three miles.

51 Mumford, *City in History*, 494.

52 Goodman, *Growing Up Absurd*, 116.

53 Gilbert, *Cycle of Outrage*.

54 Medovoi, *Rebels*.

55 Engelhardt, *End of Victory Culture*, 133.

56 Gilbert, *Cycle of Outrage,* 63–78.

57 Gilbert, *Another Chance*, 73.

58 Leerom Medovoi has argued that the image of rebellion, however, released teenage consumers from the stigma of conformity. See Medovoi, *Rebels*, 102.

59 Whyte, *Organization Man*, 10.

60 Ibid., 51–52.

61 Foundation for Research on Human Behavior, *Creativity and Conformity*, n.p.

62 Whyte commented: "From company to company, trainees express the same impatience. All the great ideas, they explain, have already been discovered and not only in physics and chemistry but in practical fields like engineering. The basic creative work is done, so the man you need—for every kind of job—is a practical, team-player fellow who will do a good shirt-sleeves job. 'I would sacrifice brilliance,' one trainee said, 'for human understanding every time.' And they do, too." *Organization Man*, 137.

63 Jancovich, "Othering Conformity in Post-war America," 12–13.

64 Guilford, "Creativity." During World War II, Guilford had directed a psychological research unit in the U.S. Army and Air Force. Charged with developing intelligence tests for incoming recruits, Guilford and his colleagues worked to create tests for creative ability. Naval research funds supported Guilford's research for

twenty years, along with grants from the National Science Foundation and the Office of Education of the Department of Health, Education, and Welfare. See Guilford, *Creative Talents*.

65 Guilford, *Nature of Human Intelligence*.

66 Eventually Guilford revised the model. By separating various memory functions, he increased the number of abilities to 180; see Guilford, "Some Changes in the Structure of Intellect Model."

67 Feist and Runco, "Trends in the Creativity Literature," 272.

68 Gardner, *Art, Mind, and Brain*, 3; and Bruner, *Acts of Meaning*, 2–4.

69 On the Utah conferences, held between 1955 and 1959, see Taylor and Barron, *Scientific Creativity*.

70 Anderson, *Creativity and Its Cultivation*, xii.

71 Brown, "Creativity." See also Guenter, "Historical Influences of Creativity and Its Measurement in American Education, 1950–1985."

72 Millar, *E. Paul Torrance, "the Creativity Man,"* 50.

73 Children in grades 1 through 6 at the University of Minnesota Laboratory Elementary School and the Sidney Pratt Elementary School in Minneapolis participated in the first study, sponsored by the U.S. Office of Education, to explore school environments and promote creative behavior. See ibid., 62.

74 Runco, Millar, Acar, and Cramond, "Torrance Tests of Creative Thinking."

75 See Millar, *Torrance Kids at Mid-life*; Millar, *Power of Creativity*; and Torrance, *Manifesto*.

76 See Lemann, *Big Test*, 119; and Sharp, *IQ Cult*.

77 Getzels and Jackson, "Meaning of 'Giftedness.'"

78 Getzels and Jackson, *Creativity and Intelligence*, 120. J. Nina Lieberman's work with New York kindergarten children from 1959 to 1961 yielded her argument not only that playfulness was an element in play, imagination, and creativity but also that it "survives play and becomes a personality trait of the individual"; see Lieberman, *Playfulness*, 5.

79 The National Science Foundation supported the Utah conferences, and corporations such as General Electric and General Motors developed training courses in creative thinking. At General Motors's AC Spark Plug division, L. L. Thurstone, a mechanical engineer turned psychologist, conducted research on personality. The prominent creativity researcher Calvin W. Taylor was one of his first students.

80 Brossard, "Creative Child," 112.

81 Barron, *Creativity and Personal Freedom*, 7.

82 Osborn, *Your Creative Power*, 355 (emphasis in original).

83 Osborn claimed that 120,000 copies of *Applied Imagination* had been printed by 1966. Scientific researchers also saw the notion of creativity as problem solving; see Newell, Shaw, and Simon, "Processes of Creative Thinking."

84 Osborn, *Your Creative Power*, 61–62.

85 Osborn, *Applied Imagination*, xxi. Trustees included cultural and business leaders as well as Sidney J. Parnes, who at the time was professor of creative studies at the State University of Buffalo. Eventually, E. Paul Torrance also became a trustee.

86 Parnes developed a course on creative thinking and eventually created a major and a graduate program in this area at Buffalo State University. He took over running the foundation after Osborn's death, in 1966; the following year, the foundation began publishing the *Journal of Creative Behavior*. See Parnes, "Programs and Courses in Creativity."

87 A 1975 scholarly volume assessing the psychological research on the subject of creativity looked back over the literature and estimated that the number of studies published in 1965–66 equaled that of the preceding five years, which equaled that of the preceding ten years, which equaled that of the preceding one hundred years. This book also explored a number of definitions of *creativity*, acknowledging the divergence in usage and systemic approaches. See Taylor and Getzels, *Perspectives in Creativity*.

88 U.S. Department of Health, Education and Welfare, Children's Bureau, *Story of the White House Conference*, 20.

89 See, for example, "News and Clues for Parents," November 1960; Ruth and Edward Brecher, "Creative Ability . . . What Is It? Who Has It? What Makes It Flourish or Falter?" November 1960; Marvin R. Weisbord, "Let's Not Stifle Our Children's Creativity," November 1961; Evelyn Seeley Stewart, "The Big Question of Creativity," June 1963; Rhoda W. Backmeister, "How to Handle a Creative Child," January 1964; Suzanne Newton, "How to Encourage Your Child's Natural Creativity," July 1968; Cynthia Lang, "Experiment in Creativity," September 1969; and Dessie-Ellen Coggins, "Five Steps to Creativity," March 1970.

90 Jane, "Are You Raising an Idea Man?" 80.

91 Newton, "How to Encourage Your Child's Natural Creativity," 83.

92 Maslow, *Farther Reaches of Human Nature*.

93 Kirkham and Bass, *Saul Bass*, 241–47.

94 Mead, *Creative Life for Your Children*, 4. Many of the themes Mead develops were discussed at the Golden Anniversary White House Conference on Children and Youth, held in 1960.

95 Ibid., 41.

96 Kuhn, review of Anderson, *Creativity and Its Cultivation*.

97 Barzun, "Cults of 'Research' and 'Creativity,'" 74.

98 Mihaly Csikszentmihalyi, a former student of Jacob W. Getzels, distinguishes the creativity of great artists and thinkers as Creativity with a capital C. The insights of children and household inventiveness are what he calls "small-c" forms. See Csikszentmihalyi, *Creativity*, 8. Skeptics of the era included Salvatore R. Maddi, who argued that motivation was more important than nurturing environments; see Maddi, "Strenuousness of the Creative Life."

99 Townsend, *Written for Children*, 308.

100 Rose, *Case of Peter Pan*.

101 McGavran, *Literature and the Child*.

102 Riesman, *Lonely Crowd*, 104–7. Sally Allen McNall argues that books for young adults, grades 5 through 7, especially between the late 1940s and 1960s, portrayed a world that was safely circumscribed and that valued conformity. She also argues

that in the 1960s there was a resurgence of a romantic image and that "a generation of writers has tried to imagine what a generation of creative, loving, autonomous children thinks and feels." See McNall, "American Children's Literature,
1880–Present," 402.

103 Mickenberg, *Learning from the Left*.

104 Lurie, *Don't Tell the Grown-Ups*, 13.

105 Lurie also argues that children's literature can renew the adult reader's own childhood and that when adults leave "the tribal culture of childhood . . . behind, we
lose contact with instinctive joy in self-expression: with the creative imagination,
spontaneous emotion, and the ability to see the world as full of wonders." Ibid.,
204.

106 See Tatar, *Enchanted Hunters*, 169–70.

107 Margret and H. A. Rey were collaborators on the Curious George and other
children's books. Although H. A. was the draftsman and composed the pictures,
Margret wrote the plots.

108 Nathalie op de Beeck points out that the first edition of *Curious George* included
the suggestion of curiosity as a fault. See op de Beeck, *Suspended Animation*, vii.

109 Greenstone, "Frightened George." As Greenstone observes, adults in the early
George titles exploit the monkey. In the later books, however, as George loses his
early bravado, adults are depicted as understanding and forgiving, going to great
lengths to rescue George.

110 Rey and Rey, *Curious George Goes to the Hospital*, 43.

111 John Rowe Townsend described *Little Blue and Little Yellow* as "offbeat. . . . It
was however truly original and stimulating." See Townsend, *Written for Children*, 316.

112 Heller, "Leo Lionni." *Little Blue and Little Yellow* won an American Institute of
Graphic Arts award for book design in 1960, and Lionni was an AIGA medalist
in 1984.

113 Johnson, *Harold and the Purple Crayon*, n.p.

114 *The Snowy Day* won the 1963 Caldecott Award for illustration.

115 Silvey, *100 Best Books for Children*, 22.

116 Lurie, *Don't Tell the Grown-Ups*, 14–15; Tatar, *Enchanted Hunters*, 169ff.

117 Tatar, *Enchanted Hunters*, 171.

118 Schramm, Lyle, and Parker, *Television in the Lives of Our Children*, 11.

119 Turow, *Entertainment, Education, and the Hard Sell*, 2.

120 This perception of a widening generation gap and suspicion around media and
mass culture are discussed in Gilbert, *Cycle of Outrage*, 63–108.

121 Sammond, *Babes in Tomorrowland*, 323ff.

122 Spigel, *Make Room for TV*, 52.

123 Spigel, *Welcome to the Dreamhouse*, 193–94.

124 Horn, "Re: 'Mr. I. Magination.'"

125 The show was revived in 1969 as five-minute stand-alone segments, but fears
that proximity to the TV screen would expose children to radiation precipitated
its end.

126 Other television shows also depended on kits for revenue. John Gnagy, who hosted a long-running art show, was paid in revenue from his art sets. See Israel, "Learn to Draw with Jon Gnagy."

127 Orme, *Television for the Family*, 7.

128 Clokey studied film at the University of Southern California under Slavko Vorkapich. See Frierson, *Clay Animation*, 116–31.

129 *The Gumby Show* ran on Saturday mornings beginning in March 1957 and was sponsored by the Sweets Company of America. In the 1950s, the twelve-minute show had a live portion that included activities in a fun shop. In the 1960s, Gumby returned to children's television, without the live host but with a greater number of characters and more exotic and complex sets. See Kaplan and Michaelsen, *Gumby*; and Frierson, ibid., 125.

130 In a later episode, Gumbasia is the name of Gumby's town and book, and it was originally the name of Clokey's first experimental animated film produced as a student at USC in 1953.

131 Frierson, *Clay Animation*, 126.

132 Art Clokey said he resisted developing Gumby merchandise for seven years. Michael Frierson, however, has argued that Lakeside Toy Company of Minneapolis helped to secure syndication and boost Gumby's appeal with toy tie-ins. When the bendable dolls (which sold for about a dollar each) appeared, in the mid-1960s, they proved tremendously popular. See ibid., 127.

133 See a 1967 advertisement, "Gumby, the TV Star," accessed June 7, 2010, in the online exhibition at http://thedeeparchivescom/ex_show_top.php4?ex_id=4.

134 Clokey, foreword to Kaplan and Michaelsen, *Gumby*, 5–6.

135 See Kaplan and Michaelsen, *Gumby*, 137–48.

136 Schramm, Lyle, and Parker, *Television in the Lives of Our Children*, 153–54.

137 Morrow, *"Sesame Street" and the Reform of Children's Television*, 46.

138 Malcolm Gladwell has argued that this is *Sesame Street*'s "stickiness," in *Tipping Point*, 106.

139 Lesser, *Children and Television*, 129–30.

140 Ibid., 113.

141 In an episode from 1985, Snuffy is revealed to the human characters, a position that reflected the producers' efforts to encourage children to tell the truth and have adults believe them.

142 Myers, "Reading Children and Homeopathic Romanticism," 45.

2. EDUCATIONAL TOYS AND CREATIVE PLAYTHINGS

1 Toy Manufacturers of the U.S.A., *Toy Purchase Habits of U.S. Families*.

2 Cross, *Kids' Stuff*, 166.

3 Ibid., 143.

4 Hewitt and Roomet, *Educational Toys in America, 1800 to the Present*. There is a voluminous bibliography on the history of toys and playthings. See, for example, Fraser, *History of Toys*; Mergen, *Play and Playthings*; Cross, *Kids' Stuff*; and Sutton-Smith, *Toys as Culture*. The merchandising strategies of American toy makers have also gained significant attention, particularly from scholars of com-

munication and media, who have traced the history and development of a widely shared children's culture. See, for example, Kline, *Out of the Garden*; Seiter, *Sold Separately*; and Spigel, *Welcome to the Dreamhouse*. Thomas J. Schlereth, asking for greater attention to be paid to the child-made toys and amusements, comments: "We need to collect and study more of this childhood material culture. While some of it may prove highly idiosyncratic, enough of it may reveal patterns that will tell us as much about creativity, imagination and aesthetics as any of the manufactured or educational toys that predominate in most museum collections." See Schlereth, "Material Culture of Childhood," 93.

5   Although there is evidence of toys from antiquity and the Middle Ages, the changing use of the word *toy* has been viewed as evidence that the modern idea of a child's plaything emerged only in the early modern period. Before the mid-eighteenth century, *toy* meant a trifle or petty commodity. See Brewer, "Childhood Revisited."

6   Sutton-Smith, *Toys as Culture*, 119. Locke's *Some Thoughts concerning Education* (1693) offers not only lessons on the alphabet but a complete program for training children.

7   As Karen Hewitt and Louise Roomet indicate, the label "educational" was applied to many kinds of different objects, from scientific instruments to miniature kitchens. See Hewitt and Roomet, *Educational Toys in America, 1800 to the Present*, 1–2. Birgitta Almqvist argues that "educational toy" as it was used in the 1960s indicated a specific agenda of postwar competition. See Almqvist, "Educational Toys, Creative Toys," 49.

8   Sutton-Smith, *Toys as Culture*, 125.

9   Baudelaire, *Painter of Modern Life*, 198.

10 Sutton-Smith, *Ambiguity of Play*.

11 Caillois, *Man, Play, and Games*.

12 Piaget, *Play, Dreams, and Imitation in Childhood*, 162.

13 Brosterman, *Inventing Kindergarten*; Beatty, *Preschool Education in America*; and Rose, *Mother's Job*.

14 John Dewey, Anna Bryan, and Patty Smith Hill all came out against the Fröbel method. In America, the Fröbel kindergarten materials were produced by Milton Bradley.

15 Brosterman, *Inventing Kindergarten*, 101.

16 Kilpatrick, *Montessori System Examined*.

17 Rose, *Mother's Job*, 100–121.

18 Beatty, *Preschool Education in America*, 137–42.

19 Patty Smith Hill also developed a series of hollow wooden blocks that became the basis for many variations of nursery school equipment.

20 Although most nursery schools were private, the model was discussed for all children. One of the pledges of the 1930 Conference on Child Health and Protection was to provide every child with early education, specifically "nursery schools and kindergartens to supplement home care." See U.S. Department of Health, Education and Welfare, Children's Bureau, *Story of the White House Conference on Children and Youth*.

21 "Holgate Brothers"; and Holgate Toy Company, *Story of Holgate Toys.*

22 Wallance, Case Study 11-A, *Shaping America's Products* Archive, Box 4. According to Wallance, Mary Frank was the daughter of the treasurer of Holgate and, after noticing that nursery schools often had toys made by local craftsmen, suggested that the company begin to manufacture objects for this market.

23 Ibid. According to Wallance, Mrs. Homer F. Barnes invented a hammer toy and Mrs. Ethel D. Mintzer designed a construction-block set for Holgate.

24 The president of Holgate, William T. Henretta, discovered Rockwell through a series of designs for dollhouses he had produced for Macy's.

25 Holder, "Story of Holgate"; and Hewitt and Roomet, *Educational Toys in America, 1800 to the Present,* 100.

26 The LSRM promoted scientific research in child development, supporting and establishing centers at Yale and Berkeley, as well as Minnesota and Toronto. See Schlossman, "Philanthropy and the Gospel of Child Development."

27 *Parents' Magazine,* originally called *Children: A Magazine for Parents* (and today called simply *Parents*), was founded in 1926. One writer has characterized it as the "most successful educational magazine in the world." The magazine covered topics that ranged from education to advice about raising children, architecture, homemaking, food, and fashion. See Hulbert, *Raising America,* 104; Schlossman, "Perils of Popularization"; Schlossman, "Philanthropy and the Gospel of Child Development," 285, 291–94; and Hawes, "Child Science, Guidance Clinics, and the Rise of Experts."

28 Knowles, "Millions of War Babies Should Have Educational Toys."

29 Moore, *American Toy Industry's Golden Era.*

30 The Midcentury White House Conference on Children and Youth, held in 1950, brought new attention to the importance of the "healthy personality." Erik Erikson, Benjamin Spock, and Margaret Mead all participated in this event.

31 Erikson, *Toys and Reasons,* 100–111.

32 Playskool toy catalog, ca. 1950, in Wallance, *Shaping America's Products* Archive (emphases in original). Ethel Kawin's essay was adapted from her 1938 book, *The Wise Choice of Toys,* which was reissued in a seventh impression in 1947.

33 Helfand, *Reinventing the Wheel.*

34 As Elizabeth Rose argues in *A Mother's Job,* this marked a change from a long history as a philanthropic enterprise aimed at poor children and their families. See also Beatty, *Preschool Education in America,* 185–92.

35 For histories of the debate around the appropriation of government money for federal day-care centers, see Rose, *Mother's Job,* 153–80; and Tuttle, *"Daddy's Gone to War,"* 69–90.

36 Scholars have pointed to the need for rethinking what was "traditional" in postwar gender roles; see Meyerowitz, *Not June Cleaver.*

37 Muncy, "Cooperative Motherhood and Democratic Civic Culture in Postwar Suburbia, 1940–1965."

38 The Play School Association advocated for community organizing of play spaces and groups for children of preschool and school age. Begun during World War II, the Play School Association stressed the idea not only that day care was a wartime

provision but that the benefits to children and parents would also serve during peacetime. See Lambert, *School's Out*.

39 See Beatty, *Preschool Education in America*, 192–200, for a discussion of the fraught history and highly debated theory behind the Head Start model.

40 Aaron, *Child's Play*, 120.

41 Spock, "Can You Raise Your Child's I.Q.?" Playskool claimed its toys could "build up your child's IQ" in an advertisement in *American Home* in December 1945, 86.

42 Holgate advertisement, *Parents' Magazine*, November 1949, 140; Playskool advertisement, *Parents' Magazine*, October 1948, 157.

43 Al Kaufman, cartoon, *Ladies' Home Journal*, December 1955, 113.

44 In 1957, two leading educators commented, "Plastic is especially suspect as a toy material. There are several kinds of plastic and some shatter far too easily." See Hartley and Goldenson, *Complete Book of Children's Play*, 6. On the kinds of plastic adopted for use in toy manufacture, see Meikle, *American Plastic*, 186–89.

45 This link between handicraft ideals of the Arts and Crafts movement and early educational toys would seem to have a legacy in the postwar suburban ideal of a workshop off the garage, but most postwar toys were mass-produced. See Cross, *Kids' Stuff*, 137–38.

46 Russell Lynes's "Highbrow, Lowbrow, Middlebrow" was first published in *Harper's* in 1949 and became the penultimate chapter in his book *The Tastemakers*. See also Menand, "Friend Writes," 143.

47 Barthes, "Toys," 54–55.

48 Gary Cross, in *Kids' Stuff*, notes that Marx aimed to appeal to a mass market, and especially to those suspicious of educational toys.

49 Frank Caplan, quoted in Johnson, "Toys Should Hold Interest Year 'Round."

50 Spock, *Baby and Child Care*, 304–5 (emphasis in original).

51 The Montessori system, once deemed by Kilpatrick as inappropriate for democratic American children, returned in the 1960s in part because of the efforts of Nancy Rambusch, who promoted Montessori ideas in the late 1950s and founded the American Montessori Society. In the 1960s, after Frank and Theresa Caplan met Maria Montessori and Rambusch, Creative Playthings manufactured many objects for this curriculum.

52 "How [the child] plays, with whom, and the material he uses—his toys—determine in large part his future social personality." Advertisement in *Parents' Magazine*, October 1953. See also Cross, *Kids' Stuff*, 160.

53 Advertisement in *Parents' Magazine*, October 1952 (emphasis in original).

54 Advertisement in *Parents' Magazine*, November 1952 (emphasis in original).

55 Advertisement in *Playthings* 54 (April 1956): 76.

56 Frank, introduction, viii.

57 Getzels and Jackson, *Creativity and Intelligence*, 121–22.

58 Brecher and Brecher, "Creative Ability," 88.

59 Playskool, *Playtools to Shape a Child's World*.

60 Almqvist, "Educational Toys, Creative Toys," 50.

61 "Magnet Master"; Daniel S. Defenbacher Correspondence, folder 1, and Carradan

Associates, 1950, folder 3, Box 21, Walker Art Center Archives. Arthur A. Carrara Papers, Box FF 6.12; Wallance, Case Study 5-A, Carradan Associates, 1948–49, *Shaping America's Products* Archive. Despite growing interest in Magnet Master, amid increasing expenses and limited income, the Carradan Associates partnership was liquidated in 1950.

62 "Magnet Master," 2.

63 Ibid., 3.

64 "New Toy."

65 Magnet Master first appeared at the Walker's Children's Fair in May 1948. The design was then refined, and national distribution began in February 1949 with the participation of the Addison Gallery of American Art, the Baltimore Museum of Art, the Colorado Fine Arts Center, the Joslyn Memorial Art Museum, and the San Francisco Museum of Art. A list of forty stores that carried Magnet Master as of September 1950 included the major department stores with toy departments as well as specialty toy shops and design stores such as Baldwin Kingery in Chicago and New Design in New York, which had had a "test sale" of two hundred sets in November 1948. Box 21, General Correspondence, folder 3, Walker Art Center Archives. Carrara also designed a series of cardboard structures in animal forms to which Magnet Master could be adapted. See a typescript to Evelyn Peterson for an unidentified article, Arthur A. Carrara Papers, Ryerson and Burnham Library Archives, 1998.1 6.12.

66 The standard Magnet Master was given a retail price of $9.95, and a junior size for children under six was priced at $4.95. This toy was selected for the "Shopping Scout" column of *Parents' Magazine,* which suggested that children could manipulate it into "endless designs."

67 Walker Art Center Archives, Box 21, General Correspondence, folder 3.

68 Hilde Reiss, curator of Everyday Art at the Walker, later mounted a traveling exhibition of toys circulated by the American Federation of Arts that included Magnet Master as well as toys from Playskool, Holgate, Tigrett, and others. See Reiss, *Toys.* In the early 1950s, Don Wallance began research for a Walker Art Center exhibition that looked at product design and the heritage of craftsmanship. He carried out several case studies of toy manufacturers, including Playskool, Holgate, and Carradan Associates, although they did not appear in his exhibition book, *Shaping America's Products.* Wallance's papers are located at the Cooper-Hewitt National Design Museum Archives, Smithsonian Institution.

69 Wallance, Box 4, Case Study 5-A, Carradan Associates, 1948–49, *Shaping America's Products* Archive.

70 The Eameses' toys were produced by Tigrett Enterprises until 1961. See Kirkham, *Charles and Ray Eames*; and Neuhart, Neuhart, and Eames, *Eames Design.*

71 Tamar Zinguer has suggested a close relationship between the Eameses' Toy, their architectural ideas, and kite design. See Zinguer, "Toy."

72 An early draft of the text for the box for the Toy suggests that the Eameses emphasized the smallness of the box and the potential for large constructions. See Box 103, Office Files, folder 12, The Work of Charles and Ray Eames Archive, Library of Congress.

73 "Industrial Design."

74 Instructions, the Little Toy, Canadian Centre for Architecture, Montreal.

75 Haber, "Designed for Play," 127.

76 The House of Cards was originally issued as two decks of fifty-four cards, one with pictures and another with patterns. The Eameses also produced a Computer House of Cards for IBM. The Giant House of Cards was a package of twenty images and patterns. An intermediate size was issued in Europe by the Otto Maier Verlag in 1960 and again in the 1980s. Otto Maier/Ravensburger also created a memory game for children using some of the same images as those on the House of Cards. Boxes 41 and 42 Office Files, The Work of Charles and Ray Eames Archive.

77 Haber, "Designed for Play," 127.

78 Bassetti suggests that Flexagons was four years in the making and that it was initially offered in 1959 in Seattle. Bassetti patented Flexagons, and his own Førde Corporation produced it. Creative Playthings eventually took over the idea and the name, and produced the set in black and white. Bassetti recalls that one of his greatest compliments came when Charles Eames told him he had sent a set to Alexander Girard for Christmas. Fred Bassetti, interview by the author, August 2010.

79 Hoffman, *Kid Stuff*, 19–21.

80 Colorforms sets cost $1.49 for a 100-shape box or $2.98 for 255 shapes. Colorforms catalog, ca. 1950s.

81 In answer to this question, the author claimed emphatically that "too many toys are designed as if for adults, with directions to match: too restrained, too tidy, too down-to-earth for a child's imagination. Too many toys are the product of a designer whose reigned-in imagination is harnessed to the pursuit of a literalness that will always outrun him. The last thing a child needs in a toy is utter realism. But the highly competitive market makes a manufacturer aim for a first-impression exterior, often to the neglect of long-term delight and creative growth." See E. P., "Child at Play in the World of Form."

82 The Playhouse was located on West Ninety-Fifth Street and eventually moved to Madison Avenue at Seventy-Second Street.

83 Frank Caplan, who had degrees from the College of the City of New York and Teacher's College, had originally begun a company called Creative Toy Makers with a Pik-a-Part Clown toy, and he ran the Playhouse with his wife, Theresa. He met Bernard Barenholtz, who also had a degree from Teacher's College and had studied for a doctorate in psychology, at the annual New York Toy Fair in 1946. Barenholtz and his wife, Edith, ran the Playroom, a toy shop in St. Louis. In 1950, Caplan and Barenholtz entered into a partnership to supply educational toys and equipment to schools. With Caplan as president and Barenholtz as vice president, the company went public in 1961 and established offices in Cranbury, New Jersey, with a factory in Herndon, Pennsylvania. In 1966, the company was acquired by Columbia Broadcasting Systems (CBS). See Theresa Caplan, *Frank Caplan, Champion of Child's Play.*

84 Press release, 1946, Caplan Archive (now dispersed).

85 Along with the shop in New York, Creative Playthings initiated an ambitious catalog business that was expanded to reach parents, teachers, and school administrators. Creative Playthings sold Pratt's Unit Blocks, as well as adaptations of Montessori equipment, by the late 1950s. In February 1950, shortly before Magnet Master was liquidated, Frank Caplan indicated that Creative Playthings was interested in collaborating for the school market. See Box 21, General Correspondence, folder 3, Walker Art Center Archives.

86 Donald Wallance, in a case study of Holgate Brothers, notes the similarity between the Hollow Block on view in Marcel Breuer's house in the Museum Garden at MoMA and a Holgate design from 1931. Wallance, Box 4, *Shaping America's Products* Archive.

87 "Creative Toy," 40.

88 The Rocking Beauty, now an iconic form in the collection of design museums worldwide, has been continually misdated. It was designed by Gloria Caranica in the mid-1960s.

89 "Experts See Toys in Stimulant Role"; "Creative Playthings"; and "Ph.D.s in Toyland." Creative Playthings also relied on experts. Among those listed on the official letterhead and in its catalogs were Lawrence K. Frank, Gerald S. Craig, Clara Lambert, and Craig Muriel Logan.

90 *Antonio Vitali*.

91 "Contemporary Object."

92 Frank Caplan was a member of the Educator's Committee of Better Playthings, along with Jane Cooper Bland, an art educator at MoMA. Bland was also listed in early publicity as a consultant for Creative Playthings.

93 Noguchi's design for a United Nations playground was never realized, although he later designed equipment for the company. Henry Moore agreed in 1953 to collaborate but never realized any designs for play equipment. Robert Winston, professor at the California College of Arts and Crafts, designed the Play Sculpture for Fairyland Park and Lakeside Park in Oakland, California. In 1961, with money from the Creative Playthings Foundation and donations in the name of the civic leader Adele Levy, Louis Kahn and Isamu Noguchi created a proposal for a sculptural playground for Riverside Park in New York City that was never realized. See Solomon, *American Playgrounds*.

94 The number of complete Play Sculpture playgrounds was limited; however, individual units of Play Sculpture were installed throughout the country, especially in play areas intended for young children. At the playground Cornelia Hahn Oberlander designed at Eighteenth and Bigler in Philadelphia, Creative Playthings installed Moeller-Nielsen's slide, the Turtle Tent, and a number of climbing designs. See "Up, Down, and Over"; and "Neighborhood Playground."

95 Play Sculptures, *New World of Play*, n.p.

96 Other members of the jury were Edith Mitchell, Delaware state director of art; Penelope Pinson, *Parents' Magazine*; and George D. Butler, director of the Department of Research at the National Recreation Association.

97 Play Sculptures, *New World of Play*, n.p.

98 See, for example, Ledermann and Trachsel, *Creative Playgrounds and Recreation Centers*; Dattner, *Design for Play*; and Miller, *Creative Outdoor Play Areas*.

99 Solomon, *American Playgrounds*, 53–62.

100 Dattner, *Design for Play*, 14.

101 Saarinen, "Playground."

102 Aaron, *Child's Play*, 37.

103 The Fröbel kindergarten was criticized in America as overly dominated by the figure of the teacher and the rigid system of the "gifts" and "occupations." See Fröbel, *Friedrich Froebel's Pedagogics of the Kindergarten*, 9.

104 See Kuznick and Gilbert, *Rethinking Cold War Culture*; Whitfield, *Culture of the Cold War*; May, *Recasting America*; Saunders, *Cultural Cold War*; and Caute, *Dancer Defects*. Saunders and Caute both discuss, though from different perspectives, the role of the Museum of Modern Art.

105 On the ideological uses of postwar modernism, see, for example, Cockcroft, "Abstract Expressionism, Weapon of the Cold War"; and Guilbaut, *How New York Stole the Idea of Modern Art*.

106 Haddow, "Victor D'Amico's Creative Center."

107 "U.S. in Moscow"; "Russian Children to Romp on Latest American Playground Gear." Creative Playthings was also invited by the interdenominational Protestant Council to design a children's center, equipped with toys, play areas, and scientific instruments designed for children's use, and a playground for the 1964–65 New York World's Fair.

108 On the discourse of competition and consumption at the Moscow Exhibition, see Marling, *As Seen on TV*. On the Cold War, design, and the role of U.S. exhibitions, see Castillo, *Cold War on the Home Front*.

109 *Creative Playthings Holiday Catalogue*, 1962, 1.

110 "Creative Toy," 42–43.

111 "Here Come the Gerbils."

112 Creative Playthings catalog, 1969, 25.

113 "Toys: Little Brother."

114 Rylands's designs were produced by Trendon Toys in the United Kingdom and won the Duke of Edinburgh's Prize for Elegant Design in 1970. In the 1960s, Creative Playthings imported large numbers of hardwood toys, dollhouse furniture, and other materials from Finland and Germany, even though it maintained its own factory in Pennsylvania.

115 The New York shop moved to Madison Avenue in the late 1940s, and in 1964 to a specially designed store in Rockefeller Plaza. In the mid-1960s, Creative Playthings set up holiday shops in the toy departments in upscale department stores such as Bloomingdale's. Around the same time, a Western division was established in Los Angeles, and in the early 1970s, after acquisition by CBS, Creative Playthings' toys and goods became available at thirteen hundred local baby shops around the country. A new shop on East Fifty-Third in New York City opened in 1969 and reinforced the company's image of providing good design as an enticement for children and their parents; see Cook, "Toy Store Designed So

That Children Can Play in It"; "Designing for the Real Customer"; and "Child's Play." Studio Works (Godard, Hodgetts, Mangurian, and Walker), the firm that designed the shop, also designed cardboard children's furniture called Punch Out in 1973, which was manufactured by Design Research. Lester Walker has designed wooden toys and has written books for children on carpentry and block building.

116 Spigel, *TV by Design*.

117 Creative Playthings catalog, 1967.

118 Meehan, "Creative (and Mostly Upper-Middle Class) Playthings."

119 See ibid.; and Zinsser, "This Year, Give Baby an Ego Expander."

120 Frank Caplan resigned in 1968, only two years after the acquisition by CBS. Bernard Barenholtz remained until 1970.

121 Frank and Theresa Caplan continued to advocate for child development and creative play through their foundation and the numerous publications of the Princeton Center for Infancy and Early Childhood. See Theresa Caplan, *Frank Caplan, Champion of Child's Play*. Among the popular books that the Caplans wrote on children and childhood, see *The Power of Play*. This was also the title of a 1967 Creative Playthings catalog. Bernard Barenholtz established the Pyne Press and continued to be an avid toy collector. By the mid-1980s, CBS had sold Creative Playthings, along with its other interests in the toy market. The name is now owned by a maker of backyard play equipment located in Framingham, Massachusetts.

122 Sutton-Smith, *Toys as Culture*, 125.

3. CREATIVE LIVING AT HOME

1 Wright, *Building the Dream*, 246. Wright has shown how suburban developments before the war also employed the rhetoric of improving family life (191–214).

2 Shanken, *194X*, 157.

3 "What's Ahead for Me?" Certain-Teed Building Products advertisement, *American Home,* March 1945 (emphasis in original).

4 Clark, "Ranch House Suburbia"; and Clark, *American Family Home, 1800–1960*. See also Gans, *Levittowners*; Hine, "Search for the Postwar House"; and Spigel, *Welcome to the Dreamhouse*.

5 Mead, *Creative Life for Your Children*, 1.

6 Clark, "Ranch House Suburbia"; and Clark, *American Family Home, 1800–1960*.

7 Cherner, *How to Build Children's Toys and Furniture*, 78.

8 See, for example, Moskowitz, *Standard of Living*.

9 Wright, *Building the Dream*, chap. 13.

10 Yost, "Homes for Our Children," 24–25.

11 Winton, "'A Man's House Is His Art.'"

12 "How Livable Is a Modern House?" 108.

13 In the survey, 68.8 percent indicated there would be "fewer rooms in the postwar

house," and 71.2 percent suggested that there would be more dual-purpose rooms. Parents' Magazine, *Parents' Magazine's Survey of Postwar Housing.*

14 Pratt, "You Can Build Your Own Home for Half the Price."

15 Guinan, "Getting Re-acquainted with the Children," 30.

16 Mock, *If You Want to Build a House*, 18. See also Kelly, *Expanding the American Dream*; and Kennedy, *House and the Art of Its Design*, 86.

17 Armstrong Linoleum advertisement, *Ladies' Home Journal,* June 1950, inside front cover.

18 Carter and Hinchcliff, *Family Housing.*

19 Adams, "Eichler Home," 170. Adams also suggests that the family, including the children, who lived in the Eichler house she discusses did not necessarily use the house as the prescriptive literature intended.

20 The title page of the 1943 edition of Gesell and Ilg's *Infant and Child in the Culture of Today* was illustrated with numerous objects, such as toys, cars, books, music, charts, a crib, bottles, a high chair, and, in the center, a playpen.

21 Hulbert, *Raising America*, 174.

22 Kennedy, *House and the Art of Its Design*, 85.

23 "How to Make Your Playpen Pay Dividends!" 42.

24 Gesell and Ilg, *Infant and Child in the Culture of Today*, 361.

25 Spock, *Baby and Child Care* (rev. ed.), 167–68. Editions of Spock's book after the first occasionally included a slight title change.

26 Snyder, "Playroom."

27 "Kitchen Is Most Popular Room in Museum's House," Department of Public Information Records, microfilm 12;12, MoMA Archives, NY.

28 Eleanor Roosevelt, "Museum Model Home Is New but Expensive," *New York World-Telegram,* June 24, 1949, PI, mf 12;2, MoMA Archives, NY.

29 MoMA's education department, under Victor D'Amico, promoted worldwide the influential notion of creative art teaching.

30 Jacobson, *Raising Consumers.* See chap. 5, "Revitalizing the American Home: Playrooms, Parenting, and the Middle-Class Child Consumer."

31 "Child's Playroom Ingeniously Set Up."

32 Joseph Aronson, quoted in Roche, "Ideas for a Playroom."

33 A property-owners' publication from 1957 noted, "Levittown is a child-centered community at this time. It is a veritable wonderland for raising children"; quoted in Kelly, *Expanding the American Dream*, 107.

34 Kelly, *Expanding the Dream*, 72, 107.

35 Price's house was estimated to cost $17,500; see "Builder House." The house, located at 1802 North Shirley Street, was outfitted as a show house and opened in late May 1954. It cost $17,999 for the house and land in 1959. See *"Parents' Magazine's* Ninth Annual Builders' Competition," 68.

36 *Shortage of Scientific and Engineering Manpower.*

37 Besser, *Growing Up with Science.* This book was also excerpted in *Parents' Magazine* as "A Space Program for Your Young Scientist," January 1962, 48.

38 West, *Growing Up in Twentieth-Century America*, 182.

39 Mead, *Creative Life for Your Children*, 20.

40 Annmarie Adams also notes that the "typical child's bedroom of the 1960s expressed, in its arrangement and decoration, the personality of its tiny inhabitant." See Adams, "Eichler Home," 173.

41 Hartley and Goldenson, *Complete Book of Children's Play*, 332.

42 This belief has returned with new enthusiasm for creating authentic aesthetic experience in children. See Spitz, *Brightening Glance*, 133–57.

43 "Better Rooms to Grow In," 47.

44 Roche, "Permanent Room for Junior."

45 Cherner, *How to Build Children's Toys and Furniture*, 82.

46 Ibid., 86.

47 Calvert, *Children in the House*, 131–35.

48 Stearns, Rowland, and Giarnella, "Children's Sleep."

49 On more elaborate nineteenth- and early twentieth-century nursery designs, see White, *World of the Nursery*; and Ottillinger, *Fidgety Philip!*

50 The exhibition *L'Enfant à travers les ages* was held at the Petit Palais in 1901, and a similar exhibition was held in Vienna the following year. Schemes for nursery designs were also submitted to the Salon d'autômne and the Société des artistes décorateurs.

51 Juliet Kepes published *Five Little Monkeys*, a children's book that revisited the monkey theme, in 1952.

52 Kepes and Kepes, "Most Important Room," 104.

53 "Fun Room." The article refers to Julie as "Judy."

54 Laverne Originals was established in 1942 by the painters Erwin and Estelle Laverne, who met at the Arts Students' League in the 1930s. The company was known for its modernist designs by Alexander Calder, Alvin Lustig, Ray Komai, and others. See Kirkham, *Women Designers in the USA, 1900–2000*, 156; and Jackson, *Twentieth-Century Pattern Design*.

55 *Interiors* announced that the design was in preparation and could be ordered in any of Laverne's forty basic ground colors; it depicted one sample in orange. See "Wallpapers," 109. From at least the 1930s onward, experts argued that illustrative wallpapers should be carefully chosen to provoke a child's imagination. See Burris-Meyer, *Color and Design in the Decorative Arts*, 230.

56 Fineberg, *Innocent Eye*. See also Fineberg, *Discovering Child Art*.

57 The utopian desire to create the world anew after the destruction of World War I was fully expressed in the numerous designs for children created at the Bauhaus by the German designer Ferdinand Kramer and the Dutch De Stijl designer Gerrit Rietveld, and in the Soviet children's books that El Lissitzky designed. See Kinchin and O'Connor, *Century of the Child*, 58–87.

58 Siedhoff-Buscher's designs were advertised as everyday products that might make money for the Bauhaus and thereby fulfill Gropius's aim of allying art and industry. Similar designs by Katt Both and Marcel Breuer were also produced in Dessau. The architectural historian Nikolaus Pevsner purchased a set of Siedhoff-Buscher's children's furniture for his son, now in the Klassik Stiftung, Bauhaus-Museum, Weimar.

59 Alma Siedhoff-Buscher, "Kindermöbel und Kinderkleidung," *Vivos Voco: Zeitschrift für neues Deutschtum* 5, no. 4 (April 1926): 156; quoted in Fiedler, "Room for Children but None for Research?" 50.

60 Siedhoff-Buscher's shipbuilding toys and throw dolls, along with Eberhardt Schrammen's blocks, were indebted to the venerable German toy industry (especially the popular nineteenth-century Anker building sets), but the Bauhaus toys did not presuppose a formal outcome. The German architect Bruno Taut produced a set of sixty-two colored glass building blocks, with Blanche Mahlberg, around 1919 called the Dandanah Fairy Palace.

61 Siedhoff-Buscher, "Kind Märchen Spiel Spielzeug."

62 László Moholy-Nagy, "Die Arbeit des Staatlichen Bauhauses," *Thüringer Allegemeinen Zeitung*, October 19, 1924, cited in Siebenbrodt, *Alma Siedhoff-Buscher*, 54.

63 The psychological benefits and ability to "grow with the child" were aspects of the industry that retailers emphasized. See Hansen, "Children's Furniture."

64 Burris-Meyer, *Color and Design in the Decorative Arts*, 232, 234–35.

65 Wilson, *Livable Modernism*, 108–9.

66 Howe, "New York World's Fair, 1940," 39.

67 Calvert, *Children in the House*.

68 S. H., "On and Off the Avenue, About the House," *New Yorker*, May 21, 1949. PI, mf 12;2, MoMA Archives, NY.

69 Pat Kirkham has noted the similarity of these designs to Marcel Breuer's Isokon furniture. See Kirkham, *Charles and Ray Eames*, 216.

70 Ibid., 218.

71 Henry P. Glass was trained as an architect in Vienna. See "Shaping the Modern."

72 The Bamboozler in the collection of the Brooklyn Museum of Art, no. 1993.6, was a prototype but was estimated to cost $14.95.

73 Glass's Swingline designs won the prestigious Industrial Design Institute's Gold Medal Award in 1952. The Eameses' children's furniture was featured in prominent displays of furniture and housing design, and even on the cover of *House and Garden* magazine in 1946, yet the edition of five thousand initially produced was the first and last.

74 Knoll Associates advertisement, *Architectural Forum* 102 (February 1955): 227.

75 Other Knoll advertising, which Matter also produced, depicted his young son enjoying adult-sized Knoll furniture as playthings.

76 See Kauffmann, "Kay Bojesen," 64–67.

77 Vedel chairs were included in a large display of Scandinavian furniture and design at Bloomingdale's in the spring of 1958.

78 These objects were imported to the United States by Hank Loewenstein of Dallas, Texas, in the late 1960s. See "In the Showrooms," 24.

79 Bliss, introduction to "Children's Furniture," n.p.

80 "Children's Rooms," 114.

81 McGrath and McGrath, *Children's Spaces*. Many of the designs depicted were conceived for urban spaces where there was no backyard.

82 Chermayeff, foreword to ibid., 5.

83 McGrath and McGrath, *Children's Spaces*, 10.

84 Norman McGrath, conversation with author, February 2012.

85 Hugh Hardy, quoted in McGrath and McGrath, *Children's Spaces*, 66.

86 Henry Smith-Miller was trained as an architect and, while living in Rome on a Fulbright scholarship, developed a series of toys. He was considered as a possible member of Dino Gavina's design group, but only a few objects were prototyped. In the early 1970s, he returned to the United States to work for the architect Richard Meier.

87 Henry Smith-Miller, quoted in McGrath and McGrath, *Children's Spaces*, 180.

88 Bradley, *Happiness through Creative Living*, 21.

89 Osborn, *Applied Imagination*, rev. ed., 76.

90 Gelber, *Hobbies*. The biting satire of John Keats condemned suburban do-it-yourself to "sterile monotony"; see Keats, *Crack in the Picture Window*, 89.

91 Cross, "Suburban Weekend."

92 Gans, *Levittowners*, 204.

93 Toy Manufacturers of the U.S.A., *So You Want to Build a Playroom*. According to the industry magazine *Playthings*, coverage of the model playroom was extensive, and "every time a magazine offered the plans, thousands of consumers wrote in requesting them—in many instances setting new records for consumer demand on subjects of specialized interest." "Model Playroom," 100.

94 See, for example, Caney, *Steven Caney's Toy Book*; Fiarotta and Fiarotta, *Snips and Snails and Walnut Whales*; Laury, *Handmade Toys and Games*; and Ritchie, *Making Scientific Toys*.

95 Bragdon, "Word from the Editor-in-Chief," 6.

96 Cherner, *How to Build Children's Furniture and Toys*, 15. Cherner's earlier book, *How to Make Your Own Modern Furniture* (1953), had already established his do-it-yourself credentials. Cherner studied at Columbia University and also taught at MoMA.

97 Cherner, *How to Build Children's Furniture and Toys*, 16.

98 Gelber cites a 1958 survey of two hundred people in Little Rock, Arkansas, who found that do-it-yourself projects gave them "a sense of creative self-fulfillment." See Gelber, *Hobbies*, 270.

99 See for example, "Secret Spaces of Childhood."

100 Van Slyck, "Spatial Practices of Privilege."

101 Jekyll, *Children and Gardens*, 27. Jekyll addressed both children and parents and acknowledged that the playhouse was "a somewhat costly toy."

102 "To Toyland, This Way"; "Next to the Pony—the Playhouse."

103 White, *Playhouse Architecture*.

104 Livingston, "Give Your Children a Playhouse," 51; and Charles, "Playhouses You Can Build Yourself," 56.

105 See Gardner, "Rainy Day Playhouse."

106 FAO Schwarz, *Fun in the Sun Catalogue*, 24.

107 *Children's Rooms and Play Yards* (1960), 70.

108 Spock, *Common Sense Book of Baby and Child Care*, 248.

109 *Sunset* noted, "Often the simplest and most inexpensive outdoor play equipment

scores the greatest success. Cardboard boxes and packing cases are turned into castles and forts and playhouses; a length of hose is a 'pretend' snake or a piece of play gas station equipment." *Children's Rooms and Play Yards* (1960), 70.

110 Smith, *"Where Did You Go?" "Out." "What Did You Do?" "Nothing,"* 71.

111 Charles, "Playhouses You Can Build Yourself," 56.

112 Strait, "Playhouse for the Kids."

113 May, *Homeward Bound*.

4. BUILDING CREATIVITY IN POSTWAR SCHOOLS

1 The population of the state of California more than doubled between 1940 and 1960; see Stoltzfus, *Citizen, Mother, Worker*, 139.

2 See statistics cited in American Association of School Administrators, *Planning America's School Buildings*, 18; and Reef, *Childhood in America*, 240.

3 Between 1949 and 1959, twenty-five thousand one-teacher schools were abandoned because of consolidation and unified districts. See American Association of School Administrators, *Planning America's School Buildings*, 19.

4 "Schools," 129.

5 American Association of School Administrators, *Planning America's School Buildings,* 20.

6 William W. Cutler and Amy S. Weisser have looked at postwar schools through the lens of earlier debates about school design; I examine the form, representation, and implications of elementary and secondary school architecture as a particular concern of the postwar era. See Cutler, "Cathedral of Culture." I am especially indebted to Weisser's discussion of Crow Island in "Institutional Revisions."

7 Cutler, "Cathedral of Culture," 4–5; and Weisser, "'Little Red School House, What Now?'" 198.

8 Cutler, "Cathedral of Culture," 10.

9 Donovan, *School Architecture*.

10 LaChance, *Schoolhouses and Their Equipment*, 19.

11 On the interwar pavilion schools in Germany, see Henderson, "'New Buildings Create New People.'"

12 See for example, Châtelet, Lerche, and Luc, *L'école de plein air*; and Gutman, "Entre moyens de fortune et constructions spécifiques."

13 Hines, *Richard Neutra and the Search for Modern Architecture*, 164–65.

14 See, for example, Cremin, *Transformation of the School*; Cuban, *How Teachers Taught*; Zilversmit, *Changing Schools*; and Reese, *America's Public Schools*.

15 The Perkins, Wheeler, Will firm had received few commissions at this point but had completed buildings for prominent figures in Winnetka. Perkins, Wheeler, Will expressed interest in the project and arranged for Saarinen to collaborate. Lawrence Perkins describes this collaboration in "Oral History of Lawrence Bradford Perkins." See also Weisser, "Institutional Revisions," 65–66, 102–5.

16 Emphasis in original. Weisser cites a letter from Pressler to the Saarinens that is worded slightly differently from the one published in the *Architectural Forum*: "Everywhere children and what they can do shall be the adornment of the structure. . . . The beauty should be a background setting kind, and one not too fin-

ished, lest children feel it beyond them to make [a] contribution." See Weisser, "Institutional Revisions," 71.

17 The curriculum covered basic subjects such as reading, writing, arithmetic, history, and science, but it allowed each pupil to advance and master subjects at his or her own rate and without letter grades or fear of failure. One of the distinctive features of the school curriculum was the designated Pioneer Room, where the children explored aspects of daily life of the past and experimented with materials. See ibid., 69–70.

18 Ibid., 71.

19 Ibid., 74–83.

20 In 1955, the *Architectural Forum* revisited the school and remarked: "Crow Island appears, if anything, more significant than it did 15 years ago. Time and use—not only here but in many hundred later schools—have proved out the workability of its innovations to a degree that only the wildest optimism in 1940 could have conjectured. The national debt owed Crow Island for ideas large and small is staggering." See "Crow Island Revisited," 130.

21 Maynard, *Buildings of Delaware*, 41–42.

22 "Color Is Key to Modern Classrooms," 38.

23 Caudill, *Space for Teaching*, 42.

24 After the war, as demand surged, school boards and local superintendents around the country raised taxes and proposed bond measures multiple times for capital building projects. U.S. Department of Health, Education and Welfare, Office of Education, *Local, State, and Federal Funds for Public School Facilities, Circular no. 558* (Washington, D.C.: Government Printing Office, 1959), cited in American Association of School Administrators, *Planning America's School Buildings*, 21.

25 An illustrated slide talk on the exhibition was also circulated widely; see Department of Circulating Exhibitions Records, II.1.75.2. MoMA Archives, NY. The exhibition did not have a catalog, but an offprint of Elizabeth and Rudolf Mock's article "Schools Are for Children" was available. A film, *Design for Learning* (1942), not produced by MoMA, also circulated with the exhibition. In addition to being in the exhibition, Crow Island was included in Mock, *Built in USA, 1932–1944*, 74–75. The exhibition charted the progress of modernism in the United States since the International Style exhibition of 1932. The advisory committee for this exhibition included Sigfried Giedion, Walter Curt Behrendt, Serge Chermayeff, John Entenza, and Kenneth Reid.

26 In addition to displaying photographs and models of forty-one schools in the United States, Europe, and Brazil, the exhibition contrasted "modern" educational theories to those of the past. "Modern Architecture for the Modern School," CE, II.1.75 1. MoMA Archives, NY. Modern school architecture had a prominent place in the museum's other postwar architecture exhibitions "Built in USA" (1944) and "Built in USA: Postwar Architecture" (1952).

27 Henry Ford Museum and Greenfield Village and *Encyclopedia Americana*, "Schoolroom Progress, U.S.A. Press and Educators Preview," EI 1929-Box 89,

Henry Ford Museum and Greenfield Village Archives. During the press preview, on September 19, 1955, in Washington, D.C., children and adults in period costume enlivened the exhibits.

28 Press release, CE,II.1.75 1. MoMA Archives, NY.

29 Perkins, Wheeler, Will became Perkins and Will after Todd Wheeler left the firm briefly in 1946. Perkins and Will eventually expanded to include offices in Chicago and White Plains, New York. John Lyon Reid was a partner in the San Francisco firm of Bamberger and Reid until 1948. The firm was later called John Lyon Reid and Partners, and Reid and Tarics after 1962. Reid designed numerous schools in the Bay Area. William Wayne Caudill was a student of Reid's at MIT. The Caudill Rowlett firm was established in Austin in 1946, moved to College Station in 1947, and was reorganized as Caudill, Rowlett, and Scott in 1948. In the late 1950s, the firm moved from Bryan to Houston, Texas, and practiced throughout the Southwest. Many other architects and firms, including Ketchum, Giná, Sharp; Maynard Lyndon; John Carl Warnecke; Mario Ciampi; Alonzo J. Harriman; and Hugh Stubbins also produced important school buildings in this period.

30 Shanken, *194X*, 109.

31 JoAnne Brown argues that civil-defense administrators viewed postwar schools as potential bomb shelters. However, most single-story postwar schools built before the mid-1960s did not have fallout-shelter provisions. See Brown, "A Is for Atom, B Is for Bomb.'" David Monteyne argues that schools were a focus of fallout-shelter debates but that competition projects produced uncongenial bunkerlike or subterranean schools. Caudill Rowlett Scott's Blackwell Senior High School (1966), in Blackwell, Oklahoma, had glass walls and windowless classroom wings. See Monteyne, *Fallout Shelter*, 170–77, 208.

32 Stairs were frequently cited as a source of injuries on the school grounds. National Council on Schoolhouse Construction, *Guide for Planning School Plants*. This idea was widely repeated; see, for example, Caudill, *Space for Teaching*, 83.

33 The 1946 *Guide for Planning School Plants*, published by the National Council on Schoolhouse Construction, emphasized expansion and flexibility as prime considerations. According to the report, a building's rigid frame, classrooms on one or two sides of the corridor, and continuous fenestration along the entire wall would all enhance a school plant's adaptability to change and expansion.

34 Davidson, "Building for War, Preparing for Peace," 202–5.

35 Montecito Elementary is today the Martinez Adult School. See "Low-Cost School."

36 Szlizewski, "Schoolhouse Architecture in America from 1830 to 1915," 137.

37 Reid had been associated with the Franklin and Kump practice from 1937 onward, and he profiled the work of the firm, including Acalanes Union High School, in "Post-war Schools" and "Perspectives."

38 "Growth of an Indoor-Outdoor Unit." Caudill Rowlett Scott's Underwood Elementary School in Andrews, Texas, also had a view of the boiler behind glass.

39 Goode, *Museums of the Future*, 427.

40 Brückner, *Geographic Revolution in Early America*. In the early 1920s, Howard Gilkey wrote, "The architecture of the school building, through daily inspira-

tion, develops good taste in the child. Pictures on the wall, copies of the Masters, stimulate aesthetic appreciation." See Gilkey, "Landscape Development of School Grounds," 61.

41 See, for example, Burke, "Light"; and Wu and Ng, "Review of the Development of Daylighting in Schools."

42 See Ogata, "Building for Learning in Postwar American Elementary Schools."

43 Bursch and Reid, *You Want to Build a School?* 7.

44 Throughout the 1940s and 1950s, research conducted by General Electric and Westinghouse into optimal lighting culminated in new designs for luminous ceilings and continuous fluorescent fixtures.

45 Manufacturers that contributed materials used the Michigan Research Laboratory Classroom in advertisements to sell their products. Congoleum-Nairn provided the asphalt tile floor, Mosaic Tile the tile for the walls, Owens-Illinois the glass block and Toplite ceiling panels, Owens-Corning the fiberglass curtains, and Brunswick the furniture.

46 Darrell B. Harmon and Faber Birren conducted extensive research on light, color, attention, and posture. See Ogata, "Building for Learning in Postwar American Elementary Schools," 569–70.

47 Caudill and Peña, "Colour in the Classroom," 123.

48 Peña, "What a Good Color Environment Can Do," 186; and Caudill and Peña, ibid., 123–24. Robert Forman, a British designer, advocated for special attention to color in nursery schools for cognitive reasons: "In more advanced schools it has been discovered that the correct use of colour greatly assists the children in becoming observant of detail which would otherwise be overlooked." See Forman, *Nursery Furnishing and Decoration*, 70. The use of vibrant color was an important aspect of the British Infant Schools; see Bonnick, "Post-war School Programme in England," 143–44.

49 "Homeliness in an American School," 14. See also "U.S. Is Building Some Fine New Schools," 82–83.

50 Zilversmit, *Changing Schools*, 9.

51 Waechter and Waechter, *Schools for the Very Young*, 152.

52 Donovan, *School Architecture*, 27.

53 Tyack and Cuban, *Tinkering toward Utopia*, 69.

54 See Ravitch, *Troubled Crusade*; and Cuban, *How Teachers Taught*. Also see Merle M. Ohlsen's handbook *Modern Methods in Elementary Education*.

55 Wilson, *Flexible Classrooms*.

56 Sanders, *Innovations in Elementary School Classroom Seating*. This study was underwritten by the American Desk Manufacturing Company. See also Pinnell, *Functionality of Elementary School Desks*; and Pinnell, "Directions in Design and Use of School Furniture."

57 In the late 1950s, American Seating developed several designs similar to the Universal model. See *Facts about School Furniture Today*; and *American Seating School Furniture*. After the mid-1950s, large corporations dominated the school-furniture market. Even before World War II, about two dozen manufacturers produced about 80 percent of all the school furniture used in the United States. After

the war, many smaller businesses were absorbed into larger corporations, such as American Seating and Brunswick. See Pinnell, *Functionality of Elementary School Desks*, 18–22.

58 American Seating Company, *American Seating School Furniture*, n.p.

59 Great Britain Ministry of Education, *Schools in the U.S.A.*, 295.

60 Korzenik, "Choices and Motives in Doing Historical Research," 267.

61 The chair design was by Dave Chapman, who was hired to conduct research for the company. Chapman continued to design Brunswick furniture into the late 1950s. He later created special furniture for classrooms designed for television. See Chapman, *Planning for Schools with Television*.

62 See advertisement in *Interiors* 116 (July 1957): 30 (emphasis in original).

63 In 1953, *Architectural Forum* held a debate on schoolhouse economy among the leading school designers. The cluster plan was the "biggest news" for that year in part because it resembled the scale and semi-isolation of the house. See "Cluster Plan."

64 Shaw and Perkins, "Planning an Elementary School," 59.

65 *Architectural Forum* suggested that the Yale Clinic of Child Development recommended the sixty-degree angles. See "Organic School," 115.

66 See Isenstadt, *Modern American House*.

67 "Organic School," 116. See also "Heathcote"; and Weinstock, *Heathcote Elementary School, Scarsdale, New York*.

68 Similar panes were also installed in the walls of the kindergarten playroom. The Heathcote bathrooms were originally brightly tiled with a repeating *H* motif. Although Perkins and Will used color sparingly, the British architects David Medd and Mary Crowley argued that the panes' color "reduces, rather than enhances, the quality of the natural materials which are so generously used." See Great Britain Ministry of Education, *Schools in the U.S.A.*, 280.

69 Lawrence B. Perkins, quoted in "Organic School," 114.

70 Pope, "What's Happened to the Little Red Schoolhouse?"

71 See American Association of School Administrators, *Cutting Costs in Schoolhouse Construction*. This pamphlet was based on a manuscript by William W. Caudill. The cost of Heathcote was $1,095,692, or $3,400 per pupil.

72 West Columbia Elementary School won the 1952 Competition for Better School Design, sponsored by *School Executive* magazine, and was included in Hitchcock and Drexler, *Built in USA*. Maynard Lyndon's Vista (California) Elementary School and Ernest J. Kump's San Jose (California) High School were also featured in this exhibition.

73 "Wirework School." See also the extensive discussions of Barthelme's work in Brazoria County in "Schools of Donald Barthelme and Associates." West Columbia won critical praise, but Barthelme created similar designs for segregated "Negro schools" in Sweeny, Texas.

74 See "Education," a special issue of *Life*, October 16, 1950. *Parents' Magazine* regularly covered educational issues in September and October but also devoted special issues to schools; see especially *Parents' Magazine*, February 1963, and September 1965. *Collier's* ran several series of articles on education in the mid-

1950s. Adam Benjamin Golub has discussed how popular media enhanced perceptions of "crisis" in American education. See "Into the Blackboard Jungle."

75 In the professional press, see, for example, *School Executive* 73 (July 1954), which devoted much of the issue to Heathcote; and Kling, "Beauty in Schools," 21–23. In the popular press, Dorothy Thompson objected to the new schools' lavish recreational facilities and the implications for adult-organized play. See Thompson, "Must Schools Be Palaces?" Heathcote (although not named) was an example of excess in a *Reader's Digest* article analyzing a number of recently constructed buildings deemed extravagant. See Harvey, "Do School Pupils Need Costly Palaces?" 39. The *Architectural Forum* devoted a long article to refuting the *Reader's Digest* allegations, charging that the *Digest* actually "set back attempts to overcome the school shortage and to aid communities in getting their money's worth for every school dollar spent." See "That 'Reader's Digest' Article."

76 With flexibility and expansibility as the watchwords, *Life* magazine published a scheme for an elementary school by Caudill Rowlett Scott and a junior high school by Perkins and Will. See "New Schools, Economy Too."

77 Tracy Myers is working on a dissertation on TAC and schools, which I have not consulted.

78 Cassler, "You Can Build a Better School House," 98–101.

79 The firm adopted aspects of this scheme in several other projects. At the West Bridgewater (Massachusetts) Elementary School (1954), TAC enlarged the grid to encompass two groups of seven classrooms placed around external courts that were connected by both glazed and open corridors. The rigid frame allowed for non-load-bearing walls and had clerestory windows and Plexiglas skylights. At the John Eliot Elementary School (1956), in Needham, Massachusetts, TAC departed from the cluster arrangement and used corridors for circulation between the segregated grade levels.

80 Harkness, "TAC's Educational Buildings," 29.

81 "The Function of Glass in School Design," September 1957, AIA File no. 26-A-9. CRS Archives, document 3000.0109, CRS Archives. The architect quoted is probably William Caudill or someone from the CRS firm. See also Thomas A. Bullock, "Design Applications in Modern School Construction," *Glass Digest* 36, no. 11 (November 1957): 46–47, 89–90, CRS Archives, document 3000.0101; and "How to Build Glass into a School," *School Management* (1962), CRS Archives, document 3000.0254.

82 Caudill, *Toward Better School Design*, 3.

83 Caudill, *Space for Teaching*, 4. Caudill's short book was well known among California school planners. Charles D. Gibson of the California State Department of Education wrote to him in 1946: "Your reputation as an authority on school design is already well established in California. We use your Bulletin 'Space for Teaching' almost as a Bible in this state." William M. Peña papers, Box 1, file 1578.0102, CRS Archives.

84 "Schools That Utilize the Prevailing Breeze," 130.

85 McQuade, "Little Red Schoolhouse Goes Modern."

86 The San Jacinto School in Liberty, Texas, had a covered assembly area; see Lopez,

"Individual School and the Delightful, Never-Ending Progress to Perfection." For the San Andres Elementary School and other schools in Andrews, Texas, CRS placed a covered "activity slab" at the entrance; see "Flexible Classrooms and an Academic Mall," 176.

87 See "Is Cooling Coming for Schools?"; "Air Conditioned Elementary School"; Clinchy, *Belaire Elementary School, San Angelo, Texas*; Roth, *New Schoolhouse*, 169–74; and Great Britain Ministry of Education, *Schools in the U.S.A.*, 54–55.

88 The circular form, unusual at the time, was indebted to a scheme for an economical circular school (eliminating the need for corridors and thereby cutting expenses) that Matthew Nowicki had published in *Architectural Forum* as a model "school for 1950." See Nowicki, "Forum's School for 1950." Nowicki died in a plane crash (returning from India, where he was planning the new capital of Chandigarh) in 1950.

89 The San Angelo School District designed and manufactured much of its school furniture. See "Staff Designs School-Built Teaching Aids," 31–32.

90 Federal Security Agency, Office of Education, *First Progress Report of the School Facilities Survey 1951–1952*; and Federal Security Agency, Office of Education, *Second Progress Report, School Facilities Survey*. At the same time, Congress approved legislation to provide money to states experiencing the impact of federal activities, such as those with military installations. These funds were used to improve and build schools and community centers for the expanding populations in previously rural places.

91 Benton, "Now the 'Cold War' of the Classrooms." Benton, who represented Connecticut from 1949 to 1953, published the *Encyclopedia Britannica* and also wrote *Teachers and the Taught in the U.S.S.R.*

92 Riesman, *Lonely Crowd* (rev. ed.), 60.

93 Ibid., 62.

94 Bestor was careful to qualify what he meant by "progressive" education. He had attended the Lincoln School, part of Teachers College at Columbia University, one of the foremost "progressive" institutions, saying, "I have not used the term 'progressive education.' I have deliberately refrained from doing so, because the phrase is vague and ambiguous. It is applied to a multitude of different programs, with many of which I am in hearty sympathy. On the other hand, many tendencies in contemporary American education that are labeled progressive can be more accurately described, I believe, as 'regressive education.'" See Bestor, *Educational Wastelands*, 44.

95 *Shortage of Scientific and Engineering Manpower*.

96 Ibid., iii.

97 Rickover, *Education and Freedom*, 130.

98 Ibid., 22.

99 Zilversmit and other historians of education have argued that the popular rejection of progressive education in the 1950s tends to exaggerate the degree to which progressivism had been embraced or sustained in the United States. In the mid-1950s, for example, even the famously progressive curriculum in Winnetka, Illinois, was redirected toward academic subjects, although it maintained indi-

vidualized instruction. See Zilversmit, *Changing Schools*, 120. William J. Reese also suggests that American education remained relatively constant despite the polarizing public debates. See Reese, *America's Public Schools*, chap. 8, "Guardians of Tradition," 251–85.

100 The denunciation of progressive education has led Diane Ravitch to argue that the progressive-education movement died in the mid-1950s. See Ravitch, *Troubled Crusade*, 78–80. She acknowledges that the more generalized emphasis on projects, individualized instruction, and antipathy for memorization are beholden to progressivism. Like Ravitch, Lawrence Cremin uses the demise of the Progressive Education Association as a marker, but points out numerous other factors; see Cremin, *Transformation of the School*, 347–53.

101 Wilt, *Creativity in the Elementary School*, 1.

102 Torrance, *What Research Says to the Teacher*, 3.

103 Kornbluth and Bard, *Creativity and the Teacher*.

104 See, for example, Wilt, *Creativity in the Elementary School;* Gowan, Demos, and Torrance, *Creativity*; and Drews, *Learning Together*.

105 Torrance, *What Research Says to the Teacher*, 3.

106 Government legislation supported the study and development of technological and curricular innovations, but private foundations, such as the Carnegie Corporation, the Rockefeller Brothers Fund, and especially the Ford Foundation, also provided substantial funding. The Rockefeller Brothers Fund's *The Pursuit of Excellence: Education and the Future of America* was a widely read response to the Sputnik crisis, and the Carnegie Corporation supported James B. Conant's report *The American High School Today*.

107 Marks, "History of Educational Facilities Laboratories." EFL had headquarters in New York City but established a regional center, the Stanford School Planning Laboratory, at Stanford University, in 1959 and another in 1962, at the University of Tennessee's School Planning Laboratory. By the 1970s, EFL also had an office in Austin, Texas, and ran project centers in other states. The EFL board of directors initially included industry leaders such as Milton Mumford of Lever Brothers, Thomas J. Watson Jr. of IBM, Clay P. Bedford of Kaiser Aircraft, and Frank Stanton of CBS, as well as the industrial designer Henry Dreyfuss and education experts.

108 Bruner, *Process of Education*. See also Dow, *Schoolhouse Politics*, 33–71.

109 Gores, "Educational Change and Architectural Consequence," 155. EFL published a pamphlet with nearly the same title in 1968.

110 Education Facilities Laboratories, *New Schools for New Education*.

111 Caudill, "Case of the Busted Box," 18.

112 John Lyon Reid, quoted in Lopez, *Schools for the New Needs*, 253.

113 "Chip Harkness and the Transitional School." Wayland Senior High School gained widespread attention from educators and administrators as well as from popular magazines. See, for example, "Crackling Excitement in School Corridors"; and Anderson and Harkness, "Planned Variability."

114 Clinchy, *Wayland Senior High School, Wayland, Massachusetts*, 1.

115 Anderson, "How We Made the Change-Over," 86.

116 "High School Plan Has Campus Look."

117 Harkness, "TAC's Educational Buildings," 30.

118 Thompson, "Toward Creative Teaching," 29.

119 At the "New Schools for New Education" conference, there was some dissent over what "flexibility" might mean. Donald Barthelme argued that the word meant nothing, whereas EFL isolated expansibility, convertibility, and versatility as the components of the idea.

120 See Educational Facilities Laboratories and Institute for Development of Educational Activities, *Open Plan School*.

121 Gross and Murphy, *Educational Change and Architectural Consequences*, 16.

122 EFL and IDEA, *Open Plan School*, 12.

123 Kohl, *Open Classroom*, 34–47, 115.

124 The investment was $680,000; see Griffin, *Systems*, 19.

125 The thirteen school districts, together with the SCSD staff as advisers, grouped together as the First California Commission on School Construction Systems. A group debate, with Gores and Ehrenkrantz, on the question of standardized components and their implications was hosted by the editors of the *Architectural Forum* in September 1961. The proceedings were published as "New Proposals to Cut School Costs."

126 The company estimated that the traditional California school cost $16.74 per square foot to build and hoped to reduce this by $1.50 per square foot through the development of component parts. See "School Component Designs, Costs Revealed," 169.

127 See Saint, *Towards a Social Architecture*; and Bullock, *Building the Post-war World*. Mary Crowley and David Medd, two of the most prominent architects and spokespersons for the British project, spent a year on a Harkness Fellowship studying American schools and comparing them to the British examples. See Medd and Crowley, "British School Architects Examine Our Work." Their formal report was published on behalf of the Great Britain Ministry of Education as *Schools in the U.S.A.: A Report*. See also Part, "What Can Be Learned from Britain's New Schools?" 126–28; and "Britain's Prefab Schools."

128 The first school was realized in 1946, one hundred by 1952, and two hundred by 1962.

129 Many schools are discussed in Educational Facilities Laboratories, *SCSD: The Project and the Schools*. The promotion of the SCSD program reached a national audience, and it attracted considerable attention. Although many praised the notion of component systems, the feasibility did not necessarily reduce overall costs. The California districts did not build cheaper schools. However, EFL argued that they received more comprehensive buildings of better quality. Thirteen, rather than the initially projected twenty-two, schools were erected with SCSD components, but aspects of the design were also installed in industrial buildings, and similar programs for school building were developed in Canada and Florida through the late 1960s. See Griffin, *Systems*, for a discussion of related projects in Toronto and Montreal, and at the University of California.

130 The school was a steel structure with brick facing. The dome, devised by Edward F. Nye, was a lamella-patterned steel form with concrete insulation.

131 "Big Top for Teaching"; Clinchy, *Schools for Team Teaching*; "Some Current

Answers for Urban Schools"; and "Shells and the Educating Process," *Technical Bulletin* 105 (September 1963): 59–61, CRS Archives, document 3000.0268.

132 William Caudill, "Eggcrates, Eggheads, and Eggshells," address given at the Sarasota Conference, Sarasota, Florida, November 17, 1960, CRS Archives, document 1079.0102.

133 Ramey and Piper, "Creativity in Open and Traditional Classrooms."

134 In its defense, SCSD countered that recommendations for acoustic ceiling panels had been made, but the panels had not been purchased.

135 Cuban, *How Teachers Taught*, 198–99.

136 Sanders, *Innovations in Elementary School Classroom Seating*, 135–36.

137 Pile, "Open Office."

138 A succession of books directed at the layperson who might be a parent, teacher, administrator, or member of a school board showed cost-benefits and plans and photographs of prominent schools. Most were written by architects, or published by architectural presses, and consistently recommended the low-rise profile, bilateral lighting, and self-contained classroom. See, for example, Caudill, *Toward Better School Design*; Bursch and Reid, *You Want to Build a School?*; Engelhardt, Engelhardt, and Leggett, *Planning Elementary School Buildings*; Perkins and Cocking, *Schools*; Lopez, *Schools for the New Needs*; Waechter and Waechter, *Schools for the Very Young*; and McQuade, *Schoolhouse*. McQuade's book was published by the Joint School Research Project, which included McQuade, Eggers and Higgins, Architects, and the Aluminum Company of America. See also Educational Facilities Laboratories, *Cost of a Schoolhouse*. More recent examples of this genre are Graves, *School Ways*; Dudek, *Architecture of Schools*; and Hille, *Modern Schools*.

139 Examples include Arne Jacobsen's Munkegårds School in Denmark, the projects of CAPFCE in Mexico, the Goethe-Schule in Kiel, Le Corbusier's school on the roof of the Unité d'Habitation in Marseille, and many others. See Roth, *New Schoolhouse*.

140 The debates around the elementary school had resonance for other educational buildings, as well as sprawling corporate complexes, suburban shopping malls, and airports.

5. LEARNING IMAGINATION IN ART AND SCIENCE

1 Efland, *History of Art Education*, 228.

2 Since at least the sixteenth century, children were believed to possess a unique vision that, if unfettered by learned conventions, had the capacity for expression. See Fineberg, *When We Were Young*, 199–200.

3 Ibid.; Fineberg, *The Innocent Eye*; and Fineberg, *Discovering Child Art*.

4 Cižek taught a private juvenile class in 1897 and began a similar class in 1904 at the Kunstgewerbeschule in Vienna, which continued until 1937. See Rochowanski, *Ein Führer durch das Österreichische Kunstgewerbe*, 28–29; Duncum, "Origins of Self-Expression," 32–35; and Smith, "Franz Cižek," 28–31.

5 Cižek's ideas were conveyed in English through Wilhelm Viola's *Child Art and Franz Cižek*. See Efland, *History of Art Education*, 198; Macdonald, *History and*

    Philosophy of Art Education, 320–54; Smith, *History of American Art Education*, 59–78; and Kelly, *Uncovering the History of Children's Drawing and Art.*

6   Although Lowenfeld enrolled in the Kunstgewerbeschule in 1921, Efland argues that Cizek's influence on him was minimal and perhaps even negative. See Efland, *History of Art Education*, 234.

7   In Austria, Lowenfeld collaborated with the art historian Ludwig Münz on interpretations of sculptural work by blind children. See Saunders, "Contributions of Viktor Lowenfeld to Art Education," 7. See also Lowenfeld, *Nature of Creative Activity.*

8   Lowenfeld, *Creative and Mental Growth*, v.

9   Ibid., 1. This statement appears in the second, third, and fourth editions of the book.

10 Lowenfeld revised *Creative and Mental Growth* in 1952 and 1957. Successive editions were prepared with his former student W. Lambert Brittain. Jonathan Fineberg has called this "perhaps the single most influential book for art educators in America in the second half of the twentieth century." See Fineberg, *When We Were Young*, 237.

11 Lowenfeld, *Your Child and His Art.*

12 Saunders, "Contributions of Viktor Lowenfeld to Art Education," 8. See also Logan, *Growth of Art in American Schools.*

13 Freedman, "Art Education and Changing Political Agendas."

14 Kern, "Purposes of Art Education in the United States from 1870 to 1980." Creative art education remained strong into the late 1970s but was joined with a greater concern for integrating art into other areas of the curriculum.

15 Denver Public Schools, *Creative Art for Use in the Elementary School*, 15, 16–17.

16 Jefferson, *Teaching Art to Children*, 40–42.

17 Lowenfeld, *Creative and Mental Growth*, 3rd ed., 5.

18 Maslow, *Farther Reaches of Human Nature*, 57. Maslow's argument about creativity dates from the late 1950s and early 1960s.

19 For a general discussion of the committee, see Freundlich, "Committee on Art Education."

20 Victor D'Amico, quoted in ibid., 329.

21 Committee on Art Education, "The Vital Role of Art Education Today," 2. Reports & Pamphlets: Educational Department, Box 14.4. MoMA Archives, N.Y.

22 Read, *Culture and Education in World Order*; MacLeish, *Art Education and the Creative Process*; and Bettelheim, "Art as a Personal Vision."

23 Freundlich, "Committee on Art Education," 331.

24 In 1934, Harry W. Jacobs, editor of *The Drawing Teacher,* suggested that a child's imaginative powers could be developed through graphic expression. See *The Drawing Teacher,* December–January (1934), in Binney & Smith Records, Series 5, Box 9, Folder 2. Jacobs directed the school of art in Buffalo and was the first editor of *The Drawing Teacher* when it began in 1926. In 1945, Marie C. Falco replaced Jacobs as editor, and the publication ended in 1949. An expanded newsletter, *The Binney & Smith Rainbow Reporter,* which was intended for the trade rather than art educators, began in 1948.

25 *The Drawing Teacher,* January–February 1946, n.p. Binney & Smith Records, Series 5, Box 9, Folder 14.

26 C. W. Knouff founded *Everyday Art* in 1922. Its aim, in addition to promoting Prang products, was to inspire art teachers with progressive ideas and bring art into everyday life.

27 Zweybruck also left a clear mark on the company. As the company art director between 1952 and her death, in 1956, she had Richard Neutra build the company's West Coast studio and participate as an art adviser along with eminent German art administrator Edwin Redslob.

28 The workshop staff collaborated with a company salesman, who arranged the workshops, ordered materials, and extolled the benefits of Binney & Smith products. The company also hoped that the teachers, comfortable with the materials they used, would have some say in which products were ordered. See S. Vere Smith, "B&S Art Workshops," *Binney & Smith Rainbow Reporter,* April 1948, 2. Binney & Smith Records, Box 11, Folder 3.

29 "Teachers Learn by Doing at B&S Workshops," *Binney & Smith Rainbow Reporter,* Spring 1956. Binney & Smith Records, Series 5, Box 11, Folder 7.

30 Ibid.

31 "Crayon Art," 14. In the 1950s, The American Crayon Company unveiled a product that transfer-printed images of children's drawings to textiles. See Zweybruck, "Experimental Fabric Design in Silk Screen Technique."

32 Binney & Smith, *Shaw Finger-Paint*, 3.

33 Stankiewicz, "Self-Expression or Teacher Influence."

34 Lowenfeld, *Creative and Mental Growth* (rev. ed.), 166, 326.

35 "Imagination," Binney & Smith advertisement for finger paint, 1958. Binney & Smith Records, Series 10, Box 34, Folder 28, Finger Paint.

36 Brochure, Binney & Smith Records, Series 10, Box 34, Folder 28, Finger Paint.

37 "Modeling clay is one of the first tools for creative self-expression we can give a child." "Clayola Modeling Clay," Binney & Smith Records, Series 10, Box 34, Folder 3.

38 *Binney & Smith Rainbow Reporter,* Spring 1958, 16. Binney & Smith Records, Series 5, Box 11, Folder 8.

39 "Review of Crayola Crayon Consumer Advertising, 1956–1979," Binney & Smith Records, Series 7, Box 22, Folder 13.

40 The company conducted test cases in radio and TV during this time. Radio spots were adaptations of the "Crayola Corner" theme, and a television spot had an art-workshop consultant as a featured guest. See ibid.

41 Seiter, *Sold Separately,* 71. Rob Goldberg, who is writing a dissertation on toys of this period, argues that the Vietnam War informed the discourse on quiet, non-violent play.

42 Charles W. Reinhart, "Monday Memo," *Broadcasting,* March 3, 1975. Binney & Smith Records, Series 6 and 7, Box 22, Folder 13.

43 "Review of Crayola Crayon Consumer Advertising, 1956–1979," 22.

44 Spigel, *TV by Design.*

45 Before the creation of the Junior Museum, the Metropolitan estimated that al-

ready it received three hundred thousand schoolchildren per year. In the 1930s, there were WPA tours in addition to in-house educational tours. See "Executive Committee Meeting, June 30, 1941," in Office of the Secretary Subject Files 1870–1950, Educational Work, Re-organization of Educational & Extension Departments, 1941–43, 1945, 1947, Ed804, Metropolitan Museum of Art Archives. See also the 1948 description of the Junior Museum in Condit, "Junior Museum at the Metropolitan."

46 Taylor, "Education and Museum Extension," 181.

47 This was part of a large program of reconstruction begun in 1950 that included new galleries for paintings, medieval art, arms and armor, and later European decorative art, as well as a restaurant decorated by Dorothy Draper (now returned to its earlier use as an antique court) and the Grace Rainey Rogers Auditorium. See Condit, "New Junior Museum."

48 A review in the *New York Herald Tribune* noted that the exhibition was "replete with push buttons, peep shows, and phonograph recordings to lure the children of an electronic age in to the joys of esthetics." See Paul V. Beckley, "Museum for Small Fry has Scores of Gadgets," *New York Herald Tribune*, October 2, 1957, Junior Museum Scrapbook, vol. 1, Thomas J. Watson Library.

49 "How to Look at Paintings" (1958–60), Junior Museum Scrapbook, vol. 2, Thomas J. Watson Library. The Junior Museum began a studio program on Saturdays for members' children in 1954. Cray-Pas was invented in Japan in the 1920s precisely to encourage free drawing and personal expression.

50 Nosan, "Women in the Galleries," 63.

51 In a 1960 memo discussing objectives for the museum, members of the Women's Board, a group of elite supporters, noted that a children's museum might "fire the imagination of the press and the public." Letter to John Maxton from Mrs. William D. Shorey, Mrs. C. E. Shorey Jr., and Mrs. James Alter, February 17, 1960. Art Institute of Chicago Archives, Subject Files Department Histories, Box 2, Folder: Museum Education, History Jr. Museum, 1960–1969.

52 "Plan and Objectives for the Junior Museum," Art Institute of Chicago Archives, Subject Files Department Histories, Box 2, Folder: Museum Education, History Jr. Museum, 1960–1969. The Women's Board and Junior League of Chicago raised $250,000 for renovation and created a full-service children's area with galleries, lunchroom, and a library.

53 "The Junior Museum of the Metropolitan Museum of Art," n.d. (before 1957). See Metropolitan Museum of Art Archives, Folder: Office of the Secretary Records, Junior Museum of Metropolitan Museum of Art, 1941–46; 1953; 1956, J958.

54 Interdepartmental memo from Louise Condit to Mr. Bach, November 5, 1943. Metropolitan Museum of Art Archives, Folder: Office of the Secretary Records, Junior Museum of Metropolitan Museum of Art, 1941–46; 1953; 1956, J958.

55 See Morgan, "From Modernist Utopia to Cold War Reality"; Shaw, "Modern Art, Media Pedagogy, and Cultural Citizenship"; and Haddow, "Victor D'Amico's Creative Center."

56 D'Amico, "What Is Creative Teaching?"; and D'Amico, *Experiments in Creative Art Teaching*.

57 Bland, *Art of the Young Child*, 33.

58 D'Amico, *Experiments in Creative Art Teaching*, 15.

59 The MoMA concept was widely covered in the press. An article in the middle-class magazine *Living for Young Homemakers* suggested adapting lessons for home; see O'Connor, "Museum Art Classes Give Ideas for Home."

60 MoMA Press Release 19, March 14, 1955. MoMA Archives, NY.

61 Kasai recounted that after the war began, the museum requested that because her name was Japanese, it should be left off the label. Amy Kasai, conversation with the author, 2004.

62 In 1949, the Committee on Art Education also developed a recommended list of "pictures for children" culled by art teachers representing the committee. These pictures were lithographed prints of famous works for children from three to twelve years of age, available through MoMA and other galleries and print societies. The works included not only images of cities, animals, young sitters, and circus themes, but also Vincent Van Gogh's *Starry Night* (for all ages) and Winslow Homer's *Gulf Stream* (for children aged nine through twelve). "Pictures for Children Aged 3–12 Years," Committee on Art Education (1949), Reports and Pamphlets: Education Department, Folder 11. MoMA Archives, NY.

63 Press Release, CE, II.1.50.7. MoMA Archives, NY.

64 "Materials for Sale from the Exhibition Designed for Children," CE, II.1.50.7. MoMA Archives, NY.

65 Maeda and Iwasaki, *Victor D'Amico*.

66 See "Children's Art Carnival," Museum of Modern Art Library Archives, 3.8 C48c; and Sahasrabudhe, "Children's Art Carnival."

67 The playground, designed by Cornelia Hahn Oberlander, was gardenlike, with flowing water, a tree house, Unit Blocks, and a sound area, and it was run by a playground leader. The notion of learning through play was no longer novel; however, the organizers argued that this approach was still not well understood or sufficiently valued, and they posed their exhibits as "a catalyst for action in education for creativity." See Hill, *Children's Creative Centre*, 48.

68 See Cockcroft, "Abstract Expressionism, Weapon of the Cold War"; and Guilbaut, *How New York Stole the Idea of Modern Art*.

69 Haddow, "Victor D'Amico's Creative Center."

70 D'Amico, *Experiments in Creative Art Teaching*, 40.

71 Harvey, "Through the Enchanted Gate," 29.

72 Louise Kainz, quoted in Council on Museums and Education in the Visual Arts, *Art Museum as Educator*, 60.

73 Council on Museums and Education in the Visual Arts, *Art Museum as Educator*, 61.

74 "Designed for Children" circulation list. CE, II. 1.50.7. MoMA Archives, NY. The museum displayed books and posted recommended lists from education specialists at the Child Study Association, the Association for Childhood Education, and the Bureau of Educational Experiments. The exhibition traveled to Walker between April 27 and May 18, 1948.

75 New examples were produced expressly for the Walker event. Carol Kottke Correspondence, Box 13, Folder 2, 1948–1950, Walker Art Center Archives.

76 Tyng, who had studied architecture at Harvard, was working in the office of Louis Kahn and Oscar Stonorov at the time. She began designing the toy around 1947 and started to seek a U.S. patent that year. Patent 2,551,071, for "Children's Furniture and Toy Construction," was issued May 1, 1951. The Tyng Toy came in sets of different sizes, ranging from six to twenty-one pieces, with accompanying pieces for adding to an original set. Tyng's family provided the initial investment and helped with aspects of the Tyng Toy's promotion and production. About one thousand pieces were produced and eventually sold. In addition to the exhibition at the Walker, Tyng exhibited the toy at the Museum of Modern Art, the Contemporary Arts Museum in Houston, the Denver Art Museum, the Wisconsin-Union, the San Francisco Museum of Modern Art, and the Institute of Contemporary Art in Boston. Documents suggest that she also held demonstrations at department stores and toy shops, and that she sought a partnership with retailers such as Creative Playthings in New York and St. Louis, as well as shops in Minneapolis; Brookline, Massachusetts; Philadelphia; and Washington, D.C. At a later point, Tyng developed an idea for a toy based on the platonic solids that she had begun to explore in her (and Kahn's) architectural work. Anne Tyng Papers, Architectural Archives, University of Pennsylvania.

77 Promotional text accompanying correspondence from Anne Tyng to D. S. Defenbacher. Walker Art Center Archives, Ex B18 F5, Children's Fair Toys. This text is also included in a printed, six-sided brochure, which was not ready at the time of the Children's Fair. See Anne Tyng Papers, 74 VI 8.

78 Carol Kottke to Robert Preusser, October 28, 1950. Carol Kottke Correspondence, Box 13, Walker Art Center Archives, DSD B13 F2.

79 It is clear that Kottke was following what D'Amico had done. Carol Kottke to Robert Preusser, October 28, 1950. Carol Kottke Correspondence, Box 13, Walker Art Center Archives, DSD B13 F2.

80 Robert Preusser, codirector, to Carol Kottke, September 29, 1950, Carol Kottke Correspondence, Box 13, Walker Art Center Archives, DSD B13 F2.

81 Brayton, "Report on Children's Museums."

82 Brayton, "Children's Work in Museums," 179.

83 See Din, "History of Children's Museums in the United States, 1899–1997"; Heine, "Making Glad the Heart of Childhood"; Zien, "Beyond the Generation Gap"; and LeBlanc, "Slender Golden Thread, 100 Years Strong."

84 See Kohlstedt, *Teaching Children Science*; and Onion, "Picturing Nature and Childhood at the American Museum of Natural History and the Brooklyn Children's Museum, 1899–1930."

85 See Alexander, *Museum in America*, 133–45; Duitz, "Soul of a Museum"; and Hein, "Progressive Education and Museum Education."

86 Tullock, "First Museum for Children," 90.

87 Ibid., 94.

88 The Boston Children's Museum began in 1913 with donated natural-history speci-

mens from other Boston-area institutions, including the University Museum at Harvard and the Peabody Essex Museum in Salem, Massachusetts.

89   Howe, "New Faces of Education."

90   Rudolph, *Scientists in the Classroom.*

91   See U.S. Department of Health, Education, and Welfare, Office of Education, *Title III Elementary and Secondary Education Act.*

92   U.S. Department of Health, Education, and Welfare, Office of Education, *Stepping Up with PACE (Projects to Advance Creativity in Education).*

93   Spock, "Michael Spock: Looking Back on Twenty-three Years."

94   Spock noted, "You have to have enough freedom of operation in the exhibit to generate the phenomena but also be able to push it past the point where the phenomenon no longer occurs. The nature of this exploration allows you to begin to really understand and explain why the button is not the method to use in a 'hands on' approach." Ibid.

95   Educational Facilities Laboratories, *Hands-On Museums.* See also Frank Oppenheimer, "The Unique Educational Role of Museums," January 1969, cited in Hein, *Exploratorium.*

96   On the foundation of the Exploratorium, see Hein, *Exploratorium*; and Ogawa, Loomis, and Crain, "Institutional History of an Interactive Science Center."

97   See Cole, *Something Incredibly Wonderful Happens.*

98   "The Palace of Arts and Science: An Exploratorium of Science, Technology and Human Perception," ca. 1969, Exploratorium Records, BANC MSS 87/148c, Carton 21, Folder 6.

99   After 1971, the museum was eligible to request government-surplus items from the General Services Administration. See Hein, *Exploratorium*, 49.

100 Ibid., 30.

101 The use of young adults as on-site guides was modeled on practices at the Palais de la Découverte in Paris.

102 "Cybernetic Serendipity" had been organized by Jasia Reichardt at the Institute of Contemporary Art in London and then mounted at the Corcoran Gallery of Art Annex, in Washington, D.C. The opening of this exhibit at the Exploratorium also constituted the official opening of the museum, on October 11, 1969. See Hein, *Exploratorium*, 32–34.

103 August Coppola was the brother of director Francis Ford Coppola. The Tactile Dome grew out of Coppola's work on tactile sensation at California State University at Long Beach. With limited funds from the National Endowment for the Arts, the production of the dome took place in a warehouse space of the American Zoetrope Company.

104 Lorenz Eitner, a Stanford University art historian, headed the Exploratorium's Art Committee, which, at least initially, selected artistic materials for the museum. The artist residencies were supported by a grant from the National Endowment for the Humanities and the California Arts Council. In a fund-raising letter, Oppenheimer noted that the Artist-in-Residence program was developed after discussions with Charles Eames, John Kerr, artists on staff, and others. See

Oppenheimer's 1974 letter to June Noble Larkin, Exploratorium Records, BANC MSS 87/148c, Carton 11, Folder 2.

105 Asawa cofounded the Alvarado Arts Workshop in 1968 using throwaway objects, including milk cartons, to create structural forms.

106 Oppenheimer, "Schools Are Not for Sightseeing."

107 Ketcham, "Visit to the Exploratorium."

108 "Field Trips, Letters of Appreciation," Exploratorium Records, BANC MSS 87/148c, Carton 42, Folder 31.

109 Edwin Schlossberg to Frank Oppenheimer, Exploratorium Records, BANC MSS 87/148c, Carton 1, Folder 5, Minutes from Board of Directors Meeting, September 1973. The Exploratorium also promoted itself as a model, preparing a list of visitors from existing and new institutions that was circulated as press material. See "The Exploratorium as a Model for Museums," July 25, 1974. Exploratorium Records, BANC MSS 87/148c, Carton 21, Folder 6. The original letter is dated March 10, 1972; see Carton 30, Folder 3.

110 The renovation of these buildings had been discussed for years without much progress. As their condition grew worse and the city moved to condemn the buildings, the trustees of the Brooklyn Institute of Arts and Sciences planned to relocate the Children's Museum to a site on Eastern Parkway, near the Brooklyn Museum and the Brooklyn Botanic Garden. Resistance from the local Crown Heights community put pressure on trustees to keep the museum in its original site, in Brower Park. Changes to the park, including the closing of a small street, were part of the new plan.

111 The staff had already moved into the museum, and the space was open for press previews in anticipation of an opening in 1974. See, for example, Funke, "Children's Museum Shows New Ideas." The 1976 opening also garnered press interest; see Educational Facilities Laboratories, *Hands-On Museums*, 34–35; and "B. C. M. für Kinder."

112 "Report on the New Building in Outline," June 1965. Brooklyn Children's Museum Archives.

113 The commission for the new building was originally given to MacFayden and Knowles under the tenure of museum director Helen Fisher. Several versions of working reports about the new building produced under both MacFayden and Knowles and Hardy Holzman Pfeiffer included the provision for a simple planetarium, which was realized only at MUSE.

114 Hardy Holzman Pfeiffer Associates, "Preliminary Program Analysis," Brooklyn Children's Museum, Brower Park Building, February 14, 1969. Brooklyn Children's Museum Archives.

115 Architecture critic Paul Goldberger called the building "one of the most effective museums of architecture imaginable." Goldberger, "Funhouse Built in a Fun Structure." See also "Esprit Grows in Brooklyn."

116 Norman Pfeiffer, quoted in Funke, "Children's Museum Shows New Ideas."

117 Edwin Schlossberg, "The Learning Environment for the Brooklyn Children's Museum," 1975. Brooklyn Children's Museum Archives.

118 The museum maintained a large permanent collection, with some five hundred specimens housed in visible storage. See Pohle, "Children's Museum as Collector."

119 Pearce received a patent for this structure. He established Synestructrics, Inc., of Chatsworth, California, to manufacture the design.

120 Jones, "Space Labyrinths Teach Children about Molecules."

121 John L. Rudolph has described the role of research scientists working in National Science Foundation groups to revise curricular materials in the mid- and late 1950s. Molecules and waves were some of the key themes of the new textbooks produced in the hopes of introducing students to larger concepts. One of the leaders of this movement, MIT physicist Jerrold Zacharias, hoped to produce a low-cost ripple tank, accompanied by photographs and other materials, to allow students to see for themselves the laws of waves as an example for other motions. See Rudolph, *Scientists in the Classroom*, 177.

122 Sally Gregory Kohlstedt argues that the environmental reformer Rachel Carson's early experiences in nature study molded her acute awareness. The sense of wonder and discovery, which Carson had first argued for in a 1956 *Ladies Home Companion* article called "Help Your Child to Wonder," was republished in 1965 after her death. See Kohlstedt, *Teaching Children Science*; and Carson, *Sense of Wonder*.

123 Kenworthy, *Teacher and the Post-war Child*, 9.

EPILOGUE

1 In the 1980s, Mark A. Runco studied parents' and teachers' perceptions of creativity in children. Both used descriptions such as "active," "adventurous," "alert," "ambitious," "artistic," "capable," "dreamy," "energetic," "enthusiastic," and "imaginative." See Runco, "Implicit Theories," 29.

2 Gowan, Demos, and Torrance, *Creativity*, viii.

3 Imagination Playground in a Box is now in use at selected sites and is in the permanent collection of the Cooper-Hewitt National Design Museum, Smithsonian Institution, New York.

4 Smith, Cowie, and Blades, *Understanding Children's Development*, 237.

5 Singer and Singer, *House of Make-Believe*, 22 (emphasis in original).

6 Sutton-Smith, *Ambiguity of Play*.

7 Ibid., 206–7.

8 Singer and Singer, *Imagination and Play in the Electronic Age*.

9 Runco estimates some nine thousand papers were published on creativity between 1960 and 1991. See Runco, "Creativity." See also Runco, preface to *Encyclopedia of Creativity*, xv. Creativity studies increased rapidly in the 1990s, and although the field is still anchored in psychology and education, it has found wide appeal in other disciplines. In addition to Osborn and Parnes's *Journal of Creative Behavior* (begun in 1967), the *Creativity Research Journal* (begun in 1998) is dedicated to the science behind creativity. The Association for Computing Machinery (ACM), the world's largest group of educational and scientific computing, has hosted a series of regular conferences on creativity and cognition since 1993.

10 Florida, *Rise of the Creative Class and How It's Transforming Work, Leisure, Community and Everyday Life*. See also Ray and Anderson, *Cultural Creatives*.

11 IBM, "*Capitalizing* on Complexity."

12 Alliance of Artists Communities, *American Creativity at Risk*.

13 Bronson and Merryman, "Creativity Crisis."

14 Ibid.

15 See Gardner, *Artful Scribbles*; Gardner, *Art, Mind, and Brain*; and Gardner, *Creating Minds*. See also Craft, Gardner, and Claxton, *Creativity, Wisdom, and Trusteeship*.

16 National Advisory Committee on Creative and Cultural Education, "All of Our Futures: Creativity, Culture and Education."

17 Obama, State of the Union address.

18 Lingo and Tepper, "Creative Campus."

19 Gill, prologue to Alliance of Artists Communities, *American Creativity at Risk*.

20 Florida, *Rise of the Creative Class and How It's Transforming Work, Leisure, Community and Everyday Life*, 317.

BIBLIOGRAPHY

ARCHIVES

Art Institute of Chicago Archives. Art Institute of Chicago, Chicago, Illinois.

Binney & Smith Records. Archive Center, National Museum of American History, Smithsonian Institution, Washington, D.C.

Brooklyn Children's Museum Archives. Brooklyn Children's Museum, New York, New York.

Caplan Archive (now dispersed).

Carrara, Arthur A. Papers. Ryerson and Burnham Library Archives, Art Institute of Chicago, Chicago, Illinois.

CRS Archives. CRS Archive Center, Texas A&M University, College Station, Texas.

Donovan, Marion O'Brien. Papers. Archive Center, National Museum of American History, Smithsonian Institution, Washington, D.C.

Eames, Charles, and Ray Eames. The Work of Charles and Ray Eames Archive. Library of Congress, Washington, D.C.

Exploratorium Records. Bancroft Library, University of California, Berkeley, California.

Henry Ford Museum and Greenfield Village Archives. The Henry Ford, Dearborn, Michigan.

Kepes, György. Papers (1825–1989). Archives of American Art, Smithsonian Institution, Washington, D.C.

Metropolitan Museum of Art Archives. Metropolitan Museum of Art, New York, New York.

Museum of Modern Art (MoMA) Archives. Museum of Modern Art, New York, New York.

Museum of Modern Art (MoMA) Library Archives. Museum of Modern Art, New York, New York.

Tyng, Anne. Papers. The Architectural Archives, University of Pennsylvania, Philadelphia, Pennsylvania.

Walker Art Center Archives. Walker Art Center, Minneapolis, Minnesota.

Wallance, Donald. Shaping America's Products Archive. Cooper-Hewitt National Design Museum Archives, Smithsonian Institution, New York, New York.

Warshaw Collection of Business Americana. Archive Center, National Museum of American History, Smithsonian Institution, Washington, D.C.

OTHER SOURCES

A. J. Wood Research Corporation and Toy Manufacturers of the U.S.A. *Toy Buying in the United States: A One Year Study Prepared for Toy Manufacturers of the U.S.A., Inc.* New York: Toy Manufacturers of the U.S.A., 1965.

Aaron, David, with Bonnie P. Winawer. *Child's Play: A Creative Approach to Playspaces for Today's Children.* New York: Harper & Row, 1965.

Abramson, Paul. *Schools for Early Childhood: Profiles of Significant Schools.* New York: Educational Facilities Laboratories, 1970.

Adams, Annmarie. "The Eichler Home: Intention and Experience in Postwar Suburbia." In *Gender, Class, and Shelter,* edited by Elizabeth Collins Cromley and Carter L. Hudgins. Perspectives in Vernacular Architecture 5. Knoxville: University of Tennessee Press, 1995.

"Air Conditioned Elementary School." *School Executive* 75 (November 1956): 62–66.

Albrecht, Donald, ed. *World War II and the American Dream: How Wartime Building Changed a Nation.* Washington, D.C., and Cambridge, Mass.: National Building Museum and MIT Press, 1995.

Alexander, Edward P. *The Museum in America: Innovators and Pioneers.* Walnut Creek, Calif.: Altamira, 1997.

Allen of Hurtwood, Lady [Marjory Gill Allen]. *Planning for Play.* Cambridge, Mass.: MIT Press, 1968.

Allen of Hurtwood, Lady [Marjory Gill Allen], Maalfrid S. Flekkoy, Jens Sigsgaard, and Aase Grunda Skard, eds. *Space for Play: The Youngest Children.* Copenhagen: World Organisation for Early Childhood Education, 1964.

Alliance of Artists Communities. *American Creativity at Risk: Restoring Creativity as a Priority in Public Policy, Cultural Philanthropy, and Education.* Providence, R.I.: Alliance of Artists Communities, 1997. Electronic report.

Almqvist, Birgitta. "Educational Toys, Creative Toys." In *Toys, Play, and Child Development,* edited by Jeffrey H. Goldstein, 46–66. Cambridge: Cambridge University Press, 1994.

Amburgy, Patricia M., ed. *The History of Art Education: Proceedings from the Second Penn State Conference, 1989.* Reston, Va.: National Art Education Association, 1992.

American Association of School Administrators. *Cutting Costs in Schoolhouse Construction.* Washington, D.C.: American Association of School Administrators, 1952.

———. *Planning America's School Buildings: A Report of the AASA School-Building Commission.* Washington, D.C.: American Association of School Administrators, 1960.

American Seating Company. *American Seating School Furniture.* Grand Rapids, Mich.: American Seating, 1959.

———. *Classroom Furniture.* Grand Rapids, Mich.: American Seating Company, 1959.

———. *Facts about School Furniture Today*. Grand Rapids, Mich.: American Seating Company, 1959.

Anderson, Edward J. "How We Made the Change-Over." *Life,* March 22, 1963.

Anderson, Edward J., and John C. Harkness. "Planned Variability." *Nation's Schools* 65, no. 4 (April 1960): 83–91.

Anderson, Harold H., ed. *Creativity and Its Cultivation: Addresses Presented at the Interdisciplinary Symposia on Creativity, Michigan State University, East Lansing, Michigan*. New York: Harper & Row, 1959.

Antonio Vitali: Spielzeugdesigner, Creator of Toys. Weingarten: Kunstverlag Weingarten, 1994.

Appadurai, Arjun, ed. *The Social Life of Things: Commodities in Cultural Perspective*. Cambridge: Cambridge University Press, 1986.

Archer, John. *Architecture and Suburbia: From English Villa to American Dream House, 1690–2000*. Minneapolis: University of Minnesota Press, 2005.

Ariès, Philippe. *Centuries of Childhood*. Harmondsworth, U.K.: Penguin, 1960.

The Art Museum as Educator. Berkeley: University of California Press, Cleveland Museum of Art, and the Council on Museums and Education in the Visual Arts, 1978.

Ashwin, Clive. "Pestalozzi and the Origins of Pedagogical Drawing." *British Journal of Educational Studies* 29, no. 2 (June 1981): 138–51.

Association for Childhood Education. *Make It for the Children*. Washington, D.C.: Association for Childhood Education, n.d.

Association for Supervision and Curriculum Development. *Growing Up in an Anxious Age*. Washington, D.C.: National Education Association, 1952.

Attfield, Judy. *Wild Things: The Material Culture of Everyday Life*. Oxford: Berg, 2000.

"B. C. M. für Kinder." *Architektur und Wohnen* 1 (1976): 170–75.

Bachelard, Gaston. *The Poetics of Reverie: Childhood, Language, and the Cosmos*. Boston: Beacon, 1971.

Ball, Donald. "Towards a Sociology of Toys: Inanimate Objects, Socialization, and the Demography of the Doll World." *Sociological Quarterly* 8 (1968): 447–58.

Barenholtz, Bernard, and Inez McClintock. *American Antique Toys, 1830–1900*. New York: Abrams, 1980.

Barrie, J. M. *Peter Pan; or, The Boy Who Wouldn't Grow Up*. 1904.

Barron, Frank X. *Creative Person and Creative Process*. New York: Henry Holt, 1969.

———. *Creativity and Personal Freedom*. Van Nostrand Insight Books 44. Princeton, N.J.: Van Nostrand, 1968.

Barth, Herbert, Anne Barth, and Norm Hesseldahl. *Building a Creative Playground: A Community-School PTA Project*. Bellingham, Wash.: Educational Design and Consultants, 1974.

Barth, P. S. *Open Education and the American School*. New York: Agathon, 1972.

Barthes, Roland. "Toys." In *Mythologies*, 53–55. Translated by Annette Lavers. New York: Noonday, 1972.

Barzun, Jacques. "The Cults of 'Research' and 'Creativity.'" *Harper's*, October 1960, 69–74.

Baudelaire, Charles. *The Painter of Modern Life. 1863.* Edited and translated by Jonathan Mayne. New York: Da Capo, 1964.

Beatty, Barbara. *Preschool Education in America: The Culture of Young Children from the Colonial Era to the Present.* New Haven, Conn.: Yale University Press, 1995.

Beauregard, Robert A. *When America Became Suburban.* Minneapolis: University of Minnesota Press, 2006.

Beckett, Sandra L., ed. *Reflections of Change: Children's Literature since 1945.* Westport, Conn.: Greenwood, 1997.

Bengtsson, Arvid, ed. *Building Adventure Playgrounds.* New York: Praeger, 1972.

Benjamin, Walter. "The Cultural History of Toys." In *Selected Writings.* Vol. 2, *1927–1934*, edited by Michael W. Jennings, Howard Eiland, and Gary Smith and translated by Rodney Livingstone et al., 113–16. Cambridge, Mass.: Belknap Press of Harvard University Press, 1999.

Benton, William. "Now the 'Cold War' of the Classrooms." *New York Times,* April 1, 1956.

———. *Teachers and the Taught in the U.S.S.R.* New York: Atheneum, 1966.

Besser, Marianne. *Growing Up with Science.* New York: McGraw-Hill, 1960.

Bestor, Arthur. *Educational Wastelands: The Retreat from Learning in Our Public Schools.* 2nd ed. Urbana: University of Illinois Press, 1985.

Bettelheim, Bruno. "Art as a Personal Vision." In *Art: As the Measure of Man; as Education; a Personal Vision,* by George D. Stoddard, Irwin Edman, and Bruno Bettelheim. New York: Museum of Modern Art and the National Committee on Art Education, 1964.

"Better Rooms to Grow In." *Parents' Magazine,* January 1953.

"Big Top for Teaching." *Architectural Forum* 114 (May 1961): 97–100.

Binkley, Sam. *Getting Loose: Lifestyle Consumption in the 1970s.* Durham, N.C.: Duke University Press, 2007.

Binney & Smith. *Shaw Finger-Paint: The Original Finger Paint.* New York: Binney & Smith, 1953.

Bird, William L., Jr. *Paint by Number.* Washington, D.C.: Smithsonian Institution, National Museum of American History, in association with Princeton Architectural Press, 2001.

Birren, Faber. *Color, Form, and Space.* New York: Reinhold, 1961.

———. "Functional Color in the Schoolroom." *Magazine of Art* 42 (1949): 136–38.

———. "Functionalism with Color." *Nation's Schools* 39, no. 5 (1947): 40–43.

———. *New Horizons in Color.* New York: Reinhold, 1955.

Bland, Jane Cooper. *Art of the Young Child: Three to Five Years.* New York: Museum of Modern Art, 1957.

Bliss, Anna Campbell. Introduction to "Children's Furniture." Special issue, *Design Quarterly* 57 (1963).

Boas, George. *The Cult of Childhood.* London: Warburg, 1966. Reprint, Dallas: Spring, 1990.

Bonnick, John H. "The Post-war School Programme in England." *Journal of the Royal Architectural Institute of Canada* 28 (May 1951).

Boyer, Paul. *By the Bomb's Early Light: American Thought and Culture at the Dawn of the Atomic Age*. New York: Pantheon, 1985.

Bradley, Ben. *Visions of Infancy*. Oxford: Blackwell, 1989.

Bradley, Preston. *Happiness through Creative Living*. Garden City, N.Y.: Hanover House, 1955.

Bragdon, Allen D. "A Word from the Editor-in-Chief." *Family Creative Workshop*. Vol. 1. New York: Plenary, 1974.

Brayton, Margaret. "Children's Work in Museums." *Museum* 1, nos. 3–4 (1948): 178–82.

———. "Report on Children's Museums." First General Biennial Conference of the International Council on Museums, July 1948. UNESCO. Accessed November 5, 2009. http://unesdoc.unesco.org/.

Brecher, Ruth, and Edward Brecher. "Creative Ability . . . What Is It? Who Has It? What Makes It Flourish or Falter?" *Parents' Magazine*, November 1960.

Breines, Wini. *Young, White, and Miserable: Growing Up Female in the Fifties*. Chicago: University of Chicago Press, 1991.

Bremner, Robert H., ed. *Children and Youth in America: A Documentary History*. Vol. 3. Cambridge, Mass.: Harvard University Press, 1974.

Brewer, John. "Childhood Revisited: The Genesis of the Modern Toy." *History Today* 30 (1980): 32–39.

"Britain's Prefab Schools." *Architectural Forum* 94 (October 1952): 129–33.

Bronfenbrenner, Urie. *The Ecology of Human Development: Experiments in Nature and Design*. Cambridge, Mass.: Harvard University Press, 1979.

———. *Two Worlds of Childhood: U.S. and U.S.S.R.* New York: Sage Foundation, 1970.

———. *The Uses of Enchantment*. New York: Vintage, 1977.

Bronson, Po, and Ashley Merryman. "The Creativity Crisis." *Newsweek*, July 10, 2010.

Brossard, Chandler. "The Creative Child." *Look*, November 7, 1961.

Brosterman, Norman. *Inventing Kindergarten*. New York: Abrams, 1997.

Brown, JoAnne. "'A Is for Atom, B Is for Bomb': Civil Defense in American Public Education, 1948–1963." *Journal of American History* 75, no. 1 (1988): 68–90.

Brown, Kenneth D. *The British Toy Business: A History since 1700*. London: Hambledon, 1996.

Brown, Robert T. "Creativity: What Are We to Measure?" In *Handbook of Creativity*, edited by John A. Glover, Royce R. Ronning, and Cecil R. Reynolds, 3–19. New York: Plenum, 1989.

Browne, Sibyl, in collaboration with Ethel Tyrrell, Gertrude M. Abbihl, Clarice Evans, et al. *Art and Materials for the Schools: Activities to Aid the War and the Peace*. New York: Progressive Education Association, 1943.

Brubaker, C. William. *Planning and Designing Schools*. New York: McGraw-Hill, 1998.

Bruce, William C., ed. *Grade School Buildings*. Milwaukee, Wis.: Bruce, n.d., ca. 1914–25.

Brückner, Martin. *The Geographic Revolution in Early America: Maps, Literacy, and National Identity*. Chapel Hill: University of North Carolina Press, 2006.

Bruner, Jerome. *Acts of Meaning*. Cambridge, Mass.: Harvard University Press, 1990.

——. "The Creative Surprise." In *Contemporary Approaches to Creative Thinking*, edited by Howard E. Gruber, Glenn Terrell, and Michael Wertheimer. New York: Atherton, 1962.

——. *The Process of Education*. New York: Vintage, 1960.

Bryson, L. "Training for Creativity." *School Arts Magazine* 60 (1960): 5–8.

Buckingham, David. *The Material Child: Growing Up in Consumer Culture*. Cambridge: Polity, 2011.

"Builder House: The Architect and His Community; Robert Billsbrough Price." *Progressive Architecture* 37 (April 1956): 110–13.

Bullock, Nicholas. *Building the Post-war World: Modern Architecture and Reconstruction in Britain*. London: Routledge, 2002.

Burger, I. *Creative Play Activity*. New York: Barnes, 1950.

Burke, Catherine. "Light: Metaphor and Materiality in the History of Schooling." In *Materialities of Schooling: Design, Technology, Objects, and Routines*, edited by Martin Lawn and Ian Grosvenor, 125–43. Oxford: Symposium, 2005.

Burke, Catherine, and Ian Grosvenor. *School*. London: Reaktion, 2008.

Burris-Meyer, Elizabeth. *Color and Design in the Decorative Arts*. The Retailing Series. New York: Prentice-Hall, 1935.

Bursch, Charles Wesley, and John Lyon Reid. *You Want to Build a School?* New York: Reinhold, 1947.

Burton, Anthony. *Children's Pleasures: Books, Toys, and Games from the Bethnal Green Museum of Childhood*. London: Victoria & Albert, 1996.

——. "Design History and the History of Toys: Defining a Discipline for the Bethnal Green Museum of Childhood." *Journal of Design History* 10, no. 1 (1997): 1–21.

——. "Looking Forward from Ariès? Practical and Material Evidence of the History of Childhood and Family Life." *Continuity and Change* 4 (1989): 203–9.

Butt, Baseden. "The Modern Nursery." *Nursery World* (1933): 620–21.

Caillois, Roger. *Man, Play, and Games*. Translated by Meyer Barash. Urbana: University of Illinois Press, 1961.

Calvert, Karin. *Children in the House: The Material Culture of Early Childhood, 1600–1900*. Boston: Northeastern University Press, 1992.

Caney, Steven. *Steven Caney's Toy Book*. New York: Workman, 1972.

Cannady, William, ed. *New Schools for New Towns*. Houston, Tex.: Department of Architecture, Rice University, 1968.

Caplan, Frank, and Theresa Caplan. *The Power of Play*. New York: Anchor, 1973.

——. *The Second Twelve Months of Life*. New York: Grosset & Dunlap, 1977.

Caplan, Theresa. *Frank Caplan, Champion of Child's Play*. New York: Vantage, 1999.

Carlson-Paige, Nancy, and Diane Levin. *The War Play Dilemma: Balancing Needs and Values in the Early Childhood Classroom*. New York: Columbia University, Teachers College Press, 1987.

Carson, Rachel. *The Sense of Wonder*. New York: Harper & Row, 1965.

Carter, Deane G., and Keith Hinchcliff. *Family Housing*. New York: Wiley, 1949.

Cassler, Sey. "You Can Build a Better School House." *Collier's*, April 30, 1954.

Castaldi, Basil. *Creative Planning of Educational Facilities*. Chicago: Rand Mc-Nally, 1969.

Castillo, Greg. *Cold War on the Home Front: The Soft Power of Midcentury Design*. Minneapolis: University of Minnesota Press, 2010.

Caudill, William W. "The Case of the Busted Box." In Educational Facilities Laboratories, *New Schools for New Education*, 17–21.

———. *Space for Teaching*. Engineering Experiment Station Series 59. College Station, Tex.: Agricultural and Mechanical College of Texas, 1941.

———. *Toward Better School Design*. New York: Dodge, 1954.

Caudill, William W., and W. M. Peña. "Colour in the Classroom." *Journal of the Royal Architectural Institute of Canada* 28, no. 2 (May 1951): 123–24.

Caute, David. *Dancer Defects: The Struggle for Cultural Supremacy during the Cold War*. Oxford: Oxford University Press, 2003.

Cech, John. *Angels and Wild Things: The Archetypal Poetics of Maurice Sendak*. University Park: Pennsylvania State University Press, 1995.

Chapman, Dave. *Planning for Schools with Television: Design for ETV*. New York: Educational Facilities Laboratories, 1960.

Charles, Robert. "Playhouses You Can Build Yourself." *Parents' Magazine*, July 1962.

Châtelet, Anne-Marie, Dominique Lerche, and Jean-Noël Luc, eds. *L'école de plein air: Une experience pédagogique et architectural dans l'Europe du XXe siècle*. Paris: Éditions Recherches, 2003.

Chermayeff, Ivan. Foreword to McGrath and McGrath, *Children's Spaces*.

Chermayeff, Serge. *A Children's Center or Nursery School*. New York: Revere Copper & Brass, 1944.

Cherner, Norman. *How to Build Children's Toys and Furniture*. New York: Mc-Graw-Hill, 1954.

"Children's Rooms." *Progressive Architecture* 33 (December 1952): 114.

Children's Rooms and Play Yards. Menlo Park, Calif.: Lane Magazine & Book Co., 1960.

Children's Rooms and Play Yards. Rev. ed. Menlo Park, Calif.: Lane Magazine & Book Co., 1970.

"Child's Play: Creative Playthings' New Store." *Industrial Design* 17 (April 1970): 38–39.

"Child's Playroom Ingeniously Set Up." *New York Times*, June 24, 1947.

"Chip Harkness and the Transitional School." In Educational Facilities Laboratories, *New Schools for New Education*, 26–27.

Chudacoff, Howard P. *Children at Play: An American History*. New York: New York University Press, 2007.

Church, Louisa Randall. "Parents: Architects of Peace." *American Home*, November 1946, 18–19.

Clark, Beverly Lyon, and Margaret R. Higonnet, eds. *Girls, Boys, Books, Toys: Gender in Children's Literature and Culture*. Baltimore: Johns Hopkins University Press, 1999.

Clark, Clifford E., Jr. *The American Family Home, 1800–1960*. Chapel Hill: University of North Carolina Press, 1986.

——. "Ranch House Suburbia: Ideals and Realities." In May, *Recasting America*, 171–91.

Cleary, Beverly. *Beezus and Ramona*. New York: Morrow, 1955.

——. *Henry and the Clubhouse*. New York: Dell, 1962.

Clements, Robert D. "Modern Architecture's Debt to Creativity Education." *Arts Magazine* 64, no. 5 (1990): 44–63.

Clinchy, Evans. *A&M Consolidated Senior High School, College Station, Texas*. Profiles of Significant Schools. New York: Educational Facilities Laboratories, 1960.

——. *Belaire Elementary School, San Angelo, Texas*. Profiles of Significant Schools. New York: Educational Facilities Laboratories, 1960.

——. *Schools for Team Teaching*. Profiles of Significant Schools. New York: Educational Facilities Laboratories, 1961.

——. *Wayland Senior High School, Wayland, Massachusetts*. Profiles of Significant Schools. New York: Educational Facilities Laboratories, 1960.

"Cluster Plan." *Architectural Forum* 99 (October 1953): 117–26.

Cockcroft, Eva. "Abstract Expressionism, Weapon of the Cold War." *Artforum* 15, no. 10 (1974): 39–41.

Cohen, Lizabeth. *A Consumer's Republic: The Politics of Mass Consumption in Postwar America*. New York: Knopf, 2003.

Cole, K. C. *Something Incredibly Wonderful Happens: Frank Oppenheimer and the World He Made Up*. Boston: Houghton Mifflin Harcourt, 2009.

Cole, Natalie Robinson. *The Arts in the Classroom*. New York: Day, 1940.

——. *Children's Arts from Deep Down Inside*. New York: Day, 1966.

Colomina, Beatriz. *Domesticity at War*. Cambridge, Mass.: MIT Press, 2007.

Colomina, Beatriz, AnnMarie Brennan, and Jeannie Kim, eds. *Cold War Hothouses: Inventing Postwar Culture, from Cockpit to Playboy*. New York: Princeton Architectural Press, 2004.

"Color Is Key to Modern Classrooms." *Nation's Schools* 43, no. 1 (January 1949): 38.

Conant, James B. *The American High School Today: A First Report to Interested Citizens*. New York: McGraw-Hill, 1959.

Condit, Louise. "The Junior Museum at the Metropolitan." *Museum* 1, nos. 3–4 (1948): 192–94.

——. "The New Junior Museum." *Metropolitan Museum of Art Bulletin* 16 (1958): 257–68.

Connelly, Frances S. *The Sleep of Reason: Primitivism in Modern European Art and Aesthetics, 1725–1907*. University Park: Pennsylvania State University Press, 1995.

"The Contemporary Object." *Arts and Architecture* 71, no. 11 (November 1954): 37.

Cook, Daniel Thomas. *The Commodification of Childhood: The Children's Clothing Industry and the Rise of the Child Consumer*. Durham, N.C.: Duke University Press, 2004.

Cook, Joan. "A Toy Store Designed So That Children Can Play in It." *New York Times,* October 21, 1969.

Cooke, Ebenezer. Preface to *How Gertrude Teaches Her Children: An Attempt to Help Mothers to Teach Their Own Children and an Account of the Method*, by Johann Heinrich Pestalozzi. Syracuse, N.Y.: Bardeen, 1898.

Coontz, Stephanie. *The Way We Never Were: American Families and the Nostalgia Trap*. New York: Basic Books, 1992.

Cooper, Patty. *Toy Buildings, 1880–1980*. Atglen, Penn.: Schiffer, 2000.

Cottle, Thomas J. *Time's Children: Impressions of Youth*. Boston: Little, Brown, 1971.

———. "True Creativity Can Emerge Anytime—at Age Six, or at Forty." *Life*, December 17, 1971.

Council of Educational Facility Planners. *Guide for Planning Educational Facilities*. Columbus, Ohio: Council of Educational Facility Planners, 1969.

Council on Museums and Education in the Visual Arts. *The Art Museum as Educator*. Cleveland: Cleveland Museum of Art for the Council on Museums and Education in the Visual Arts, 1978.

"Crackling Excitement in School Corridors." *Life*, March 22, 1963.

Craft, Anna, Howard Gardner, and Guy Claxton, eds. *Creativity, Wisdom, and Trusteeship: Exploring the Role of Education*. Thousand Oaks, Calif.: Corwin, 2008.

"Crayon Art." *Interiors* 117 (January 1958).

"Creative Playthings: An Object Lesson with an Academic Approach." *Interiors* 113, no. 7 (1954): 88–93.

"The Creative Toy." *Science Digest* 56, no. 6 (December 1964): 40–43.

Cremin, Lawrence A. *American Education, 1876–1980: The Metropolitan Experience*. New York: Harper & Row, 1988.

———. *The Transformation of the School: Progressivism in American Education, 1876–1957*. New York: Knopf, 1961.

Cross, Gary. *All-Consuming Century: Why Commercialism Won in Modern America*. New York: Columbia University Press, 2000.

———. *The Cute and the Cool: Wondrous Innocence and Modern American Children's Culture*. Oxford: Oxford University Press, 2004.

———. *Kids' Stuff: Toys and the Changing World of American Childhood*. Cambridge, Mass.: Harvard University Press, 1997.

———. "The Suburban Weekend: Perspectives on a Vanishing Twentieth Century Dream." In *Visions of Suburbia*, edited by Roger Silverstone, 108–31. London: Routledge, 1997.

"Crow Island Revisited." *Architectural Forum* 103 (October 1955): 130–37.

Csikszentmihalyi, Mihaly. *Creativity: Flow and the Psychology of Discovery and Invention*. New York: HarperCollins, 1996.

Cuban, Larry. *How Teachers Taught: Constancy and Change in American Classrooms, 1880–1990*. 2nd ed. New York: Teachers College Press, 1993.

Cunningham, Hugh. *Children and Childhood in Western Society since 1500*. London: Longman, 1995.

Curtis, Eleanor. *School Builders*. Chichester, U.K.: Wiley-Academy, 2003.

Cutler, William W. "Cathedral of Culture: The Schoolhouse in American Educational Thought and Practice since 1820." *History of Education Quarterly* 29 (Spring 1989): 1–40.

Dal Fabbro, Mano. *How to Make Children's Furniture and Play Equipment*. New York: McGraw-Hill, 1963.

D'Amico, Victor. *Creative Teaching in Art*. Scranton, Penn.: International Textbook, 1942.

———. *Experiments in Creative Art Teaching: A Progress Report on the Department of Education, 1937–1960*. New York: Museum of Modern Art, 1960.

———. "What Is Creative Teaching?" *School Arts* 54 (January 1955): 3–8.

D'Amico, Victor, and Arlette Buchman. *Assemblage: A New Dimension in Creative Teaching in Action*. New York: Museum of Modern Art and New York Graphic Society, 1972.

D'Amico, Victor, Frances Wilson, and Moreen Maser. *Art for the Family*. New York: Museum of Modern Art and Simon & Schuster, 1954.

Dattner, Richard. *Design for Play*. Cambridge, Mass.: MIT Press, 1969.

Davidson, Joel. "Building for War, Preparing for Peace." In *World War II and the American Dream: How Wartime Building Changed a Nation*, edited by Donald Albrecht. Washington, D.C., and Cambridge, Mass.: National Building Museum and MIT Press, 1995.

Davini, William C., et al. *Color Planning for School Interiors*. St. Paul, Minn.: Board of Education, 1948.

Davis, Mary Dabney. *Schools for Children under Six: A Report on the Status and Need for Nursery Schools and Kindergartens*. Bulletin 5. Washington, D.C.: Federal Security Agency, 1947.

Davis, Michael. *Street Gang: The Complete History of Sesame Street*. New York: Viking, 2008.

De Mause, Lloyd, ed. *The History of Childhood*. New York: Psychohistory Press, 1974.

Denver Public Schools. *Creative Art for Use in the Elementary School*. Denver: Denver Public Schools, 1949.

"Designing for the Real Customer." *Progressive Architecture* 51 (November 1970): 74–77.

Dewey, John. *The School and Society*. Rev. ed. Chicago: University of Chicago Press, 1943. First published 1900.

Dillard, Annie. *An American Childhood*. New York: HarperPerennial, 1988.

Din, Herminia Weihsin. "A History of Children's Museums in the United States, 1899–1997: Implications for Art Education and Museum Education in Art Museums." PhD diss., Ohio State University, 1998.

Donovan, John J. *School Architecture: Principles and Practices*. New York: Macmillan, 1921.

Dow, Peter B. *Schoolhouse Politics: Lessons from the Sputnik Era*. Cambridge, Mass.: Harvard University Press, 1991.

Drews, Elizabeth Monroe. *Learning Together: How to Foster Creativity, Self-Fulfillment, and Social Awareness in Today's Students and Teachers*. Englewood Cliffs, N.J.: Prentice-Hall, 1972.

Dudek, Mark. *Architecture of Schools: The New Learning Environment*: Architectural Press, 2000.

Duitz, Mindy. "The Soul of a Museum: Commitment to Community at the Brooklyn Children's Museum." In *Museums and Communities: The Politics of Public Culture*, edited by Ivan Karp, Christine Mullen Kreamer, and Steven D. Lavine, 242–61. Washington, D.C.: Smithsonian Institution Press, 1992.

Duncum, Paul. "The Origins of Self-Expression: A Case of Self-Deception." *Art Education* 35, no. 5 (September 1982).

"Education." Special issue, *Life*, October 16, 1950.

Educational Facilities Laboratories. *The Cost of a Schoolhouse*. New York: Educational Facilities Laboratories, 1960.

———. *Hands-On Museums: Partners in Learning*. New York: Educational Facilities Laboratories, 1975.

———. *New Schools for New Education*. New York: Educational Facilities Laboratories, 1960.

———. *The Place of the Arts in New Towns*. New York: Educational Facilities Laboratories, 1973.

———. *School Construction Systems Development*. Palo Alto: School Planning Laboratory, Stanford University, 1962.

———. *SCSD: The Project and the Schools*. New York: Educational Facilities Laboratories, 1967.

Educational Facilities Laboratories and Experimental Schools Program, U.S. Office of Education. *Places and Things for Experimental Schools*. New York: Educational Facilities Laboratories, 1972.

Educational Facilities Laboratories and Institute for Development of Educational Activities. *The Open Plan School: Report of a National Seminar*. New York: Educational Facilities Laboratories and Institute for Development of Educational Activities, 1970.

Efland, Arthur D. *A History of Art Education: Intellectual and Social Currents in Teaching the Visual Arts*. New York: Teachers College Press, 1990.

———. "History of Art Education as Criticism: On the Use of the Past." In *The History of Art Education: Proceedings from the Second Penn State Conference, 1989*, edited by Patricia M. Amburgy, 1–11. Reston, Va.: National Art Education Association, 1992.

Ehrenkrantz, Ezra. "What's Happening to SCSD—and Why." *Nation's Schools* 83, no. 4 (1969): 55–57.

Engelhardt, Nickolaus L. *Complete Guide for Planning New Schools*. West Nyack, N.Y.: Parker, 1970.

Engelhardt, Nickolaus L., N. L. Engelhardt Jr., and Stanton Leggett. *Planning Elementary School Buildings*. New York: Dodge, 1953.

———. *School Planning and Building Handbook*. New York: Dodge, 1956.

Engelhardt, Tom. *The End of Victory Culture: Cold War America and the Disillusioning of a Generation*. Rev. ed. Amherst: University of Massachusetts Press, 2007.

Erikson, Erik H. *Childhood and Society*. 2nd ed. New York: Norton, 1963. First edition published 1950.

———. *Dimensions of a New Identity: The 1973 Jefferson Lectures in the Humanities*. New York: Norton, 1974.

———. *Toys and Reasons: Stages in the Ritualization of Experience*. New York: Norton, 1977.

"Esprit Grows in Brooklyn." *Progressive Architecture* 59, no. 5 (1978): 62–67.

Evett, Elisa. *The Critical Reception of Japanese Art in Late Nineteenth-Century Europe*. Ann Arbor, Mich.: UMI Research Press, 1982.

"Experts See Toys in Stimulant Role." *New York Times*, October 5, 1948.

FAO Schwarz. *One Hundred Years of Fun in the Sun, 1862–1962*. New York: FAO Schwarz, 1962.

———. *Toys and Children's Books, Educational Playthings, Games, Sporting Goods, Children's Clothes, and Accessories*. New York: FAO Schwarz, 1964.

Fass, Paula S., and Mary Ann Mason, eds. *Childhood in America*. New York: New York University Press, 2000.

Federal Security Agency, Office of Education. *First Progress Report of the School Facilities Survey, 1951–1952*. Washington, D.C.: Federal Security Agency, Office of Education, 1952.

———. *Second Progress Report, School Facilities Survey*. Washington, D.C.: Federal Security Agency, Office of Education, 1952.

Feist, Gregory J., and Mark A. Runco. "Trends in the Creativity Literature: An Analysis of Research in the *Journal of Creative Behavior* (1967–1989)." *Creativity Research Journal* 6, no. 3 (1993): 271–86.

Fiarotta, Phyllis, and Noel Fiarotta. *Snips and Snails and Walnut Whales: Nature Crafts for Children*. New York: Workman, 1975.

Fiedler, Jeannine. "Room for Children but None for Research? Children's Furniture at the Bauhaus." In Ottillinger, *Fidgety Philip!*

Fineberg, Jonathan, ed. *Discovering Child Art: Essays on Childhood, Primitivism, and Modernism*. Princeton, N.J.: Princeton University Press, 1998.

———. *The Innocent Eye: Children's Art and the Modern Artist*. Princeton, N.J.: Princeton University Press, 1997.

———, ed. *When We Were Young: New Perspectives on the Art of the Child*. Berkeley: University of California Press, 2006.

Finkelstein, Barbara. "Uncle Sam and the Children: A History of Government Involvement in Child Rearing." In *Growing Up in America: Children in Historical Perspective*, edited by N. Ray Hiner and Joseph M. Hawes, 255–66. Urbana: University of Illinois Press, 1985.

Fleming, Dan. *Powerplay: Toys as Popular Culture*. Manchester, U.K.: Manchester University Press, 1996.

Flesch, Rudolf. *Why Johnny Can't Read—and What You Can Do About It*. New York: Harper, 1955.

"Flexible Classrooms and an Academic Mall." *Architectural Record* 126 (August 1959).

Florida, Richard. *The Rise of the Creative Class and How It's Transforming Work, Leisure, Community, and Everyday Life.* New York: Basic Books, 2002.

Folk, Fantasy, and Play: Selections from the Caplan Collection. Indianapolis: Children's Museum of Indianapolis, 1991.

Forman, Robert. *Nursery Furnishing and Decoration.* London: Country Life, 1950.

Foundation for Research on Human Behavior. *Creativity and Conformity: A Problem for Organizations.* Ann Arbor, Mich.: Foundation for Research on Human Behavior, 1958.

Frank, Lawrence K. Introduction to Hartley and Goldenson, *Complete Book of Children's Play.*

Frank, Thomas. *The Conquest of Cool: Business Culture, Counterculture, and the Rise of Hip Consumerism.* Chicago: University of Chicago Press, 1997.

Franklin, Adele. *Home Play and Play Equipment.* Washington, D.C.: U.S. Department of Health, Education, and Welfare, 1959.

Fraser, Antonia. *A History of Toys.* London: Weidenfeld & Nicolson, 1966.

Frean, F. Merle, and D. M. Calderwood. *Colour and the Child: Colour and Its Contribution to School and Hostel Buildings.* Pretoria: South African Council for Scientific and Industrial Research, 1959.

Freedman, Kerry. "Art Education and Changing Political Agendas: An Analysis of Curriculum Concerns of the 1940s and 1950s." *Studies in Art Education* 29, no. 1 (1987): 17–29.

Frenkel-Brunswik, Else. "Differential Patterns of Social Outlook and Personality in Family and Children." In Mead and Wolfenstein, *Childhood in Contemporary Cultures.*

Freundlich, August L. "The Committee on Art Education." In *The History of Art Education: Proceedings from the Penn State Conference,* edited by Brent Wilson and Harlan Hoffa, 329–33. Reston, Va.: National Art Education Association, 1985.

Friedman, Alice T. "Model Homes and Dream Houses." In *Dream Houses, Toy Homes.* Montreal: Canadian Centre for Architecture, 1995.

Frierson, Michael. *Clay Animation: American Highlights, 1908 to the Present.* New York: Twayne, 1994.

Fröbel, Friedrich. *Friedrich Froebel's Pedagogics of the Kindergarten; or, His Ideas concerning the Play and Playthings of the Child.* Translated by Josephine Jarvis. New York: Appleton, 1904.

Funke, Phyllis. "Children's Museum Shows New Ideas." *New York Times,* March 24, 1974.

"Fun Room: Child Can Climb and Romp in Her Novel Nursery." *Life,* August 22, 1949, 49–51.

Gabor, Andrea. *The Capitalist Philosophers: The Geniuses of Modern Business, Their Lives, Times, and Ideas.* New York: Times Business, 2000.

Gaitskell, Charles D. *Children and Their Art.* New York: Harcourt, Brace, 1958.

Galbraith, John Kenneth. *Affluent Society.* Boston: Houghton Mifflin, 1958.

Gallagher, Winifred. *House Thinking: A Room-by-Room Look at How We Live*. New York: HarperCollins, 2006.

Gans, Herbert J. *The Levittowners: Ways of Life and Politics in a New Suburban Community*. 1967. Reprint, New York: Columbia University Press, 1982.

Gardner, Howard. *Art, Mind, and Brain: A Cognitive Approach to Creativity*. New York: Basic Books, 1982.

——. *Artful Scribbles: The Significance of Children's Drawings*. New York: Basic Books, 1980.

——. *Creating Minds: An Anatomy of Creativity Seen through the Lives of Freud, Einstein, Picasso, Stravinsky, Eliot, Graham, and Gandhi*. New York: Basic Books, 1993.

——. *The Mind's New Science: A History of the Cognitive Revolution*. New York: Basic Books, 1985.

Gardner, Martin. "Rainy Day Playhouse." *Parents' Magazine*, November 1953, 54–55.

Gelber, Steven M. *Hobbies: Leisure and the Culture of Work in America*. New York: Columbia University Press, 1999.

Gell, Alfred. *Art and Agency: An Anthropological Theory*. New York: Oxford University Press, 1998.

Genter, Robert. *Late Modernism: Art, Culture, and Politics in Cold War America*. Philadelphia: University of Pennsylvania Press, 2010.

Geronimi, Clyde, Wilfred Jackson, and Hamilton Luske, directors. *Peter Pan*. Walt Disney Productions, 1953.

Gesell, Arnold, and Frances L. Ilg, with Janet Learned and Louise B. Ames. *Infant and Child in the Culture of Today: The Guidance of Development in Home and Nursery School*. New York: Harper & Brothers, 1943.

Gesell, Arnold, Frances L. Ilg, Louise Bates Ames, and Glenna E. Bullis. *The Child from Five to Ten*. New York: Harper & Brothers, 1946.

Getzels, Jacob W. "Learning Environments." *School Review* 82, no. 4 (1974): 527–40.

Getzels, Jacob W., and Philip W. Jackson. *Creativity and Intelligence: Explorations with Gifted Students*. New York: Wiley, 1962.

——. "The Meaning of 'Giftedness'—an Examination of an Expanding Concept." *Phi Delta Kappan* (1958): 40, 75–77.

Gilbert, James. *Another Chance: Postwar America, 1945–1985*. 2nd ed. Chicago: Dorsey, 1986.

——. *A Cycle of Outrage: America's Reaction to the Juvenile Delinquent in the 1950s*. New York: Oxford University Press, 1986.

——. *Men in the Middle: Searching for Masculinity in the 1950s*. Chicago: University of Chicago Press, 2005.

Gilkey, Howard. "Landscape Development of School Grounds." In Donovan, *School Architecture*, 61–69.

Gill, Brendan. Prologue to Alliance of Artists Communities, *American Creativity at Risk*.

Gitlin, Todd. Foreword to Riesman, *The Lonely Crowd: A Study of the Changing American Character* (rev. ed.).

Gladwell, Malcolm. *The Tipping Point: How Little Things Can Make a Big Difference*. New York: Little, Brown, 2000.

Glick, Paul. *American Families*. New York: Wiley, 1957.

Glover, John A., Royce R. Ronning, and Cecil R. Reynolds, eds. *Handbook of Creativity*. New York: Plenum, 1989.

Goldberger, Paul. "A Funhouse Built in a Fun Structure." *New York Times,* May 29, 1977.

Goldhagen, Sarah Williams, and Réjean Legault, eds. *Anxious Modernisms: Experimentation in Postwar Architectural Culture*. Cambridge, Mass., and Montreal: MIT Press and the Canadian Centre for Architecture, 2000.

Goldstein, Jeffrey H., ed. *Toys, Play, and Child Development*. Cambridge: Cambridge University Press, 1994.

Golub, Adam Benjamin. "Into the Blackboard Jungle: Educational Debate and Cultural Change in 1950s America." PhD diss., University of Texas at Austin, 2004.

Goode, G. Brown. *The Museums of the Future.* Reprinted from *Report of the National Museum, 1888–1889*, by Smithsonian Institution, 427–45. Washington, D.C.: Government Printing Office, 1891.

Goodman, Paul. *Growing Up Absurd: Problems of Youth in the Organized System*. Rev. ed. New York: Random House, 1960.

Goodwin, Doris Kearns. *Wait Till Next Year: A Memoir*. New York: Simon & Schuster, 1997.

Gordon, Lesley. *Peepshow into Paradise: A History of Children's Toys*. London: Harrap, 1953.

Gores, Harold B. "Educational Change and Architectural Consequence." *Architectural Record* 126 (1959): 154–58.

———. "Where the Schoolhouse Goes from Here." *Architectural Record* 136 (1964): 225–27.

Gowan, John Curtis, George D. Demos, and E. Paul Torrance, eds. *Creativity: Its Educational Implications*. New York: Wiley, 1967.

Grant, Julia. *Raising Baby by the Book: The Education of American Mothers*. New Haven, Conn.: Yale University Press, 1998.

Graves, Ben E. *School Ways: The Planning and Design of America's Schools*. New York: McGraw-Hill, 1993.

Great Britain Ministry of Education. *Schools in the U.S.A.: A Report*. Building Bulletin 18. London: HMSO, 1961.

Greenstone, Daniel. "Frightened George: How the Pediatric-Educational Complex Ruined the Curious George Series." *Journal of Social History* 39, no. 1 (Fall 2005): 221–28.

Griffin, C. W., Jr. *Systems: An Approach to School Construction*. New York: Educational Facilities Laboratories, 1971.

Griffiths, R. *A Study of Imagination in Early Childhood*. London: Kegan Paul, 1935.

Gropius, Walter, et al., eds. *The Architects Collaborative, 1945–1965*. New York: Architectural Book Publishing, 1966.

Gross, Ronald, and Judith Murphy. *Educational Change and Architectural Con- sequences: A Report on Facilities for Individualized Instruction.* New York: Educational Facilities Laboratories, 1968.

"Growth of an Indoor-Outdoor Unit." *Architectural Record* 115 (February 1954): 172–77.

Gruber, Howard E., Glenn Terrell, and Michael Wertheimer, eds. *Contemporary Approaches to Creative Thinking: A Symposium Held at the University of Colorado.* New York: Atherton, 1962.

Gruen, Victor, and Larry Smith. *Shopping Towns USA: The Planning of Shopping Centers.* New York: Reinhold, 1960.

Guenter, Cris Eileen. "The Historical Influences of Creativity and Its Measurement in American Education, 1950–1985." EdD diss., University of Wyoming, 1985.

Guilbaut, Serge. *How New York Stole the Idea of Modern Art: Abstract Expression- ism, Freedom, and the Cold War.* Translated by Arthur Goldhammer. Chicago: University of Chicago Press, 1983.

Guilford, J. P. "Can Creativity Be Developed?" *Art Education* 11 (1956): 14–18.

———. *Creative Talents: Their Nature, Uses, and Development.* Buffalo, N.Y.: Bearly, 1986.

———. "Creativity." *American Psychologist* 5 (1950): 444–54.

———. *Intelligence, Creativity, and Their Educational Implications.* San Diego, Calif.: Knapp, 1968.

———. *The Nature of Human Intelligence.* New York: McGraw-Hill, 1967.

———. "Some Changes in the Structure of Intellect Model." *Educational and Psy- chological Measurement* 48 (1980): 1–4.

———. "Traits of Creativity." In Anderson, *Creativity and Its Cultivation.*

Guinan, Patricia. "Getting Re-acquainted with the Children." *House Beautiful*, Janu- ary 1945.

Gutman, Marta. "Entre moyens de fortune et constructions spécifiques: Les écoles de plein-air aux États-Unis à l'époque progressiste (1900–1920)." *Histoire de l'Éducation* 102 (2004): 157–80.

Gutman, Marta, and Ning de Coninck-Smith, eds. *Designing Modern Childhoods: History, Space, and the Material Culture of Children.* New Brunswick, N.J.: Rutgers University Press, 2008.

Haber, Michael. "Designed for Play." *Graphis* 14 (March–April 1958): 126–33.

Haddow, Robert H. "Victor D'Amico's Creative Center." In *Pavilions of Plenty: Ex- hibiting American Culture Abroad in the 1950s*, 112–34. Washington, D.C.: Smithsonian Institution Press, 1997.

Halberstam, David. *The Fifties.* New York: Fawcett Columbine, 1994.

Halliwell, Martin. *American Culture in the 1950s.* Edinburgh: Edinburgh Univer- sity Press, 2007.

Halpern, Sydney A. *American Pediatrics: The Social Dynamics of Professionalism, 1880–1980.* Berkeley: University of California Press, 1988.

Hansen, Esther Skaar. "Children's Furniture: A Big Market That Gets Little Atten- tion." *Retailing*, Home Furnishings ed., May 8, 1933.

Hardyment, Christina. *Dream Babies: Three Centuries of Good Advice on Child Care*. New York: Harper & Row, 1983.

Harkness, John C. "TAC's Educational Buildings." In Gropius et al., *Architects Collaborative, 1945–1965*.

Harmon, D. B. "Lighting and Child Development." *Illuminating Engineering*, April 1945.

———. "Lighting and the Eye." *Illuminating Engineering*, September 1944.

Harris, Dianne, ed. *Second Suburb: Levittown, Pennsylvania*. Pittsburgh: Pittsburgh University Press, 2010.

Hartley, Ruth E., Lawrence K. Frank, and Robert M. Goldenson. *Understanding Children's Play*. New York: Columbia University Press, 1952.

Hartley, Ruth E., and Robert M. Goldenson. *The Complete Book of Children's Play*. New York: Crowell, 1957.

Hartmann, Susan M. *The Home Front and Beyond: American Women in the 1940s*. Boston: Twayne, 1982.

Harvey, Brett. *The Fifties: A Women's Oral History*. New York: HarperCollins, 1993.

Harvey, Holman. "Do School Pupils Need Costly Palaces?" *Readers Digest*, September 1957, 37–42.

Harvey, Michelle. "Through the Enchanted Gate: The Modern on TV." *MoMA: The Museum of Modern Art* 4, no. 7 (September 2001): 29–30.

Hawes, Joseph M. "Child Science, Guidance Clinics, and the Rise of Experts: The Reconstruction of Childhood in the United States." In *Children between the Wars: American Childhood, 1920–1940*, 65–85. New York: Twayne, 1997.

Hayden, Dolores. *Building Suburbia: Green Fields and Urban Growth, 1820–2000*. New York: Vintage, 2004.

———. *Redesigning the American Dream: The Future of Housing, Work, and Family Life*. New York: Norton, 1984.

"Heathcote: A Pioneering School in Plan and Atmosphere." *Architectural Forum* 101 (July 1954): 98–105.

Hechinger, Fred M. *The Big Red School House*. Gloucester, Mass.: Smith, 1968.

———, ed. *Pre-school Education Today: New Approaches to Teaching Three-, Four-, and Five-Year-Olds*. Garden City, N.Y.: Doubleday, 1966.

Hechinger, Fred M., and Grace Hechinger. *Growing Up in America*. New York: McGraw-Hill, 1975.

Hein, George E. "Progressive Education and Museum Education: Anna Billings Gallup and Louise Connolly." *Journal of Museum Education* 31, no. 3 (2006): 161–74.

Hein, Hilde. *The Exploratorium: The Museum as Laboratory*. Washington, D.C.: Smithsonian Institution Press, 1990.

Heine, Aalbert. "Making Glad the Heart of Childhood." *Museum News* 58, no. 2 (November–December 1979): 23–25.

Heingold, Ehrhardt. *Holtzspielzeug aus aller Welt*. Weingarten, Ger.: Kunstverlag Weingarten, 1983.

Helfand, Jessica. *Reinventing the Wheel*. New York: Princeton Architectural Press, 2006.

Heller, Steven. "Leo Lionni." AIGA Web site. 1984. http://www.aiga.org/content. cfm/medalist-leolionni.

Henderson, Susan R. "'New Buildings Create New People': The Pavilion Schools of Weimar Frankfurt as a Model of Pedagogical Reform." *Design Issues* 13, no. 1 (Spring 1997): 27–38.

Henriksen, Margot A. *Dr. Strangelove's America: Society and Culture in the Atomic Age.* Berkeley: University of California Press, 1997.

Henry, J. "The Problem of Spontaneity, Initiative, and Creativity in Suburban Classrooms." *American Journal of Orthopsychiatry* 29 (1959): 266–79.

"Here Come the Gerbils." *Newsweek*, December 27, 1965.

Herman, Ellen. *The Romance of American Psychology: Political Culture in the Age of Experts.* Berkeley: University of California Press, 1995.

Hewes, Jeremy Joan. *Build Your Own Playground! A Source Book of Play Sculptures, Designs, and Concepts from the Work of Jay Beckwith.* Boston: Houghton Mifflin, 1974.

Hewitt, Karen, and Louise Roomet, eds. *Educational Toys in America, 1800 to the Present.* Burlington, Vt.: Robert Hull Fleming Museum, University of Vermont, 1979.

Highmore, Ben. "A Sideboard Manifesto: Design Culture in an Artificial World." In *The Design Culture Reader*, edited by Ben Highmore, 1–11. London: Routledge, 2009.

"High School Plan Has Campus Look." *New York Times*, April 26, 1959.

Higonnet, Anne. *Pictures of Innocence: The History and Crisis of Ideal Childhood.* London: Thames & Hudson, 1998.

Hill, Polly. *Children's Creative Centre: Methods and Objectives.* Montreal: Canadian Government Pavilion, 1967.

Hille, R. Thomas. *Modern Schools: A Century of Design for Education.* Hoboken, N.J.: Wiley, 2011.

Hine, Thomas. "The Search for the Postwar House." In *Blueprints for Modern Living: History and Legacy of the Case Study Houses*, edited by Elizabeth A. T. Smith. Los Angeles: Museum of Contemporary Art; Cambridge, Mass.: MIT Press, 1989.

Hiner, N. Ray, and Joseph Hawes, eds. *Growing Up in America: Children in Historical Perspective.* Urbana: University of Illinois Press, 1985.

Hines, Thomas S. *Richard Neutra and the Search for Modern Architecture: A Biography and History.* New York: Oxford University Press, 1982.

Hirsch, Elisabeth S., ed. *The Block Book.* Washington, D.C.: National Association for the Education of Young Children, 1984.

Hitchcock, Henry-Russell, and Arthur Drexler, eds. *Built in USA: Post-war Architecture.* New York: Museum of Modern Art, 1952.

Hoffa, Harlan. "From the New Deal to the New Frontier: The Role of Government in Arts Education." In *The History of Art Education: Proceedings from the Penn State Conference*, edited by Brent Wilson and Harlan Hoffa, 338–45. Reston, Va.: National Art Education Association, 1985.

Hoffman, David. *Kid Stuff: Great Toys from our Childhood*. San Francisco: Chronicle, 1996.

Holder, Robert. "The Story of Holgate: An American Industrial Saga." *Playthings* 44 (December 1946): 172–74.

"Holgate Brothers: Creators of Toys, Craftsmen in Woodwork." *Commonwealth Magazine*, December 1946.

Holgate Toy Company. *The Story of Holgate Toys*. Kane, Penn.: Holgate Toy Co., 1990.

Holland, Thomas W., ed. *Boys' Toys of the Fifties and Sixties: Memorable Catalogue Pages from the Legendary Sears Christmas Wishbooks, 1950–1969*. Sherman Oaks, Calif.: Windmill, 1997.

———, ed. *Girls' Toys of the Fifties and Sixties: Memorable Catalog Pages from the Legendary Sears Christmas Wishbooks, 1950–1969*. Sherman Oaks, Calif.: Windmill, 1997.

"Homeliness in an American School." *Interiors* 109 (February 1950).

Hopkins, L. T. "Classroom Climate Can Promote Creativeness." *Educational Leadership* 13 (1956): 279–82.

Horn, John. "Re: 'Mr. I. Magination,'" *New York Times*, July 31, 1949.

Howe, George. "The New York World's Fair, 1940." *Architectural Forum*, July 1940, 31–39.

Howe, Harold. "The New Faces of Education." *American Education* 4 (April 1968): 2–3. Reprinted in *The Impact of War on American Life: The Twentieth-Century Experience*, edited by Keith L. Nelson, 250–53. New York: Holt, Rinehart, & Winston, 1971.

"How Livable Is a Modern House?" *Life*, October 18, 1948.

"How to Make Your Playpen Pay Dividends!" *Baby Talk*, August 1949.

Huizinga, Johan. *Homo Ludens: A Study of the Play-Element in Culture*. New York: Roy, 1950.

Hulbert, Ann. *Raising America: Experts, Parents, and a Century of Advice about Children*. New York: Knopf, 2003.

Hyman, Isabelle. *Marcel Breuer, Architect: The Career and the Buildings*. New York: Abrams, 2001.

IBM. "*Capitalizing* on Complexity" (global CEO survey). 2010.

Illick, Joseph. *American Childhoods*. Philadelphia: University of Pennsylvania Press, 2002.

"Industrial Design: Another Toy to Tinker With." *Interiors* 111, no. 2 (September 1951): 10.

"In the Showrooms: Market Report." *Interiors*, April 1967.

"Is Cooling Coming for Schools?" *Architectural Forum* 105 (July 1956): 124–27.

Isenstadt, Sandy. *The Modern American House: Spaciousness and Middle-Class Identity*. New York: Cambridge University Press, 2006.

Israel, Mei-Ling. "Learn to Draw with Jon Gnagy: The Legacy of America's First Television Artist." MA qualifying paper, Bard Graduate Center, 2011.

Jaber, William. *Tree Houses: How to Build Your Own Tree House*. New York: Drake, 1975.

Jackson, Kenneth T. *Crabgrass Frontier: The Suburbanization of the United States*. New York: Oxford University Press, 1985.

Jackson, Lesley. *Twentieth-Century Pattern Design*. New York: Princeton Architectural Press, 2007.

Jacobson, Lisa. *Children and Consumer Culture in American Society: A Historical Handbook and Guide*. Westport, Conn.: Praeger, 2008.

———. *Raising Consumers: Children and the American Mass Market in the Early Twentieth Century*. Popular Cultures, Everyday Lives. New York: Columbia University Press, 2004.

———. "Revitalizing the American Home: Children's Leisure and the Revaluation of Play, 1920–1940." *Journal of Social History* 30, no. 3 (1997): 581–96.

James, Allison. *Theorizing Childhood*. Cambridge, U.K.: Polity Press in association with Blackwell, 1998.

James, Allison, and Alan Prout, eds. *Constructing and Reconstructing Childhood*. Basingstoke, U.K.: Falmer, 1990.

Jancovich, Mark. "Othering Conformity in Post-war America: Intellectuals, the New Middle Classes, and the Problem of Cultural Distinctions." In *Containing America: Cultural Production and Consumption in Fifties America*, edited by Nathan Abrams and Julie Hughes, 12–28. Birmingham, U.K.: University of Birmingham Press, 2000.

Jane, Mary C. "Are You Raising an Idea Man?" *Parents' Magazine*, July 1950, 29, 80.

Jefferson, Blanche. *Teaching Art to Children: The Values of Creative Expression*. Boston: Allyn & Bacon, 1959.

Jekyll, Gertrude. *Children and Gardens*. 1908. Reprint, Woodbridge, U.K.: Antique Collector's Club, 1982.

Jenks, Chris. *Childhood*. London: Routledge, 1996.

Johnson, Crockett. *Harold and the Purple Crayon*. New York: HarperCollins, 1955.

Johnson, Hope. "Toys Should Hold Interest Year 'Round." *New York World-Telegram*, November 13, 1947.

Jones, Landon Y. *Great Expectations: America and the Baby Boom Generation*. New York: Coward, McCann & Geoghegan, 1980.

Jones, Stacy V. "Space Labyrinths Teach Children about Molecules." *New York Times*, January 17, 1976.

Kaban, Barbara. *Choosing Toys for Children*. New York: Schocken, 1979.

Kagan, Jerome, ed. *Creativity and Learning*. Daedalus Library. Boston: Houghton Mifflin, 1967.

Kaledin, Eugenia. *Daily Life in the United States, 1940–1959: Shifting Worlds*. Westport, Conn.: Greenwood, 2000.

———. *Mothers and More: American Women in the 1950s*. American Women in the Twentieth Century. Boston: Twayne, 1984.

Kaplan, Louis, and Scott Michaelsen, with Art Clokey. *Gumby: The Authorized Biography of the World's Favorite Clayboy*. New York: Harmony, 1986.

Katz, Donald. *Home Fires: An Intimate Portrait of One Middle-Class Family in Postwar America*. New York: HarperCollins, 1992.

Kauffmann, Edgar, Jr. "Kay Bojesen: Tableware to Toys." *Interiors* 112 (February 1953): 64–67.

Kaufman, Irving. "Education and the Imagination." *School Arts Magazine* 56 (1957): 5–8.

———, ed. *Education and the Imagination in Science and Art*. Ann Arbor: University of Michigan and National Committee on Art Education, 1958.

Kawin, Ethel. *The Wise Choice of Toys*. Chicago: University of Chicago Press, 1938.

Keats, Ezra Jack. *The Snowy Day*. New York: Viking, 1962.

Keats, John. *The Crack in the Picture Window*. Cambridge, Mass.: Riverside, 1957.

Keiler, Manfred L. *Art in the Schoolroom*. Lincoln: University of Nebraska Press, 1951.

Kelly, Barbara M. *Expanding the American Dream: Building and Rebuilding Levittown*. Albany: State University of New York Press, 1993.

Kelly, Donna Darling. *Uncovering the History of Children's Drawing and Art*. Westport, Conn.: Praeger, 2004.

Kennedy, Robert Woods. *The House and the Art of Its Design*. New York: Reinhold, 1953.

Kenworthy, Leonard S. *The Teacher and the Post-war Child*. Paris: UNESCO, 1946.

Kepes, György, and Juliet Kepes. "The Most Important Room." *Interiors*, January 1949.

Kepes, Juliet. *Five Little Monkeys*. Boston: Houghton Mifflin, 1952.

Kern, Evan J. "The Purposes of Art Education in the United States from 1870 to 1980." In *The History of Art Education: Proceedings from the Penn State Conference*, edited by Brent Wilson and Harlan Hoffa, 40–52. Reston, Va.: National Art Education Association, 1985.

Kertzer, David I., and Marzio Barbagli, eds. *Family Life in the Twentieth Century: The History of the European Family*. New Haven, Conn.: Yale University Press, 2003.

Ketcham, Hank. "Visit to the Exploratorium." *Dennis the Menace*, no. 135, November 1974.

Kilpatrick, William Heard. *Foundations of Method: Informal Talks on Teaching*. New York: Macmillan, 1925.

———. *The Montessori System Examined*. Riverside Educational Monographs. Boston: Houghton Mifflin, 1914.

Kimmel, Chad M. "Re-reading the History of Levittown, One Voice at a Time." In Harris, *Second Suburb*, 17–40.

Kinchin, Juliet, and Aidan O'Connor, eds. *Century of the Child: Growing by Design, 1900–2000*. New York: Museum of Modern Art, 2012.

Kindermöbel und Spielobjekte. Cologne, Ger.: Kunstgewerbemuseum, 1973.

King, Jonathan, and Philip Langdon, eds. *The CRS Team and the Business of Architecture*. College Station: Texas A&M Press, 2002.

Kirkham, Pat. *Charles and Ray Eames: Designers of the Twentieth Century*. Cambridge, Mass.: MIT Press, 1995.

———. *Women Designers in the USA, 1900–2000: Diversity and Difference*. New Haven, Conn.: Yale University Press, 2000.

Kirkham, Pat, and Jennifer Bass. *Saul Bass: A Life in Film and Design*. London: King, 2011.

Kismaric, Carole, and Marvin Heiferman. *Growing Up with Dick and Jane: Learning and Living the American Dream*. San Francisco: Harper, 1996.

Kline, Stephen. *Out of the Garden: Toys and Children's Culture in the Age of TV Marketing*. London: Verso, 1993.

Kling, Vincent G. "Beauty in Schools." *School Executive* 78 (August 1959): 21–23.

Knowles, Eleanor N. "Millions of War Babies Should Have Educational Toys." *Playthings* 43 (June 1945): 120–21.

Koerner, Michael. *Die Architektur des Kindergartens im 20. Jahrhundert: Eine Untersuchung im hinblick auf konzeptionelle qualitaeten im spektrum individueller Plannungsvielfalt und Baukastensystemen*. Berlin: Logos Verlag, 2000.

Kohl, Herbert R. *The Open Classroom: A Practical Guide to a New Way of Teaching*. New York: Random House, 1969.

Kohlstedt, Sally Gregory. *Teaching Children Science: Hands-On Nature Study in North America, 1890–1930*. Chicago: University of Chicago Press, 2010.

Konigsburg, E. L. *From the Mixed-Up Files of Mrs. Basil E. Frankweiler*. New York: Atheneum, 1968.

Kornbluth, Frances S., and Bernard Bard. *Creativity and the Teacher*. Curricular Viewpoints. Chicago: American Federation of Teachers, AFL-CIO, 1966.

Korzenik, Diana. "Choices and Motives in Doing Historical Research." In *The History of Art Education: Proceedings from the Second Penn State Conference, 1989*, edited by Patricia M. Amburgy, 264–68. Reston, Va.: National Art Educators Association, 1992.

———. *Objects of American Art Education: Highlights from the Diana Korzenik Collection*. San Marino, Calif.: Huntington Library Press, 2004.

Kuhn, Manford H. Review of *Creativity and Its Cultivation*, by Harold H. Anderson, and *Recognition of Excellence: Working Papers of a Project of the Edgar Stern Family Fund. Annals of the Academy of Political and Social Science* 335 (May 1961): 232.

Kuznick, Peter J., and James Gilbert, eds. *Rethinking Cold War Culture*. Washington: Smithsonian Institution Press, 2001.

LaChance, W. W. *Schoolhouses and Their Equipment: With Plans and Illustrations of the Newest Schoolhouse Architecture*. Niagara Falls, N.Y.: White & LaChance, 1925.

Lambert, Clara. *School's Out: Child Care through Play Schools*. New York: Harper and Play Schools Association, 1944.

Lamprecht, Barbara Mac. *Richard Neutra: Complete Works*. Edited by Peter Goessel. Cologne, Ger.: Taschen, 2000.

Latour, Bruno. *Reassembling the Social: An Introduction to Actor-Network-Theory*. Oxford: Oxford University Press, 2005.

Laury, Jean Ray. *Handmade Toys and Games: A Guide to Creating Your Own.* Garden City, N.Y.: Doubleday, 1975.

Lawn, Martin, and Ian Grosvenor, eds. *Materialities of Schooling: Design, Technology, Objects, Routines.* Oxford: Symposium, 2005.

Leach, William. *Land of Desire: Merchants, Power, and the Rise of a New American Culture.* New York: Vintage, 1993.

LeBlanc, Suzanne. "The Slender Golden Thread, 100 Years Strong." *Museum News* 78 (November–December 1999): 48–55, 63.

Ledermann, Alfred, and Alfred Trachsel. *Creative Playgrounds and Recreation Centers.* Rev. ed. New York: Praeger, 1968.

Lefaivre, Liane, and Ingeborg de Rood, eds. *Aldo van Eyck: The Playgrounds and the City.* Amsterdam: Stedelijk Museum, 2002.

Leggett, Stanton, C. William Brubaker, Aaron Cohodes, and Arthur S. Shapiro. *Planning Flexible Learning Places.* New York: McGraw-Hill, 1977.

Lehane, Stephen, *The Creative Child: How to Encourage the Natural Creativity of Your Preschooler.* Englewood Cliffs, N.J.: Prentice-Hall, 1979.

Lemann, Nicholas. *The Big Test: The Secret History of the American Meritocracy.* New York: Farrar, Strauss & Giroux, 1999.

Lerner, Max. *America as a Civilization: Life and Thought in the United States.* 2 vols. New York: Simon & Schuster, 1957.

Lescaze, William. "Types of Schools to Serve Tomorrow's Needs." *American School and University* 15 (1943): 33–36.

Lesser, Gerald S. *Children and Television: Lessons from "Sesame Street."* New York: Vintage, 1974.

Leu, Donald J. *Planning Educational Facilities.* New York: Center for Applied Research in Education, 1965.

Levine, Ellen. *Children's Rooms: How to Decorate Them to Grow with Your Child.* Indianapolis: Bobbs-Merrill, 1975.

Lewis, Michael J, and Yvan Rompré, eds. *Apprendre de toutes pieces / Toys That Teach.* Montreal: Canadian Centre for Architecture, 1992.

Lieberman, J. Nina. *Playfulness: Its Relationship to Imagination and Creativity.* New York: Academic Press, 1977.

Lienhard, John H. *Inventing Modern: Growing Up with X-Rays, Skyscrapers, and Tailfins.* New York: Oxford University Press, 2003.

Lingo, Elizabeth Long, and Steven J. Tepper. "The Creative Campus: Time for a 'C' Change." *Chronicle of Higher Education,* October 10, 2010.

Linn, Susan. *Consuming Kids: The Hostile Takeover of Childhood.* New York: New Press, 2004.

Lionni, Leo. *Little Blue and Little Yellow.* New York: McDowell & Obolensky, 1959.

Livingston, Maxine. "Give Your Children a Playhouse." *Parents' Magazine,* November 1950, 50–51, 134.

Locke, John. *Some Thoughts concerning Education.* 1693. Reprint edited by Ruth W. Grant and Nathan Tarcov. Indianapolis: Hackett, 1996.

Logan, Frederick M. *Growth of Art in American Schools.* New York: Harper, 1955.

Long, Elizabeth. *The American Dream and the Popular Novel*. Boston: Routledge & Kegan Paul, 1985.

Lopez, Frank G. "Improving Secondary Schools." In Lopez, *Schools for the New Needs*.

———. "The Individual School and the Delightful, Never-Ending Progress to Perfection." *Architectural Record* 120 (July 1956): 151–60.

———, ed. *Schools for the New Needs: Educational, Social, Economic*. New York: Dodge, 1956.

"Low-Cost School." *Architectural Forum* 91 (October 1949): 111–14.

Lowenfeld, Viktor. *Creative and Mental Growth*. New York: Macmillan, 1947.

———. *Creative and Mental Growth*. Rev. ed. New York: Macmillan, 1952.

———. *Creative and Mental Growth*. 3rd ed. New York: Macmillan, 1957.

———. *The Nature of Creative Activity*. New York: Harcourt, Brace, 1939.

———. *Your Child and His Art: A Guide for Parents*. New York: Macmillan, 1954.

Lowenfeld, Viktor, and W. Lambert Brittain. *Creative and Mental Growth*. 4th ed. New York: Macmillan, 1964.

Luke, Carmen. *Constructing the Child Viewer: A History of the American Discourse on Television and Children, 1950–1980*. New York: Praeger, 1990.

Lurie, Alison. *Don't Tell the Grown-Ups: Subversive Children's Literature*. Boston: Little, Brown, 1990.

Lynes, Russell. *The Tastemakers*. New York: Grosset & Dunlap, 1954.

MacConnell, James D. *Dr. Mac, Planner for Schools*. Palo Alto, Calif.: Johnson/Dole, 1988.

Macdonald, Stuart. *History and Philosophy of Art Education*. 1970. Reprint, Cambridge: Lutterworth, 2004.

MacLeish, Archibald. *Art Education and the Creative Process*. New York: Committee on Art Education and Museum of Modern Art, 1954.

Maddi, Salvatore R. "The Strenuousness of the Creative Life." In Taylor and Getzels, *Perspectives in Creativity*, 173–90.

Maeda, Chimako, and Kiyoshi Iwasaki, eds. *Victor D'Amico: Art as Human Necessity*. Tokyo: Child Welfare Foundation of Japan, 1995.

"Magnet Master." *Everyday Art Quarterly* 8 (Summer 1948): 1–4.

Maier, Thomas. *Dr. Spock: An American Life*. New York: Harcourt, Brace, 1998.

Marks, Judy. "A History of Educational Facilities Laboratories." National Clearinghouse for Educational Facilities. Accessed June 2006. http://edfacilities.org/pubs/pubs_html.

Marling, Karal Ann. *As Seen on TV: The Visual Culture of Everyday Life in the 1950s*. Cambridge, Mass.: Harvard University Press, 1994.

Maslow, Abraham. *The Farther Reaches of Human Nature*. New York: Viking, 1971.

May, Elaine Tyler. *Homeward Bound: American Families in the Cold War Era*. Rev. ed. New York: Basic Books, 1999.

May, Lary, ed. *Recasting America: Culture and Politics in the Age of Cold War*. Chicago: University of Chicago Press, 1989.

Mayfield, Margie I. "Children's Museums: Purposes, Practices, and Play?" *Early Childhood Development and Care* 175, no. 2 (2005): 179–92.

Maynard, W. Barksdale. *Buildings of Delaware*. Charlottesville: University of Virginia Press, 2008.

McClary, Andrew. *Toys with Nine Lives: A Social History of American Toys*. North Haven, Conn.: Linnet, 1997.

McClintock, Marshall, and Inez McClintock. *Toys in America*. Washington, D.C.: Public Affairs, 1961.

McCormick, Virginia E. *Educational Architecture in Ohio: From One-Room Schools and Carnegie Libraries to Community Education Villages*. Kent, Ohio: Kent State University Press, 2001.

McGavran, James Holt. *Literature and the Child: Romantic Continuations, Postmodern Contestations*. Iowa City: University of Iowa Press, 1999.

McGrath, Molly, and Norman McGrath. *Children's Spaces: Fifty Architects and Designers Create Environments for the Young*. New York: Morrow, 1978.

McNall, Sally Allen. "American Children's Literature, 1880–Present." In *American Childhood: A Research Guide and Historical Handbook*, edited by Joseph M. Hawes and N. Ray Hiner. Westport, Conn.: Greenwood, 1985.

McQuade, Walter. "The Little Red Schoolhouse Goes Modern." *Collier's*, September 9, 1950, 42–43, 65–67.

———, ed. *Schoolhouse: A Primer about the Building of the American Public School Plant*. New York: Simon & Schuster, 1958.

Mead, Margaret. *And Keep Your Powder Dry: An Anthropologist Looks at America*. New York: Morrow, 1965. Reprint, New York: Berghahn, 2000.

———. *The Changing Cultural Patterns of Work and Leisure*. Washington, D.C.: U.S. Department of Labor, 1967.

———. *A Creative Life for Your Children*. Washington, D.C.: U.S. Department of Health, Education, and Welfare, 1962.

———. *The School in American Culture*. Cambridge, Mass.: Harvard University Press, 1951.

Mead, Margaret, and Elena Calas. "Child-Training Ideals in a Postrevolutionary Context: Soviet Russia." In Mead and Wolfenstein, *Childhood in Contemporary Cultures*.

Mead, Margaret, and Martha Wolfenstein, eds. *Childhood in Contemporary Cultures*. Chicago: University of Chicago Press, 1955.

Medd, David L., and Mary Crowley. "British School Architects Examine Our Work." *Progressive Architecture* 41 (March 1960): 125–35.

Medovoi, Leerom. *Rebels: Youth and the Cold War Origins of Identity*. Durham, N.C.: Duke University Press, 2005.

Meehan, Thomas. "Creative (and Mostly Upper-Class) Playthings." *Saturday Review*, December 16, 1972, 42–47.

Meikle, Jeffrey L. *American Plastic: A Cultural History*. New Brunswick, N.J.: Rutgers University Press, 1995.

Menand, Louis. "Cat People: What Dr. Seuss Really Taught Us." *New Yorker*, December 23, 2002, 148.

———. "A Friend Writes: The Old *New Yorker*." In *American Studies*, 125–45. New York: Farrar, Straus & Giroux, 2002.

Mergen, Bernard. "Made, Bought, and Stolen." In *Small Worlds: Children and Adolescents in America, 1850–1950*, edited by Elliott West and Paula Petrik, 86–106. Lawrence: University Press of Kansas, 1992.

———. *Play and Playthings: A Reference Guide*. Westport, Conn.: Greenwood, 1982.

———. "Toys and American Culture: Objects as Hypotheses." *Journal of American Culture* 3, no. 4 (1980): 743–51.

Mertins, Detlef. "Playing at Modernity." In *Toys and the Modernist Tradition*. Montreal: Canadian Centre for Architecture, 1993.

Meyerowitz, Joanne, ed. *Not June Cleaver: Women and Gender in Postwar America, 1945–1960*. Philadelphia: Temple University Press, 1994.

Mickenberg, Julia L. *Learning from the Left: Children's Literature, the Cold War, and Radical Politics in the United States*. Oxford: Oxford University Press, 2006.

Midcentury White House Conference on Children and Youth. *Personality in the Making: The Fact-Finding Report of the Midcentury White House Conference on Children and Youth*. Edited by Helen Leland Witmer and Ruth Kotinsky. New York: Harper, 1952.

Milam, Jennifer D. *Fragonard's Playful Paintings: Visual Games in Rococo Art*. Manchester, U.K.: Manchester University Press, 2006.

Millar, Garnet W. *E. Paul Torrance, "the Creativity Man": An Authorized Biography*. Norwood, N.J.: Ablex, 1995.

———. *The Power of Creativity*. Bensenville, Ill.: Scholastic Testing Services, 2010.

———. *The Torrance Kids at Mid-life: Selected Case Studies of Creative Behavior*. Westport, Conn.: Ablex, 2002.

Miller, Daniel. *Material Culture and Mass Consumption*. Oxford: Blackwell, 1987.

Miller, Daniel, and Guy Swanson. *The Changing American Parent: A Study in the Detroit Area*. New York: Wiley, 1958.

Miller, Douglas T., and Marion Nowak. *The Fifties: The Way We Really Were*. Garden City, N.Y.: Doubleday, 1977.

Miller, Peggy L. *Creative Outdoor Play Areas*. Englewood Cliffs, N.J.: Prentice-Hall, 1972.

Miner, Claudia Ann. "What about the Children? Americans' Attitudes toward Children and Childhood in the 1950s." PhD diss., Washington State University, 1986.

Ministry of Education. *Building Bulletin: Schools in the USA*. London: Ministry of Education, 1961.

Mintz, Steven. *Huck's Raft: A History of American Childhood*. Cambridge, Mass.: Belknap Press of Harvard University Press, 2004.

Mitchell, Claudia, and Jacqueline Reid-Walsh. *Researching Children's Popular Culture: The Cultural Spaces of Childhood*. London: Routledge, 2002.

Mock, Elizabeth, ed. *Built in USA, 1932–1944*. New York: Museum of Modern Art, 1944.

———. *If You Want to Build a House*. New York: Museum of Modern Art, 1946.

Mock, Elizabeth, and Rudolf Mock. "Schools Are for Children." In *The American School and University*, 37–43. New York: American School Publishing Corporation, 1943.

"Model Playroom." *Playthings* 47 (July 1949).

Monteyne, David. *Fallout Shelter: Designing for Civil Defense in the Cold War.* Minneapolis: University of Minnesota Press, 2011.

Moore, Thornton B. *The American Toy Industry's Golden Era.* Washington, D.C.: Business Information Service, U. S. Department of Commerce, 1949.

Morgan, Carol. "From Modernist Utopia to Cold War Reality: A Critical Moment in Museum Education." In *The Museum of Modern Art at Mid-century: Continuity and Change*, 151–73. New York: Museum of Modern Art and Abrams, 1995.

Morisseau, James J. *The New Schools.* Design and Planning. New York: Van Nostrand Reinhold, 1972.

Morrow, Robert W. *"Sesame Street" and the Reform of Children's Television.* Baltimore: Johns Hopkins University Press, 2006.

Moskowitz, Marina. *Standard of Living: The Measure of the Middle Class in Modern America.* Baltimore: Johns Hopkins University Press, 2004.

Mumford, Lewis. *The City in History: Its Origins, Its Transformations, and Its Prospects.* New York: Harcourt Brace Jovanovich, 1961.

Muncy, Robyn. "Cooperative Motherhood and Democratic Civic Culture in Postwar Suburbia, 1940–1965." *Journal of Social History* 38, no. 2 (2004): 285–310.

Munro, Thomas. *Art Education: Its Philosophy and Psychology.* New York: Liberal Arts Press, 1956.

Myers, Mitzi. "Reading Children and Homeopathic Romanticism: Paradigm Lost, Revisionary Gleam; or, 'Plus ça change, plus c'est la même chose'?" In McGavran, *Literature and the Child.*

Nadel, Alan. *Containment Culture: American Narratives, Postmodernism, and the Atomic Age.* Durham, N.C.: Duke University Press, 1995.

National Advisory Committee on Creative and Cultural Education. "All of Our Futures: Creativity, Culture and Education." May 1999.

National Council on Schoolhouse Construction. *Guide for Planning School Plants.* Part 2 of *Proceedings of the 22nd Meeting.* N.p.: National Council on Schoolhouse Construction, 1946.

National Education Association of the United States, Department of Rural Education. *PACE: A Guide for Developing Projects to Advance Creativity in Education.* Washington, D.C.: National Education Association of the United States, Department of Rural Education, 1966.

"Neighborhood Playground." *Progressive Architecture* 36 (December 1955): 102–3.

Nel, Philip. *Dr. Seuss: American Icon.* New York: Continuum, 2004.

Neuhart, John, Marilyn Neuhart, and Ray Eames. *Eames Design: The Work of the Office of Charles and Ray Eames.* New York: Abrams, 1989.

Neutra, Richard. *Life and Shape.* New York: Appleton-Century-Crofts, 1962.

Newell, Allen, J. C. Shaw, and Herbert A. Simon. "The Processes of Creative Thinking." In *Contemporary Approaches to Creative Thinking*, edited by Howard E. Gruber, Glenn Terrell, and Michael Westheim. New York: Atherton, 1962.

New England School Development Council. *The Elementary School Classroom.* Cambridge, Mass.: New England School Development Council, 1950.

"New Proposals to Cut School Costs." *Architectural Forum* 115 (November 1961): 111–28.

"New Schools, Economy Too." *Life*, February 1, 1954, 74–80.

Newson, John, and Elizabeth Newson. *Toys and Playthings in Development and Remediation*. Harmondsworth, U.K.: Penguin, 1979.

Newton, Suzanne. "How to Encourage Your Child's Natural Creativity." *Parents' Magazine*, July 1968.

"New Toy." *Look*, February 15, 1949.

"Next to the Pony—the Playhouse." *House and Garden*, August 1916, 26.

Nodelman, Perry. "The Other: Orientalism, Colonialism, and Children's Literature." *Children's Literature Association Quarterly* 17, no. 1 (1992): 29–35.

Norfleet, Barbara. *When We Liked Ike: Looking for Postwar America*. New York: Norton, 2001.

Nosan, Gregory. "Women in the Galleries: Prestige, Education, and Volunteerism at Mid-century." *Museum Studies* 29, no. 1 (2003).

Nowicki, Matthew. "Forum's School for 1950." *Architectural Forum* 91 (October 1949): 134–37.

Obama, Barack. State of the Union address. January 25, 2011. Accessed March 2011. http://www.whitehouse.gov/the-press-office/2011/01/25/remarks-president-state-union-address.

O'Connor, Barbara. "Museum Art Classes Give Ideas for Home." *Living for Young Homemakers*, October 1952, 146–47.

Ogata, Amy F. *Art Nouveau and the Social Vision of Modern Living: Belgian Artists in a European Context*. Cambridge: Cambridge University Press, 2001.

———. "Building for Learning in Postwar American Elementary Schools." *Journal of the Society of Architectural Historians* 67, no. 4 (2008): 562–91.

———. "Building Imagination in Postwar American Children's Rooms." *Studies in the Decorative Arts* 16, no. 1 (2008): 126–42.

———. "Creative Playthings: Educational Toys and Postwar American Culture." *Winterthur Portfolio* 39, nos. 2–3 (2004): 129–56.

Ogawa, Rodney T., Molly Loomis, and Rhiannon Crain. "Institutional History of an Interactive Science Center: The Founding and Development of the Exploratorium." *Science Education* 93, no. 2 (2009): 269–92.

Ohlsen, Merle M., ed. *Modern Methods in Elementary Education*. New York: Holt, 1959.

Olofsson, Ulla Keding, ed. *Museums and Children*. Paris: UNESCO, 1979.

Onion, Rebecca Stiles. "Picturing Nature and Childhood at the American Museum of Natural History and the Brooklyn Children's Museum, 1899–1930." *Journal of the History of Childhood and Youth* 4, no. 3 (2011): 434–69.

op de Beeck, Nathalie. *Suspended Animation: Children's Picture Books and the Fairy Tale of Modernity*. Minneapolis: University of Minnesota Press, 2010.

Opinion Research Corporation and Toy Manufacturers of the U.S.A. *Toy Purchase Habits of U.S. Families, 1954*. New York: Toy Manufacturers of the U.S.A., and American Toy Association, 1955.

Oppenheimer, Frank. "Schools Are Not for Sightseeing." In *Opportunities for Ex-*

tending Museum Contributions to Pre-college Science Education: Summary Report of a Conference Supported by the National Science Foundation, January 26–27, 1970, edited by Katherine J. Goldman. Washington, D.C.: Smithsonian Institution, 1970.

"Organic School: Humanist Approach Yields Bold New Ideas for Classrooms and Auditorium." *Architectural Forum* 94 (October 1952): 114–18.

Orme, Frank. *Television for the Family*. Los Angeles: National Association for Better Radio and Television, 1965.

Osborn, Alex F. *Applied Imagination: Principles and Procedures of Creative Thinking*. Rev. ed. New York: Scribner, 1963.

———. *Your Creative Power: How to Use Imagination*. New York: Scribner, 1948.

Osmon, Fred Linn. *Patterns for Designing Children's Centers*. New York: Educational Facilities Laboratories, 1971.

Ott, Robert W. "Art Education in Museums: Art Teachers as Pioneers in Museum Education." In *The History of Art Education: Proceedings from the Penn State Conference*, edited by Brent Wilson and Harlan Hoffa, 286–94. Reston, Va.: National Art Education Association, 1985.

Ottillinger, Eva B., ed. *Fidgety Philip! A Design History of Children's Furniture*. Vienna: Böhlau Verlag, 2006.

Owen, David. "Where Toys Come From." *Atlantic Monthly*, October 1986.

P., E. "The Child at Play in the World of Form: A Catalogue of Architectural Toys." *Progressive Architecture* 47 (April 1966): 191–98.

Packard, Vance. *The Hidden Persuaders*. New York: McKay, 1957.

———. *Our Endangered Children: Growing Up in a Changing World*. Boston: Little, Brown, 1983.

———. *The Status Seekers: An Exploration of Class Behavior in America and the Hidden Barriers That Affect You, Your Community, Your Future*. New York: McKay, 1959.

Palmer, Bruce. *Making Children's Furniture and Play Structures*. New York: Workman, 1974.

"*Parents' Magazine*'s Ninth Annual Builders' Competition." *Parents' Magazine*, February 1959.

Parents' Magazine's Survey of Postwar Housing. New York: Parents' Magazine, 1943.

Parnes, Sidney J. "Programs and Courses in Creativity." In *Encyclopedia of Creativity*, 2:465–77. San Diego: Academic Press, 1999.

Parr, Joy. *Domestic Goods: The Material, the Moral, and the Economic in the Postwar Years*. Toronto: University of Toronto Press, 1999.

Parsons, Talcott. *Essays in Sociological Theory*. 2nd ed. Glencoe, Ill.: Free Press, 1954.

Part, Antony. "What Can Be Learned from Britain's New Schools?" *Architectural Forum* 94 (October 1952): 126–28.

Passantino, Richard J. *Found Spaces and Equipment for Children*. New York: Educational Facilities Laboratories, 1972.

Patterson, James T. *Grand Expectations: The United States, 1945–1974*. New York: Oxford University Press, 1996.

Peña, William M. "What a Good Color Environment Can Do." *Childhood Education*, December 1952.

Perkins, Lawrence B. "Oral History of Lawrence Bradford Perkins." Interview by Betty J. Blum. Chicago Architects Oral History Project, Ernest R. Graham Study Center for Architectural Drawings, Department of Architecture, Art Institute of Chicago.

———. *Work Place for Learning*. New York: Reinhold, 1957.

Perkins, Lawrence B., and Walter D. Cocking. *Schools*. Progressive Architecture Library. New York: Reinhold, 1949.

Perkins & Will. *Selected and Current Works*. Edited by Renée Otmar. Master Architect Series 5. Mulgrave, Australia: Images, 2000.

"Ph.D.s in Toyland." *Newsweek*, May 29, 1967.

Piaget, Jean. *The Origin of Intelligence in the Child*. Translated by Margaret Cook. Middlesex, U.K.: Penguin, 1977.

———. *Play, Dreams, and Imitation in Childhood*. Translated by C. Gattegno and F. M. Hodgson. New York: Norton, 1962.

Pile, John F. "The Open Office: Does It Work?" *Progressive Architecture* 58 (June 1977): 68–81.

Pinnell, Leroy K. "Directions in Design and Use of School Furniture." *American School and University* 32 (1960–61).

———. *Functionality of Elementary School Desks*. Austin: University of Texas Press, 1954.

Play Sculptures. *A New World of Play*. New York: Play Sculptures, 1957.

Playskool. *Playtools to Shape a Child's World: A Program for the Home Recommended by Playskool Research*. N.p.: Playskool, 1972.

Plucker, Jonathan A., and Ronald A. Beghetto. "Why Creativity Is Domain General, Why It Looks Domain Specific, and Why the Distinction Does Not Matter." In *Creativity: From Potential to Realization*, edited by Robert J. Sternberg et al. Washington, D.C.: American Psychological Association, 2004.

Pohle, Gabrielle V. "The Children's Museum as Collector." *Museum News* 58, no. 2 (November–December 1979): 32–37.

Pope, Elizabeth. "What's Happened to the Little Red Schoolhouse?" *McCall's*, October 1955, 52–60.

Postman, Neil. *The Disappearance of Childhood*. New York: Delacorte, 1982.

Potter, David. *People of Plenty: Economic Abundance and the American Character*. Chicago: University of Chicago Press, 1954.

Powers, Alan. *Serge Chermayeff: Designer, Architect, Teacher*. London: RIBA, 2001.

Pratt, Richard. "You Can Build Your Own Home for Half the Price." *Ladies' Home Journal*, April 1950, 46–49.

Pressler, Frances. Letter. In "Crow Island School." *Architectural Forum* 75 (August 1941): 80–81.

Pugh, Allison J. *Longing and Belonging: Parents, Children, and Consumer Culture*. Berkeley: University of California Press, 2009.

Ramey, Craig T., and Vera Piper. "Creativity in Open and Traditional Classrooms." *Child Development* 45 (June 1974): 557–60.

Ravitch, Diane. *The Troubled Crusade: American Education, 1945–1980.* New York: Basic Books, 1983.

Ray, Paul H., and Sherry Ruth Anderson. *The Cultural Creatives: How Fifty Million People Are Changing the World.* New York: Three Rivers, 2000.

Read, Herbert. *Culture and Education in World Order.* New York: Museum of Modern Art and Committee on Art Education, 1948.

———. *Education through Art.* New York: Pantheon, 1956.

Reef, Catherine. *Childhood in America.* New York: Facts on File, 2002.

Reese, William J. *America's Public Schools: From the Common School to "No Child Left Behind."* Baltimore: Johns Hopkins University Press, 2005.

Reid, John Lyon. "Perspectives: He Sees Farther through a Sieve than Most: Ernest Joseph Kump." *Pencil Points / Progressive Architecture* 26 (April 1945): 87–88.

———. "Post-War Schools." *Architect and Engineer* 153, no. 2 (May 1943): 12–24, 32.

Reid, Kenneth, ed. *School Planning: The Architectural Record of a Decade.* New York: Dodge, 1951.

Reiss, Hilde. *Toys: A Group of American Toys Selected for their Educational Value.* San Francisco: American Federation of Arts, 1960.

Retter, Hein. *Speilzeug: Handbuch zur Geschichte und Paedagogik der Spielmittel.* Basel: Beltz, Weinheim, 1979.

Rey, Margret, and H. A. Rey. *Curious George.* Boston: Houghton Mifflin, 1941.

———. *Curious George Goes to the Hospital.* Boston: Houghton Mifflin, 1966.

———. *Curious George Rides a Bike.* Boston: Houghton Mifflin, 1952.

———. *Curious George Takes a Job.* Boston: Houghton Mifflin, 1947.

Richards, Ruth, ed. *Everyday Creativity and New Views of Human Nature: Psychological, Social, and Spiritual Perspectives.* Washington, D.C.: American Psychological Association, 2007.

Richter, N. "Construction Toys at the Octagon 'Just for Fun': An Exhibit Combines Historic Examples with Contemporary Creations." *AIA Journal* 68 (1979): 54–55.

Rickover, Hyman George. *Education and Freedom.* New York: Dutton, 1959.

Riesman, David. *Abundance for What? and Other Essays.* Garden City, N.Y.: Doubleday, 1964.

———. *Individualism Reconsidered, and Other Essays.* Glencoe, Ill.: Free Press, 1954.

Riesman, David, in collaboration with Reuel Denney and Nathan Glazer. *The Lonely Crowd: A Study of the Changing American Character.* Studies in National Policy 3. New Haven, Conn.: Yale University Press, 1950.

Riesman, David, with Nathan Glazer and Reuel Denney. *The Lonely Crowd: A Study of the Changing American Character.* Rev. ed. New Haven, Conn.: Yale University Press, 1961.

Ritchie, Carson I. A. *Making Scientific Toys.* New York: Dutton, 1975.

Robinson, Ken. *Out of Our Minds: Learning to Be Creative.* Oxford: Capstone, 2001.

———. *Out of Our Minds: Learning to Be Creative.* Rev. ed. Oxford: Capstone, 2011.

Roche, Mary. "Ideas for a Playroom." *New York Times*, October 5, 1947.

——. "A Permanent Room for Junior." *New York Times*, September 18, 1949.

Rochowanski, L. W., ed. *Ein Führer durch das Osterreichische Kunstgewerbe.* Leipzig, Ger.: Heinz, 1930.

Rockefeller Brothers Fund. *The Pursuit of Excellence: Education and the Future of America.* Special Studies Report 5. Garden City, N.Y.: Doubleday, 1958.

Ronard, Marguerite. *Children's Play Spaces, from Sandbox to Adventure Playground.* Woodstock, N.Y.: Overlook, 1977.

Rose, Elizabeth. *A Mother's Job: The History of Day Care, 1890–1960.* New York: Oxford University Press, 1999.

Rose, Jacqueline. *The Case of Peter Pan; or, The Impossibility of Children's Fiction.* London: Macmillan, 1984.

Rose, Nikolas. *Governing the Soul: The Shaping of the Private Self.* 2nd ed. London: Free Association Books, 1999.

Rosenberg, Charles E., ed. *The Family in History.* Philadelphia: University of Pennsylvania Press, 1975.

Rosenblum, Robert. *The Romantic Child: From Runge to Sendak.* New York: Thames & Hudson, 1988.

Roth, Alfred. *The New School.* Winterthur, Switz.: Gemsbergdruck der Geschwister Ziegler, 1950.

——. *The New Schoolhouse / Das neue schulhaus / La nouvelle école.* Rev. ed. New York: Praeger, 1966.

Rousseau, Jean-Jacques. *Émile; or, On Education.* 1762. Reprint, translated by Allan Bloom. New York: Basic Books, 1979.

Rowe, Peter G. *Making a Middle Landscape.* Cambridge, Mass.: MIT Press, 1991.

Rudolph, John L. *Scientists in the Classroom: The Cold War Reconstruction of American Science Education.* New York: Palgrave, 2002.

Rudy, Willis. *Schools in an Age of Mass Culture: An Exploration of Selected Themes in the History of Twentieth-Century American Education.* Englewood Cliffs, N.J.: Prentice-Hall, 1965.

Runco, Mark A. "Creativity." *Annual Review of Psychology* 55 (2004): 657–87.

——. "Implicit Theories." In *Encyclopedia of Creativity.* Vol. 2. San Diego: Academic Press, 1999.

——. Preface to *Encyclopedia of Creativity.* Vol. 1. San Diego: Academic Press, 1999.

Runco, Mark A., Garnet W. Millar, Selcuk Acar, and Bonnie Cramond. "The Torrance Tests of Creative Thinking as Predictors of Personal and Public Achievement: A Fifty-Year Follow-Up." *Creativity Research Journal* 22, no. 4 (2010): 361–68.

Russell, Irene, and Blanche Waugaman. "A Study of the Effect of Workbook Copy Experiences on the Creative Concepts of Children." *Research Bulletin of the Eastern Arts Association* 3, no. 1 (1952).

Russell, Mable. *Art Education for Daily Living.* Peoria, Ill.: Bennett, 1946.

"Russian Children to Romp on Latest American Playground Gear." *New York Times*, April 3, 1959.

Saarinen, Aline D. "Playground: Function and Art." *New York Times,* July 4, 1954.

Sahasrabudhe, Prabha. "The Children's Art Carnival: Windows on Creative Art Teaching." In Maeda and Iwasaki, *Victor D'Amico,* 19–28.

Saint, Andrew. *Towards a Social Architecture: The Role of School-Building in Postwar England.* New Haven, Conn.: Yale University Press, 1987.

Sammond, Nicholas. *Babes in Tomorrowland: Walt Disney and the Making of the American Child, 1930–1960.* Durham, N.C.: Duke University Press, 2005.

Sanders, David C. *Innovations in Elementary School Classroom Seating.* Bureau of Laboratory Schools Publications 10. Austin: University of Texas Press, 1958.

Saunders, Frances Stonor. *The Cultural Cold War: The CIA and the World of Arts and Letters.* New York: New Press, 1999.

Saunders, Robert J. "The Contributions of Viktor Lowenfeld to Art Education, Part I: Early Influences on His Thought." *Studies in Art Education* 2, no. 1 (1960): 6–15.

———. "The Contributions of Viktor Lowenfeld to Art Education, Part II: Creative and Mental Growth." *Studies in Art Education* 2, no. 2 (1961): 7–13.

Schlereth, Thomas J. "The Material Culture of Childhood: Research Problems and Possibilities." In *Cultural History and Material Culture: Everyday Life, Landscapes, Museums,* edited by Thomas J. Schlereth, 86–111. Ann Arbor, Mich.: UMI Research Press, 1990.

Schlossman, Steven L. "Perils of Popularization: The Founding of *Parents' Magazine.*" In *History and Research in Child Development,* edited by Alice Boardman Smuts and John W. Hagen, 65–77. Monographs of the Society for Research in Child Development 50, nos. 4–5, serial no. 211. Chicago: University of Chicago Press, 1986.

———. "Philanthropy and the Gospel of Child Development." *History of Education Quarterly* 21, no. 3 (1981): 275–99.

"School Component Designs, Costs Revealed." *Architectural Record* 135 (February 1964): 166–72.

"Schools: A Look Backward and Forward." *Architectural Forum* 103 (October 1955): 129–45.

Schools for the New Needs: Educational, Social, Economic. New York: Architectural Record and F. W. Dodge, 1956.

"The Schools of Donald Barthelme and Associates." *School Executive* 72 (June 1953): 66–86.

"Schools That Utilize the Prevailing Breeze." *Architectural Record* 105 (March 1949).

Schor, Juliet B. *Born to Buy: The Commercialized Child and the New Consumer Culture.* New York: Scribner, 2004.

Schramm, Wilbur, Jack Lyle, and Edwin B. Parker. *Television in the Lives of Our Children.* Stanford, Calif.: Stanford University Press, 1961.

Seagers, Paul W. "Developing the Color Treatment for Schoolrooms." *Illuminating Engineering,* June 1953.

Sears, Robert, et al. *Patterns of Child Rearing.* Stanford, Calif.: Stanford University Press, 1957.

"Secret Spaces of Childhood." Special issue, *Michigan Quarterly Review* 39, nos. 2–3 (Spring–Summer 2000).

Seiter, Ellen. *Sold Separately: Children and Parents in Consumer Culture*. New Brunswick, N.J.: Rutgers University Press, 1993.

Sendak, Maurice. *Caldecott & Co: Notes on Books and Pictures*. New York: Farrar, Straus & Giroux, 1988.

——. *Where the Wild Things Are*. New York: Harper & Row, 1963.

Seuss, Dr. [Theodore Geisel]. *The Cat in the Hat*. New York: Random House, 1957.

Shanken, Andrew M. *194X: Architecture, Planning, and Consumer Culture on the American Home Front*. Minneapolis: University of Minnesota Press, 2009.

"Shaping the Modern: American Decorative Arts at the Art Institute of Chicago, 1917–65." *Art Institute of Chicago Museum Studies* 27, no. 2 (2001): 90–91.

Shapiro, Michael. *Child's Garden: The Kindergarten Movement from Froebel to Dewey*. University Park: Pennsylvania State University Press, 1983.

Sharp, Evelyn. *The IQ Cult*. New York: Coward, McCann & Geoghegan, 1972.

——. *Thinking Is Child's Play*. New York: Dutton, 1969.

Shaw, Archibald B., and Lawrence B. Perkins. "Planning an Elementary School." *School Executive* 73 (July 1954).

Shaw, Nancy Alison. "Modern Art, Media Pedagogy, and Cultural Citizenship: The Museum of Modern Art's Television Project, 1952–1955." PhD diss., McGill University, 2000.

"Shopping Scout." *Parents' Magazine*, April 1949, 14.

Shortage of Scientific and Engineering Manpower: Hearings before the Subcommittee on Research and Development of the Joint Committee on Atomic Energy of the Congress, April and May 1956. Washington, D.C.: U.S. Government Printing Office, 1956.

Siebenbrodt, Michael. *Alma Siedhoff-Buscher: Eine neue Welt für Kinder*. Weimar, Ger.: Stiftung Weimarer Klassik und Kunstsammlungen, 2004.

Siedhoff-Buscher, Alma. "Kind Märchen Spiel Spielzeug." *Junge Menschen* 5, no 8 (1924). Reprint, Munich: Kraus, 1980.

Silber, Käte. *Pestalozzi: The Man and His Work*. 3rd ed. New York: Schocken, 1973.

Silvey, Anita. *One Hundred Best Books for Children*. New York: Houghton Mifflin, 2004.

Singer, Dorothy G., and Jerome L. Singer. *The House of Make-Believe: Children's Play and the Developing Imagination*. Cambridge, Mass.: Harvard University Press, 1990.

——. *Imagination and Play in the Electronic Age*. Cambridge, Mass.: Harvard University Press, 2005.

——. *Partners in Play: A Step-by-Step Guide to Imaginative Play in Children*. New York: Harper & Row, 1977.

Singer, Jerome L. *The Child's World of Make-Believe: Experimental Studies of Imaginative Play*. New York: Academic Press, 1973.

Smith, Paul, ed. *Creativity: An Examination of the Creative Process*. Communication Arts Books. New York: Hastings House, 1958.

Smith, Peter. "Franz Cižek: The Patriarch." *Art Education* 38, no. 2 (March 1985).

——. *The History of American Art Education: Learning about Art in American Schools*. Westport, Conn.: Greenwood, 1996.

Smith, Peter K., Helen Cowie, and Mark Blades. *Understanding Children's Development*. 4th ed. Malden, Mass.: Blackwell, 2003.

Smith, Robert Paul. *"Where Did You Go?" "Out." "What Did You Do?" "Nothing."* New York: Norton, 1957.

Snyder, David. "Playroom." In Colomina, Brennan, and Kim, *Cold War Hothouses*, 124–42.

Sobel, David. *Children's Special Places: Exploring the Role of Forts, Dens, and Bush Houses in Middle Childhood*. Tucson, Ariz.: Zephyr, 1993.

Solomon, Susan G. *American Playgrounds: Revitalizing Community Space*. Hanover, N.H.: University Press of New England, 2006.

"Some Current Answers for Urban Schools." *Architectural Record* 142 (October 1967): 177–79.

Spigel, Lynn. *Make Room for TV: Television and the Family Ideal in Postwar America*. Chicago: University of Chicago Press, 1992.

——. *TV by Design: Modern Art and the Rise of Network Television*. Chicago: University of Chicago Press, 2008.

——. *Welcome to the Dreamhouse: Popular Media and Postwar Suburbs*. Durham, N.C.: Duke University Press, 2001.

Spitz, Ellen Handler. *The Brightening Glance: Imagination and Childhood*. New York: Pantheon, 2006.

Spock, Benjamin. *Baby and Child Care*. Rev. ed. New York: Pocket Books, 1968.

——. "Can You Raise Your Child's I.Q.?" *Ladies' Home Journal*, October 1962, 112, 114.

——. *The Common Sense Book of Baby and Child Care*. New York: Duell, Sloan & Pearce, 1946.

Spock, Michael. "Michael Spock: Looking Back on Twenty-Three Years." *Hand to Hand* 2 (Spring 1988).

"Staff Designs School-Built Teaching Aids." *Nation's Schools* 62, no. 2 (August 1958).

Stanford University, School Planning Laboratory. *School Construction Systems Development*. Stanford, Calif.: School Planning Laboratory, 1962.

Staniszewski, Mary Anne. *The Power of Display: A History of Exhibition Installations at the Museum of Modern Art*. Cambridge, Mass.: MIT Press, 1998.

Stankiewicz, Mary Ann. "Self-Expression or Teacher Influence: The Shaw System of Finger Painting." *Art Education* 37, no. 2 (1984): 20–24.

Starr, Paul. *The Social Transformation of American Medicine*. New York: Basic Books, 1982.

Stearns, Peter N. *American Cool: Constructing a Twentieth-Century Emotional Style*. New York: New York University Press, 1994.

——. *Anxious Parents: A History of Modern Childrearing in America*. New York: New York University Press, 2003.

——. *Childhood in World History*. New York: Routledge, 2006.

Stearns, Peter N., Perrin Rowland, and Lori Giarnella. "Children's Sleep: Sketching Historical Change." *Journal of Social History* 30, no. 2 (1996): 345–66.

Stein, Morris I. *Stimulating Creativity*. Vol. 1. New York: Academic Press, 1974.

Stephens, Sharon. "Nationalism, Nuclear Policy, and Children in Cold War America." *Childhood* 4, no. 1 (February 1997): 103–23.

Stern, Sydney Ladensohn, and Ted Schoenhaus. *Toyland: The High-Stakes Game of the Toy Industry*. Chicago: Contemporary, 1990.

Stoddard, Alexander J. *Schools for Tomorrow: An Educator's Blueprint*. New York: Fund for the Advancement of Education, 1957.

Stoddard, Alexandra. *A Child's Place: How to Create a Living Environment for Your Child*. Garden City, N.J.: Doubleday, 1977.

Stoddard, George D., Irwin Edman, and Bruno Bettelheim. *Art as the Measure of Man; as Education; a Personal Vision*. New York: Museum of Modern Art, 1964.

Stoltzfus, Emilie. *Citizen, Mother, Worker: Debating Public Responsibility for Child Care after the Second World War*. Chapel Hill: University of North Carolina Press, 2003.

Stone, Jeannette Galambos, and Nancy Rudolph. *Play and Playgrounds*. Washington, D.C.: National Association for the Education of Young Children, 1970.

Stouffer, Samuel A. *Communism, Conformity, and Civil Liberties: A Cross-Section of the Nation Speaks Its Mind*. Gloucester, Mass.: Smith, 1963.

Strait, Suzanne Hart. "Playhouse for the Kids." *Parents' Magazine*, August 1958, 42–43, 44, 90–91.

Strickland, Charles E., and Andrew M. Ambrose. "The Baby Boom, Prosperity, and the Changing Worlds of Children, 1945–1963." In *American Childhood: A Research Guide and Historical Handbook*, edited by Joseph M. Hawes and N. Ray Hiner, 533–85. Westport, Conn.: Greenwood, 1985.

Sutton-Smith, Brian. *The Ambiguity of Play*. Cambridge, Mass.: Harvard University Press, 1997.

———. "The Role of Toys in the Instigation of Playful Creativity." *Creativity Research Journal* 5, no. 1 (1992): 3–11.

———. *Toys as Culture*. New York: Gardner, 1986.

Szlizewski, Lucian August. "Schoolhouse Architecture in America from 1830 to 1915." PhD diss., Miami University, 1989.

Tanner, Daniel, and Laurel Tanner. *History of the School Curriculum*. New York: Macmillan, 1990.

Tatar, Maria. *Enchanted Hunters: The Power of Stories in Childhood*. New York: Norton, 2009.

Taylor, Calvin W., and Frank Barron, eds. *Scientific Creativity: Its Recognition and Development*. New York: Wiley, 1963.

Taylor, Francis Henry. "Education and Museum Extension." *Metropolitan Museum of Art Bulletin* 36 (1941): 179–81.

Taylor, Irving A., and J. W. Getzels, eds. *Perspectives in Creativity*. Chicago: Aldine, 1975.

"That 'Reader's Digest' Article." *Architectural Forum* 107 (November 1957): 118–21.

Thompson, Benjamin. "Toward Creative Teaching." In Gropius et al., *Architects Collaborative, 1945–1965*.

Thompson, Dorothy. "Must Schools Be Palaces?" *Ladies' Home Journal*, August 1957, 11, 13, 88.

Todd, Jessie. "Children Need to 'Feel at Home' in School." *American Childhood* 41 (1956): 18–20.

Torrance, E. Paul. *Assessing the Creative Thinking Abilities of Children*. Minneapolis: University of Minnesota Press, 1960.

——. *Guiding Creative Talent*. Englewood Cliffs, N.J.: Prentice-Hall, 1962.

——. *The Manifesto: A Guide to Developing a Creative Career*. Westport, Conn.: Ablex, 2001.

——. *Rewarding Creative Behavior: Experiments in Classroom Creativity*. Englewood Cliffs, N.J.: Prentice-Hall, 1965.

——. *Torrance Tests of Creative Thinking: Verbal Forms A and B*. Princeton, N.J.: Personnel Press, 1966.

——. *What Research Says to the Teacher: Creativity*. Washington, D.C.: National Education Association, 1963.

"To Toyland, This Way." *Vogue*, August 15, 1915, 44, 94.

Townsend, John Rowe. *Written for Children: An Outline of English-Language Children's Literature*. Philadelphia: Lippincott, 1975.

Toy Manufacturers of the U.S.A. *How to Sell Toys*. New York: Toy Manufacturers of the U.S.A., 1949.

——. *So You Want to Build a Playroom*. New York: Toy Manufacturers of the U.S.A., 1947.

——. *Toy Purchase Habits of U.S. Families, Christmas Season 1954: A Market and Opinion Survey Conducted by Opinion Research Corporation*. New York: Toy Manufacturers of the U.S.A., 1955.

"Toys: Little Brother." *Time,* November 10, 1967.

Toys of the Avant-Garde. Malaga, Spain: Museo Picasso, 2010.

Trump, J. Lloyd. *Images of the Future: A New Approach to the Secondary School*. Urbana, Ill.: National Association of Secondary School Principals, Commission on the Experimental Study of the Utilization of the Staff in the Secondary School, 1959.

Tullock, Margaret DeWolf. "The First Museum for Children." *Museums Journal* 51 (July 1951): 90–94.

Turmel, André. *A Historical Sociology of Childhood: Developmental Thinking, Categorization, and Graphic Visualization*. Cambridge: Cambridge University Press, 2008.

Turow, Joseph. *Entertainment, Education, and the Hard Sell: Three Decades of Network Children's Television*. New York: Praeger, 1981.

Tuttle, William M., Jr. *"Daddy's Gone to War": The Second World War in the Lives of America's Children*. New York: Oxford University Press, 1993.

——. "The Homefront Children's Popular Culture: Radio, Movies, Comics—Adventure, Patriotism, and Sex-Typing." In *Small Worlds: Children and Adolescents in America, 1850–1950*, edited by Elliott West and Paula Petrik, 143–63. Lawrence: University Press of Kansas, 1992.

Tyack, David B., and Larry Cuban. *Tinkering toward Utopia: A Century of Public School Reform*. Cambridge, Mass.: Harvard University Press, 1997.

Tyng, Anne Griswold, ed. *Louis Kahn to Anne Tyng: The Rome Letters, 1953–1954*. New York: Rizzoli, 1997.

"Up, Down, and Over: Philadelphia's Children Get Exciting Set of Playgrounds." *Life*, September 13, 1954.

U.S. Children's Bureau. *Home Play and Play Equipment for the Preschool Child*. Washington, D.C.: Government Printing Office, 1937.

———. *Toys in Wartime: Suggestions to Parents on Making Toys at Home*. Washington, D.C.: Children's Bureau, U.S. Department of Labor, 1942.

U.S. Department of Health, Education and Welfare, Children's Bureau. *The Story of the White House Conference on Children and Youth*. Washington, D.C.: U.S. Department of Health, Education and Welfare, Children's Bureau, 1967.

U.S. Department of Health, Education, and Welfare, Office of Education. "A Manual for Project Applicants and Grantees, Title III Elementary and Secondary Education Act." Washington, D.C.: U.S. Department of Health, Education, and Welfare, 1967.

———. *Stepping up with PACE (Projects to Advance Creativity in Education): Supplementary Centers and Services Program; Title III of the Elementary and Secondary Education Act of 1965*. Washington, D.C.: U.S. Department of Health, Education, and Welfare, 1967.

———. *Title III Elementary and Secondary Education Act: Supplementary Centers and Services Program; A Manual for Project Applicants*. Washington, D.C.: U.S. Department of Health, Education, and Welfare, Office of Education, 1965.

"The U.S. in Moscow: Russia Comes to the Fair." *Time*, August 3, 1959.

"U.S. Is Building Some Fine New Schools: School Is Made Gay and Homey." *Life*, October 16, 1950.

Utzinger, Robert C. *Some European Nursery Schools and Playgrounds: Early Childhood Facilities*. Ann Arbor: University of Michigan Press, 1970.

Van Slyck, Abigail A. *A Manufactured Wilderness: Summer Camps and the Shaping of American Youth, 1890–1960*. Minneapolis: University of Minnesota Press, 2006.

———. "The Spatial Practices of Privilege." *Journal of the Society of Architectural Historians* 70, no. 2 (June 2011): 210–39.

Vincent, William S. *Tomorrow's School Building*. New York: School Executive, 1947.

Viola, Wilhelm. *Child Art*. 2nd ed. Peoria, Ill.: Bennett, 1944.

———. *Child Art and Franz Cižek*. Vienna: Austrian Junior Red Cross, 1936.

Waechter, Heinrich, and Elisabeth Waechter. *Schools for the Very Young*. New York: Dodge, 1951.

Walker, Nancy A. "The *Ladies' Home Journal*: 'How America Lives' and the Limits of Cultural Diversity." *Media History* 6, no. 2 (2000): 129–38.

Wallance, Don. *Shaping America's Products*. New York: Reinhold, 1956.

"Wallpapers." *Interiors*, February 1950.

Weinstein, Carol Simon, and Thomas G. David, eds. *Spaces for Children: The Built Environment and Child Development*. New York: Plenum, 1987.

Weinstock, Ruth. *Heathcote Elementary School, Scarsdale, New York*. Profiles of Significant Schools. New York: Educational Facilities Laboratories, Inc., 1960.

Weiss, Jessica. *To Have and to Hold: Marriage, the Baby Boom, and Social Change*. Chicago: University of Chicago Press, 2000.

Weiss, Nancy Pottishman. "Mother, the Invention of Necessity: Dr. Benjamin Spock's 'Baby and Child Care.'" In *Growing Up in America: Children in Historical Perspective*, edited by N. Ray Hiner and Joseph M. Hawes, 283–303. Urbana: University of Illinois Press, 1985.

Weisser, Amy S. "Institutional Revisions: Modernism and American Public Schools from the Depression to the Second World War." PhD diss., Yale University, 1995.

———. "'Little Red School House, What Now?': Two Centuries of American Public School Architecture." *Journal of Planning History* 5 (August 2006): 196–217.

Wells, William. "Children's Marketing." *Journal of Advertising Research*, March 1965.

West, Elliott. *Growing Up in Twentieth-Century America: A History and Reference Guide*. Westport, Conn.: Greenwood, 1996.

West, Elliott, and Paula Petrik, eds. *Small Worlds: Children and Adolescents in America, 1850–1950*. Lawrence: University Press of Kansas, 1992.

Wheelis, Allen. *The Quest for Identity*. New York: Norton, 1958.

Whitaker, Jan. *Service and Style: How the American Department Store Fashioned the Middle Class*. New York: St. Martin's, 2006.

Whitcomb, Mildred. "Classroom Lighting: The Harmon Technic." *Nation's Schools* 39, no. 5 (1947): 34–39.

White, Anthony G. *Architectural Toys: A Selected Bibliography*. Monticello, Ill.: Vance Bibliographies, 1984.

———. *Playhouse Architecture: A Selected Bibliography*. Monticello, Ill.: Vance Bibliographies, 1986.

White, Colin. *The World of the Nursery*. London: Dutton, 1984.

Whitfield, Stephen J. *The Culture of the Cold War*. 2nd ed. Baltimore: Johns Hopkins University Press, 1996.

Whitney Carriage Company. "Whitney Catalogue for the Year 1950." Leominster, Mass.: Whitney Carriage Co., 1950.

Whitton, Blair. *Paper Toys of the World*. Cumberland, Md.: Hobby House Press, 1986.

Whyte, William Hollingsworth. *The Organization Man*. New York: Simon & Schuster, 1956.

Wiencek, Henry. *The World of Lego Toys*. New York: Abrams, 1987.

Wilkinson, Paul F., ed. *Innovation in Play Environments*. New York: St. Martin's, 1980.

Williams, Anthony. "Toward a Geometry of Childhood: The Visual Culture of Toy Bricks in Britain, c. 1900–1940." MA thesis, Bath Spa University College, 1999.

Wilson, Brent, and Harlan Hoffa, eds. *The History of Art Education: Proceedings from the Penn State Conference*. Reston, Va.: National Art Education Association, 1985.

Wilson, Kristina. *Livable Modernism: Interior Decorating and Design during the Great Depression*. New Haven, Conn.: Yale University Press and Yale University Art Gallery, 2004.

Wilson, Robert F. *Colour in Industry Today*. London: Allen & Unwin, 1960.

Wilson, Russell E. *Flexible Classrooms: Practical Ideas for Modern Schoolrooms*. Detroit: Carter, 1953.

Wilson, Sloan. *The Man in the Grey Flannel Suit*. New York: Simon & Schuster, 1955.

Wilt, Miriam E. *Creativity in the Elementary School*. New York: Appleton-Century-Crofts, 1959.

Winton, Alexandra Griffith. "'A Man's House Is His Art': The Walker Art Center's Idea House Project and the Marketing of Domestic Design, 1941–1947." *Journal of Design History* 17, no. 4 (2004): 377–96.

"Wirework School." *Architectural Forum* 97 (October 1952): 103–9.

Wolfenstein, Martha. "Fun Morality: An Analysis of Recent American Child-Training Literature." In Mead and Wolfenstein, *Childhood in Contemporary Cultures*, 168–78.

Wood, Robert C. *Suburbia: Its People and Their Politics*. Boston: Houghton Mifflin, 1958.

Woods, William Crawford. "The Littlest Arms Race." *Harper's*, April 1983.

Wright, Gwendolyn. *Building the Dream: A Social History of Housing in America*. Cambridge, Mass.: MIT Press, 1981.

Wright, H. Myles, and R. Gardner-Medwin. *The Design of Nursery and Elementary Schools*. London: Architectural Press, 1938.

Wrigley, Julia. "Do Young Children Need Intellectual Stimulation? Experts' Advice to Parents, 1900–1985." *History of Education Quarterly* 29, no. 1 (1989): 41–75.

Wu, Wei, and Edward Ng. "A Review of the Development of Daylighting in Schools." *Lighting Research Technology* 35, no. 2 (2003): 111–25.

Young, Milton A. *Buttons Are to Push: Developing Your Child's Creativity*. New York: Pitman, 1970.

Yost, L. Morgan. "Homes for Our Children." *Small Homes Guide*, Spring 1944.

Zarchy, Harry. *Creative Hobbies*. New York: Knopf, 1953.

Zelizer, Viviana A. *Pricing the Priceless Child: The Changing Social Value of Children*. New York: Basic Books, 1985.

Ziegfeld, Edwin, ed. *Education and Art: A Symposium*. Paris: UNESCO, 1952.

Zien, Jim. "Beyond the Generation Gap." *Museum News* 58, no. 2 (November–December 1979): 26–31.

Zilversmit, Arthur. *Changing Schools: Progressive Education Theory and Practice, 1930-1960*. Chicago: University of Chicago Press, 1993.

Zinguer, Tamar. "Toy." In Colomina, Brennan, and Kim, *Cold War Hothouses*, 143–67.

Zinsser, William K. "This Year, Give Baby an Ego Expander." *Life*, December 16, 1966.

Zuckerman, Michael. "Dr. Spock: The Confidence Man." In *The Family in History*, edited by Charles E. Rosenberg. Philadelphia: University of Pennsylvania Press, 1975.

Zukowsky, John, ed. *1945: Creativity and Crisis: Chicago Architecture and Design of the World War II Era*. Chicago: Art Institute of Chicago, 2005.

Zweybruck, Emmy. "Experimental Fabric Design in Silk Screen Technique." *Arts and Architecture* 71 (March 1954): 22–23.

INDEX

AMY F. OGATA is associate professor at the Bard Graduate Center: Decorative Arts, Design History, Material Culture in New York City. She is the author of *Art Nouveau and the Social Vision of Modern Living*.